SOAS SOUTH ASIAN TEXTS NO. 2

THE HINDI CLASSICAL TRADITION
A BRAJ BHĀṢĀ READER

SOAS SOUTH ASIAN TEXTS NO. 2

The Hindi Classical Tradition

A Braj Bhāṣā Reader

Rupert Snell

Reader in Hindi, School of Oriental and African Studies, University of London

SCHOOL OF ORIENTAL AND AFRICAN STUDIES
UNIVERSITY OF LONDON
London

1991

Published by The School of Oriental and African Studies,
(University of London),

Published by Routledge
2 Park Square, Milton Park, Abingdon, Oxon, OX14 4RN
270 Madison Ave, New York NY 10016

Transferred to Digital Printing 2006

British Library Cataloguing in Publication Data

Snell, Rupert
The Hindi classical tradition: a Braj Bhāṣā reader.
I. Title
491.43
ISBN 0-7286-0175-3

Publisher's Note
The publisher has gone to great lengths to ensure the quality of this reprint but points out that some imperfections in the original may be apparent

Printed and bound by CPI Antony Rowe, Eastbourne

To Mahesh Patel

बिनती रसिकनि सौं करौं हों अति मति करि हीन ।
भूल्यों होंहु सुधारियों कोबिद परम प्रबीन ॥

धरणीधरदास

SOAS South Asian Texts

During the period of British colonial rule in India, members of the education services and others felt it to be a natural part of their duties to edit important works of South Asian literature, so as to make them accessible to English-speaking readers. The initiative represented by these nineteenth century editions, which are now difficult to obtain, has sadly long been allowed to lapse.

The present series of SOAS South Asian Texts represents an attempt to revive this tradition in such a way as to meet the rather different requirements and expectations of students of South Asian literature today. The series is designed for those who have a basic reading knowledge of the language, but require the assistance of explanatory material in English in approaching original literary texts.

All volumes in the series accordingly begin with an editorial introduction in English, followed by the text itself, which is accompanied by explanatory notes and a glossary. It has not been thought necessary to provide translations of modern prose, but older verse texts are accompanied by full English translations. Though these renderings are primarily designed to assist understanding of the original, and themselves make no claim to any literary merit, it is hoped that they and the editorial introductions may serve to introduce some of the classics of South Asian literature to those unable to read them in their original language.

Christopher Shackle
Rupert Snell

Series Editors

Preface

In modern usage, the name 'Hindi' refers increasingly narrowly to the Kharī Bolī dialect which underlies Modern Standard Hindi (MSH) both in its spoken and its literary forms. Yet until about the middle of the nineteenth century, the literatures of the 'Hindi'-speaking area were dominated by other dialects, principal of which were Braj Bhāṣā and Avadhī. Braj Bhāṣā in particular gained a literary currency well beyond the borders of the area where it was (and is) spoken as a mother-tongue; the association of the cultural district of Braj, centred on the towns of Mathura and Vrindaban, with the Kṛṣṇa religion made it a natural choice as the vehicle for devotional verse, and its linguistic and literary conventions were enthusiastically adopted for a wider range of court and popular verse.

This book seeks to introduce some of the main genres and styles of Braj Bhāṣā literature to readers already having a confident grasp of MSH. Though obviously falling far short of being fully representative, the choice of works excerpted here is intended to reflect a standard repertory of the classical, or pre-modern, tradition. Texts for which full and annotated translations are already published elsewhere (e.g. the major Braj Bhāṣā texts of Tulsīdās and Nanddās) have not been included; and considerations of space have excluded other major figures such as Haridās, Keśav, and Ghanānand. The natural juxtapositioning of devotional poems with examples of a more worldly or even decadent taste has not been interrupted by any attempt to delineate literary 'eras' (*kāl*), since traditional designations such as *bhakti kāl, rīti kāl* disguise the natural heterogeneity of the literature under review. Several of the works reproduced here include some verses whose popular attribution to a particular author may rest on dubious — if time-honoured — assumptions about literary and religious history: this aspect of the texts, so typical a feature of Indian literary history, is discussed in the Introduction.

The Introduction has a practical emphasis, being intended to service an appreciation of the texts included in the reader rather than to attempt the kind of exhaustive coverage of Braj Bhāṣā grammar and literary history already available elsewhere. It falls into three main parts. The first, in which a familiarity with MSH (and such grammatical features as the formation of causative verbs) is assumed, is an outline grammar of Braj Bhāṣā, drawing heavily on the texts themselves for examples. The second introduces Hindi metrics, concentrating primarily (but not exclusively) on metres exemplified in this book. The third part attempts a survey history of the literature of the period, and gives brief introductions to the authors and the texts, with reference to other English-medium introductory materials; it concludes with a note of some textual conventions and dating systems. This section is followed by concordances to the published texts from which the extracts have been drawn, and by a select bibliography. While the scope of the Introduction has been defined by the contents of the texts themselves, it is hoped that it may also be found helpful in approaching parallel literatures such as the Avadhī verse of Tulsīdās and the Sufi poets.

The first two texts are in prose (a rarity in pre-modern writing) and consequently offer a more accessible entrée into the literature than can be hoped for in the formalized and elliptical contexts of verse, where word order and syntax are often subjugated to the different requirements of literary rhetoric. The prose selections are not translated, but annotations at the foot of the page gloss any obscurities of lexis or phrasing; line numbers have been added for ease of reference, and are in Nagari to avoid confusion with the annotation references, which are marked by superscript footnote numbers in this 'prose' section. The remaining texts, all in verse, are arranged chronologically and follow a standard format: Braj Bhāṣā text on the left-hand page is faced by an English translation, and by annotations which refer to verse and line number (e.g. '12.4') such that they can be approached from either the original or the translation. It must be emphasized that the translations have been kept deliberately literal, as they are intended as a key to the meaning and, where possible, the syntax of the Braj verses: no attempt has been made to echo the poetic diction of the originals.

A brief Index of Epithets and Motifs lists the most common of the allusive titles, patronymics etc. which throng any traditional poem to the exasperation of the novice reader. Finally, a complete Glossary lists all the words in the texts; etymologies following the English definitions are based closely on CDIAL.

The Introduction is best used by reference from the texts themselves, and the first of the prose texts, *Rāj-nīti*, makes a more accessible starting-point than the necessarily dry paragraphs of Part I; *Rāj-nīti* is relatively straightforward linguistically, and its Aesop-like contexts require no background information. Once *Rāj-nīti* and the following *Vārtā* episodes have introduced the morphology of Braj Bhāṣā, the reader should confidently be able to begin on the verse texts, beginning perhaps with the *Sūr-sāgar*. Readers looking for a limited sampling of verse types might usefully take verses from *Sūr-sāgar*, *Sujān-Raskhān* and the *Satsaī* of Bihārīlāl as a 'core' selection, light relief being always available in the *Sabhā-bilās* poems.

I am grateful to a number of colleagues who have commented on various parts of this book: the heaviest debt of gratitude is due to Professor J.C. Wright, whose scrupulous examination of the etymologies in the Glossary has provided much enlightenment and saved me from many an embarrassment. I am also grateful to Professor C. Shackle for numerous suggestions on the presentation of the material; to Mr S.C.R. Weightman for championing the cause of the *Bhāṣā-bhūṣaṇ* and for loans of numerous books; to Dr R.D. Gupta for his discussion of textual problems; and to Mr Simon Digby for providing a photograph of a folio from a Raskhān manuscript in his collection.

The physical production of the book has been made possible by Apple Macintosh software devised by Dr K.E. Bryant of the University of British Columbia ('Jaipur' Devanagari font) and by Mr K.R. Norman of Cambridge University ('Norman' font for Roman transliteration with diacritical marks); I am grateful to the SOAS Research and Publications Committee for meeting the full costs of production, and to Martin Daly, Diana Matias, Alison Surry and Susan Madigan for their help in preparing the text for publication. Shortcomings in the book are, needless to say, all my own work.

The shared enthusiasms of those for whom the contents of this book are part of a living culture have been a great incentive in the preparation of the material. In particular, an unseen debt of gratitude is due to Mahesh Patel, to whom the book is consequently dedicated.

Rupert Snell

CONTENTS

INTRODUCTION

THE TEXTS

ABBREVIATIONS

abs.	absolutive	MSH	Modern Standard Hindi
Add.	Addenda of CDIAL	num.	numeral
Add²	Turner 1985 (see Bibliography)	obj.	object(ive)
adj.	adjective, adjectival	obl.	oblique
Ar.	Arabic	part.	particle
aux.	auxiliary (verb)	Pers.	Persian
BhP	*Bhāgavata Purāṇa*	pl.	plural
CDIAL	Turner 1966 (see Bibliography)	poss.	possessive
emph.	emphatic	ppn.	postposition(al)
enc.	enclitic	pr.	pronoun, pronominal
esp.	especially	pref.	prefix(ed)
f.	feminine	ptc.	participle, participial
foll.	following	rh.	form found in rhyme only
indef.	indefinite	S	[in Glossary] Sanskrit
inf.	infinitive	sg.	singular
interj.	interjection	Skt	Sanskrit
interr.	interrogative	subj.	subjunctive
KhB	Khaṛī Bolī	suf.	suffix(ed)
lit.	literally	vi.	intransitive verb
m.	masculine	vt.	transitive verb

SIGLA OF READER TEXTS

AP	*Arill-pacīsī* (Nāgarīdās)	RN	*Rāj-nīti* (Lallūlāl)
AY	*Aṣṭayām* (Dev)	RP	*Ras-prabodh* (Raslīn)
BhBh	*Bhāṣā-bhūṣaṇ* (Jasvant Siṁh)	SB	*Sabhā-bilās* (Lallūlāl)
BS	*Satsaī* (Bihārīlāl)	SR	*Sujān-raskhān* (Raskhān)
MP	*Padāvalī* (Mīrā)	SS	*Sūr-sāgar* (Sūrdās)
NS	*Nīti-satsaī* (Vṛnd)	VV	*Caurāsī vaiṣṇavan kī vārtā* & *Do sau bāvan vaiṣṇavan kī vārtā* (Gokulnāth/Harirāy)
RAM	*Rasik-ananya-māl* (Bhagvat Mudit)		
RB	*Barvai* (Rahīm)		

SYSTEM OF TRANSLITERATION

Textual references are transliterated with 'inherent' *a*. Elsewhere, 'inherent' *a* is shown only after conjuncts (as in *bhakta*), in Sanskrit titles, and in some short words to follow established usage (e.g. *rasa*). Unmarked transliteration has been used for well-known place names and historical characters. Certain letters such as *ḥ* and *ṣ* are used to transliterate both Sanskrit and Arabic/Persian phonemes, since no confusion is possible in context.

INTRODUCTION

I GRAMMAR[1]

Braj Bhāṣā is a member of the group of languages and dialects descended from the western form of Prakrit called Śaurasenī. In terms of the genealogical model on which Indo-Aryan languages are traditionally categorized, Braj Bhāṣā occupies a place parallel with such neighbouring dialects as Khaṛī Bolī (KhB), Hariyānī, Kanaujī, etc., and also with such languages as Panjabi, Rajasthani, Gujarati, Marathi, and Bengali. These and other such languages constitute the 'New Indo-Aryan' (NIA) group; NIA languages, though individually distinct, share features of phonology and morphology which characterize them as parallel descendants of 'Middle Indo-Aryan' (MIA) languages, i.e. the Prakrits and various forms of Apabhraṁśa, which are themselves descended from Old Indo-Aryan (OIA), i.e. Vedic and the later forms of Sanskrit. This descent from OIA to NIA is typified by a gradual and progressive process of linguistic simplification, as is clearly seen in the example of grammatical inflexion, where the two main cases of Hindi (direct and oblique) are a distant echo of the fully inflecting syntax of Sanskrit with its eight distinct cases.

In terms of phonology and morphology also, NIA languages show a process of simplification wherein, for example, the often complex consonant clusters of Sanskrit are reduced to more readily pronounceable forms. Paradoxically, however, the new demands put on NIA languages by twentieth-century contexts of language use has led to an unprecedented reliance on borrowings from Sanskrit and on the coining of neologisms from the inexhaustible stocks of the Sanskrit lexicon. As a result of this process, which is particularly conspicuous in the 'standardized' modern forms of Hindi and Bengali, the true NIA quality of these vernaculars tends to be disguised by the high proportion of Sanskrit loanwords. In comparison with Modern Standard Hindi (MSH), then, the Braj Bhāṣā of the 'classical' period of Hindi literature exhibits in relatively chaste form the true vernacular phonology and lexicon of NIA.

Various sound changes characteristic of the NIA phonology of Braj are appropriately exemplified in the Kṛṣṇa epithet *sā̃varo* 'the dark one', a derivative of Sanskrit *śyāmala* through MIA *sāmala* : the replacement of *ś* by *s* ; the simplification of an initial conjunct to a single consonant; the replacement of a medial consonant by a semivowel, and the accompanying nasalization of the preceding long vowel; the replacement of original final *l* by *r* ; and a direct case m.sg. ending in *-o/-au* (cf. MSH *-ā*).

[1]**Bibliographical Note.** The development of Indo-Aryan is summarized in G.A. Zograph 1982 and with greater detail in J. Bloch 1965; J. Beames 1966 follows a comparative approach to NIA grammar. For the wider Indo-European perspective see W.B. Lockwood 1969. H.S. Kellogg 1938 is a grammar of the various Hindi dialects, and includes useful comparative tabulations of grammatical forms. C. Shackle and R. Snell 1990 analyse the component elements of Hindi-Urdu and trace the divergent development of the two languages since 1800. R.S. McGregor 1968, an analysis of a sixteenth-century prose text, is the standard Braj Bhāṣā grammar; its categories have been usefully applied to a body of religious verse in M. Thiel-Horstmann 1983.

Broadly speaking, three levels of Indo-Aryan vocabulary appearing in Braj are to be distinguished: tatsama, i.e. unchanged Sanskrit words (e.g. *puṣpa* 'flower', *patra* 'leaf'); semitatsama or ardhatatsama, i.e. those loanwords from Sanskrit whose spelling has been superficially altered but which have not been subject to a full process of sound change (e.g. *bhagata* < *bhakta* 'votary', *darasana* < *darśana* 'seeing'); and tadbhava, i.e. vernacular words derived from OIA etymons via the MIA stage (e.g. *sā̃varo* < *sāmala* < *śyāmala*; *puhupa* < *puppha* < *puṣpa* 'flower'; *pāta* < *patta* < *pattra* 'leaf'). As is seen here, the tatsama and tadbhava forms of some words may be synonymous (though often distinct in register); elsewhere, the tadbhava comprises an etymological doublet to the tatsama, e.g. *bhā̃ti* 'type, manner' versus its etymon *bhakti* 'devotion'. Depending on the nature of their constituent consonants, some tadbhavas will have little obvious similarity to their etymons, e.g. *ahū̃ṭha* < *ardhacaturtha* 'three and a half'; other words, having a simple tatsama form, will not change at all in their tadbhava stage, e.g. *nīla* 'blue', *jāla* 'net', *bila* 'mouse-hole', *chala* 'deceit'.

The tripartite scheme of tatsama, semi-tatsama and tadbhava accounts for the majority of words encountered in the texts included in the book; but loans from Persian and from Arabic (through Persian) are also commonplace, especially in those texts which are not self-consciously based on Sanskrit models. The widespread borrowings from European languages which are so prominent in the twentieth-century lexicon were still some way off in the period covered by our texts, which include only a single isolated example (SB *tamākū* 'tobacco', from the Portuguese). Finally, there is the smaller category of so-called *desī* words, i.e. those Indian words not deriving from Sanskrit but from ancient 'local' dialects (which may include those from pre-Aryan speech).

The processes of Indo-Aryan word derivation are demonstrated with great clarity by the comparative etymological dictionary CDIAL, whose presentation of the full range of NIA derivatives under their OIA etymon (as headword) allows sound changes to be observed in both their chronological and their geographical perspectives. The comparative approach of CDIAL also makes it possible for hypothetical etymons, marked with an asterisk, to be reconstructed on the basis of the evidence of MIA and NIA forms.

I.1 PHONOLOGY AND ORTHOGRAPHY

This section outlines the most important characteristics of Braj morphology, often by comparison with MSH equivalents. Orthographic conventions in Braj are far from standardized. The forms which appear in published texts are the product of successive centuries of scribal copying and re-copying, and do not necessarily represent accurately the conventions in which a work was originally composed; forms preserved in manuscripts may represent genuine linguistic features, or may simply reflect scribal whim. Because of the diversity of texts included here (some of which, for example, include KhB forms), a complete analysis of all occurring grammatical forms is not practicable: major exceptions to the general outline given here (which follows closely the categories established by R.S. McGregor 1968 and M. Thiel-Hortsmann 1983) are noted in the annotations to the texts.

I.1.1 Vowels

(a) *i* may replace *a* in a palatal environment, e.g. *china* (Skt *kṣaṇa*).

(b) Short vowels may be arbitrarily lengthened for metre and/or rhyme, e.g. *cārī* for *cāri.*

(c) Tatsama *ṛ* (ऋ) is frequently represented by *ri.*

(d) *e* and *ai* are often interchangeable, as e.g. *ke/kai* (MSH *ke*).

(e) *o* and *au* are likewise interchangeable in final position, e.g. in m. perf. ptc. such as *āyau/āyo* (MSH *āyā*).

(f) Elision of an initial *a*- (following final -*a* in the previous word) may be shown by *avagraha*: *dharama 'ru* (धरम ऽरु, SS 30.2).

(g) Unstressed vowels may be subject to metathesis, e.g. *lapaṭā- / lipaṭā-.*

I.1.2 Consonants

(a) Arabic and Persian *kh*, *z* are usually assimilated to their Indo-Aryan counterparts and are not distinguished by the use of diacritical dots: thus ख्याल, हजार.

(b) Tatsama *kṣ* yields tadbhava *kh* (e.g. *kṣaṇa* > *khana*); but *ch* or *cch* also appears as a semitatsama for *kṣ*, e.g. *china, kaṭāccha, chīra.*

(c) *jñ* is usually represented by *gy*, e.g. *gyāna.*

(d) *ṛ, ṛh* are not consistently distinguished from *ḍ, ḍh.*

(e) Original retroflex *ṇ* usually appears as *n* : e.g. *kārana.*

(f) *y* is usually represented by *j* in stressed positions, e.g. *jamunā*; but *y* is retained in pr., e.g. *yaha.* (In some manuscripts the graphs य़ and य represent *y* and *j* respectively.)

(g) Similarly *v* is represented by *b* in stressed positions, e.g. *basana*; but with *v* retained in pr., e.g. *vaha.* Little consistency in *b/v* appears in e.g. verbal nouns in *-bau/-vau.*

(h) *l* > *r* is a common sound change in a final syllable: *gālī* > *gārī, dhūli* > *dhūri.*

(i) Medial or final -*aya*- is often represented as -*ai*-, e.g. *samai, udai*; and -*ava*- becomes -*au*-, e.g. *ūdhau.*

(j) *ś* is largely replaced by *s*, e.g. *syāma*; it is maintained regularly only in the prestigious formula/title *śrī*, with its distinctive grapheme (श्री).

(k) *ṣ* may be represented by *kh*, e.g. *bhākhā*, reflecting pronunciation. In manuscripts, [kh] may be written with the graph ष, e.g. षात 'eats'. (A convention in the published text of BhBh, wherein [kh] is written ष़, is not followed in the transcription in this book.)

(l) Aspirate consonants may be reduced to *h*, e.g. *gahiro* < *gabhīra.*

I.1.3 Conjuncts

(a) Consonant clusters are often resolved into their components, e.g. *janma* > *janama.*

(b) Simplification of a conjunct to a single consonant may be accompanied by a lengthening of a preceding short vowel, e.g. *karma* > *kāma*, *patra* > *pāta*.

(c) Conjuncts of *r* with *y*, common in perf. ptc. from verb roots in *-r*, are written not with a superscript *repha* but with a modified य, appearing in the printed text as e.g. करयौ.

I.1.4 Nasality

(a) Many manuscripts and printed texts make no use of *candrabindu*, and so do not distinguish vowel nasality from homorganic nasals. Usage in this book follows the source texts as printed, without attempting any standardization on metrical or phonetic grounds.

(b) Nasalization of a vowel before or after a nasal consonant, or occurring spontaneously in a long vowel, is commonly shown in manuscripts (e.g. करनां, स्यांम, पांइ), but this convention is not usually carried through into printed texts.

(c) Nasalization of verb endings is largely random, and does not usually distinguish pl. from sg. with any consistency. Similarly, nasality in the final vowels of nouns, adj., etc. has little consistent morphological value; though adverbs in *-e* / *-ai* are often nasalized (e.g. *pahalẽ, āgaĩ*).

I.1.5 Sanskritization

The authentic vernacular quality of Braj phonology tends to become disguised by the imposition of Sanskritic orthographies (though the process is not nearly as advanced as it is in MSH); this tendency is found in manuscript copyists and modern editors/typesetters alike. Thus many of the tatsama forms found in the texts may represent Sanskritizations of semi-tatsamas or tadbhavas.

I.2 NOUNS

(a) Nouns with *-a* stems may show *-u*, normally in the direct case: e.g. *aṁjanu*. This remnant of the fuller inflexional system of the older language is common in the orthography of BS (as appearing in the edition used here), more random elsewhere.

(b) Alongside m. nouns in *-ā* (which may retain *-ā* in obl.) are some in *-au* (or *-o*): e.g. *pahũcau* 'wrist', *mātho* 'head'.

(c) Obl.pl. nouns take the suffix *-na, -nu* or *-ni* (= MSH *-õ*). No consistent distinction is usually apparent between the three forms of the suffix. As in MSH, *-ī* and *-ū* stems are usually shortened before the suffix: *dinani, bhãtina, sakhinu.*

(d) Obl.sg. nouns may take the suffix *-hi* /*-hī* (often nasalized): *manahi cori* 'stealing the mind' (SS 30.2); *jasodā syāmahĩ kaṁṭha lagāyau* 'Yaśodā embraced Śyām' (SS 25.6).

(e) Used nominally, *baḍau* (MSH *baṛā*) has the obl.pl. *baḍena* (/*-ni* /*-nu*).

(f) Various case functions are carried by obl. without ppn., reflecting the fact that the language has yet to develop a fully analytic syntax (where case relationships are indicated through the use of ppn., as in MSH).

(g) Verbal nouns: see I.5.11.

I.3 ADJECTIVES

(a) *-au* / *-o* endings are the equivalent to MSH *-ā* : *bahirau, chabīlau, sūno.*

(b) Both *-ai* and *-e* appear as m. obl. endings; they may be nasalized, though nasality often indicates adverbial use: see I.6.1.

(c) Ptc. adj. in *-ita* are frequently borrowed from Sanskrit: *śobhita, racita, ānandita.*

(d) Pronominal adj. (*merau* etc.) are included in the following section.

I.4 PRONOUNS

The following is a summary of occurring forms, and does not list all variants: the texts show much orthographic variation, particularly in respect of vowel length, of *e/ai* and *o/au* vowel values, and of nasality. Many forms here listed as s. also appear as pl.

I.4.1 Demonstrative, near reference (MSH यह etc.)

	Sg.	Pl.
Dir.	यह, ए	ये
Obl.	या, इहिं	इन
Obj.	याहि	इन्हें

I.4.2 Demonstrative, distant reference (MSH वह etc.)

Dir.	वह	वे, वै
Obl.	वा, उहिं	उन, विन
Obj.		उन्हें

I.4.3 Demonstrative-correlative (MSH वह [सो] etc.)

Dir.	सो, सु	ते
Obl.	ता, तिहि	तिन
Obj.		तिन्हैं

I.4.4 **Relative** (MSH जो etc.)

Dir.	जो, जु	जो, जे
Obl.	जा, जिहिं	

I.4.5a **Personal, 1st person** (MSH मैं etc.)

Dir.	हौं, मैं	हम
Obl.	मो	हम
Obj.	मोहि	
Poss.	मेरौ, मेरो, मोर, मोरौ, मम	हमारौ, हमरौ
Agent.	मैं	

I.4.5b **Personal, 2nd person** (MSH तू, तुम etc.)

Dir.	तू	तुम
Obl.	तो	
Poss.	तेरौ, तुव, तो, तिहारौ	तुम्हरौ, तुम्हारौ
Agent.	तैं	

I.4.6a **Interrogative, animate/inanimate** (MSH कौन etc.)

Dir.	को, कौन	
Obl.	का, कौन	किन

I.4.6b **Interrogative, inanimate** (MSH क्या etc.)

Dir.	कहा, कह, का, कौन	
Obl.	काहे, काहें , किहिं	

I.4.7 **Indefinite** (MSH कोई etc.)

Dir.	कोइ, कोय, कोई, कोउ, कोऊ	
Obl.	काहू	

The examples given here follow the above categories (but do not represent all classes):

I.4.1 इहिं बँसुरी सखि सबै चुरायौ 'this flute, friend, has stolen everything' (SS 30.1)
याही कौ राज 'his own kingdom' (SS 16.3)

I.4.3 सो छबि कहत न बनियाँ 'that splendour cannot be described' (SS 14.6)
दियौ तिहि निर्वान पद हरि 'to her Hari gave salvation' (SS 28.7)
तिन मैं मुख्य 'chief amongst them' (SS 13.4)
तिन्हैं छाँड़ि 'forsaking them' (SS 5.8)

I.4.4 जो/ जौ / जु may be used as an emphatic restatement of a subject noun:

अपने या बालक की करनी जौ तुम देखौ आनि 'you come and see the deed ("which is") of your son' (SS 18.3)

I.4.5a मोहिं उधारि 'save me' (SS 4.1)
यह मेरो घर है 'this is my house' (SS 17.5)
महामोह मम देस 'great infatuation is my homeland' (SS 6.2)
ताते आइ शरण मैं गही 'so I came and took refuge' (RAM 55)
मैं ...राख्यौ माखन 'I placed the butter' (SS 18.5)

I.4.5b कहा कहौं हरि के गुन तोसौं 'what could I tell you of Hari's qualities?' (SS 20.1)
यह तेरे सुत की घात 'this is your son's ploy' (SS 20.7)
तैं बहुतै निधि पाई 'you have found great treasure indeed' (SS 23.5)

I.4.6a को है जनक कौन है जननी 'who is his father, who is his mother?' (SS 36.3)
अब तुम काकौ नाउँ लेउगे 'now whose name will you take?' (SS 17.4)
कौन पुन्य तप तैं 'through what merit or penance?' (SS 27.3)

I.4.6b मुख करि कहा कहौं 'what should I say with my mouth?' (SS 9.2)
कहा चाहत से डोलत 'with what desire do you roam about?' (SS 17.1)
तुम्हरे दरस को का बरनौं 'what shall I describe of your appearance?' (SS 29.4)
किहिं रस मैं अभिलाषी 'in what sentiment is he desirous?' (SS 36.4)
अब काहैं नहिं बोलत 'why do you not speak now?' (SS 37.6)

I.4.7 कोउ न उतारै पार 'no-one may transport you across' (SS 2.6)
नाहिंन कोऊ साथ 'there is no-one with you' (SS 17.4)

I.5 VERBS

I.5.1 Root, Theme, and Stem

The composition of verb forms is described on the basis of the following tables:

Roots ending in a consonant:

ROOT	THEME		
bol-	*-i, -a*	STEM:	*boli, bola*
bol-	*-a-*	ACTIVE STEM:	*bola-*
bol-	*-iya-*	PASSIVE STEM:	*bolī̌ya-, bolī̌ja-*

Roots ending in a vowel:

ROOT	THEME		
ā-	*-i, -ya*	STEM:	*āi, āya*
ā-	zero, *-va-*	ACTIVE STEM:	*ā-, āva-*
ā-	*-iya-*	PASSIVE STEM:	*āiya-*

Note the following points:

(a) The stem form of the verb *ho-* is *hvai* in many contexts.

(b) Final *-ā* of a root may coalesce with thematic *-i*, forming stems in *ai-*: root *khā-* > stem *khai-*, etc.

(c) Braj retains many verb stems which have been replaced by phrase verbs in KhB: Braj *pūj-, bhaj-, baran-* vs. KhB *pūrā karnā, bhajan karnā, varṇan karnā* respectively.

I.5.2 The Substantive Verb, *ho-*

Used both independently and as auxiliary with ptc., the following forms are found:

	Present		**Imperfective Past** (MSH *thā* etc.)	
	Sg.	Pl.	Sg.	Pl.
1st	हौं	है, हैं	हतौ, हती	हते, हती
2nd	हो	हौ		
3rd	है, हौ, आहि	है, हैं	हतौ, हो, हती	हते, हती

hutau etc. also occur alongside *hatau*.

I.5.3 General Present, and Past Imperfective

The imperf. ptc. is formed from active stem + *-ta*, *-ti* (e.g. *kahata*, *kahati*). The weak f. ending *-ti* is often replaced by *-ta* ; *-tu* (*kahatu*) sometimes appears with m. subjects; *-tī/-te* also occur, especially when for metre or rhyme and/or through MSH influence.

Past and present tenses may be distinguished by the auxiliary (present *hai*, etc., past *hatau*, etc.), though in verse this is usually absent. The general present covers the functions of the MSH present imperf. and continuous, including use as a historic present.

कछुक खात कछु धरनि गिरावत 'some he eats, some he throws to the floor' (SS 14.2)
घरही घर डोलतु 'he roams from house to house' (SS 23.4)
जानत हौ दुख सुख सब जन के 'you know the sorrows and joys of all' (SS 9.2)
देखत हौं गोरस में चींटी 'I see there's an ant in the milk' (SS 17.6).
मनहीं मन बलबीर कहत हैं 'Balbīr says to himself' (SS 11.5)
दो वैष्णव आपस में बतरात हुते 'two Vaiṣṇavas were talking together' (VV 174)

I.5.4 Subjunctive-present

1st	root + *-aũ* / *-õ*/ *-ũ*/ *-ū̃*
2nd	root + *-e*
3rd	root + *-ai*, *-e*, *-i* (sometimes written *-ya*, e.g. *hoya* = *hoi*)

Nasality of the 3rd person ending does not consistently indicate plurality. The 3rd person *-i* ending is most commonly found in verbs with *-ā* root; it is sometimes hardly to be distinguished from the stem used as abs., e.g. in BS 3 *māri* /*ḍāri*, and is particularly common in such rhyme-words requiring the metrical pattern / - ˘ /.

Usage of the subjunctive-present is often indistinguishable from that of the general present, although subjunctive force is sometimes to be understood from context. The subjunctive-present is often preferred, however, when the force of the verb is rhetorical or declamatory rather than narrative: compare the examples below with the narrative contexts of those in section I.5.3.

बंदौं तिहिं पाइ 'I bow to those feet' (SS 1.4)
मैं उनकों कैसे जानों 'how might I know him?' (VV 187)
जो पशु हौं तौ...चरौं 'if I am an animal, then...may I graze' (SR 1.2)
समुझै नहिं कोइ 'no-one understands/can understand' (BS 11.1)
को कहि सकै बड़ेनु सौं 'who could speak to the great?' (BS 41.1)

I.5.5 Perfective

The perf. ptc. is formed from root + *-au* /*-o*, *-e* (m.), *-ī* (f.): *hutau, kiyo, chā̃ṛe, gaī*; *-ā* sometimes occurs, through MSH influence. The addition of *-y-* to the root before a m.sg. ending is regular in *-ā* roots, and also occurs in some consonant roots: *āyau, kahyau, jānyau.* The endings of f.pl. ptc. are not regularly nasalized. Note the following ptc.:

हो-	भयौ (= MSH हुआ)
कर-	कीनौ, कीन, कीन्हौ, कर्‌यौ
जा-	गयौ
दे-	दीनौ
ले-	लियौ, लीन्ह(ौ)

As in MSH, an agentive construction applies with most transitive verbs in perf. tenses; the ppn. *ne*, however, is not an essential component in this construction, nouns and pr. which in MSH would take *ne* being simply in the agentive case. In the first person, *maĩ* is the agentive pr., *haũ* the nominative (though *maĩ* is nominative also in the later language, as in MSH). Some intransitive verbs with *-ā* stems have *-n-* added before the perfective ptc. termination, particularly in rhyme contexts: thus *lajāne, samānī*, *etc.*

मैं नहिं माखन खायौ 'I didn't eat the butter' (SS 25.1)
मैं जान्यौ यह मेरौ घर है 'I thought this was my house' (SS 17.5)
जसोदा ऊखल बाँधे स्याम 'Yaśoda tied Śyām to the mortar' (SS 26.1)
रूप सों दीनी चिनौती अनंगहिं 'with your beauty you gave a challenge to Anaṅga' (SR 15.1)
रावन हरन सिया कौ कीन्हौ 'Rāvaṇ perfomed the abduction of Sītā' (SS 13.7)
भई ब्याकुल...कुमारि 'the girls...became disturbed' (SS 28.3)
जब जानति आधीन भए हैं 'when she knows he has become dependent' (SS 31.5)

Verbs of 'saying', 'thinking', etc. may show concord with f. *bāta* as implicit direct object:

देसाधिपति नें सूरदास सों कही 'the emperor said to Sūrdās' (VV 23)
मन में बिचारी 'he thought to himself' (VV 206)
देसाधिपति के मन में आई 'it occurred to the emperor' (VV 6).

Some transitive verbs in VV are in concord with clause subject (though the ptc. may be read as a present-subjunctive, used as historic present, in some contexts — see VV 79):

तब वा गोपाल सों सूरदासजी कहे 'then Sūrdās said to that Gopāl' (VV 60)
कृष्णदास अपने मन में विचारे 'Kṛṣṇadās thought to himself' (VV 145)

I.5.6 Participial Constructions

Non-finite participial constructions using the imperf. ptc. -*ta* are the equivalents of MSH constructions with invariable -*te* ptc.; less common are those those in which the ptc. shows adj. agreement with the noun it governs, as *būṛato* in the last example below.

टेरत हेरत हारि परयौ 'calling and searching I suffered defeat' (SR 5.3)
मरत जियौ 'on the point of dying, I lived' (RAM 56)
सोवत लरिकनि छिरकि मही सौं हँसत चलै 'having sprinkled the sleeping boys with earth, he went off laughing' (SS 22.4)
कहत न बनै सकुच की बातें 'my anxieties could not be expressed' (SS 20.6)
दु:ख कछु टरत न टारे 'his grief cannot be removed, despite trying' (SB 8.5)
तब फिरत फिरत एक दिन गोवर्द्धन पर्वत पैं यह चढ्यो 'then wandering about, one day he ascended Govardhan hill' (VV 202)
यह वेणुनाद सुनत ही 'immediately on hearing this flute-playing' (VV 219)
नगर के निवासी...वाकौ शब्द सदा सुन्यौ करैं 'the townsfolk always hear its sound' (RN 18)
तीन दिन कौ भूखौ बैठो है 'he has been sitting [there] hungry for three days' (VV 227)
बूड़तो गजराज राख्यौ 'you saved the drowning elephant' (MP 3.5)

Non-finite constructions with the obl.sg. perf. ptc. in -*e* are, as in MSH, mostly adv.:

और भजे तैं काम सरै नहिं 'through other worshipping, one's aim is not achieved' (SS 2.2.)
वाकौ बंधे बहुत दिन बीते 'many days passed by with him tied up' (RAM 27)
तीनि दिन याकों भूखे होइ गए है 'three days have passed with him being hungry' (VV 215)
तेरे कहे 'on your say-so' (SR 3.3)

The m.sg. perf. ptc. combines with *cāh-* to give the sense 'to want to X', a usage largely replaced in MSH by dir. infinitive + *cāhnā*. Thus *bhayau cāhata* (cf. MSH *honā cāhtā*).

I.5.7 Future

I.5.7a -*h*- forms.

Sg. and pl. (nasality does not consistently designate pl. number)

1st	stem + -*haũ*
2nd	stem + -*hu*
3rd	stem + -*hai*

मोर पखा सिर ऊपर राखिहौं 'I shall place a peacock-feather [crown] on my head' (SR 3.1)
जैसें राखहु तैसें रहौं 'as you shall maintain me so I remain' (SS 9.1)

भूषन भारु सँभारिहै क्यौं 'how will she bear the burden of her ornaments?' (BS 28.1)
ह्वैहैं फेरि बसंत ऋतु 'there will be the spring season once more' (BS 42.2)

(In some published texts the 3rd person *-hai* ending is sometimes printed separately from the verb stem, through confusion with auxiliary *hai.*)

I.5.7b Subjunctive-future. Hardly to be distinguished from subjunctive-present (I.5.4) in usage. Formed from active stem + *-hi, -hī, -hĩ, -hī̃* (though nasality does not consistently indicate pl. number). The examples are 3rd person:

बेस्या बरस घटावही 'the whore will reduce her years' (NS 24.2)
(दृग) सर से जाहिं '(the eyes) go like arrows' (SR 23.2)
धात तन लावहीं 'he smears pigment on his body' (AP 16.1)

I.5.7c Extended *-g-* forms. Equivalent to MSH future forms (*karū̃gā* etc.), these comprise present subjunctive + *-gau, gī, -ge* (again with sporadic nasality):

गुंज की माल गरें पहिरौंगी 'I shall wear a necklace of seeds around my neck' (SR 3.1)
अब हम कहा करेंगे 'now what shall we do?' (VV 160)

I.5.8 Passives

I.5.8a Synthetic passive A general present tense in the passive is formed from passive stem + the imperf. ptc. endings *-ta, -ti* (e.g. *suniyata, boliyata*), with or without auxiliary. Stems in *-āi*, such as *pāi-*, may be contracted to *pai-* etc.

अब हीं चलाइयति...चलन की बात 'is talk of going already set in motion?' (BS 15.2)
ओढ़ियत है कि बिछैयत है 'is it worn, or spread over one?' (SS 39.2)
दलमलियतु...कुसुम सौ गातु 'her flower-like body is crushed' (BS 69.1)
मन्दिर में सामग्री चहियत हती 'provisions were needed in the temple' (VV 102)

A subjunctive-present tense in the passive is formed from passive stem + *-i.* (MSH *cāhie* 'is wanted' is a survival of such a form.) As with the active subjunctive-present, mood is often inexplicit, indicative or subjunctive senses applying equally well. This tense may also be indistinguishable from an imperative (cf. MSH *'āp'* imperatives in *-ie*).

पत्रा हीं तिथि पाइयै 'only with an almanac is the date found' (BS 9.1)
क्यौं बसियै क्यौं निबहियै 'how can one dwell, how can one survive?' (BS 37.1)
बात प्रेम की राखिए अपने ही मन माँहि 'matters of love are kept within one's own heart' [= 'keep matters of love...'] (NS 16.1)

I.5.8b Periphrastic passive (with *jā*-) The periphrastic or analytic passive formed from perf. ptc. + *jā-* is equivalent to the MSH passive; in the negative it often expresses incapacity or unwillingness to do something.

भूषन पिछाने जात 'her ornaments are distinguished' (BS 30.2)
जात नहिं उलँघी '[the threshold] cannot be crossed' (SS 11.3)
बोल्यौ न जाय 'he could not speak' (VV 65)

I.5.9 Absolutives

The commonest form is the verb stem alone:

ओढ़ि पितंबर लै लकुटी 'donning his sash and taking his stick' (SR 3.2)
कुच गिरि चढ़ि अति थकित ह्वै 'climbing her breast-mountains, being most tired' (BS 5.1)
गाय गाय हरि के गुन 'constantly singing of Hari's qualities' (MP 4.4)

Alongside this is the extended form with *-kari*, or *-kai/-ke* (which may be nasalized):

सूरदास महाप्रसाद लैकैं आये 'Sūrdās arrived after taking *mahāprasād*' (VV 69)
तब ऐसे कहि कै खडग उठाय लियो 'then so saying he drew his sword' (VV 182)

I.5.10 Imperatives

The verb stem is frequently an imperative: *suni, dekhi,* etc.
An imperative-subjunctive is formed from stem + *-hu*, *-hi*, *-u*, *-o*/*-au*, these endings often being nasalized. *-y-* may be suffixed to the stem before *-o* or *-au*.
Forms in *-ie* often operate as imperatives, as in MSH, though their original passive force is also often apparent.

सुनि सुत 'listen, son' (SS 13.1)
तू मिश्री...लें आउ 'bring...the sugar-candy ' (VV 115)
हरि तुम हरो जन की पीर 'Hari, you remove people's pain' (MP 3.1)
करौ कुबत जगु 'though the world speak ill' (BS 66.1)
जैसें राखहु 'as you may maintain [me]' (SS 9.1)
इनकों मन्दिर में लें आइयो 'take him into the temple' (VV 246)
सुतहिं बरजौ नँदरानी 'restrain your son, Yaśodā' (SS 24.8)
सुनहु न बचन 'listen to my words, won't you?' (SS 23.7)

I.5.11 Verbal Nouns and Infinitives

Forms with functions equivalent to MSH infinitives in *-nā* (*karnā* etc.) are as follows:

(a) stem + *-bau*/ *-vau* : forms a m. noun which inflects to *-e* in obl.

(b) active stem + *-na* . used in composition with *de-* ('to allow to'), with *pā-* ('to manage to, be able to'), and with *lāg-* ('to begin to'); and with a following finite verb in purpose expressions. An extended form in *-nau* (cf. MSH *-nā*) is also found.

(c) active stem + *-ni* : forms a f. noun.

गढ़ लैबे की घात 'the stratagem for taking a fort' (NS 11.1)
कन दैबौ सौंप्यौ ससुर 'father-in-law entrusted alms-giving' (BS 23.1)
वह् मोकों पकरन कों आयो 'he came to catch me' (VV 227)
मोकों स्पर्स करिवे कों दोरचो 'he ran to touch me' (VV 230)
बास छुड़ावन काज 'with the purpose of removing [her] clothes' (BS 48.1)
वा वेस्या की माता रोवन लागी 'that prostitute's mother began to cry' (VV 160)
तन की तपनि 'the burning of her body' (BS 71.1)
भृकुटि मटकनि 'the dancing of her brow' (BS 24. 1)

The m. perf. ptc. can be used nominally, as in MSH:

पावैगौ पुनि कियौ आपनौ 'you will reap later your own deeds' (SS 36.5)
मारचौ फिरि फिरि मारियै 'the stricken one is struck time and again' (BS 29.2)
पिय के बिछुरे 'in the lover's absence' (AY 2.1)

Forms in *-ana* such as *bināsana, prakāsana,* originally adj. ('destroying, illuminating'), function most commonly as verbal agent — thus 'destroyer, illuminator' etc. Several examples appear in RB and elsewhere. While most are Sanskrit loans, some are based on Braj verb stems, and are hardly to be distinguished from Braj verbal nouns.

I.6 ADVERBS

I.6.1 For the most part, adverbs resemble their MSH equivalents. Those having invariable obl. endings (MSH *-e*) are often nasalized: *kaisaĩ, pāchaĩ, āgaĩ, aba kaĩ, pahalẽ.*

I.6.2 Among the negatives, equivalents for MSH *nahĩ* appear variously, as required by metre: *nahĩ, nāhĩ, nāhĩna* etc. Note the 1st person use of *mati* (MSH *mat*) in the sense 'lest' (e.g. BS 20.2). The prohibitive particle is often *jini, jina* (not found in MSH).

I.6.3 The emph. enclitics of the groups *ĭ, hi, hī* and *ŭ, hu, hū* (often nasalized) are equivalents to MSH *hī* and *bhī* respectively. They often coalesce with a preceding final vowel. Final *-ī* + emph. *hī* may yield *-iyai*; final *-ī* + emph. *hū* may yield *-iyau*. Examples:

UNMARKED	EMPHATIC	UNMARKED	EMPHATIC
सब	सबै	अज, आज	अजौं
वह	वहै	नैंक	नैंकौ
इत	इतै	तो, तौ	तऊ
पून्यौ	पून्यौई	दूरि	दूरयौ
नाव	नावै	बड़ी	बड़ीयौ
भली	भलियै	कब	कबौं
परी	परियै	कै	कैयौ
कछु, कछू	कछुवै	दहि	दह्यौ

I.7 POSTPOSITIONS

Ppn. operate as in MSH, though it must be remembered that obl. case alone often has greater syntactic function than it can in MSH: see I.2(f). Note that *binā* and *sahita* also function as prepositions. Some ppn. — mostly those based on nouns — may appear with preceding *kaĩ/ke, kī.*

अंतर 'within'

ऊपर 'above, on, for'

ओर 'towards, in the direction of'

करि 'by, with respect to', (often to be interpreted as the abs. from *kar-*)

(के) काज 'for, for the sake of'

(के) कारन 'for, for the sake of'

कौं, कूँ object marker, cf. MSH *ko*

कौ, की, के poss. part., cf. MSH *kā* etc.

(के) ढिक, ढिग 'near, with', cf. MSH *pās*

तरे, तरै 'beneath, under'

ताई 'to, up to, until'

तैं, तै, तें, ते 'by, with, from, since'

(की) नाई 'like, in the manner of'

(के) निमित 'for the purpose of'

ने ppn. of agentive case

पर, पै 'to, towards, at, from,'

(के) पाछै 'after'

पै 'to, for, by, from'

बिना, बिनि, बिनु 'without, but for'

बिषै 'in, within'

बीच, बिच 'in, between'

के भाई	'like, in the manner of'	(के) समान	'like'
भीतर	'in, inside'	समीप	'near'
(के) मिस	'on the pretext of'	समेत	'with'
मंह, महिं, मधि, मध्य, महि, माँह, माहीं, में, मैं; मंझारन (rh.)	'in, into'; = MSH *mẽ*	सहित	'with'
		साथ	'with'
(के) मारे	'through, because of'	सौं, सों, सूँ	'with, by means of'
लगि, लग; लौं	'up to, as far as, until (cf. MSH *tak*); like'	के हाथ तें	'through, because of'
(के) लिए	'for'	(के) हित	'for the sake of'
(के) संग	'with, in company of'		

I.8 SUMMARY OF THE BRAJ VERB

Only the most common forms are listed. Finite examples are 3rd-person s.; main examples are based on धर- vt. 'hold, place'. Further examples requiring special note are in square brackets.

Stem	धरि, धर	[कै, ह्वै, खै, दै, लै; आय = आइ]		
Imperfective ptc.	धरत (f. धरति)	[आवत etc. show medial व]		
Perfective ptc.	धर्‍यौ (f. धरी)	[भयौ (f. भई), कर्‍यौ etc., दीनौ]		
General present	धरत (f. धरति),	धरत है,	धरत हतौ	
Subj.-present	धरै / धरे			
Future	धरिहै	धरैगौ		
Passive	धरियै	धरियत	धर्‍यौ जात	
Absolutive	धरि	धरिकै, धरि करि		
Imperative	धरि / धर	धरिहि, धरिहु	धरो	धरिये
Infinitive	धरिबौ (obl. धरिबे)	धरन / धरनि		

II PROSODY

II.1 BASIC ELEMENTS

Hindi metres derive from those of Sanskrit, Prakrit and Apabhraṁśa, and are described according to the Sanskrit terminology. Metre is not based on stress accent as in English verse, but on the intrinsic length of the syllables which make up the line. Long syllables are called *guru*, 'heavy' (hereafter '*G*'), and short syllables are called *laghu*, 'light' ('*L*'). The basic units of measurement are the *mātrā* or 'metrical instant' and the *varṇa* or 'syllable'. All syllables, including final *-a* (as in *kāma*) are counted in scanning a line.

The rules governing quantity can be summarized as follows:

1 Short vowels are of one *mātrā* : ⏑ अ ⏑ इ ⏑ उ ⏑ ऋ

2 Long vowels are of two *mātrās* : – आ – ई – ऊ – ए – ऐ – ओ – औ

3 A short vowel becomes long 'by position' when followed in the same word by a conjunct consonant, by *anusvār*, or by *visarga* :

– ⏑ भक्त   – ⏑ ⏑ पल्लव   – ⏑ नंद [= नन्द]   – ⏑ अंग [= अङ्ग]   – ⏑ दुःख

Rule 3 does not usually apply in the following circumstances:

(a) if the second member of a conjunct is the semivowel य ;

(b) before the conjunct न्ह or म्ह ;

(c) when *anusvār* stands for *candrabindu*, representing vowel nasality rather than a nasal consonant.

⏑ – कह्यौ   ⏑ – – कन्हैया   ⏑ ⏑ ⏑ हंसत [= हँसत]

Note the following exceptions which may apply if the metre requires it:

(a) ए, ऐ, ओ and औ may be counted as short, especially in unstressed positions;

(b) The diphthongs ऐ and औ may be dissolved into their two component short vowels (see note to BS 29.2);

(c) a nasal consonant in a conjunct may be reduced to vowel nasality, allowing e.g. अंग to be read as अँग (two short syllables).

In some metres, long and short syllables combine to form feet called *gaṇas*, of which the most important are listed here with their Indian and Greek names:

- -	*GG*	spondee
- ⏑	*GL*	trochee
⏑ -	*LG*	iambus
⏑ ⏑ ⏑	*na-gaṇa*	tribrach
- ⏑ ⏑	*bha-gaṇa*	dactyl
⏑ - ⏑	*ja-gaṇa*	amphibrach
- ⏑ -	*ra-gaṇa*	cretic
⏑ ⏑ -	*sa-gaṇa*	anapaest

A poetic line (*dala* or *pankti*) is typically divided into two or more sections (*pāda*) whose internal arrangement may be in feet (*caraṇ*) comprising the various *gaṇas*. *Pāda*-boundaries will usually coincide with word-breaks, but *caraṇ*-boundaries need not do so. Adjacent *pādas* may be separated by a caesura (*yati*). Odd and even lines are followed by single and double *daṇḍas* respectively; and verses are numbered at the end by numerals between double *daṇḍas*, e.g. ॥२६॥. Further features of the line are described in II.2 below.

II.2 *MĀTRIK* METRES

Metres of this category are measured by the number of *mātrās* to the line. In many *mātrik* metres, the arrangement of long and short syllables within the line or the *pāda* is not fixed, so that a line defined as '16+12 *mātrās*' may have any arrangement of syllables yielding the appropriate total of *mātrās*. In metres where the *mātrās* do fall into groups or '*mātrik gaṇas*' (as in II.2.1), the internal composition of these is typically not specified; thus a *mātrik gaṇa* of six *mātrās* may comprise /⏑ - ⏑ -/, /⏑ ⏑ ⏑ ⏑ ⏑ ⏑/, /- - -/, /⏑ ⏑ - ⏑ ⏑/, etc.

II.2.1 *Dohā*

This is the most common couplet metre, ubiquitous throughout early Hindi poetry. Each of the two lines consists of 24 *mātrās* in the arrangement 6+4+3, 6+4+1 (the comma indicates a caesura, shown in the scansion below by a double oblique line). The 'odd' *pādas*, i.e. the first and third quarters of the couplet, should not begin with an amphibrach (*ja-gaṇa*, ⏑ - ⏑) or end with a trochee (*GL*, - ⏑). The rhyme is in a trochee (*GL*, - ⏑).

⏑ - - ⏑ / ⏑ ⏑ - /⏑ ⏑ ⏑// ⏑ ⏑ ⏑ - ⏑ / - -/⏑
इहीं आस अटक्यौ रहतु अलि गुलाब कैं मूल ।
- - -/⏑ ⏑ -/⏑ ⏑ ⏑// ⏑ ⏑ - ⏑ ⏑/ - -/⏑
ह्वैहैं फेरि बसंत ऋतु इन डारनु वे फूल ॥

In a *dohā*, the four quarters (*pāda*) very commonly comprise discrete clauses: thus the caesura, though not necessarily shown graphically, elucidates the syntax of the line. Some modern editions show the caesura with a comma, a practice which has been followed, where appropriate, in this book.

II.2.2 *Sorṭhā*

This is an inverted *dohā* : that is, in each line the two *pādas* are transposed, leaving the rhyme in the middle of the line, and a *mātrā* construction of 6+4+1, 6+4+3.

– ⏑ ⏑ –/– –/⏑// ⏑ ⏑ – –/ ⏑ ⏑ –/⏑ ⏑⏑
मैं लखि नारी ज्ञानु करि राख्यौ निरधारु यह ।

⏑⏑– –/⏑ ⏑ –/⏑ // ⏑– –⏑/ – ⏑ ⏑/ ⏑–
बहई रोग निदानु वहै बैदु औषधि वहै ॥

II.2.3 *Barvai* (*Barvā, Barvau*)

A compact couplet of 12+7 *mātrās* (6+4+2, 4+2+1) to the line, rhyming like the *dohā*.

⏑⏑ – ⏑⏑ ⏑⏑ –⏑⏑ //⏑⏑⏑ ⏑ – ⏑
भज रे मन नँदनंदन बिपति बिदार ।

– – ⏑⏑ ⏑⏑ –⏑⏑//⏑⏑⏑ ⏑ –⏑
गोपी जन मन रंजन परम उदार ॥

(Note how the nasal in the initial unstressed syllable of *nãdanandana* (= *nandanandana*) is here reduced to vowel nasality, such that the syllable is metrically short.)

II.2.4 *Arill*

This is usually defined as a 16-*mātrā* metre; but as used by Nāgarīdās in the *Arill-pacīsī* the name is applied to a quatrain with a line length of 21 *mātrās* (11+10 or 12+9), rhyming in couplets (a metre elsewhere called *Cāndrāyaṇ*).

– ⏑ ⏑ –⏑ ⏑ – ⏑ //–⏑ ⏑⏑ – ⏑–
टोकत गैल गुपाल दान मिस लैं छरी ।

⏑⏑⏑⏑ ⏑⏑ ⏑ ⏑ – ⏑ //–⏑ ⏑⏑ – ⏑–
गहबर बन अँधियार हार तिय हैं करी ॥

–⏑ –⏑ ⏑⏑ ⏑⏑⏑⏑ // ⏑⏑ ⏑⏑ –⏑–
नैन बैन तन उरझन मन उरझाइयैं ।

⏑⏑ –⏑⏑ ⏑⏑ –⏑ // ⏑ ⏑⏑ ⏑⏑ –⏑–
ब्रजनागर नँदलाल सु निस दिन गाइयैं ॥

II.2.5 *Caupāī and Caupaī*

Each of the four *pādas* is effectively a self-contained line of 16 *mātrās*. The construction is often 6+4+4+2 *mātrās*; rhyme is AAAA or AABB. Rhyme is usually – –, sometimes – ⏑ ⏑

Though the name *Caupāī* clearly defines a quatrain stanza, the couplet (*dvipadī*), rather than the quatrain, is often taken as the basic unit for the purposes of verse numbering.

– – ⏑⏑⏑ ⏑ – ⏑⏑ – – // ⏑⏑⏑ – ⏑ – – ⏑ ⏑ – –
सेवा करन लग्यौ मन लाई । करत भावना नाहिं अघाई ॥

– – – ⏑ ⏑ – – – – // – – – ⏑ – ⏑ ⏑⏑ – –
आयो एक बड़ौ व्यौपारी । लादैं नाव सौंज बहु भारी ॥

Couplets of *caupāī* may alternate with a 15-mātrā variant, *caupaī*, ending – ⏑ or ⏑ – .

– ⏑ ⏑ – ⏑ ⏑ ⏑⏑ – ⏑ – // ⏑⏑⏑ ⏑ – ⏑⏑ – ⏑⏑ ⏑ –
देहि जगात न सब सों अरै । तुपक जमूरन सौं बहु लरै ॥

II.2.6 *Mukrī* (*Mukṛī, Kah-mukṛī*)

The *Mukrī* is a riddle cast in a quatrain. In the first three lines the heroine seems to speak of her lover, but in the final line denies it (*mukar-* means 'to deny, to go back on one's word'), predicating her descriptions to some innocent subject. The length of that subject word, which provides the final rhyme in the AABB rhyme-scheme, will determine the metrical length of the second couplet. Most examples seem to conform roughly to a pattern of 16 or 15 *mātrās* to the line; none conform strictly to the definition given in Platts (1930:1059) and elsewhere, according to which each line consists of four trochees, though the lines can often be read with a trochaic stress.

– – – – ⏑ – ⏑ – –
लंबी लंबी डगों जु आवै ।

– – ⏑⏑ – – ⏑ ⏑ – –
सारे दिन की हौस बुझावै ॥

⏑⏑ – ⏑ – – ⏑⏑ – – ⏑
उठकै चला तो पकड़ा खूंट ।

– ⏑⏑ – ⏑⏑ – ⏑ – – ⏑
क्यौं सखि सज्जन ना सखी ऊंट ॥

II.2.7 *Kuṇḍaliyā*

A composite metre, consisting of a *dohā* followed by one *rolā* quatrain (of 11+13 *mātrās* to the line). The first *pāda* of the *rolā* is a repeat of the last *pāda* of the *dohā*, and the last word of the whole stanza returns to the word or phrase with which it started: thus the stanza resembles a coiled serpent (*kuṇḍalī*).

⏑ –   ⏑ – / –   – / ⏑ – //   –   – – / ⏑ ⏑ – /⏑
बिना बिचारै जो करै सो पाछैं पछिताय ।
– ⏑   ⏑ – / –   – /⏑ – // ⏑ ⏑   –   – / ⏑   ⏑ – /⏑
काम बिगारे आपनौ जग में होत हँसाय ॥
⏑ ⏑   –   – ⏑   ⏑ – ⏑ // – ⏑   –   – ⏑   ⏑   – –
जग में होत हँसाय चित्त में चैन न पावै ।
– ⏑   – ⏑   ⏑ ⏑ – ⏑ // – ⏑   ⏑ ⏑   ⏑ ⏑ ⏑   ⏑   – –
खान पान सनमान राग रँग मनहि न आवै ॥
⏑ ⏑   ⏑ ⏑ ⏑ ⏑   ⏑ ⏑ – ⏑ // – ⏑   ⏑ ⏑   ⏑ ⏑ ⏑   ⏑   – –
कह गिरधर कविराय दुःख कछु टरत न टारे ।
⏑ ⏑ ⏑ ⏑   –   ⏑ ⏑   – ⏑ // ⏑ –   –   ⏑ –   ⏑ – –
खटकत है जिय माहिं कियौ जो बिना बिचारै ॥

II.2.8 *Chappay*

Another composite metre, consisting of a *rolā* quatrain (of 11+13 *mātrās* to the line) plus an *ullāl* couplet. The *ullāl* has 15+13 *mātrās* to the line, sometimes reckoned as 4+4+4+3, 6+4+3; a variant has 13+13 *mātrās*, as in the example here from the *Bhakta-māl* of Nābhādās (Nābhājī n.d.:290):

⏑ ⏑ ⏑   – ⏑ –   – ⏑ / ⏑ ⏑ ⏑   ⏑ ⏑ ⏑ ⏑ ⏑   ⏑ – –
सदृश गोपिका प्रेम प्रगट कलिजुगहिं दिखायौ ।
⏑ ⏑ – ⏑ ⏑   ⏑ ⏑   ⏑ ⏑ ⏑ / ⏑ ⏑ ⏑   ⏑ ⏑   ⏑ ⏑ –   – –
निर-अंकुश अति निडर रसिक जस रसना गायौ ॥
– ⏑ ⏑   – ⏑   ⏑ – ⏑ / – ⏑   –   – ⏑ ⏑   – –
दुष्टनि दोष बिचारि मृत्यु को उद्दिम कीयौ ।
– ⏑ ⏑   – –   ⏑ – / ⏑ ⏑ ⏑   ⏑ ⏑ ⏑   –   – –
बार न बांकौ भयौ गरल अमृत ज्यौं पीयौ ॥
– ⏑   ⏑ – ⏑   ⏑ – ⏑   – / – –   –   – ⏑ ⏑   ⏑ –
भक्ति निसान बजाय कै काहू ते नाहिन लजी ।
– ⏑   – ⏑ ⏑ ⏑   – ⏑ – / ⏑ ⏑   – –   ⏑ ⏑ ⏑ ⏑   ⏑ –
लोक लाज कुल श्रृंखला तजि मीरा गिरिधर भजी ॥

II.3 *MĀTRIK* METRES USED IN *PADAS*

A *pada* is a lyric hymn, performed in one of the many rhythmic cycles (*tāla*) of Indian music. Though metres such as *Caupāī* may be used in *padas*, the metres described below are more commonly encountered: they do not really constitute a metrical type distinct from II.2, but are here separately categorized for convenience. The *mātrik* metres used in *padas* are of a simple construction, usually being defined only in terms of the overall line length and the position of a single caesura. A *pada* may consist of any number of couplets, a typical length being three or four (i.e. six or eight lines). Occasionally an odd number of lines is encountered, especially in Mīrā's poems, which generally follow the metrical 'rules' only very loosely; but generally the couplet construction holds good. (The convention of marking odd and even lines with single and double *daṇḍas* respectively has necessarily been dropped in the Mīrā poems in this book.)

The rhyme scheme is AABBCC etc., or simply AAAAAA etc. The first line, as in the example below, is often short, and acts as a refrain, called *ṭeka* or *sthāyī* (though these terms may also be applied to the whole of the first couplet): its length usually approximates to the length of the first *pāda* of a full line, i.e. 16 *mātrās* in the case of *Sār.*

II.3.1 *Sār*

This has 16+12 *mātrās* to the line (often arranged as 6+4+4+4+4+4+2), with rhyme in *GG* (- -) or less commonly in a *bha-gaṇa* (- ⏑ ⏑).

⏑⏑ ⏑⏑ ⏑⏑⏑⏑ –⏑ ⏑– –
निसि दिन बरषत नैन हमारे।

⏑– ⏑⏑⏑ ⏑⏑– ⏑⏑ ⏑⏑ ⏑⏑//⏑⏑ – –⏑ ⏑– –
सदा रहति बरषा रितु हम पर जब तैं स्याम सिधारे ॥

⏑⏑ –⏑⏑ ⏑ ⏑⏑⏑ ⏑ ⏑ –⏑⏑//⏑⏑ ⏑–⏑ ⏑– – –
दृग अंजन न रहत निसि बासर कर कपोल भए कारे ।

–⏑⏑ ⏑⏑ –⏑⏑ ⏑⏑ ⏑⏑– // ⏑⏑ ⏑ ⏑ ⏑⏑⏑ ⏑– –
कंचुकि-पट सूखत नहिं कबहूँ उर बिच बहत पनारे ॥

– – ⏑⏑⏑ ⏑– ⏑⏑ – – //⏑⏑ ⏑ –⏑ ⏑ ⏑ – –
आसूँ सलिल सबै भइ काया पल न जात रिस टारे ।

–⏑–⏑ ⏑⏑ ⏑⏑ ⏑– – // –⏑⏑ – – ⏑– –
सूरदास प्रभु यह परेखौ गोकुल काहैं बिसारे ॥

The 16-*mātrā* base of this metre is typical of many *pada* metres, and corresponds to the use in sung performance of the commonest *tāla,* the 16-beat *tīntāl.* The following example shows how the first couplet of a *pada* might be set to the *tāla* cycle: note that the poetic line often begins at some medial point in the cycle (*āvarta*), typically allowing a long syllable to fall on beat 1, the so-called *sama,* which bears the strongest stress. In the second line of the traditional transcription given below, the *sama* is marked '×', subsidiary strong beats or *tālīs* are marked numerically '2' and '3', and the de-stressed or 'empty' beat *khālī,* at the beginning of the third section, is shown with a zero. (It is the three *tālīs* — often marked by hand-claps, or by the *jhā̃jh* cymbals — which give *tīntāl* its name.)

Tīntāl :	१	२	३	४	५	६	७	८	९	१०	११	१२	१३	१४	१५	१६
	×				२				•				३			
									नि	सि	दि	न	ब	र	ष	त
	नै	ऽ	न	ह	मा	ऽ	रे	ऽ	स	दा	ऽ	र	ह	ति	ब	र
	षा	ऽ	रि	तु	ह	म	प	र	ज	ब	तैं	ऽ	स्या	ऽ	म	सि
	धा	ऽ	रे	ऽ	*नि*	*सि*	*दि*	*न*	दृ	ग	अं	ऽ	ज	न	न	र
	(etc.)															

The first four *mātrās* of the *ṭeka* are here used as a makeweight, shown in italics, to fill the discrepancy between the 12-*mātrā ṭeka* line and the 16-beat cycle. (See R.Snell 1983.)

II.3.2 *Sarasī*

Identical to *Sār* but with final syllable short: 16+11 *mātrās* with trochee rhyme (*GL,* – ⏑). (In this and following examples, couplets exemplify the metre of whole stanzas.)

– ⏑⏑ ⏑ – – ⏑ ⏑ ⏑ – – //⏑⏑ ⏑⏑ ⏑⏑ ⏑⏑ – ⏑
कोटिक कला काछि दिखराई जल थल सुध नहिं काल ।

–⏑ –⏑ – ⏑– ⏑– – // – ⏑ ⏑ – ⏑⏑ – ⏑
सूरदास की सबै अबिद्या दूरि करौ नँदलाल ॥

Sarasī and *Sār* are often mixed within the same stanza: SS 15, for example, starts with a *Sār* couplet, and continues with two couplets in *Sarasī.*

II.3.3 *Samān savaiyā*

16+16 *mātrās* to the line, as in the first couplet of SS 32, whose *ṭeka* has 16 *mātrās,* i.e. half the length of the full line:

⏑⏑⏑⏑ –⏑ ⏑– ⏑⏑ –⏑⏑
नटवर वेष धरे ब्रज आवत ।

–⏑ ⏑⏑⏑ ⏑⏑ –⏑⏑ –⏑⏑ // ⏑⏑⏑ ⏑⏑⏑ ⏑⏑ ⏑⏑ ⏑⏑ –⏑⏑
मोर मुकुट मकराकृत कुंडल कुटिल अलक मुख पर छबि पावत ॥

II.3.4 *Bīr*

16+15 *mātrās* to the line.

– – – ⏑ ⏑ – ⏑⏑ – ⏑ ⏑ //⏑⏑⏑⏑ – ⏑⏑ – ⏑ ⏑ – ⏑
कैसी टेव परी इन गोपिनि उरहन कैं मिस आवतिं प्रात ।
–⏑ ⏑ ⏑⏑ ⏑ ⏑ –⏑ ⏑ –⏑⏑ //⏑⏑– – – ⏑⏑ ⏑⏑ –⏑
सूर सु कत हठि दोष लगावति घरही कौ माखन नहिं खात ॥

II.3.5 *Karkhā*

20+17 *mātrās* to the line (perhaps 8+12, 8+9):

⏑⏑⏑ – –⏑ – ⏑ – ⏑⏑⏑⏑ ⏑ – // ⏑ – – – ⏑ – – ⏑ – –
अनुभवी जानही बिना अनुभव कहा प्रिया जाकौ नहीं चित्त चोरै ।
–⏑ – –⏑ – –⏑ – – ⏑ – //– ⏑ ⏑ ⏑ – ⏑ ⏑ –⏑ – –
प्रेम के सिंधु कौ मर्म जान्यौ नहीं सूर कहि कहा भयौ देह बोरैं ॥

II.3.6 *Śaṅkar*

16+10 *mātrās* to the line.

⏑⏑⏑ ⏑⏑⏑ ⏑⏑ – ⏑ ⏑ –⏑⏑ //⏑⏑⏑⏑ ⏑ – ⏑ –
कमल नयन घनस्याम मनोहर अनुचर भयौ रहौं ।
–⏑–⏑ ⏑⏑ –⏑ ⏑ – ⏑ ⏑ // ⏑⏑– ⏑⏑⏑ ⏑ –
सूरदास प्रभु भक्त कृपानिधि तुम्हरे चरन गहौं ॥

II.3.7 *Rūp-mālā*

14+10 *mātrās* to the line (and accordingly sung to 14- or 7-beat *tāla*).

⏑ – –⏑ ⏑ – ⏑ ⏑⏑⏑⏑ // ⏑ – ⏑⏑ – –⏑
थक्यौ बीच बिहाल बिह्वल सुनौ करुना मूल ।
–⏑ ⏑⏑ ⏑ ⏑ – ⏑ – – // –⏑ ⏑⏑ – –⏑
स्याम भुज गहि काढ़ि लीजै सूर ब्रज कैं कूल ॥

II.4 *VARṆIK* METRES

Metres of this species are measured according to the number and arrangement of syllables (*varṇa*) to the line. They include some *pada* metres, such as the following:

II.4.1 *Pada* metre with trochee base (*GL*)

Seven repeats of the *gaṇa* /– ⏑ – ⏑/, + *G.* Though the conventional printed layout of this metre follows that of the *kavitt* (II.4.4), its structure is seen most clearly when laid out in four lines. Caesuras after the second and fourth *gaṇas* are often bolstered by the strong internal rhyme or alliteration which is a common feature of this type, as in the following example (from the sixteenth-century poet Harirām Vyās, see V. Gosvāmī 1952:269):

˘˘˘ ˘ ˘ ˘/– ˘ – ˘ //– ˘ – ˘/– ˘ – ˘//˘˘˘ – ˘/ – ˘ – ˘/ – ˘ – ˘/–
सुरँग कुच उतंग अंग माधुरी तरंग रंग सुरत रंग मान भंग काम कामिनी ।

– ˘ – – ˘/– ˘ – ˘//˘˘˘ – ˘/– ˘ – ˘//˘˘˘ ˘˘˘/˘ ˘ ˘ – ˘/– ˘ – ˘/–
मंदहास भ्रू बिलास मधुर बैन नैन सैन बिबस करत पियहिं व्यासदास स्वामिनी ॥

II.4.2 *Pada* metre with cretic base (*GLG*)

Eight repeats of the *gaṇa* / ¯ ˘ ¯ /. Caesura divisions follow the pattern of II.4.1. In the following example (from the *Caurāsī-pad* of Hit Harivaṁś, see R. Snell 1991a) the cretic rhythm is most fully represented in the *ṭeka* :

– ˘ –/– ˘ – //– ˘ – /– ˘ –
आजु नीकी बनी राधिका नागरी ।

˘˘ ˘˘˘ / – ˘ – //– ˘ ˘˘/ ˘˘˘– //– ˘ –/– ˘ ˘˘/ ˘˘˘ – / – ˘ –
ब्रज जुवति जूथ मैं रूप अरु चतुरई सील सिंगार गुन सबन तें आगरी ॥

˘˘˘ –/˘ ˘ ˘ – //– ˘ ˘˘ /– ˘ ˘ ˘// – ˘ – /˘˘˘ ˘ ˘/˘˘˘ ˘˘/– ˘ –
कमल दक्षिन भुजा बाम भुज अंस सखि गावती सरस मिलि मधुर सुर राग री ।

˘˘ ˘ – /– ˘ ˘ ˘//˘˘˘ ˘ ˘/– ˘ ˘˘//˘ ˘ ˘ ˘˘/– ˘ ˘˘ / – ˘ ˘˘/– ˘ –
सकल बिद्या बिदित रहसि हरिबंश हित मिलत नव कुंज बर स्याम बड़भाग री ॥

II.4.3 *Savaiyā*

Not to be confused with the *mātrik* metre *samān savaiyā* described above (II.3.3), this is a quatrain having AAAA rhyme and a characteristic rhythm of single long syllables alternating with paired short syllables. There are three main varieties:

(a) *Matta-gayand* or *Māltī* : seven dactyls (*bha-gaṇa,* – ˘ ˘) + a final spondee (*GG*, – –);
(b) *Kirīṭ* : eight dactyls (*bha-gaṇa,* – ˘ ˘);
(c) *Durmilā* : eight anapaests (*sa-gaṇa,* ˘ ˘ –).

Rather more than the usual amount of licence seems to be allowed in this metre in the counting of long vowels (especially *ī*) as short: a stress-based rhythm is perhaps here beginning to displace the strictly-measured syllabic basis of conventional Indo-Aryan metrics. Thus in the following *Matta-gayand* of Raskhān (SR 7), those unstressed long vowels marked ⩦ must be counted as short:

– ⏑ ⏑/– ⏑⏑ / – ⏑⏑/– ⏑=/ – ⏑= /– ⏑ ⏑ / –⏑ ⏑/– –
आजु भटू इक गोपबधू भई बावरी नेकु न अंग सम्हारै ।
– ⏑ ⏑/–⏑ ⏑/ –⏑⏑ / –⏑⏑ / – ⏑ ⏑/– = ⏑ /– = ⏑/– –
मात अघात न देवनि पूजत सासु सयानी सयानी पुकारै ॥
– ⏑⏑/– ⏑ ⏑/ – ⏑ ⏑/– ⏑⏑/ –⏑ = / – ⏑ ⏑/–⏑ ⏑/ – –
यों रसखानि घिरचो सिगरो ब्रज कौन को कौन उपाय बिचारै ।
– ⏑ ⏑/ – ⏑⏑/– ⏑⏑/– ⏑⏑/ – ⏑ ⏑/ –⏑ ⏑/– ⏑ ⏑/ – –
कोउ न कान्हर के कर तें वह बैरिनि बाँसुरिया गहि जारै ॥

Note how the *chāp 'rasakhāna'*, fits into the *savaiyā* rhythm. Different *savaiyā* types may be mixed within a single stanza: thus in SR 25, the *Matta-gayand* rhythm of lines 1, 2 and 4 is interrupted by line 3 in *Durmilā* (with an extra *guru*).

II.4.2 *Kavitt* or *Ghanākṣarī*

A quatrain in which each line has 31 or 32 syllables, whose value is not prescribed: counting is simply by the number of the syllables, regardless of length. A caesura usually follows the 16th syllable, where the line is usually split graphically on the printed page; secondary caesuras may appear after the 8th and/or 24th syllables. Caesuras are sometimes marked with internal rhyme. As the length of the syllables is immaterial, and the main caesuras are shown by line-breaks, the example is given without scansion:

गोरज बिराजै भाल लहलही बनमाल
        आगे गैया पाछे ग्वाल गावै मृदु तान री ।
तैसी धुनि बाँसुरी की मधुर मधुर तैसी
        बंक चितवनि मंद मंद मुसकानि री ॥
कदम विटप के निकट तटनी के तट
        अटा चढ़ि चाहि पीत पट फहरानि री ।
रस बरसावै तन तपन बुझावै नैन
        प्राननि रिझावै वह आवै रसखानि री ॥

III BRAJ BHĀṢĀ LITERATURE

III.1 LITERARY GENRES OF THE SIXTEENTH TO EIGHTEENTH CENTURIES[1]

The texts included in this reader represent some of the principal genres of devotional, court and other traditional poetry which came into prominence from the first half of the sixteenth century. Vernacular literature in the diverse regional languages of what is now called, with a misleading implication of linguistic and cultural homogeneity, the 'Hindi' area, was well established by this time: Sufi poetry written in Avadhī comprised one major tradition of the eastern part of the region, while eclectic traditions of Sant verse, in a mixed language often based on the Khaṛī Bolī dialect of the Delhi region, were a major current in the more westerly stream. In Rajasthan, centuries-old genres of epic and heroic verse flourished in vernaculars which would hardly be comprehensible to the residents of Banaras or Agra; and from West to East there existed vigorous styles of orally-composed

[1] **Bibliographical Note**: Braj Bhāṣā poetry is hardly to be appreciated without a familiarity with the main episodes of the life of Kṛṣṇa, whose *līlā* features so prominently in the majority of poems. A convenient summary is given in W.G. Archer 1957. The concept of *līlā* is discussed in D.R. Kinsley 1979. A. Dallapiccola 1982, and P. Banerjee 1978, give a full synopsis, with examples of the rich tradition of painting and iconography of Kṛṣṇa-*bhakti* ; Dallapiccola also introduces the various sectarian traditions with which so much devotional literature is connected. N. Sheth 1984 (especially last chapter) and B. Preciado-Solis 1984 review Puranic developments; the *Bhāgavata* is translated by G.V. Tagare 1976-78; F. Hardy 1983 gives a full treatment of the Āḻvār tradition. E. Zelliott 1976 gives a very useful (though now dated) bibliographical essay on *bhakti* traditions.

F.S. Growse 1882 is still an invaluable resource on Braj traditions; for more recent encyclopaedic coverage see A.W. Entwistle 1987. K.Klostermaier 1969 gives a comparative perspective; M. Singer 1966 includes articles on various aspects of Kṛṣṇaism; N. Hein 1972 gives a classic account of Braj performance traditions; C. Vaudeville 1976 describes the establishment of sectarian traditions in Braj, and 1980 reveals the complexity of religious reference underlying the Govardhan site and its myth. M. Corcoran 1980 discusses developments in the portrayal of Vrindaban in Vaiṣṇava literature.

On the Vallabha sect see R. Barz 1976 for an essential background to Kṛṣṇaite hagiography; J.D. Redington 1983 for Vallabha's theology; R.J. Cohen 1984 for a particularly useful and succinct summary of sectarian history and practice; A. Ambalal 1987, P.J. Bennett 1983 and 1990, and A.-M. Gaston [1992] for temple traditions; K. Mulji 1865 for a celebrated nineteenth-century scandal relating to the temple priests.

On the Caitanya sect, see J.T. O'Connell 1976 for a useful introduction; for more detail, see M.T. Kennedy 1925, S.K. De 1961, E.C. Dimock 1966, D.L. Haberman 1988a, N. Hein 1976, D.M. Wulff 1984. D.L. Haberman 1988b gives an extract from the hagiography *Caitanya-caritāmṛta*. Articles on Rādhā appear in J.S. Hawley and D.M. Wulff 1982; Jayadeva is discussed in R. Sarkar 1974, B.S. Miller 1977, L. Siegel 1978 and S. Kakar 1985.

For the Sanskrit antecedents of Braj Bhāṣā court poetry see D.H.H. Ingalls 1965 and J. Brough 1968. The fullest coverage of the entire pre-modern period of Hindi literature is given in R.S. McGregor 1984, the standard reference work. Musical settings of Braj verse are discussed in Peter Manuel 1989. An essential corrective to the view suggested so far that Hindu culture was predominant throughout our period and area is given by R. Russell and K. Islam in their classic 1968 account of late Mughal poetry.

poetry which modern taxonomies would label as 'folk' literature — another important source for the more self-consciously literary verse later patronized by the temple and the royal court. The diversity of these complementary varieties of literature typifies the heterogeneity of the cultural amalgam which existed in the late medieval period.

III.1.1 The Cultural Significance of Braj and its Language

The area of Braj (Sanskrit 'Vraja') has an ancient and culturally complex history, having sustained over the centuries a wide array of religious traditions both local and classical. Yet despite its ancient importance as a centre of Buddhism, and despite the continuing centrality of *devī*-worship among its rural inhabitants, Braj is now virtually synonymous with the traditions of devotional Vaiṣṇavism — more specifically, Kṛṣṇaism — which arose during the first decades of the sixteenth century; and it is through this Kṛṣṇaite association that Braj Bhāṣā, of all the regional varieties of 'Hindi' used for literary composition, came to its position as a first among equals.

While Vaiṣṇava sectarian and pilgrimage activity in the Braj region dates back only to the late medieval age, the region had long been eulogized in the Sanskrit *Purāṇas* on the basis of its identification as the site of Kṛṣṇa's earthly incarnation. Modern redactions of the Kṛṣṇa myth tend to present it as a coherent and monolithic narrative, derived ready-made, as it were, from classical sources. But the portrayal of Kṛṣṇa through the successive *Purāṇas,* and later through the more condensed chronology of sectarian reworkings of the Kṛṣṇa myth, can be seen developing and growing with the passage of time — a process of change which the devout Vaiṣṇava, of course, would see as one of progressive revelation and discovery rather than of invention and embellishment. Thus through the early medieval period the portrayal of Kṛṣṇa's character developed from that of folk hero to divinity, as the robust and earthy narrative of the fourth-century *Harivaṁśa* gave way to the transcendental devotionalism of the enormously influential *Bhāgavata Purāṇa* (BhP), composed in South India sometime around the ninth century. The *Harivaṁśa,* a kind of appendix to the *Mahābhārata*, emphasizes the rustic aspect of the Kṛṣṇa myth, with Kṛṣṇa's miraculous accomplishments being described as the acts of a folk hero; the *Bhāgavata*, by comparison, describes Kṛṣṇa in a sublime haze of spirituality, his superhuman deeds being represented as *līlā* or 'divine sport' undertaken without purpose. The *Viṣṇu Purāṇa* occupies an intermediate position in this development, both chronologically and in content.

A catalyst of this process of change was the devotional tradition of the Āḻvārs, a group of non-brahmanical Vaiṣṇava poets active in the Tamil country from about the sixth century, whose *bhakti* was marked by an intensely personal and emotional character stressing the pain felt by the human soul in separation from God. Another important influence on the development of Vaiṣṇava *bhakti* and its literature was the Sanskrit lyric poem *Gītagovinda*, written by Jayadeva in Orissa in the twelfth century, which depicts Rādhā and Kṛṣṇa's clandestine love-making in the lush and paradisiac setting of a grove on the bank of the Yamuna river. This text, which quickly became popular in dance and song traditions all over India, emphasizes the erotic element in the Kṛṣṇa myth and establishes in particular the central role of Rādhā as Kṛṣṇa's beloved; for up to this point Rādhā, though mentioned in Prakrit poems as early as the second century, had yet to appear in mainstream Vaiṣṇava sources — to the embarrassment of later theologians, who had to contrive explanations for her absence from even the authoritative BhP.

Despite the widespread influence of the BhP and the *Gītagovinda*, there was little cultic activity in the geographical area of Braj until several centuries after their composition. But the favourable political and cultural circumstances of the late medieval period were to see the rapid development of Vaiṣṇavism throughout India, leading to the rise of major traditions of devotional poetry in a range of vernacular languages from West to East. Two principal varieties of *bhakti* — the *saguṇ* type, dedicated primarily to the worship of Rāma and Kṛṣṇa as incarnate deities, and the *nirguṇ* type, which perceived God in abstract, non-anthropomorphic terms — became established, not as discrete alternatives to each other but rather as complementary modes of religious thought with a broad popular base. Focal points for these traditions were provided by sectarian communities called *sampradāy* (to be translated as 'sect' only with the caveat that the sense 'splinter group of an established church' does not apply here); each of the various Kṛṣṇaite *sampradāys* stems from the teachings of a spiritual leader who in some way wrought a variation on the Kṛṣṇaism of the BhP by emphasizing one or other aspect of its devotional teaching, or whose charisma was of itself sufficient to attract a substantial and coherent following. The Kṛṣṇa *sampradāys* have the additional focus of one or more of the particular Kṛṣṇa-images (*svarūp*), whose temples form the centre of sectarian activity.

It was against this background that the South Indian theologian Vallabha (1479-1531) and the Bengali mystic Kṛṣṇa Caitanya (1486-1533) gave a newly literal interpretation to the significance of Braj by identifying particular geographical localities as the very places where Kṛṣṇa's *līlā*, graphically portrayed in the BhP, had actually been enacted in historical time; by so doing, they established Braj as an important Vaiṣṇava centre in which the local vernacular, Braj Bhāṣā, came naturally to be regarded as the appropriate vehicle for contemporary devotional literature. The Vallabha *sampradāy* (often called 'Puṣṭi Mārg', interpreted as 'path of grace') and the Caitanya *sampradāy* (or 'Gauḍīya *sampradāy*', named after the Bengal province of Gauḍ from where many early adherents came) are two of the many sects whose presence and activities in Braj extend into the modern era. Such sectarian traditions of Kṛṣṇa-worship first flourished in Braj during the more tolerant phases of Muslim rule, whose power-bases of Delhi and Agra were only a short distance from this Vaiṣṇava holy land; numerous temples were built from the early decades of the sixteenth century; and although the catholic policies of Akbar's administration were reversed by later emperors (notably by the iconoclastic Aurangzeb), Braj was to remain an important centre of Vaiṣṇava pilgrimage to be compared with the *tīrthas* of Dwarka and Puri.

Thus it was that Braj Bhāṣā found itself elevated to the status of a major literary language cultivated well beyond the borders of its own spoken currency, and later adapted to literary uses only remotely related to the devotionalism which accounted for its initial rise as a poetic medium. Its supremacy was to remain unchallenged until the nineteenth century, when increasing contact with Western culture caused the ground-plan of written literature to be re-drawn, with Kharī Bolī coming into prominence as both lingua franca and literary language throughout the Hindi-speaking area. Insofar as it is maintained as the language of lyrics in the twentieth-century repertoire of classical Hindustani music, and because devotional Kṛṣṇaism continues to be a major aspect of the living Hindu tradition, Braj Bhāṣā can still lay claim to a position of prominence in the culture of Northern India.

III.1.2 Principal Trends in Braj Bhāṣā Literature

The Kṛṣṇa literature of the period under discussion was the product of various elements inherited from preceding centuries. In language and prosody it was the descendant of the Middle Indo-Aryan Apabhraṁśa; in lexicon it added to this heritage the resources of indigenous vocabulary, of literary loans from Sanskrit, and of current loans from Persian (including many Arabic words); in content it drew heavily on the Sanskrit Vaiṣṇava literature, particularly the *Purāṇas*, and on the elaborately described contexts and rhetorical categories of Sanskrit court poetry; and in style, imagery and sentiment it owed much to the timeless themes of folksong, whose lovers' laments and romantic imagery reflect the cycle of the seasons in a rural setting. All these elements are to be found in the lyric form known as the *pada*, a metrically simple song composed in rhyming couplets, comprising the most ubiquitous form in *bhakti* verse. A corpus of devotional *padas* is typically referred to as *bānī* (Skt *vāṇī*), 'speech', implying 'divinely inspired utterance'.

The collections of *padas* and other verse types which have come down to us through the centuries have been subject to influences of many kinds, notably the changing vagaries of scribal convention in respect of orthography, the priorities of compilers as they assembled collections intended to reflect a particular sectarian theology, and the various changes to wording and metre which result from a verse being handed on orally from one generation of singers to another. Thus there is often a question-mark hanging over individual poems in respect of their 'authenticity', if by that term we mean the certain and verifiable attribution of a poem to a given historical figure. The situation is further complicated by the fact that the traditional sectarian hagiologies are themselves based on piously optimistic expectations as to the manner (and length!) of a poet's life, and are hardly to be relied upon as historical accounts: thus neither the biography of a poet nor the literary corpus attributed to him can be used as a reliable yardstick against which to assess the other. The concerns of objective historicity are of course both irrelevant and irreverent in the eyes of the *bhakta*, for whom a poem's spiritual authority alone is sufficient testimony to its pedigree; but the more sceptical outside observer must have recourse to the manuscript tradition, whose evidence can often help to build up a historically accurate genealogy for the poems, and which can often be used to postulate reconstructions of a corrupt text. This book includes some texts whose attribution to named authors is beyond reasonable doubt, and others whose attribution, though long-standing, may have been as much a part of the formulaically creative element of tradition as the composition of the poem itself.

Both in terms of their content and in terms of the textual problems of the kind just outlined, the *padas* of the sixteenth-century poets Sūrdās (3) and Mīrā (4) are typical of their genre. Their themes centre on descriptive eulogies of Kṛṣṇa, often alluding to the numerous *līlās* too well known to the *bhakta* audience to call for a full serial narrative. Starting points for the poems are some of the mental attitudes of Vaiṣṇava devotionalism: *vinay* or humble entreaty to a loving deity; *vātsalya* or the feeling of parental fondness felt towards Kṛṣṇa as divine child; *mādhurya*, the sentiment of romantic and erotic love which the devotee achieves by assuming the attitude of a gopi; and the concomitant sensation of *virah*, the pain of separation felt by the gopis when deserted by their lover. Though apparently simple in their narrative and descriptive registers, poems of this kind bear — for their intended audience at least — levels of meaning and symbolic devotional significance hard to suggest through their inevitably banal translations in English. Much of the charm of the poems derives from the homely idiom in which they are couched, as the human aspect of Kṛṣṇa is stressed in such a way as to make him accessible to the lay devotee: devotional poets such as Sūr make much of their fascination with the paradox of epiphany — that Kṛṣṇa, who is the supreme God, can appear manifest in human form. Sūrdās and Mīrā may be said together to represent the exemplar of Kṛṣṇa-*bhakti* poets: much imitated, they maintain an enormous popularity to the present day.

In view of recent South Asian realities it may seem surprising to find Muslim poets prominent amongst the prime creators of Kṛṣṇa-*bhakti* literature: but the combination of a Muslim-dominated political structure with a largely Hindu populace fostered a cultural symbiosis which was richly productive in the interconnected realms of music, art and literature. Though hardly a 'melting-pot of cultures', as it is sometimes described, the relatively liberal ambiance of Akbar's reign (1556-1605) in particular made possible a commonality of culture hardly to be found in the literary traditions of the modern sub-continent. Nowhere is this tendency better illustrated than in the literary output of Akbar's courtier and general Abdurrahīm K͟hānk͟hānā, known to Hindi literature as the poet Rahīm (**6**). That the characteristics of noble birth, military prowess and poetic talent should all be so conspicuously present in the same person was symptomatic of the cultural sophistication of the age — a feature shared with so many European courts of the same period. Rahīm took enthusiastically to Kṛṣṇaite themes in his poetry, though unsurprisingly he tended to tone down their religious aspect in favour of a more generalized portrayal of the feelings of *virah* occasioned by Kṛṣṇa's absence. A less circumspect adoption of Vaiṣṇava attitudes is apparent in the lyrical verses of Raskhān (**5**), allegedly a Pathan convert to Vaiṣṇavism and an initiate of the Vallabha *sampradāy*. His spry, elegant and often highly alliterative poems describe the gopis' relationship with Kṛṣṇa as cowherd, together with stylistically elaborate praise of Kṛṣṇa himself and of the benefits of devotion to him.

While many Kṛṣṇa-*bhakti* poets were 'freelance' in respect of sectarian allegiance, the *sampradāys* deriving from the charismatic religious leadership of such figures as Vallabha and Caitanya continued to flourish and expand during the sixteenth and seventeenth centuries. Their development can be traced in the contemporary hagiologies, whose quasi-historical chronicles aimed to incite devotion through an idealized portrayal of the more-or-less sanctified figures of sectarian leaders, divines, teachers, and poets. Little or no distinction is made in these texts between mythological and historical figures, and as noted earlier, such hagiologies cannot be regarded as historical sources in the strict sense; but they give a valuable insight into the psychology of *bhakti*, and are often the only contemporary sources of any kind relating to the lives of *bhakti* poets. The Vallabhan *vārtā* chronicles (**2**), which constitute an early example of Braj Bhāṣā prose, are among the most important of such texts; a later hagiology, the *Rasik-ananya-māl* of Bhagavat Mudit (**7**), portrays early devotees of the Rādhāvallabh sect and is written in a workaday style in the *caupāī* metre (with its variant *caupaī*), whose vigorous rhyming rhythm had established it as a favourite narrative metre in the prestigious Avadhī models of Tulsīdās and the Sufi poets.

Rahīm's exploitation of the ambivalent sensuality of Kṛṣṇaite themes shows how readily the rhetoric of *bhakti* can be transferred to a more secular context. In the court poetry of the seventeenth century we see the coming together of conventionally devotional themes with a wide range of aphoristic and romantic conceits both ancient and contemporary. Traditional histories of Hindi literature tend to classify the so-called *rīti* or 'mannerist' court poetry, in which content is secondary in importance to the style of its expression, as a development chronologically distinct from the '*bhakti* era'. But in fact the composition of devotional verse was never fully superseded by that of the more secular genres, and much verse is in any case ambiguous in terms of its position on the 'secular'/'religious' continuum. Thus among the romantic situations comprising the stock-in-trade of such *rīti* poets as Bihārīlāl (**8**) are many which retain the figures of Kṛṣṇa and Rādhā as hero and heroine. Bihārī is truly one of the brightest stars of Braj Bhāṣā poetry. His couplets are compiled in the form of a *Satsaī*, a collection of (nominally) 700 couplets in the *dohā* metre which, with its inverted variant the *soṛṭhā*, had long been the staple of Hindi poets of all styles: whether in the pithy aphorisms of Kabīr, or in the connected narrative of epic poems (where it provides a foil to the *caupāī*'s pounding beat), or in the condensed brilliance of Bihārī's verses, the *dohā* has proved itself the ideal couplet form (and a verse type never adequately to be replaced in the rather different world of modern Hindi poetics). Bihārī is unsurpassed in his use of the *dohā*, matching originality of thought with vividness and aptness of expression in a way designed to gratify the courtly patron and, given the timelessness of his subject-matter, equally certain to delight the modern reader. The masterly compression of literal and implied meaning into two brief lines leads Bihārī's poems to be popularly characterized by the phrase *gāgar mẽ sāgar*— 'an ocean in a pitcher'. Many of the tropes and poetic conceits adopted by Bihārī and his contemporaries can be shown to derive from Sanskrit court poetry: but in no sense is this a pastiche literature, for poets such as Bihārī bring to their verse all the freshness and spontaneity of the vernacular tradition.

It is easy to imagine that many of Bihārī's couplets may have been inspired by incidents at the various courts in which he received patronage. The same applies with the *Nīti-satsaī* of Vṛnd (**10**), a poet from the Rajput court of Kishengarh, whose couplets on 'polity' are the stuff of metaphor and offer a kind of training in the art of lifemanship within the prescriptive norms of *dharma*. Texts of this *satsaī* type again owe much to Sanskrit and Prakrit models, both in terms of their imagery and in terms of their character as compendiums of independent aphorisms on loosely connected themes.

The reflection in vernacular court poetry of its Sanskrit exemplars led inevitably to its analysis in terms of the traditional conventions of *alaṅkāraśāstra*, the science of Sanskrit literary rhetoric. This had two main facets: a detailed taxonomy of hero and heroine (*nāyak* and *nāyikā*, the genre being known as *nāyak-nāyikā bhed*) which categorized the various types of poetic characters, differentiating for example between such varieties as *proṣitapatikā* — 'she whose husband is abroad', and *kalahāntaritā* — 'the one separated by a quarrel'; and secondly the analysis of linguistic and literary figures of speech, with careful distinctions of the various types of alliteration, metaphor, *double entendre* and so on. A third type dealt with prosody. This analytical literature virtually eclipsed in prominence the verse it purported to analyse; it is to be seen as a genre in its own right rather than as a secondary literature comparable to Western literary criticism. Rhetorical works typically alternated verses of definition and example, often with extreme minuteness of detail and at challenging length; one of the more concise texts is the *Bhāṣā-bhūṣaṇ* of Jasvant Siṁh, maharajah of Jodhpur in the mid seventeeth century (**9**).

The proclivities of courtly entertainment underlie much poetry of the seventeenth and eighteenth centuries. While devotional poetry continued to be written in large quantities, often within the framework of sectarian traditions whose autonomy one from another was jealously maintained, courtly fashions required a less pious and more overtly secular bias to be given to the old *bhakti* contexts. An almost impudently overt adaptation of a traditional theme is found among the large output of the early eighteenth-century poet Dev, whose poem *Aṣṭayām* (**11**) describes the hedonistic daily routine of a palace-dwelling heroine in terms of a ritual programme borrowed from the daily round of temple sacraments.

As the rhetoricians' codifying of poetic conventions led to an inevitable stereotyping of poetic composition, poetry began increasingly to contain set-pieces of rhetorical description, often following Sanskrit models, though blended with elements of regional or 'folk' culture: favourite subjects were 'toe-to-head' (*nakh-śikh*) descriptions of the heroine, poetic listings of attributes such as the 'sixteen adornments' (*solah śṛṅgār* or *nav-sat śṛṅgār*), and two related season-cycles — 'songs of the twelve months' (*bārah-māsā*) and 'descriptions of the six seasons' (*ṣaḍ-ṛtu-varṇan*) — in which *virah* lamentations are set against the imagery of the successive seasons. An example of this last type is found in a mid eighteenth century *rīti* work, the *Ras-prabodh* of G̲ulām Nabī Raslīn (**12**). Though nominally devotional in terms of subject matter, such poems are artistic creations first and foremost, and do not attempt to reproduce the devout intensity of Mīrā and Sūr. Nevertheless, *bhakti* continued to inspire the more pious poets such as Sāvant Siṃha, ruler of the Rajput state of Kishengarh in the mid eighteenth century, who wrote with great energy and some skill under the name 'Nāgarīdās' ('Rādhā's slave'); his *Arill-pacīsī* (**13**) is a deft synopsis of aspects of Kṛṣṇa's *līlā*, making up for any lack of originality in thematic treatment with a proficient hand in the composition of the *arill* quatrain.

'Popular wisdom' literature of the type exemplified in Vṛnd's couplets reappears in the serpentine verses of Giridhar 'Kavirāy', self-styled 'Prince of poets', or perhaps 'Poet Laureate', who was probably active in the mid-eighteenth century. His verses exploit the unsatiable public appetite for sententious verse of a type which makes its point more through nimbleness of phrasing than through any real cogency of thought: though they are infinitely memorable and useful rhetorically for the clinching of an argument, one feels that the drift of poems such as Giridhar's might readily be reversed if metre or rhyme were to require it. A selection of Giridhar's poems was included in an early nineteenth-century chrestomathy of Braj Bhāṣā verse, the *Sabhā-bilās* (**14**) of Lallūlāl, whose output also included a Braj prose version of Sanskrit fables, here entitled *Rāj-nīti* (**1**). Alongside Giridhar's pat aphorisms, the *Sabhā-bilās* included also some of the risqué riddles called *Mukṛī* or *Kah-mukṛī*, whose attribution to the thirteenth century polymath Amīr Khusrau seems to be belied by the relatively modern dress of the poems themselves, at least in their received form.

Like Giridhar, many minor poets continued to re-work the old themes and conceits; but increasing contact with Western culture in the nineteenth century was eventually to lead to new perceptions as to the nature and purpose of literature, and to signal the end of a poetical tradition which was already well advanced down a path of decadent decline.

III.2 POETS AND TEXTUAL SOURCES

III.2.1 Lallūlāl: *Rāj-nīti* (RN)

Lallūlāl ('Lallūjī Lāl'), c. 1763-1825, was a 'bhakha munshi' at the College of Fort William, founded in Calcutta in 1800, whose task was to produce language-teaching texts for the British employees of the Raj. He is best known for his *Prem-sāgar* — a Khaṛī Bolī prose version of the tenth book of the BhP — which despite its original pedagogical purpose achieved and retains wide popularity as a fluent and accessible version of the great devotional classic. Other works were similarly based ultimately on Sanskrit originals: the 'Hindustani' (i.e. Urdu) *Siṁhāsan-battīsī* and *Baitāl-paccīsī;* and two principal texts in Braj Bhāṣā — a commentary on the *Satsaī* of Bihārīlāl (**8**), in the introduction to which he describes his early career, and *Rāj-nīti* published in 1809. *Rāj-nīti* is a collection of fables from the Sanskrit *Hitopadeśa*, with some additions from the *Pañcatantra* (itself the source for the *Hitopadeśa*). The tales, narrated by the Brahmin preceptor of the sons of a king called Amaraśakti, are often told in a 'story within a story' format, though for present purposes the core stories have been separated out from their frame stories for clarity. Lallūlāl retains many characteristics of the Sanskrit originals, such as the frequent use of synonyms. His Braj Bhāṣā shows some of the modernizing influence of contemporary Khaṛī Bolī, for example in his use of the Persian cj. *ki* 'that' (cf. *jo* in VV etc.).

The text is from Lallu Lal 1854, selections being from the pages here indicated: 1—p.84; 2—p.47; 3—p.57; 4—p.55; 5—p.123; 6—p.89; 7—p.65. For Lallūlāl's career see R.S. McGregor 1973b. Various translations of RN were made during its currency as a set book, though all are long since out of print; that of J.R.A.S. Lowe (1853) is an example. For a translation of the *Pañcatantra* see A. Ryder 1955; for the *Hitopadeśa* see C. Wilkins 1885 or F. Johnson 1928. The tradition of Indian 'beast' stories is discussed in H.H. Gowen 1968, chapter XXX; for the comic element of the stories see L. Siegel 1987:61 (and passim).

III.2.2 Gokulnāth/Harirāy: *Caurāsī / Do sau bāvan vaiṣṇavan kī vārtā* (VV)

The early history of the sect of Vallabha centres on Vallabha himself, and on his son Viṭṭhalnāth (c.1515-88) who succeeded him as leader of the sect and who greatly expanded its activities and influence. Incidents in the lives of Vallabha and Viṭṭhalnāth, and of their 84 and 252 disciples respectively, are related in the prose hagiologies entitled respectively *Caurāsī vaiṣṇavan kī vārtā* and *Do sau bāvan vaiṣṇavan kī vārtā*. Both texts are ascribed to Viṭṭhalnāth's son Gokulnāth (c. 1551-1647), though their actual history is uncertain: in modern editions, the texts are accompanied by the *Bhāv-prakāś* commentary of Harirāy, Gokulnāth's disciple who was probably also responsible for compiling the original texts from oral traditions deriving from Gokulnāth's time. Many of the episodes in these two texts relate closely to the sectarian image of Śrīnāth, whose temple at Govardhan in Braj formed the original centre of the sect (though Aurangzeb's iconoclastic policies in the late seventeenth century meant that Śrīnāth, along with many other Braj deities, had to be spirited away to the safe refuge of neighbouring Rajput states: Śrīnāth was taken from Govardhan in 1669, eventually to be installed in a new temple at what was to become the pilgrimage town of Nathdwara, near Udaipur).

The *vārtā* texts form a popular source of information about the sect's history and attitudes, and are intended as an aid to the devotional life. Though at best quasi-historical, the loosely linked stories of the *vārtās* are often the only available source for 'biographies' of the sectarian poets. The narratives rest on an underlying assumption as to the nature of reality as perceived through *bhakti,* namely that each devotee living out a life in the mundane or *laukika* realm exists also in a transcendental or *alaukika* mode of reality in which he or she is one of the characters in the eternal *līlā* of Kṛṣṇa. Harirāy's *Bhāv-prakāś* commentary has recourse to this concept when justifying any incongruities in the worldly attitudes of the devotees: apparent deviations of behaviour in their *laukika* lives are simply attributed to causes in the *alaukika* sphere. Because of the so-called 'three lives' of the devotees (before and after initiation, and in the *līlā* mode), the *vārtās* are designated *tīn janma kī līlā vālī.* Further features of the chronicles are the prominence of the *guru* as intermediary between Kṛṣṇa and devotee, with the text stressing always the hereditary authority of Vallabha's descendants in the *gosvāmī* lineage; and the use of narrative context to put a particular gloss on verses ascribed to the sectarian poets.

Three selections are given here, the first two from *Caurāsī vaiṣṇavan kī vārtā*, the third from *Do sau bāvan vaiṣṇavan kī vārtā*: (i) a pair of incidents from the *vārtā* of Sūrdās (**3**), treating firstly his alleged meeting with the emperor Akbar (a chronological possibility if not a historical reality), and secondly a domestic crisis resolved by the compassionate intervention of Śrīnāth himself; (ii) the sectarian initiation of a dancing girl through the good offices of Kṛṣṇadās, a contemporary of Sūr and fellow-member of the so-called *Aṣṭachāp* group of poets whose texts form the mainstay of sectarian Vallabhite hymnody; (iii) the conversion of Raskhān (**4**), the Pathan who became a devotee of Śrīnāth and one of the most popular of Braj Bhāṣā poets. The commentary is here distinguished from the main text by smaller type and indented paragraphs.

The sections on Sūrdās and Kṛṣṇadās are from P.D. Mītal 1951:27-32, 41-43 and D. Parīkh 1970:546-549 respectively; some of the *Bhāv-prakāś* glosses have here been excised, as shown by dots [...]. These texts are translated, with introduction, in R. Barz 1976; Shyam Das 1985 gives a very free English synopsis of the *Caurāsī vaiṣṇavan kī vārtā* (but removes the vital distinction between text and commentary). For further discussion of the Sūrdās *vārtā* see J.S. Hawley 1984 (chapter 1), and of the Kṛṣṇadās *vārtā* see R. Barz 1987. The section on Raskhān is from B. Śarmā and D. Parīkh 1951-53:299-304; for discussion and synopsis see M. Corcoran 1983 and R. Snell 1989. The broader background to the history of the sect is given in A.W. Entwistle 1987 (chapter 5); and see *ibid.* pp. 91-95 on the sublimation of Raskhān's stereotyped homosexuality in the context of the 'femininity' of the human soul.

III.2.3 Sūrdās: *Sūr-sāgar* (SS)

The traditional account of the life of Sūrdās is that given in the *vārtā* discussed above (2): born in 1478 to a Brahmin family in a village near Delhi, he was blind from birth, but blessed with an inner vision through which he perceived the divinity of Kṛṣṇa, of whom he sang devotional songs; contact with Vallabha led him to follow the BhP as a model for his songs and to dedicate himself in service of the sectarian deity of Śrīnāth at Govardhan; he was one of the *aṣṭachāp* group of eight poets convened there by Viṭṭhalnāth; though not mentioning Vallabha by name in any of his verses, Sūrdās proclaimed in a death-bed statement that he perceived no distinction between Kṛṣṇa and Vallabha and that all his hymns in praise of Kṛṣṇa related equally to Vallabha.

Perhaps no single aspect of the *vārtā* account summarized here is historical. The hagiography has grown in the telling within a sectarian tradition anxious to claim Sūrdās as its own; and likewise the number of *padas* attributed to Sūr has grown in the singing, verses bearing the *chāp* or 'poetic signature' of Sūrdās having swelled *bhajan* repertoires for centuries. The published text of the *Sūr-sāgar* must accordingly be seen as representing the 'Sūr tradition' rather than an integral corpus attributable to any one historical figure.

Included here are poems of four main types: those of humble supplication or *vinay* (1-10), often using extended metaphors in confessions of impiety and in entreaty for salvation; those depicting the child Kṛṣṇa (11-27), especially as 'butter-thief' (*mākhan-cor*) and in the related *ūkhal-bandhan* episode; Kṛṣṇa's youth, his flute as summoner to the dance and as rival for the gopis' affections, his consort Rādhā, and his beauty as a cowherd (28-34); and the gopis' complaint to Uddhava, who tries to persuade them to the *nirguṇ* view in which Kṛṣṇa is to be perceived as an abstract entity (35-40). A verse in which Kṛṣṇa as king of Dwarka nostalgically recalls his days in Braj concludes the selection (41).

The text is taken from N.D. Vajpeyi 1972-76 (see Concordance, p. 51). For translation and evaluation of Sūrdās see C. Vaudeville 1971, K.E. Bryant 1978, J.S. Hawley 1983 and 1984. A facsimile of an important early *Sūrsāgar* manuscript is given in G.N. Bahura 1984. Recent research on the history of the text is summarized in J.S. Hawley 1979 and K.E. Bryant 1983. The theme of Kṛṣṇa as 'divine child' is discussed in C.S.J. White 1970.

III.2.4 Mīrā: *Padāvalī* (MP)

Mīrā, or Mīrābāī, a near contemporary of Sūrdās, was born in the Rajput royal family of Merta, and was betrothed (perhaps unwillingly) in a marriage alliance with the royal house of Mewar. Many of her poems contain references to the persecution she received from her husband's family, who apparently objected to her abandonment of worldly values as she gave herself over completely to her religious calling. It is difficult to know to what extent her own poetic references to this persecution, including an attempted poisoning (see the *chappay* of Nābhādās, II.2.8 above) are metaphorical; but she has come to be regarded as the exemplar of single-minded spiritual dedication, a theme constantly voiced in her *padas.*

Mīrā's songs have been handed down largely through oral tradition, and there is no definitive text. Gujarati, Rajasthani and Braj Bhāṣā versions of her *padas* exist, but even these traditions do not cohere as discrete recensions, and they no doubt include much material from later centuries. The poems given here, taken from an edition which has collected them under the blanket title *Padāvalī*, can at least claim the authority attributable to a received text in current use: the popular vote, rather than the scholarly imprimatur.

All of Mīrā's verses express her love for Kṛṣṇa, usually addressed as 'Giridhar' — though the salvific aspect of Kṛṣṇa as 'mountain-holder' is not otherwise prominent in her poems. Her devotion is expressed in the outspoken terms of a lover beset by the pain of separation, especially as set in stark contrast to the socially conventional expectations of the world around her. She flaunts her attitude challengingly, stressing the efficacy of time spent in the company of the devout; and her tone is a mixture of celebration and lament, its expression of *virah* often seeming to reflect the tone, though not necessarily the theology, of the Sant poets. In language and content, the poems included here are close to those poems of Sūr most likely to represent an early stratum of the *Sūr-sāgar*; their rhetorical structure is simple, making only very limited use of extended metaphor or linear narrative, the imagery being typically compounded rather than developed in any systematic way. Occurrences of the retroflex nasal (as in *pāṇī, naiṇā*) reflect the Rajasthani origin of or Gujarati influence on these Braj Bhāṣā versions of the poems, a reminder of the uncertainty surrounding the history of these most abidingly popular of devotional songs.

The text is taken from P. Caturvedī 1954 (see Concordance, p.51). (A later edition, 1973, has a markedly greater proportion of retroflex forms, but without any convincing evidence of greater textual authenticity.) The materials for Mīrā's biography are reviewed in H. Goetz 1966, A.J. Alston 1980 (from whom the apt 'courtly' has been borrowed as a translation for *nāgara*) and J.S. Hawley & M. Juergensmeyer 1988; for translations see Alston, Hawley, and U.S. Nilsson 1969.

III.2.5 Raskhān: *Sujān-raskhān* (SR)

Raskhān's *vārtā* hagiography is included in this reader (**2**); it portrays him as a lusty and somewhat gauche Pathan paedophile converted to Kṛṣṇa-*bhakti* by the sight of a portrait of Śrīnāth; but this account must of course be read with the usual caution as regards historicity. A heading to the *vārtā* text gives his name as Saiyid Ibrahīm; 'Raskhān', an epithet of Kṛṣṇa meaning 'mine of *rasa*' and so used as the poet's *chāp*, can be read as including, by design or convenient coincidence, the Persian title *khān* often suffixed to Pathan names. In a poem entitled *Prem-vāṭikā*, Raskhān alludes to his leaving Delhi following an insurrection which turned the capital into a 'burning-ground', and perhaps dateable to the 1550s.

The *Prem-vāṭikā* is in *dohās*; but Raskhān is best known for his poems in the *savaiyā* and *kavitt* quatrain metres which, with their distinctly contrasted rhythmic cadences, are often used as complementary styles within a single work (though more typically by *rīti* poets such as Ghanānand and Dev than in *bhakti* verse). Individual stanzas in these metres, mixed with occasional *dohās* and *sorṭhās*, are assembled in a collection sometimes given the title *Sujān-raskhān*. They portray Kṛṣṇa as cowherd and as lover, sometimes as saviour, their overall mood being celebratory and playful; even in a *virah* context the tone remains bright and light-hearted, quite free of the mournful plangency of poets such as Mīrā. Raskhān is more concerned to celebrate the beauty of Kṛṣṇa and the perfection of love for him than to retail episodes from his *līlās*. He also seems less restrained in his use of sensual imagery than many contemporary poets, for whom devotionalism perhaps entails a more stringently pious tone. Raskhān's use of language is witty and elegant, full of alliteration and rhythmic invention. He is fond of capping the first three lines of a poem with some sort of dénouement of the final line (e.g. stanzas 3, 5, 9, 15). Certain of his verses encapsulate the very essence of Braj Kṛṣṇaism and are hence among the most popular of all *bhakti* lyrics: verses 5 and 9 celebrate the paradox of epiphany, verse 1 declares that devotion to Kṛṣṇa yields joys so great as to outstrip salvation.

Editions vary widely as to their total number of verses. The text is taken from Bābū Amīr Siṁh 1956 (see Concordance, p. 51); all 25 stanzas are also included in V.P. Miśra 1947 and D.S. Bhāṭī 1977, with the exception of 22 (absent in Miśra); some readings from these editions have been followed as noted. The regular disposition of *savaiyās* and *kavitts* given in this book is for convenience of layout only. For a discussion of the *vārtā* of Raskhān see M. Corcoran 1983 and R. Snell 1989.

III.2.6 Rahīm: *Barvai* (RB)

Abdurrahīm 'Khānkhānā' (1556-1627) was the son of Bairam Khān, who was a courtier of the Mughal emperor Humayun and later guardian and regent to the young Akbar: Bairam Khān was, until his fall from power, the most powerful man in the Mughal court. The young Abdurrahīm was thus brought up in a situation of unique privilege and high culture, where he acquired proficiency in numerous languages and arts.

Rahīm's wide poetic gifts embraced the languages of his own cultural heritage — Persian, Turkish and Arabic — as well as what must have appeared the relatively parochial tradition of Braj Bhāṣā and Avadhī. His modest collection of Braj poetry consists mainly of couplets; universality of idiom and clarity of language ensure his continuing popularity. He was among the first to harness the *dohā* as a vehicle for aphorisms straddling sacred and profane contexts, epitomized in the following well-known verse (S.B. Siṁh 1961:309):

अब रहीम मुसकिल पड़ी, गाढ़े दोऊ काम ।
साँचे से तो जग नहीं, झूठे मिलें न राम ॥

Perplexity must be our lot, whichever way we turn.
If true, we lose the world we love: if false, then God we spurn.

Rahīm is particularly associated with the tiny couplet called *barvai,* in which a maximum of sentiment is compressed into a very brief metrical line: it was perhaps under Rahīm's influence that Tulsī wrote a miniature *Rāmāyaṇ* in this metre. Two *barvai* collections exist: one is a rhetorical work on *nāyikā-bhed* ; the other, drawn on here, is a loosely connected series of verses on the Kṛṣṇa theme. With their descriptions of *virah* against the background of the changing seasons, these verses resemble a *bārahmāsā* lament, though they do not amount to a systematic treatment of that theme.

Our selection opens with the first six verses of the full poem, comprising a conventional salutation to Gaṇeś and other deities (see III.3.1). The subsequent verses deal mostly with the *virah* theme; abrupt changes of context, such as that between verses 16 and 17, are found as much in the full text as in this selection — evidence that this work is to be seen as 'theme and variations' rather than as a structured piece of rhetorical or narrative composition. The fact that the text includes couplets in Persian (obviously not included here) again suggests that this is a compilation of only loosely connected verses.

The effectiveness of these couplets derives largely from their succinctness. The second *pāda* of the *barvai* line, being only seven *mātrās* in length, usually comprises only three or two words (or even a single word, as in line 2.1 etc.) such that the syntax of the whole poetic line is much less evenly balanced than in, say, the relatively four-square construction of the *dohā*: this gives the closing cadence of the line a laconic effect which Rahīm exploits to the full, often reserving this space for the semantic burden of the line.

The text is taken from S.B.Siṁh 1961 (see Concordance, p. 51). A summary of Rahīm's life and of works by and about Rahīm is given in J.B.Chaudhurī 1954 (whose contention that 'Barves of Rahīm are composed in Abadhī Hindī; Barve cannot be composed in Vraja Bhāṣā' seems however to relate to the *nāyikā-bhed* verses rather than those included here — though the diminutive suffix *-vā*, a feature of both texts, is indeed an eastern feature). R. Snell 1991b discusses metrical and other aspects of RB.

III.2.7 Bhagvat Mudit: *Rasik-ananya-māl* (RAM)

Bhagvat Mudit, a member of the Caitanya *sampradāy* who lived in Agra, is known as the author of a *Vṛndāvan-śatak* (1650) and of an important if rather prosaic hagiology of Rādhāvallabhīs, the undated *Rasik-ananya-māl.* (Bhagvat Mudit is himself the subject of a stanza in that exemplar of Hindi hagiologies, the *Bhaktamāl* of Nābhādās, though the authenticity of this verse has been questioned on chronological grounds.) The Rādhāvallabh *sampradāy* is a sect whose origins lie in the devotional attitude of Hit Harivaṁś (1502-52), especially as expressed through his Braj Bhāṣā work *Caurāsī-pad* ; the present-day activities of the sect, which has produced enormous quantities of devotional verse, centre on the Vrindaban temple dedicated to the image of Kṛṣṇa as Rādhāvallabh, 'lover of Rādhā', maintained by descendants of Hit Harivaṁś. The fact that one of the earliest Rādhāvallabhī hagiologies should have been written by a Caitanyite suggests that contemporary relations between the *sampradāys* had not yet degenerated to the routine antagonism which sadly typifies later sectarian developments.

The importance of the RAM lies in its being a source for sectarian history, rather than in any literary sophistication; it should be remembered that the traditional history of sectarian institutions and their (alleged) members rests largely on just such texts as this. It is written in *caupāī* and *dohā*, a favourite combination for narrative verse. The text contains brief biographies, called *paracaī*, of 36 devotees, including well-known poets such as Dhruvdās and Harirām Vyās as well as sectarian figures such as the *kāyasth* Sundardās, builder of the original temple of Rādhāvallabh and *dīvān* of Abdurrahīm 'K̲h̲ānk̲h̲ānā' (**6**). The *paracaī* given here is the first in the text, and tells the story of a local rajah named Narvāhan, a convert to the Rādhāvallabh sect, who imprisoned a Jain trader only to release him when the prisoner (deceitfully) professed himself a fellow-disciple of Hit Harivaṁś. At the happy outcome of the tale, Harivaṁś rewarded Narvāhan by dedicating to him two *padas* which appear in the *Caurāsī-pad* with the *chāp* 'Narvāhan'.

The text is taken from L.P. Purohit 1960:1-4. For discussion of the Rādhāvallabh sect and the 'Narvāhan' verses in the *Caurāsī-pad* see C.S.J. White 1977 and R. Snell 1991a.

III.2.8 Bihārīlāl: *Satsaī* (BS)

Bihārīlāl, born at the beginning of the seventeenth century near Gwalior, was a court poet under the patronage of Jaisingh at Amber (the old capital, superseded by Jaipur). He represents the culmination of the various elements which go to make up his ingeniously effective poetry: traditions of gnomic verse inherited from Sanskrit and Prakrit; the immense resources of literary rhetoric from that same source; contexts of courtly life reflecting the sophistications of Mughal and Rajput high culture; and the elaborate narrative and devotional structures of Rādhā-Kṛṣṇa *bhakti*.

Bihārī is first and foremost a love poet, for whom all romantic situations, whether secular, mythic or devotional, provide copy for the poetic imagination. The strict social code which circumscribed a free mixing of the sexes made sweet longing and anguished *virah* natural poetic subjects, with boundless scope for lovelorn glances, desperate messages and secret trysts. The commentators subject Bihārī's poetry to ever more contrived interpretations (including several probably undreamed of by the poet himself): but the charm of the verses lies rather in the fresh spontaneity of their images, the aptness of their metaphors, and the succinctness of their expression.

The *Satsaī* model, which dates back to Prakrit verse, does not necessarily imply a number of verses fixed absolutely at 700. The edition followed here, with the modern Hindi prose commentary of Jagannāth Dās 'Prabhākar' (see Concordance, p. 52), has a total of 713 *dohās* and *soṛṭhās*. G.A. Grierson's 1896 edition of the text has a useful introduction; B. G. Holland 1975 and K.P. Bahadur 1990 both give a complete translation; for an outline of the language of the text see V. Miltner 1962, and for a list of Perso-

Arabic loanwords in the *Satsaī* see R.P. Dewhurst 1915. M.S. Randhawa 1966 introduces paintings based on the poems; a miscellany of papers on Bihārī edited by Nagendra (1981) serves only to underline the ineffable quality of the poet's talent.

III.2.9 Jasvant Siṁh: *Bhāṣā-bhūṣaṇ* (BhBh)

Jasvant Siṁh (b. 1626) was maharajah of the great Rajput kingdom of Marwar, with its capital at Jodhpur, which he ruled from 1640. His fortunes were bound up with those of various factions of the imperial Mughal power, and he was particularly closely involved in the struggle for empire among Shahjahan's sons (among whom Aurangzeb was, of course, finally to emerge victorious). J. Tod's colourful account of Jasvant Siṁh's reign includes the following passage (1902:I, chapter 6):

> The life of Jeswunt Sing is one of the most extraordinary in the annals of Rajpootana, and a full narrative of it would afford a perfect and deeply interesting picture of the history and manners of the period. Had his abilities, which were far above mediocrity, been commensurate with his power, credit, and courage, he might, with the concurrent aid of the many powerful enemies of Arungzeb, have overturned the Moghul throne.

This warrior king, at whose death fifteen queens and concubines committed suttee, was also a scholar of distinction. Braj Bhāṣā texts attributed to him include commentaries on the *Bhagavad Gītā*; a version, mostly in prose, of the Sanskrit drama *Prabodhacandrodaya*; discussions on metaphysics, such as the prose *Siddhānt-bodh* composed in 'question-answer' (*praśnottar*) format as a debate between student and teacher; and the celebrated work on rhetoric, *Bhāṣā-bhūṣaṇ*, written in *dohās*. BhBh is described by G.A. Grierson (1896:23-24) as follows:

> The Bhāṣā-bhūṣaṇa deserves its reputation. It is a miracle of compactness. Its author contrives, generally most successfully, to contain the definition of each rhetorical figure, together with an example, within the limits of a single *dōhā*. At the same time, the language is usually remarkably simple, and the style pleasing...
>
> The work is divided into five lectures. The first is merely introductory. The second deals with Heroes and Heroines. Their classification is carried out to a minuteness even greater than that of the [tenth-century] Sanskrit authority on the subject, entitled the *Daça-rūpa*, or its follower the *Sāhitya-darpaṇa* [fifteenth-century]. The third deals with the various essentials of a poem, — the flavours, the emotions and the various modes of their expression, the essential and enhancing excitants, the accessories and ensuants. Then follows the fourth lecture, the main portion of the work, in which the various rhetorical ornaments of sense, the simile, metaphor, and so forth, are defined and illustrated. The fifth lecture deals with verbal ornaments, — alliteration and the like. The fourth lecture (on Rhetorical Ornaments) is based on, and might almost be called a free translation of, the fifth chapter of a well-known Sanskrit work on Rhetoric, entitled *Candrāloka*, written by Pīyuṣa-varṣa...

The text given here (from V.P.Miśra 1972: see Concordance, p. 52) comprises the first 44 *dohās* of the fourth 'lecture', framed by the first and fifth 'lectures' in their brief entirety. G.A. Grierson 1896 translates the whole text, with extensive reference to other works on rhetoric (but note that his identification of the historical Jasvant Siṁh is not correct). The works of the illustrious Keśavdās (K.P. Bahadur 1972) may be compared to BhBh. The Sanskrit tradition of poetics is surveyed in E. Gerow 1977; and individual figures of speech are fully defined and analysed, with examples from both Sanskrit and English (and American) literature, in E. Gerow 1971.

III.2.10 Vṛnd: *Nīti-satsaī* (NS)

Vṛnd, whose full name was perhaps Vṛndāvan (-dās?), was attached to the Jodhpur court from c. 1661, where his father was a poet at the court of the poet-king Jasvant Siṁh (9); in 1663 Vṛnd moved to Delhi as tutor, or guardian, to Aurangzeb's grandson Azim-ush-Shan. His duties took him to cities far from the imperial capital, and the *Nīti-satsaī* was composed in Dhaka in 1704, when Azim-us-Shan was subedar of Bengal. He was later employed at the Rajasthan court of Kishengarh, by the father of the poet Nāgarīdās (13).

The various texts attributed to Vṛnd include a *Bārah-māsā*, and a *Yamak-satsaī* exemplifying rhetorical figures; but he is best known for his *Nīti-satsaī*, a compendium of *dohās* recounting worldy wisdom. The construction of these couplets is rather more stereotyped than those of, say, Bihārī: almost invariably, the first line voices a contention of some kind, while the second supports it with a concrete illustration drawn from everyday life. The poetic skill lies largely in the aptness of the illustration.

The text is taken from J.R. Celer 1971 (see Concordance, p. 52).

III.2.11 Dev: *Aṣṭayām* (AY)

The traditionally accepted dates of Dev's life are 1673-1745. Dev, or Devdatt, from Etawah, represents a more decadent phase of the tradition of *rīti* verse than that of his forebear Bihārī, with whom he is frequently compared. The fifteen or so texts attributed to Dev cover a range of subjects from the religious (usually Kṛṣṇaite in context) to *nāyikā-bhed* description; he also wrote in praise of some of the patrons under whom he served. The poem *Aṣṭayām* exemplifies the originality which Dev could bring to conventional themes. The daily routine in a Kṛṣṇaite temple follows a cycle of ritual dividing the day into eight 'watches' or *yām*; the minutiae of these observances, and the appropriate mental attitudes to be assumed by the devotee, are described in a genre of sectarian verse called *aṣṭayām*, 'the eight watches'. This genre is the model for Dev's poem, in which he adapts the temple programme to a secular purpose in describing — perhaps with an element of satire — the self-indulgently hedonistic daily routine of a palace *nāyikā* and her beloved. Each *yām* occupies three hours, the cycle beginning notionally at 6 a.m., and is sub-divided into eight equal periods called *ghaṛī*. In Dev's poem, each *ghaṛī* is described in a *dohā* (which acts as a statement of theme) and a *savaiyā* or a *kavitt* (which expands on the narrative and description).

The eight *yām* describe the following procedures. 1: when the couple arises at dawn, signs of the night's love-making infuriate the heroine's jealous co-wives but delight her *sakhīs*. 2: she bathes, does *pūjā*, eats, dresses elaborately in a mirrored hall, meets her husband in an arbour, and goes with him to listen to music. 3: they embrace, play dice, go to a gallery where pictures of *viprīt-rati* (love-making with the female superincumbant) embarrass the heroine, visit an aviary, wear clothes of each other's colour. 4: the heroine resents the time spent with her elders; winning her freedom, putting on new unguents and clothes, she prepares herself for the tryst. 5: she goes to the 'palace of delight' (*raṅg-bhavan*) and sits with her husband, who begins romancing; the *sakhīs* leave; the couple make love. 6: they talk about the joys of love-making, but his teasing puts her into a fit of jealous pique (*mān*); he appeases her. She weeps at the thought of parting. 7: talking, kissing, telling stories, they finally fall asleep. 8: she tells him that she dreamed he was going abroad; further love-games, including *viprīt-rati* ; seeing the coming dawn, the heroine tricks her husband into thinking it still night, and he sleeps.

Our text is the fourth *yām*, and is taken from R. Tripāṭhī 1978. Some discussion on Dev is given in K.B. Jindal 1955:182-88; the *aṣṭayām* convention of Vallabhite temples is outlined in R. Barz 1976:48-49 and A. Ambalal 1987:21-25; its application in the Caitanya sect is described in D.L. Haberman 1988a: 126-29 and 161-63; for details of other *aṣṭayām* literature see A.W. Entwistle 1987:55-56 and 251.

III.2.12 Raslīn: *Ras-prabodh* (RP)

Saiyid G̱ulāmnabī, who assumed the poetic name 'Raslīn', was born in Bilgram (to the north-west of Lucknow), an important centre of Islamic culture and scholarship to which he was himself heir. He is the author of two Braj Bhāṣā texts, both composed in *dohās* : *Aṅg-darpan* (1737), comprising elegant poetic descriptions of the female figure and attire; and *Ras-prabodh* (1741), a treatise on rhetoric.

The *Ras-prabodh* begins with the praise of Allah, of the Prophet, and of Husain, from whom, as a 'Saiyid', the poet claims descent (see III.3.3). The text then treats such themes as the *rasas* and the categories of *nāyikā* and *nāyak*, the various sections of the text being headed by Sanskritized editorial rubrics (Braj forms are routinely replaced by their Sanskrit equivalents in all such contexts). A section on the *rasa* theory of poetics includes the *Saṭ-ṛtu-varṇan* included here, this 'description of the six seasons' being included in the category of *uddīpan*, i.e. the 'excitants' or contributory elements which promote aesthetic sentiment.

The text is taken from S. Pāṇḍey 1969:130-133. The conventions of 'seasonal' descriptive verse are discussed in C. Vaudeville 1986.

III.2.13 Nāgarīdās: *Arill-pacīsī* (AP)

'Nāgarīdas' is the poetic name of Sāvant Siṁh, born in 1699 in a Rajput dynasty whose capital was Kishengarh. Along with the throne of Kishengarh, which was a dependency of the Mughal empire, Sāvant Siṁh inherited also a family allegiance to the Vallabha *sampradāy*; portraits of Rādhā and Kṛṣṇa in the well-known Kishengarh school of miniature painting are said to be based on likenesses of Sāvant Siṁh and his queen (or concubine) 'Banī Ṭhanī'. Apparently a reluctant monarch who hankered after a life of devotion and study — more savant than *sāvant* — he turned his back on the strife-ridden role of kingship when his throne was usurped in 1757, and took up residence in Vrindaban.

The literary output of Nāgarīdās, which fills two published volumes, includes some short prose texts, some anthologies of earlier Braj poets, and some stanzas by 'Banī Ṭhanī' bearing the *chāp* 'Rasik Bihārī'. References within his work demonstrate his continuing allegiance to the Vallabha *sampradāy*, but he was in no way a narrowly sectarian poet: his themes are drawn from the full breadth of the Braj Kṛṣṇaite tradition, and the status given to Rādhā in particular suggests influences other than that of Vallabhan theology.

The brief *Arill-pacīsī* praises the efficacy of *bhakti*, and surveys the various Kṛṣṇa *līlās* whose climax, the *rāsa* dance, recalls the *Rās-pañcādhyāyī* of Nanddās. A coherence is given to the various component parts of the poem by the appearance in every stanza of a common fourth line.

The text is from K. Gupta (ed.) 1965; Nāgarīdās is discussed by A.W. Entwistle 1991. The *rāsa* descriptions may be compared with their BhP exemplar, translated in R. Mukerjee 1957 and in G.V. Tagare 1976-78; and with those of Nanddās, R.S. McGregor 1973a.

III.2.14 Lallūlāl: *Sabhā-bilās* (SB)

Lallūlāl has already been encountered as the author of RN (1). His *Sabhā-bilās* is an anthology of Braj Bhāṣā poetry assembled for language students; authorship of the various component texts has to be deduced from the poems themselves, since no references are given by the compiler. The text was however mostly studied with the help of English glosses, such as that of G.W. Gilbertson's 1900 edition, whose introduction indicates contemporary attitudes:

> Some of the pieces possess undoubted merit, and are well fitted to grace any language, the couplets of Tulsí Dáss and the *Kundaliyas* of Giridhar being, perhaps, among the best; others again are insipid stuff, and furnish but poor reading. But it is this incongruity, this mixture of the sublime with the ridiculous, that makes the *Sabhá Bilása* a very suitable text-book. To know a people it is necessary to be with them in their weak moments as well as in their strong; to sympathise with their levity while ready to praise their gravity.

More levity than gravity is provided by the two brief extracts given here. The first nine verses are from the *Kuṇḍaliyās* praised by Gilbertson. Their author, the poet Giridhar 'Kavirāy', is celebrated for this one verse-form; little is known of his life, though he is said to have been active in the mid eighteenth century (he is among the first Hindi poets to allude to the European presence in India). His language admits Khaṛī Bolī forms, especially when convenient for rhyme. In sentiment, Giridhar's verses belong to the aphoristic tradition of such poets as Vṛnd, though his tone is more tongue-in-cheek.

The last selection in this book has the earliest attribution: the so-called *Mukṛīs* or *Kah-mukṛīs* included in SB are ascribed to Amīr Khusrau (1253-1325, poet of the Delhi

Sultanate court), though it is quite apparent from their language that any connexion with an author of such early date must be tenuous at best. The verses are a kind of riddle (several varieties of which are included in works attributed to Khusrau): a woman suggestively recites a saucy list of characteristics which seem to describe her lover, but which, in the dénouement of the final line, are innocently ascribed to some other subject — hence the *mukrī* or 'denial' of the genre name.

The texts are from the 1900 edition of Gilbertson's *Assembly of mirth* (see Concordance, p. 52). Giridhar's poems, though widely praised, are hard to find in published form, and no recent edition has been traceable. Amīr Khusrau's Hindi works are available in Vrajratna Dās 1953 and are discussed in P. Machwe 1975; his riddles are discussed in V.P. Vatuk 1969/71. (For a recent pastiche from an unexpected source, see Aṭalbihārī Vājpeyī 1978, whose (defective) *kuṇḍaliyās* were inspired by Indian politics in the 1970s.)

III.3 SOME TEXTUAL CONVENTIONS

III.3.1 Opening Formulae

Texts having a formal composed structure, i.e. those other than the loosely compiled anthologies of the SS or MP type, often begin with a formulaic dedication to Gaṇeś, or to some other figure according to the poet's own tradition. Jasvant Siṁh's *Ānand-vilās* opens with a *barvai* (V.P. Miśra 1972:115), to which RB 1-6 may be compared:

एकदंत गजबदन सु गवरीनंद ।
बिघन हरत अति गनपति करत अनंद ॥

Single-tusked, elephant-faced, he the son of Gaurī:
Gaṇapati removes obstacles and gives great joy.

The seventeenth-century autobiographer Banārsīdās pays homage to two Jain divinities in the opening *dohā* of his *Ardhakathānak* (M. Lath 1981:223):

पानि जुगल पुट सीस धरि, मानि अपनपौ दास ।
आनि भगति चित जानि प्रभु बंदौं पास सुपास ॥

Holding my joined hands to my brow, I consider myself a slave;
with devotion in my mind I pay homage to Pārśva and Supārśva.

Raslīn's RP begins with an extended salutation to Allah, to the Prophet, and to Husain, beginning with the following verse (S. Pāṇḍey 1969:3):

अलह् नाम छबि देत यौं ग्रंथन के सिर आइ ।
ज्यों राजन के मुकुट तें अति सोभा सरसाइ ॥

Allah's name at the head of a work lends it an elegance
like the great splendour radiating from a king's crown.

Dhruvdās honours both mentor and deity in his *Premāvalī līlā* (L.C. Gosvāmī 1971:169):

प्रगट प्रेम कौ रूप धरि, श्री हरिबंश उदार ।
श्री राधाबल्लभ लाल कौ प्रगट कियो रस सार ॥

Taking the form of manifest love, the noble Śrī Harivaṁś
made manifest the quintessence of beloved Śrī Rādhāvallabh.

III.3.2 Colophons

A text is often concluded with some claim to its spiritual or aesthetic efficacy, often linked to a plea for a diligent reading. Dhruvdās closes his *Man-śikṣā-līlā* (ibid. p. 12) as follows:

मन शिक्षा के सुनत ही, ढरचौ न नैननि नीर ।
पाठ भजन ऐसो भयो जैसें पढ़त है कीर ॥

When one hears the 'Soul's Instruction', tears stop flowing from the eyes
— if the reading of the text is done in the manner that a parrot recites.

A bold claim is made by Jasvant Siṁh for his *Aparokṣasiddhānt* (V.P. Miśra 1972: 151):

या अपरोछसिधाँत कौ अरथ धरै मन माँहि ।
छूटै सो संसार तैं फिरि फिरि आवैं नाँहि ॥

He who holds the meaning of this *Aparokṣasiddhānt* in his heart
escapes from *saṁsāra*, and is no longer reborn over and over.

Banārsīdās closes his autobiography with a more general statement of benevolence, linked to a conventional totting up of verse numbers (M. Lath 1981:275):

सब दोहा अरु चौपाई छसै पिचत्तरि मान ।
कहहिं सुनहिं बांचहिं पढ़हिं तिन सबकौ कल्याण ॥

The *dohās* and *caupāīs* total six hundred and seventy-five;
good fortune to all who recite, hear, read or study them.

Court poetry often includes a diplomatic reference to a patron, as in the last couplet of Matirām's florid *Phūl-mañjarī* (K.Miśra and B.Miśra 1964:435):

हुकुम पाइ जहाँगीर कौ नगर आगरे धाम ।
फूलन की माला करी मति सों कबि मतिराम ॥

On Jahangir's command, while residing in the city of Agra
the poet Matirām created this 'garland of flowers' using all his wit.

Tulsīdās ends his *Vairāgya-sandīpanī* (R. Śukla 1958:II,14) with conventional modesty:

यह बिराग संदीपनी सुजन सुचित सुनि लेहु ।
अनुचित बचन विचारि कै जस सुधारि तस लेहु ॥

Kind sir, hear this 'Kindler of detachment' sympathetically,
and mulling over its solecisms, revise it as you will.

Formulaic apologia of this kind may equally well come at the opening of a text, as in Matirām's rhetorical work *Ras-rāj* (K. Miśra & B. Miśra 1964:201):

कवितार्थ जानों नहीं कछुक भयो संबोध ।
भूल्यो भ्रम ते जो कछुक सुकबि पढ़ैगे सोध ॥

I know nothing of the poetic muse, save what little I have picked up;
the skilled poet, reading this work, will emend it where I have erred.

At the beginning of his *Rāj-nīti* (1854:4), Lallūlāl takes a similar stance, adopting the metaphor of the narrow world of the well as compared to the breadth of the ocean:

कवि बासी गृहकूप कौ कथा अपार समंद ।
तैसीयै कछु कहत हौं मति है जैसी मंद ॥

The poet dwells in his well-like house, yet his tale is as vast as the sea;
I have said what little I could, within the limits of my intellect.

Following the text proper, a separate scribal colophon may record the date and circumstances of the copying of the manuscript (and often denying responsibility for the content or state of the text). Such colophons do not appear in printed texts, though a brief Sanskrit phrase including the formula *iti*, 'finis', may be retained.

III.3.3 Dates and Chronograms

A colophon verse may include the year of composition according to the the Vikramāditya calendar, as in the *Rasānand-līlā* of Dhruvdās (L.C. Gosvāmī 1971:251):

रसानन्द याकौ नाम कहावै । कहत सुनत आनँद रस पावै ॥
सम्वत सौ षोदस पंचासा । वरनत जस ध्रुव जुगल बिलासा ॥

Reciting or hearing this [poem] called 'Ambrosial joy' yields the joy of ambrosia;
in *samvat* sixteen hundred and fifty Dhruv described the glory of the couple's sport.

A *samvat* date is converted to A.D. by subtracting 57 (but 56 at the end of the year, i.e. in the dark half of the month Pauṣa, and in the months Māgha and Phālguṇa). The month is often included in the colophon, as in the *Ardhakathānak* (M. Lath 1981:275):

सोलह् सै अट्ठानबै संबत अगहन मास ।
सोमबार तिथि पंचमी सुकल पक्ष परगास ॥

In *samvat* sixteen hundred and ninety-eight, in the month of Āgrahāyaṇa,
on Monday, the fifth day of the bright fortnight, [this poem] is finished.

The year itself may be expressed cryptically in a chronogram. Numerals are expressed symbolically through brief ciphers (whose lexical meaning is not usually significant in the line of verse) such as the following:

0 *kha* 'sky, infinite';
1 *śaśi, vidhu* 'moon';
2 *netra* ' eyes';
3 *guṇa* 'the constituent elements of the phenominal universe';
4 *yuga* 'the ages of creation';
5 *indrī* 'the senses';
6 *rasa* 'the flavours' (sweet, sour, salt, bitter, acrid, astringent);
7 *vāra* 'the days of the week', or *sāgara* 'the oceans';
8 *gaja* 'the elephants supporting the cardinal points of the universe';
9 *chidra* 'the orifices of the body'.

(There are many variants: for a versified list see Keśavdās, *Kavi-priyā* II.5-21 (V. Miśra 1954:161-62); see also L. Renou & J. Filliozat 1953:II,708.) The numbers yielded by a chronogram are read in reverse order to reveal the year: thus the following from the *Prem-vāṭikā* of Raskhān (A. Siṁh 1956:12) dates the text as samvat 1671 (= AD 1614).

बिधु सागर रस इंदु सुभ बरस सरस रसखानि ।
प्रेमबाटिका रचि रुचिर चिर हिय हरख बखानि ॥

In the auspicious year 'Moon [1], ocean [7], flavour [6], moon [1]', Raskhān joyously extolls the 'Garden of Love', relishable to the taste, ever joyful to the heart.

Concordances

Sūrdās, *Sūr-sāgar* (N.D. Vājpeyī , ed., 1972-76)

1...........1	8.......153	15.....886	22.....935	29...1825	36...4249
2.........68	9.......161	16.....895	23.....943	30...1911	37...4306
3.........87	10.....222	17.....897	24.....945	31...1943	38...4350
4.........99	11.....743	18.....898	25.....952	32...1986	39...4583
5.......103	12.....815	19.....923	26.....997	33...2007	40...4687
6.......141	13.....816	20.....924	27...1040	34...2375	41...4891
7.......144	14.....856	21.....926	28...1625	35...3854	

Mīrā, *Padāvalī* (P. Caturvedī, ed., 1954)

1.......161	4.........16	7.........56	9.......103	11.....155	13.....177
2...........3	5.........39	8.........15	10.....125	12.....163	14.....199
3.........63	6.........50				

Raskhān, *Sujān Raskhān* (Bābū A. Siṁh, ed., 1956)

1...........1	6.........74	10.......60	14.....125	18.....106	22.....100
2.........65	7.........61	11.........7	15.....105	19.......16	23.......43
3...........3	8.......121	12.........9	16.......18	20.......17	24.......45
4.........88	9.........32	13.....107	17.......77	21.......19	25.........2
5.........28					

Rahīm, *Barvai* (S.B. Siṁh, ed., 1961)

1...........1	7...........8	13.......24	19.......42	25.......58	31.......67
2...........2	8...........9	14.......25	20.......43	26.......62	32.......78
3...........3	9.........10	15.......29	21.......47	27.......64	33.......80
4...........4	10.......11	16.......31	22.......50	28.......66	34.......81
5...........5	11.......16	17.......33	23.......52	29.......72	35.......92
6...........6	12.......22	18.......38	24.......54	30.......73	

Bihārīlāl, *Satsaī* (J. Dās 'Ratnākar' , ed., n.d.)

1...........2	14.....689	27.....315	40.....623	53.....488	66.....425
2...........7	15.....203	28.....322	41.....431	54.....512	67.....638
3.........17	16.....234	29.....325	42.....437	55.....515	68.....643
4.........22	17.....255	30.....333	43.....442	56.....159	69.....651
5.........26	18.....261	31.....344	44.....449	57.....538	70.....659
6.........38	19.....262	32.....356	45.....459	58.....557	71.....667
7.........57	20.....281	33.....361	46.....461	59.....573	72.....674
8.........70	21.....285	34.....364	47.....463	60.....575	73.....680
9.........73	22.....292	35.....373	48.....464	61.....576	74.....193
10.......87	23.....295	36.....391	49.....465	62.....601	75.....201
11.....121	24.....302	37.....407	50.....469	63.......18	76.....621
12.....519	25.....303	38.....413	51.....473	64.....635	
13.....687	26.....313	39.....423	52.....476	65.....622	

Jasvant Siṁh, *Bhāṣā-bhūṣan* (V.P. Miśra , ed., 1972)

1-5 1-5	6-49 42-85	50-64 197-211

Vṛnd, *Nīti-satsaī* (J.R. Celer, ed., 1971)

1...........4	7.........70	13.....165	19.....295	25.....477	31.....692
2...........5	8.........79	14.....202	20.....347	26.....501	32.....713
3.........22	9.........80	15.....204	21.....348	27.....503	
4.........39	10.......93	16.....245	22.....349	28.....513	
5.........54	11.......95	17.....250	23.....350	29.....567	
6.........56	12.....157	18.....254	24.....436	30.....671	

Lallūlāl, *Sabhā-bilās* (G.W. Gilbertson, ed., 1900). 1-9, chapter 8; 10-21, chapter 13.

1........8:6	5......8:18	9......8:40	13..13:21	16..13:14	19..13:19
2........8:5	6......8:24	10....13:1	14..13:10	17..13:16	20..13:20
3......8:16	7......8:38	11....13:3	15..13:13	18..13:17	21..13:23
4......8:17	8........8:2	12....13:7			

Select Bibliography

Bibliographical footnotes outlining the main sources for grammar and literature are given on pp. 3 and 29 respectively; the main primary and secondary sources for each of the textual extracts are noted at the end of the various subsections of III.2.

V.S. imprint dates have been converted to A.D. by the mechanical subtraction of 57.

Alston, A.J., 1980: *The devotional poems of Mīrābāī* (Delhi: Motilal Banarsidass).

Ambalal, Amit, 1987: *Krishna as Shrinathji: Rajasthani paintings from Nathdvara* (Ahmedabad: Mapin Publishing).

Archer, W.G., 1957: *The loves of Krishna in Indian painting and poetry* (London: George Allen & Unwin).

Bahadur, K.P., 1972: *The Rasikapriyā of Keshavadāsa* (Delhi: Motilal Banarsidass).

—— 1990: *The Satsai of Biharilal* (Delhi: Penguin Books).

Bahura, Gopal Narayan (ed.), 1984: *Pad Sūrdāsjī kā: the padas of Sūrdās* (Jaipur: Maharaja Sawai Man Singh II Museum).

Balasubhramanyan, V., 1989: *Narayana Hitopadesa* (Calcutta: M.P.Birla Foundation).

Banerjee, P., 1978: *The life of Krishṇa in Indian art* (New Delhi: National Museum).

Barz, R., 1976: *The bhakti sect of Vallabhācārya* (Faridabad: Thompson Press India).

—— 1987: 'Kṛṣṇadās Adhikārī: an irascible devotee's approach to the divine', *Journal of Comparative Sociology and Religion*, Vol.14, pp.35-54.

Beames, John, 1966: *A comparative grammar of the modern Aryan languages of India* [reprint] (Delhi: Munshiram Manoharlal).

Bennett, P.J., 1983: 'Temple organisation and worship among the Puṣṭimārgīya-Vaiṣṇavas of Ujjain' (PhD thesis, University of London).

—— 1990: 'In Nanda Baba's house: the devotional experience in Pushti Marg temples' in *Divine passions: the social construction of emotion in India,* ed. Owen M. Lynch (Berkeley: University of California Press) pp. 182-211.

Bhagvat Mudit: see Lalitā Prasād Purohit (ed.), 1960.

Bhāṭī, Deśrāj Siṁh, 1977: *Raskhān granthāvalī saṭīk* [3rd edn.] (New Delhi: Aśok Prakāśan).

Bihārīlāl: see Jagannāth Dās 'Ratnākar' (ed.), n.d.

Bloch, Jules, 1965: *Indo-Aryan from the Vedas to modern times* [trans. Alfred Masters] (Paris: Adrien-Maisonneuve).

Brough, John, 1968: *Poems from the Sanskrit* (Harmondsworth: Penguin Books).

Bryant, Kenneth E., 1978: *Poems to the child-god: structures and strategies in the poetry of Sūrdās* (Berkeley: University of California Press).

—— 1983: 'The Fatehpur manuscript and the Sūrasāgara critical edition project', in *Bhakti in current research, 1979-82*, ed. Monika Thiel-Horstmann (Berlin: Dietrich Reimer Verlag), pp. 37-52.

Burrow, T., and M.B. Emeneau, 1961: *A Dravidian etymological dictionary* (Oxford: Clarendon Press).

Caturvedī, Paraśurām (ed.), 1954: *Mīrābāī kī padāvalī* (Allahabad: Hindī Sāhitya Sammelan).

Celer, Janārdan Rāv (ed.), 1971: *Vṛnd granthāvalī* (Agra: Vinod Pustak Mandir).

Chaudhuri, J.B., 1954: *Khān Khānān Abdur Rahim (1557 A.D.-1630 A.D.) and contemporary Sanskrit learning (1551-1650 A.D.)* (Calcutta: Prācyavidyā Mandir).

Cohen, Richard J., 1984: 'Sectarian Vaishnavism: the Vallabha *sampradāya*', in *Identity and division in cults and sects in South Asia*, ed. Peter Gaeffke and David A. Utz (Philadelphia: University of Pennsylvania), pp. 65-72.

Corcoran, Maura, 1980: 'Vṛndāvan in Vaiṣṇava Braj literature' (PhD thesis, University of London).

—— 1983: 'The life and poetry of Rasakhāna', in *Bhakti in current research, 1979-82*, ed. Monika Thiel-Horstmann (Berlin: Dietrich Reimer Verlag), pp. 75-84.

Dallapiccola, Anna (ed.), 1982: *Krishna the divine lover* (London: Serindia Publications).

Dās, Jagannāth, 'Ratnākar' (ed.), N.d.: *Bihārī ratnākar* (Varanasi: Ratna Publications).

Das, Shyam, 1985: *Eightyfour Vaishnavas* (Baroda: Shri Vallabha Publications).

Dās, Vrajratna, 1921: *K͟husro kī hiṁdī kavitā* (Varanasi: Nāgarī Pracāriṇī Sabhā).

De, Sushil Kumar, 1961: *Early history of the Vaiṣṇava faith and movement in Bengal*, 2nd. edn. (Calcutta: Firma K.L. Mukhopadhyay).

Dev: see Ramānāth Tripāṭhī, 1978.

Dewhurst, R.P., 1915: 'Persian and Arabic words in the Satsai of Bihari Lal', *Journal of the Royal Asiatic Society*, Part 1, pp. 122-27.

Dhruvdās: see Lalitā Caraṇ Gosvāmī (ed.), 1971.

Dimock, Edward C., 1966: *The place of the hidden moon: erotic mysticism in the Vaiṣṇava-Sahajiyā cult of Bengal* (Chicago: University of Chicago Press).

Dowson, John, 1982: *A classical dictionary of Hindu mythology and religion, geography, history, and literature* [reprint] (Calcutta: Rupa).

Eck, Diana, 1981: *Darśan: seeing the divine image in India* (Chambersburg: Anima Books).

Entwistle, A.W., 1982: 'Vaiṣṇava tilakas: sectarian marks worn by worshippers of Viṣṇu', special issue of *IAVRI Bulletin* XI and XII (December 1981-June 1982).

——1983: *The Rāsa māna ke pada of Kevalarāma: a medieval Hindi text of the eighth gaddī of the Vallabha sect* (Groningen: Rijksuniversiteit te Groningen).

—— 1987: *Braj: centre of Krishna pilgrimage* (Groningen: Egbert Forsten).

—— 1991: 'The cult of Krishna-Gopāl as a version of pastoral', in *Devotion divine: bhakti traditions from the regions of India*, ed. Diana L. Eck and Françoise Mallison (Groningen: Egbert Forsten; and Paris: École Française d'Extrême Orient), pp.73-90.

Gambhir, Vijay, 1983: 'Theme-focusing in Hindi', *Indian Linguistics* 44, 1-4 (March/December 1983), pp. 27-38.

Garg, Lakṣmīnārāyaṇ, 1981: *Kathak nṛtya* [4th edn.] (Hathras, Saṅgīt Kāryālay).

Gaston, Ann-Marie, [1991]: *Krishna's musicians: a study of the kirtankars of Nathdvara, Rajasthan* [Provisional title: forthcoming]

Gerow, Edwin, 1971: *A glossary of Indian figures of speech* (The Hague: Mouton).

—— 1977: *Indian poetics* (Wiesbaden: Otto Harrassowitz).

Gilbertson, G.W., 1900: *The assembly of mirth: a literal translation into English of the Sabhá Bilása* (Benares: Medical Hall Press).

Goetz, Hermann: 1966: *Mira Bai: her life and times* (Bombay: Bharatiya Vidya Bhavan).

Gokulnāth: see Brajbhūṣaṇ Śarmā and Dvārkādās Parīkh (eds.) 1951-53.

Gosvāmī, Lalitā Caraṇ (ed.), 1971: *Śrī Bayālīs līlā tathā Padyāvalī* [of Dhruvdās] (Vrindaban: Baba Tulsidas).

Gosvāmī, Vāsudev, 1952: *Bhakta-kavi Vyās jī*, ed. Prabhudayāl Mītal (Mathura: Agravāl Press).

Gowen, Herbert H., 1968: *A history of Indian literature from Vedic times to the present day* [reprint of 1931 edn.] (New York: Greenwood Press).

Grierson, G.A., 1896: *The Satsaiya of Bihari* (Calcutta: Superintendent of Government Printing).

Growse, F.S., 1882: *Mathurá: a district memoir* [3rd. edn.] (Allahabad: North-Western Provinces and Oudh Government Press).

Gupta, Kiśorīlāl (ed.), 1965: *Nāgarīdās granthāvalī* (Varanasi: Nāgarī Pracāriṇī Sabhā).

Gupta, Rākeśa, 1967: *Studies in nāyaka-nāyikā-bheda* (Aligarh: Granthayan).

Haberman, David, 1988a: *Acting as a way of salvation: a study of rāgānugā bhakti sādhana* (New York: Oxford University Press).

—— 1988b: 'The Bengali tradition', in *Textual sources for the study of Hinduism* , ed. W.D. O'Flaherty (Manchester: Manchester University Press), pp.151-68.

Hardy, Friedhelm, 1983: *Viraha-bhakti: the early history of Kṛṣṇa devotion in South India* (Delhi: Oxford University Press).

Harirāy: see Brajbhūṣaṇ Śarmā and Dvārkādās Parīkh (eds.) 1951-53; and Dvārkādās Parīkh (ed.) 1970.

Hawley, John Stratton , 1979: 'The early *Sūr Sāgar* and the growth of the Sūr tradition', *Journal of the American Oriental Society,* 99, no.1, pp. 64-72.

—— 1981: *At play with Krishna: pilgrimage dramas from Brindavan* (Princeton: Princeton University Press).

—— 1983: *Krishna, the butter thief* (Princeton: Princeton University Press).

—— 1984: *Sūrdās: poet, singer, saint* (Seattle: University of Washington Press).

—— & Mark Juergensmeyer, 1988: *Songs of the saints of India* (New York: Oxford University Press).

—— & Donna Marie Wulff (eds.), 1982: *The divine consort: Rādhā and the goddesses of India* (Berkeley: Graduate Theological Union).

Hein, Norvin, 1972: *The miracle plays of Mathurā* (New Haven: Yale University Press).

—— 1976: 'Caitanya's ecstasies and the theology of the name', in *Hinduism: new essays in the history of religions,* ed. Bardwell L.Smith (Leiden: E.J.Brill) pp. 15-32.

Holland, Barron G., 1975: 'The Satsaī of Bihārī: Hindi poetry of the early Rīti period' (PhD thesis, University of Washington).

Ingalls, Daniel H.H., 1965: *An anthology of Sanskrit court poetry: Vidyākara's "Subhāṣitaratnakoṣa"* (Cambridge, Mass.: Harvard University Press).

Jasvant Siṁh: see Viśvanāth Prasād Miśra (ed.), 1972.

Jāyasvāl, Puṣpārānī (ed.), 1974: *Dev granthāvalī* (Allahabad: Sāhitya Academy).

Jindal, K.B., 1955: *A history of Hindi literature* (Allahabad: Kitab Mahal).

Johnson, Francis, 1928: *Hitopadeśa: the book of wholesome counsel* (London: Chapman & Hall).

Kakar, Sudhir, 1985: 'Erotic fantasy: the secret passion of Radha and Krishna', *Contributions to Indian Sociology* (New Series) Vol.19, No.1 (January-June 1985), pp. 75-94.

Kellogg, S.H., 1938: *A grammar of the Hindí language* [3rd edn.] (London: Kegan Paul, Trench, & Trubner).

Kennedy, Melville T., 1925: *The Chaitanya movement* (Calcutta: Association [Y.M.C.A.] Press).

Keśavdās: see Miśra, Viśvanāth Prasād (ed.), 1954.

Kinsley, David, 1979: *The divine player: a study of Kṛṣṇa-līlā* (Delhi: Motilal Banarsidass).

Kippen, James, 1988: *The tabla of Lucknow: a cultural analysis of a musical tradition* (Cambridge: Cambridge University Press).

Klaiman, M.H. (trans.), 1984: *Singing the glory of Lord Krishna: the Śrīkṛṣṇakīrtana* (Chico: Scholars Press).

Klostermaier, Klaus, 1969: *Hindu and Christian in Vrindaban* (London: SCM Press).

Lallu Lal, 1854: *Rája-níti; a collection of Hindu apologues, in the Braj Bháshá language* [Revised edn.] (Allahabad: Presbyterian Mission Press).

[Lallūlāl: see also G.W.Gilbertson, 1900.]

Lath, Mukund, 1981: *Half a tale* [the *Ardhakathānaka* of Banārsīdās]: *a study in the interrelationship between autobiography and history* (Jaipur: Rajasthan Prakrit Bharati Sansthan).

Lockwood, W.B., 1969: *Indo-European philology, historical and comparative* (London: Hutchinson).

Lowe, J.R.A.S., 1853: *The Rajnítí* [sic]; *or tales, exhibiting the moral doctrines and the civil and military policy of the Hindoos* (Calcutta: P.S.D'Rozano & Co).

Machwe, Prabhakar, 1975: 'Amir Khusrau's Hindi poetry' in *Amir Khusrau* (New Delhi: Ministry of Information and Broadcasting, Government of India), pp. 93-102.

Mahesh, Maheshwari Sinha, 1964: *The historical development of mediæval Hindi prosody* (Bhagalpur: Bhagalpur University).

Manuel, Peter, 1989: *Ṭhumrī in historical and stylistic perspectives* (Delhi: Motilal Banarsidass).

Mathur, Ramesh, 1974: *Padmāvata: an etymological study* (Calcutta: Simant Publications (for Intercultural Research Institute)).

Matirām: see Kṛṣṇabihārī Miśra and Brajkiśor Miśra (eds.), 1964.

McGregor, R.S., 1968: *The language of Indrajit of Orcha* (Cambridge: Cambridge University Press).

—— 1973a: *The round dance of Krishna and Uddhav's message* (London: Luzac & Co).

—— 1973b: *Hindi literature of the nineteenth and early twentieth centuries* (Wiesbaden: Otto Harrassowitz).

—— 1984: *Hindi literature from its beginnings to the nineteenth century* (Wiesbaden: Otto Harrassowitz).

Miller, Barbara Stoler, 1977: *Love songs of the dark lord: Jayadeva's Gītagovinda* (New York: Columbia University Press).

Miltner, Vladimir, 1962: 'Old Braj morphology in the Bihārī-Satsaī', *Archiv Orientalni,* 30, pp.494-504.

Mīrā: see Paraśurām Caturvedī (ed.), 1954.

Miśra, Kṛṣṇabihārī, and Brajkiśor Miśra (eds.), 1964: *Matirām (granthāvalī)* (Varanasi: Nāgarī Pracāriṇī Sabhā).

Miśra, Viśvanāth Prasād (ed.), 1947: *Rasakhāni* (Varanasi: Vāṇī Vitān).

—— 1954: *Keśav granthāvalī*, I (Allahabad: Hindustani Academy).

—— 1972: *Jasvantsiṁh granthāvalī* (Varanasi: Nāgarī Pracāriṇī Sabhā).

Mītal, Prabhu Dayāl, 1951: *Sūrdās kī vārtā* (Mathura: Agravāl Press).

—— 1968: *Braj ke dharma-sampradāyõ kā itihās* (Delhi: National Publishing House).

Molesworth, J.T., 1857: *A dictionary, Marathi and English* [2nd edn.] (Bombay: Government of India).

Monier-Williams, Monier, 1974: *A Sanskrit-English dictionary* [reprint of 1899 edn.] (Oxford: Oxford University Press).

Mukerjee, Radhakamal, 1957: *The lord of the autumn moons* (Bombay: Asia Publishing House).

[Mulji, Karsendas], 1865: *History of the sect of the maharajas* [published anonymously] (London: Trübner).

Nābhājī, n.d.: *Śrī bhaktamāl* (Govardhan: Devīdās Gupta).

Nāgarīdās: see Kiśorīlāl Gupta (ed.), 1965.

Nagendra (ed.), 1981: *Bihārī: an anthology* (Delhi: Bansal).

Nārāyaṇa: see V. Balasubhramanyan, 1989.

Nilsson, Usha S., 1969: *Mira Bai* (New Delhi: Sahitya Akademi).

O'Connell, J.T., 1976: 'Caitanya's followers and the Bhagavad Gītā', in *Hinduism: new essays in the history of religions,* ed. Bardwell L.Smith (Leiden: E.J.Brill) pp. 33-52.

Pāṇḍey, Sudhākar (ed.), 1969: *Raslīn granthāvalī* (Varanasi: Nāgarī Pracāriṇī Sabhā).

Parīkh, Dvārkādās (ed.), 1970: *Caurāsī vaiṣṇavan kī vārtā* (Mathura: Śrī Govardhan Granthamālā Kāryālay).

Platts, John T., 1968: *A dictionary of Urdū, classical Hindī, and English* [Reprint of 1930 edn.] (London: Oxford University Press).

Prasād, Jagannāth, 'Bhānu Kavi', 1935: *Chandaḥprabhākar* [8th edn.] (Bilaspur: the author).

Preciado-Solis, Benjamin, 1984: *The Kṛṣṇa cycle in the Purāṇas: themes and motifs in a heroic saga* (Delhi: Motilal Banarsidass).

Purohit, Lalitā Prasād (ed.), 1960: *Rasik-ananya-māl* (Vrindaban: Veṇu Prakāśan).

Rahīm: see Samar Bahādur Siṁh (ed.), 1961.

Randhawa, M.S., 1966: *Kangra paintings of the Bihārī Sat Saī* (Delhi: National Museum).

Raskhān: see Bābū Amīr Siṁh (ed.), 1956.

Raslīn: see Sudhākar Pāṇḍey (ed.), 1969.

Redington, James D., 1983: *Vallabhācārya on the love games of Kṛṣṇa* (Delhi: Motilal Banarsidass).

Renou, Louis, & Jean Filliozat (eds.), 1953: *L'Inde classique: manuel des études indiennes* [2 vols.] (Paris: École Française d'Extrême-Orient).

Russell, Ralph, & Khurshidul Islam, 1969: *Three Mughal poets: Mir, Sauda, Mir Hasan* (London: George Allen & Unwin).

Ryder, Arthur W., 1955: *The Panchatantra* (Chicago: Chicago University Press).

Sarkar, Ranajit, 1974: *Gītagovinda: towards a total understanding* (Groningen: Rijksuniversiteit te Groningen).

Śarmā, Brajbhūṣaṇ, & Dvārkādās Parīkh (eds.) 1951-53: *Do sau bāvan vaiṣṇavan kī vārtā* [3 vols.] (Kankaroli: Śuddhādvaita Academy).

Shackle, Christopher, 1981: *A Gurū Nānak glossary* (London: School of Oriental and African Studies).

—— 1984: 'The non-Sanskritic vocabulary of the later Sikh gurūs', *Bulletin of the School of Oriental and African Studies,* XLVII, Part 1, pp.76-107.

—— and Rupert Snell, 1990: *Hindi and Urdu since 1900: a common reader* [SOAS South Asian Texts 1] (London: School of Oriental and African Studies).

Shapiro, Michael, 1986: 'On the semantics of Hindi *āge/ke āge*', *Studien zur Indologie und Iranistik,* 11-12, pp. 233-43.

Sheth, Noel, S.J., 1984: *The divinity of Krishna* (Delhi: Munshiram Manoharlal).

Siegel, Lee, 1978: *Sacred and profane dimensions of love in Indian traditions as exemplified in the Gītagovinda of Jayadeva* (Delhi: Oxford University Press).

—— 1987: *Laughing matters: comic tradition in India* (Chicago: University of Chicago Press).

Siṁh, Bābū Amīr (ed.), 1956: *Raskhān aur Ghanānand* (Varanasi: Nāgarī Pracāriṇī Sabhā).

Siṁh, Samar Bahādur, 1961: *Abdurrahīm Khānkhānā* (Chirganv: Sāhitya Sadan).

Singer, Milton (ed.), 1966: *Krishna: myths, rites and attitudes* (Chicago: Chicago University Press).

Smith, Bardwell L. (ed.), 1976: *Hinduism: new essays in the history of religions* (Leiden: Brill).

Smith, J.D., 1976: *The Vīsaḷadevarāsa: a restoration of the text* (Cambridge: Cambridge University Press).

Snell, Rupert, 1983: 'Metrical forms in Braj Bhāṣā verse: the *Caurāsī pada* in performance', in *Bhakti in current research, 1979-82*, ed. Monika Thiel-Horstmann (Berlin: Dietrich Reimer Verlag), pp. 353-84.

—— 1989: 'Raskhān the neophyte: Hindu perspectives on a Muslim Vaishnava', in *Urdu and Muslim South Asia: studies in honour of Ralph Russell*, ed. C.Shackle (London: School of Oriental and African Studies), pp. 29-37.

—— 1991a: *The eighty-four hymns of Hita Harivaṃśa: an edition of the Caurāsī pada.* (Delhi: Motilal Banarsidass; and London: School of Oriental and African Studies).

—— 1991b: 'Barvai metre in Tulsīdās and Rahīm', paper for presentation at the Fifth International Conference on Early Devotional Literature in New Indo-Aryan Languages, Paris, July 1991.

Śukla, Rāmcandra, et. al. (eds.), 1958: *Tulsī-granthāvalī* [2 vols.] (Varanasi: Nāgarī Pracāriṇī Sabhā).

Sūrdās: see Nand Dulāre Vājpeyī (ed.), 1972-76.

Tagare, Ganesh Vasudeo (trans.), 1976-78: *Bhāgavata Purāṇa* [5 vols.; vols. 7-11 of *Ancient Indian tradition and mythology*] (New Delhi: Motilal Banarsidass).

Ṭaṇḍan, Premnārāyaṇ, 1974: *Brajbhāṣā Sūr-koś* [2 vols.] (Lucknow: Lucknow University).

Thiel-Horstmann, Monika, 1983: *Crossing the ocean of existence: Braj Bhāṣā religious poetry from Rajasthan. A reader* (Wiesbaden: Otto Harrassowitz).

Tod, James, 1902: *Annals and antiquities of Rajasthan, or the central & western Rajpoot states of India* ['Coronation edition', 2 vols.] (Calcutta: The Society for the Resuscitation of Indian Literature).

Tripāṭhī, Ramānāth, 1978: *Devakavi: Aṣṭayām tathā Jasrāj Savāī kā pandrahtithi-virah-varṇan* (New Delhi: Kumār Prakāśan).

Tulsīdās: see Rāmcandra Śukla et. al. (eds.), 1958.

Turner, R.L., 1966: *A comparative dictionary of the Indo-Aryan languages* (London: Oxford University Press).

—— 1985: *A comparative dictionary of the Indo-Aryan languages: addenda and corrigenda*, ed. J.C.Wright (London: School of Oriental and African Studies).

Vājpeyī, Aṭalbihārī, 1978: *Kaidī Kavirāy kī kuṇḍaliyā̃*, 2nd. edn. (New Delhi: Sarasvatī Vihār).

Vājpeyī, Nand Dulāre (ed.), 1972-76: *Sūr-sāgar* [Vol. I, 4th edn.; Vol. II, 5th edn.] (Varanasi: Nāgarī Pracāriṇī Sabhā).

Varma, Dhirendra, 1935: *La langue Braj (dialecte de Mathurā)* (Paris: Librairie d'Amerique et d'Orient).

Vatuk, V.P., 1969/71: 'Amir Khusrau and the Indian riddle tradition', *Journal of American Folklore*, pp. 142 ff.; II, 24, 1971, nos. 3-4. [cited R.S.McGregor 1984:24n.].

Vaudeville, Charlotte, 1971: *Pastorales par Soûr-Dâs* (Paris: Gallimard).

—— 1976: 'Braj, lost and found', *Indo-Iranian Journal*, 18, pp. 195-213.

—— 1980: 'The Govardhan myth in Northern India', *Indo-Iranian Journal*, 22, pp. 1-45.

Vaudeville, Charlotte, 1986: *Bārahmāsā in Indian literatures: songs of the twelve months in Indo-Aryan literatures* (Delhi: Motilal Banarsidass).

Vṛnd: see Janārdan Rāv Celer (ed.), 1971.

White, Charles S.J., 1970: 'Kṛṣṇa as divine child', *History of Religions* X.2, pp. 156-177.

—— 1977: *The Caurāsī Pad of Śrī Hit Harivaṁś* (Honolulu: University Press of Hawaii).

Wilkins, Charles, 1885: *Fables and proverbs from the Sanskrit, being the Hitopadesa* (London: George Routledge).

Wulff, Donna Marie, 1984: *Drama as a mode of religious realization: the Vidagdha-mādhava of Rūpa Gosvāmī* (Chico: Scholars Press).

Zelliot, Eleanor, 1976: 'The medieval bhakti movement in history: an essay on the literature in English', in *Hinduism: new essays in the history of religions*, ed. B.L.Smith (Leiden: Brill), pp. 143-168.

Zograph, G.A., 1982: *Languages of South Asia: a guide* [*Languages of Asia and Africa*, Vol. 3] (London: Routledge & Kegan Paul).

THE TEXTS

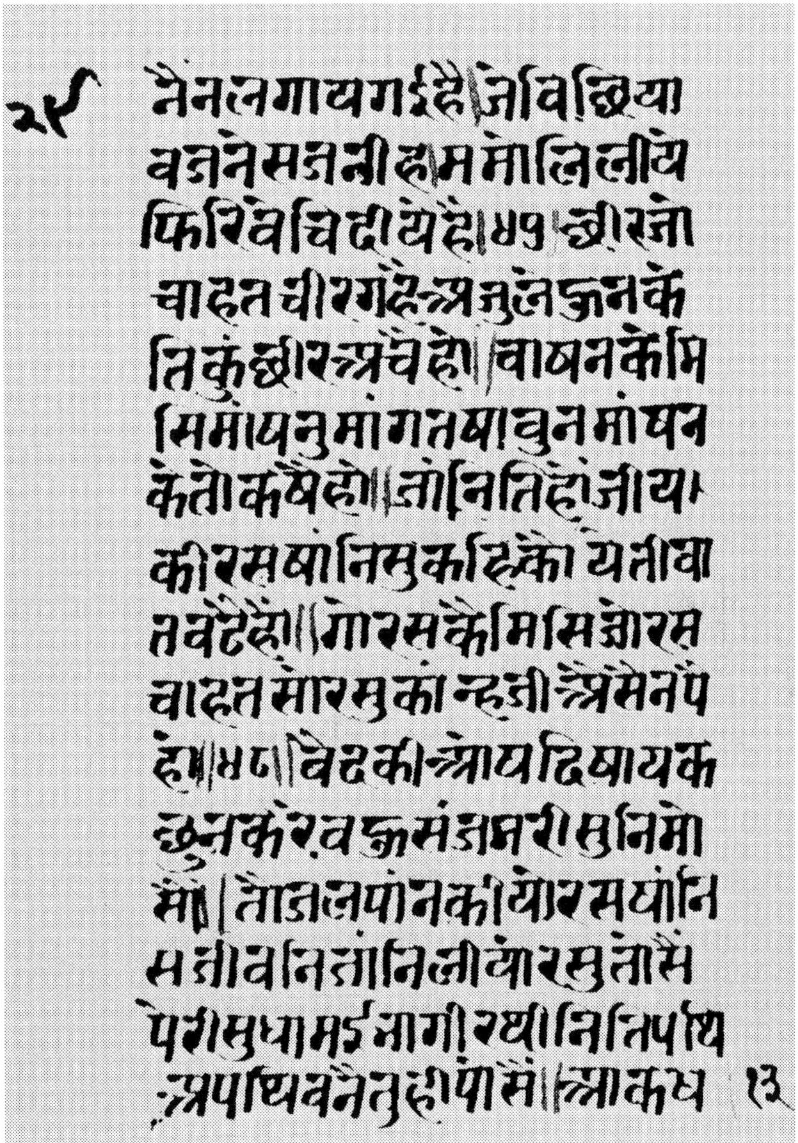

Folio of a manuscript including verses by Raskhān; SR 4, here numbered '48', begins on the third line. The undated MS (from the collection of Mr Simon Digby) was probably copied in the Jaipur area in the late eighteenth century.

राजनीति

लल्लूलाल

- १ -

हस्तिनापुर में एक बिलास नाम धोबी रहै । ताके घर एक गदहा । वा पै बोझ लादतु लादतु जद वाकी पीठ पर चांदी परी तब वह धुबिया गदहा कौं रात्रि के समय बाघ कौ चाम उढ़ाय काहू जव के खेत में छोड़ि आयौ [1]। वा खेत कौ रखवारौ ताहि देखत ही परायौ । या ही भांति यह नित नित वाकौ खेत खाय खाय आवै । तद वा रखवारे नें नाहर मारवे कौ यत्न कियौ औ वा ही खेत की पगार के निकट भूरी कामरी ओढ़ि धनुष चढ़ाय आप हू काहू झुंड तरें दबकि रह्यौ । द्वै पहर रात के समें अंधेरे में गदहा आयौ औ याकी भूरी कमरिया कौं देखि गदही जानि [2] वह कामांध होय रैंकतु धायौ । पुनि रखवारे नें जान्यौ कि यह तौ गदहा है पर बाघ कौ चाम ओढ़ि आयौ है । ऐसें कहि क्रोध करि रखवारे नें वाहि लौठियन लौठियन [3] मारि गिरायौ । वाकौ प्रान गयौ । तातें हौं कहतु हौ [4] कि आपनौ बल बिचारि काज कीजै ।

- २ -

मगध देस में सुभदत्त नाम कायथ । तिन धर्मारन्य बन में क्रीड़ा की ठौर बनावन कौ आरम्भ कियौ । तहां कोऊ बढ़ई काठ चीरतु चीरतु वा मांहिं लकरी की कील दै काहू काम कौं गयौ । अरु एक बन कौ बानर चपलाई करतु करतु कालबस [5] वा ही काठ पर कील पकरि आय बैठ्यौ । अरु वाके अंडकोष वा काठ की संधि मांहिं लटकि परे । ज्यौं उनि

[1] *choṛi āyau* : 'left and came', i.e. 'went and left'. Cf. 4 *khāya khāya āvai*, 24 *māri āū̃* etc.

[2] *gadahī jāni* : 'thinking [the watchman] a she-ass' — a typical use of *jān-* with the sense 'assume wrongly, misconstrue'. But cf. *jānyau* as 'realized' in the next sentence.

[3] *lauṭhiyana lauṭhiyana* : 'with repeated blows of a stick'.

[4] *tātẽ haũ kahatu hau* : 'therefore I say' — a formula which typically introduces the moral at the end of the tale.

[5] *kālabasa* : 'in the grip of fate', i.e. 'as fate would have it'.

चंचलता सों युक्ति करि कील काढ़ी त्यौं काढ़त प्रमान [6] अंडकोष चपे औ मरचौ । तातें हौं कहतु हौं कि बिन स्वारथ चेष्टा न करियै ।

- ३ -

श्रीपर्वत में ब्रह्मपुर नाम नगर । अरु वा पहाड़ की चोटी पै एक घंटाकरन नाम राक्षस रहै । सो[7] वा नगर के निवासी सब जानैं क्यौंकि वाकौ शब्द सदा सुन्यौ करैं । एक दिन नगर में तें चोर घंटा चुराय गिर पर लियै जातु हो । ताहि तहां बाघ नें मारि खायौ अरु वह घंटा बानर के हाथ आई । जब वह बजावै तब नगरनिवासी जानैं कि राक्षस डोलतु है । काहू दिन कोऊ वा मरे मनुष [8] कौं देखि आयौ । तिन सब तें कह्यौ कि अब घंटाकरन रिसाइकै नर खानि लाग्यौ । यह मैं स्वदृष्टि देखि आयौ । वाकी बात सुनि मारे भय के [9] नगर के सब लोग भजवे लागे । तब कराला नाम एक कुटनी नें वा घंटा के बजवे कौ कारन जानि राजा सों जाय कह्यौ कि महाराज मोहि कछु देउ तौ घंटाकरन कौं मारि आऊं । यह सुनि राजा नें वाहि लाख रुपैया दिये अरु वाके मारिवे कौं बिदा कियौ । तद वा नें धन तौ निज मंदिर [10] मांहिं राख्यौ अरु बहुत सी खैवे [11] की सामा लै बन की गैल गही [12] । ह्वां जाय देखै तौ एक मरकट रूख पर बैठ्यौ घंटा बजावतु है । वाहि देखि या नें एक ऊंचे पर[13] सब सामा बिथराय दई । वह बंदरा देखतु ही बृक्ष तें कूदि ह्वां आयौ । पकवान मिठाई फल मूल देखि घंटा पटकि खैवे कौं जौं उनि हाथ चलायौ त्यौं घंटा अलग भई । तब या नें [14] घंटा लै आपनी गैल गही । नगर में आय वा ने वह राजा के हाथ दई अरु यह बात कही कि महाराज हौं वाहि मारि आई । यह सुनि औ घंटा देखि राजा नें वाकी बहुत प्रतिष्ठा करी अरु नगर के लोगन हू वाहि पूज्यौ । तातें हौं कहतु हौं कि महाराज [15] केवल शब्द ही तें न डरियै । प्रथम वाकौ कारन बिचारियै पुनि उपाय करियै ।

[6] *pramāna* : used adverbially after a ptc., this has the sense 'immediately on' (but only in RN).

[7] *so* : 'that [fact]', referring back to the statement of the previous sentence.

[8] *mare manuṣa* : 'dead man', the ptc. qualifies the noun.

[9] *māre bhaya ke* : 'because of fear, through fear' — an inverted ppn.

[10] *maṁdira*: 'house', not the sense 'temple' as in the modern language.

[11] *khaibe* : a contraction of *khāibe*, obl. inf.

[12] *bana kī gaila gahī* : 'took the forest path', i.e. 'set off for the forest'. Cf. 30 *āpanī gaila gahī* , 55 *āpanau pantha liyau* 'went on his/her way'.

[13] *eka ū̃ce para* : 'on a high [place]'.

[14] *yā nẽ* : the pr. refers to the *kuṭanī.*

[15] *mahārāja* : the storyteller addresses his patron, the king Amaraśakti.

- ४ -

अर्बुद परवत की कंदरा में एक महाबिक्रम नाम सिंह रहै । जब वह वहां सोवै तब एक मूसा बिल तें निकरि वाके केस काटै । जद वह जागै तद बिल में भजि जाय । कह्यौ है[16] छोटे शत्रु बड़ेनि[17] तें न मरैं । वा मूषक की दुष्टता देखि बाघ नें निज मन में बिचार्यौ कि याके समान कौ कोऊ ल्याऊं [18] तौ यह मार्यौ जाय । ना तौ याके हाथ तें सोवन न पायहौं। यह बिचारि गांव में जाय एक दधिकरन नाम बिलाव कौं अति आदर सों ल्यायौ अरु राख्यौ । वह हू वा कंदरा के द्वार पर बैठ्यौ रहै अरु बिलाव के भय तें मूसा बिल सों बाहर न निकरै । सिंह सुखनीद सोवै। यातें मूसा के डर तें बाघ बिलाव कौ अति आदर करै । आगै कितेक दिन पाछै [19] एक दिन दाव पाय वा मूसा कौं बिलाव नें मारि खायौ । जब सिंह नें मूषक कौ शब्द न सुन्यौ तब उनि मन मांहिं बिचार्यौ कि जाके कारन याहि ल्यायौ हो सो काम तौ सिद्ध भयौ । अब याहि राखिवे तें कहा प्रयोजन । बाघ नें ऐसें बिचारि वाकौ अहार बंद कियौ । तब बिलाव वा ठौर तें भूख्यौ मरि मरि परायौ । यातें हौं कहतु हौं कि ठाकुर कौं कबहू निचतौ न राखियै ।

- ५ -

गौतमारन्य में एक ब्राह्मन यज्ञ के निमित्त बोकरा माथे लिये आवतु हो । वाहि तीन ठगनि देखि बोकरा लैन कौ आपस में मतौ कियौ [20] अरु वे तीनौं साध कौ भेष बनाय तीन ठौर जाय बैठे । जब वह ब्राह्मन पहिले साध के निकट गयौ तब उन कह्यौ अरे ब्राह्मन यह कूकर माथे धरि[21] काहे लिये जातु है । इन कही कूकर नाहिं । यज्ञ कौ बोकरा है । यह सुनि वह साध चुप रह्यौ । आगे दूसरे के पास गयौ। पुनि उन हू कह्यौ रे देवता मूंड़ पै स्वान क्यौं चढ़ायौ । इतनौ सुनि इन बुरौ मानि वाहि सीस तें उतारि देख्यौ अरु संदेह करतु चल्यौ कि जो देखतु है सो याहि कूकर कहतु है पर मेरी दृष्टि में तौ बोक जनातु है । ऐसें

16 *kahyau hai*: 'it is said [that]...'.

17 *bareni*: obl. pl. of *barau*. The adj. is used nominally: 'small enemies do not die at the hands of big ones'.

18 *yāke samāna kau koū lyāū̃*: 'if I could get someone similar [in size] to him'.

19 *kiteka dina pāchai* : 'after a certain time'.

20 *bokarā laina kau āpasa mẽ matau kiyau*: 'conspired together to get the goat'.

21 Following the fondness of the Skt original for multiple synonyms, each of the three rogues is given a distinct vocabulary for the three key items in the story: *brāhmana / devatā / bipra* for 'brahmin', *kūkara / svāna / kūkarā* for 'dog', and *māthau / mūṛa / sira* for 'head'.

सोचतु सोचतु वह तीजे के निकट जाय पहुंच्यौ । तद उन हू कह्यौ अहो बिप्र कूकरा सिर तें डारि दै । तैं यह कहा अनर्थ कियौ जो स्वान मूंड़ पै धरि लियौ[22] । यह बात वाके मुख तें सुनत प्रमान वाहि कूकर जानि बिप्र नें माथे तें पटक आपनौ पंथ लियौ । अरु विननि बोक लै आपनौ मनोरथ पूरौ कियौ । तातें हौं कहतु हौं कि दुष्ट के बचन तें साध हू की बुद्धि चलै [23] ।

- ६ -

श्रीनगर में मंदबुद्धि नाम एक खाती रहै । सो आपनी नारी कौं बिभचारिनी जानै पर वाहि जार समेत कबहू न पावै । एक दिन वा नें वाके जार कौं पकरवे के लियै वा सों कह्यौ कि आज हौं गांव जातु हौं । सु तीन चार दिन में आयहौं । इतनौ कहि वह बाहर जाय फेरि घर में आय खटिया तरै छिप रहचौ । वाकी स्त्री नें ताहि गांव गयौ जानि[24] निज जार कौं बुलायौ अरु क्रीड़ा के समें कछु आहट पाय जान्यौ कि यह मेरी परीक्षा लैन कौं खटिया तरै लुक्यौ है । यौं जानि वह मन में चिंतित भई । अरु जब जार कही रमति क्यौं नाहीं तब वह बोली आज मेरे घर कौ धनी घर नाहीं। यातें मेरे भायें [25] आज गांव सूनौ बनखंड सौ लगतु है । पुनि जार कही जौ तेरौ वा सों ऐसौ ही सनेह हो[26] तौ वह तोहि काहे छांड़ि गयौ । उनि कही अरे बावरे तू यह नाहीं जानतु । सुनि । कहचौ है कि स्वामी स्त्री कौं चाहै कै न चाहै[27] पर नारी कौ यह धर्म है जु पति कौं एक पल हू न बिसारै अरु भर्त्तार की मार गारी सिंगार जानै[28] । सो धर्म कौं पावै औ कुलवंती सती कहावै । धनी घर में रहै कै बाहर पापी होय कै पुन्यात्मा पर नारी वाहि न बिसारै क्योंकि स्त्री कौ अलंकार भर्त्तार है । पतिहीन अति सुंदरी हू नीकी न लागै । औ तू जार है । सो तौ पान फूल के समान एक घरी कौ पाहुनौ[29] दैव के संजोग आनि मिल्यौ । कर्म की रेख मेटी न जाय । बिधाता सों काहू की कछु न

22 'What is this absurdity that you have done, putting a dog on your head!'

23 *sādha hū kī buddhi calai* : 'even a good man loses his wits' (*sādha* here does not have the technical sense 'holy man' which applies in line 47).

24 *tāhi gā̃va gayau jāni* : 'thinking him gone to the village'.

25 *mere bhāyẽ* : 'in my view, according to my feelings'.

26 *jau terau vā sõ aisau hī sancha ho* : 'if your love for him is such'.

27 *svāmī strī kaũ cāhai kai na cāhai* : 'whether a husband loves his wife or not'.

28 *bharttāra kī māra gārī siṁgāra jānai* : 'should consider her husband's beatings and abuse as ornaments'.

29 *pāna phūla ke samāna eka gharī kau pāhunau* : 'like *pān* or a flower, an hour's guest' — a fleeting pleasure.

बसाय [30]। अरु वह मेरौ स्वामी, हौं वाकी दासी । जौ लौं वह [31] तौ लौं मेरौ जीव है । वाके मरे हौं सती [32] हौऊंगी । कह्यौ है जो सती होय सो प्रथम तौ आपने कुकर्म तैं छूटै । दूजै कैसौ हू वाकौ भर्त्तार दुष्कर्मी पापी होय [33] तौ हू जेते देह में रोम हैं तेते बर्ष [34] वह निज स्वामी कौं साथ लै स्वर्ग भोग करै । औ जैसें गारड़ू सांप कौं मंत्र की शक्ति करि पाताल तें बुलावै तैसें ही सहगामिनी आपने पति कौं नरक सों काढ़ि परम गति [35] दिवावै । यह बात सुनि वह खाती आपने जी मांहिं कहनि लाग्यौ धन्य मेरे भाग जु ऐसी नारी पाई कि आप तरै औ मोहि तरावै [36] । वह ऐसें बिचारि उछाह कौ मारचौ उन दोउअन समेत खाट माथे लै[37] नाच्यौ । तातें हौं कहतु हौं कि मूरख दोष देखि हू स्तुति किये [38] प्रसन्न होय ।

- ७ -

द्वारिका नगरी में एक घोस की नारि बिभचारिनी ही [39] । सु कोटवार औ वाके मौंड़ा तें रहै । एक दिन रात्रि की बेला कोटवार के छोहरा तें भोग करि रही ही । ता मांहिं [40] कोटवार आय बार पर पुकारचौ । तब या नें वाके ढोटा कौं कोठी में लुकाय द्वार खोल दियौ अरु ता हू कौ भलौ मनायौ । [41] इतेक में वाकौ धनी आयौ । तद इन कोटवार कौं यह सिखायौ कि हौं तौ बार उघारनि जाति हौं । पर तुम लौठिया कांधे पै धरि क्रोध करि घर तें निकरौ । ता पाछै हौं बात बनाय लैउंगी [42]। उनि वैसें ही करी । तब अहीर नें घर में आय आपनी स्त्री तें कह्यौ कि आज कोटवार हमारे घर तें रिसायकै क्यौं गयौ ।

30 *bidhātā sõ kāhū kī kachu na basāya* : 'nothing anyone does can influence the creator at all' (implicit *bāta* is subject).

31 *jau laũ vaha* : 'as long as he [lives]'.

32 *satī* : here in the technical sense, 'suttee, wife who immolates herself on husband's funeral pyre' — vs. the more general sense of 68 *satī* as 'faithful wife'

33 *kaisau hū vākau bharttāra duṣkarmī pāpī hoya* : 'no matter what kind of wicked sinner her husband may be'.

34 *jete deha mẽ roma haĩ tete varṣa* : 'for as many years as there are hairs on the body'.

35 *parama gati* : 'the supreme state', i.e. salvation from rebirth.

36 *āpa tarai au mohi tarāvai* : 'gets across [the ocean of existence] herself, and gets me across too' — i.e. 'brings both of us to salvation'.

37 *una douana sameta khāṭa māthe lai* : 'taking the bed with both of them in it onto his head'.

38 *stuti kiye* : 'on being praised'.

39 *hī* : f. past tense of the verb *ho-*, MSH *thī*. Cf. 81 *bhoga kari rahī hī* .

40 *tā māhĩ* : 'meanwhile, at that moment'; cf. 83 *iteka mẽ*, 88 *iteka māhĩ*.

41 'Then she hid his son in a storeroom, opened the door and gave him [the father] a good time also'.

42 *haũ bāta banāya laiũgī* : 'I'll make up an excuse, explain it away, sort it out'.

अहीरी बोली कोटवार हमारे घर तें क्यौं रिसायगौ [43] । वाकौ पूत वा तें रिसाय मेरे घर मांहिं आय छिप्यौ है । सु वह आपने मौंडा कौं मो सों मांगतु हो । इतेक मांहिं तुम जो आये सो तुम्हैं देखि चल्यौ गयौ । यह कहि घुसायन नें कोटवार के पुत्र कौं कोठी तें निकारि कह्यौ कि तू कछू भय मत कर । मैं तोहि बाहर निकारि देति हौं । जित तेरे सींग समाय [44] तित चल्यौ जा । ऐसें कहि वाहि घर तें निकारि दियौ । कह्यौ है,

दोहा[45]

पुरुषनि तें दुगनी क्षुधा, बुद्धि चौगुनी होय ।
काम आठ साहस छगुन, या बिधि तिय सब कोय ॥

तातें हौं कहतु हौं काम परे जाकी बुद्धि फुरै सोई पंडित ।

[43] *koṭavāra hamāre ghara tẽ kyaũ risāyagau* : future tense shows the question to be rhetorical, 'Why would the kotwal be angry with our household?'

[44] *jita tere sĩga samāya* : lit. 'wherever your horns may fit', i.e. 'anywhere you can find refuge'.

[45] See II.2.1 for a description of the *dohā* form. The couplet may be translated:

In appetite, double the menfolk, in cleverness fourfold;
in lust, eight-, and in courage, six- : woman are thus, all told.

चौरासी (तथा) दो सौ बावन वैष्णवन की वार्ता

गोकुलनाथ / हरिराय

१. सूरदास (८४ वैष्णवन की वार्ता)

[सूरदास] के पद जहाँ तहाँ लोग सीखिकै गावन लागे । सो तब एक समय तानसेन [1] नें एक पद सूरदास कौ सीखिकै अकबर बादसाह के आगै गायौ । यह सुनि देसाधिपति अकबर नें कह्यौ जो ऐसे लक्षनबारे भक्तन [2] सों मिलाप होय तौ कहा कहियै [3] । सो तानसेन नें कही [4] जो [5] जिननें यह कीर्तन कियौ है [6] सो ब्रज में रहत हैं और सूरदासजी उनकौ नाम है ।

यह सुनि देसाधिपति के मन में आई जो कोई उपाय करिकै सूरदास सों मिलियै । पाछै देसाधिपति दिल्ली तें आगरा आयौ । तब अपने हलकारान सों कह्यौ जो ब्रज में सूरदासजी श्रीनाथजी के पद गावत हैं सो तिनकी ठीक पारिकै मोकों श्रीमथुराजी [7] में खबर दीजियो और यह बात सूरदास जानैं नाँहीं ।

तब उन हलकारान नें श्रीनाथजी द्वार[8] में आयकै खबर काढ़ी । तब सुनी जो सूरदासजी तौ मथुराजी गये हैं । सो तब वे हलकारा श्री मथुरा में आयकै सूरदास कों नजर में राखे, जो या समय यहाँ बैठे हैं । तब उन हलकारान नें देसाधिपति कों खबर करी जो अजी साहब, सूरदासजी तौ मथुराजी में हैं । तब सूरदास कूँ अकबर बादशाह ने दस पाँच मनुष्य बुलायवे कों पठाये । सो सूरदासजी देसाधिपति के पास आये । तब देसाधिपति नें उनकौ [9] बहौत आदर सन्मान कियौ । पाछै सूरदासजी सों देसाधिपति नें कह्यौ जो

[1] *tānasena* : Tānsen, Akbar's principal musician and one of the 'nine jewels' of the Mughal court. A composer of *dhrupad* compositions, he is said to have been the disciple of Svāmī Haridās of Vrindaban.

[2] *aise lakṣanabāre bhaktana* : 'devotees of such qualities'.

[3] *kahā kahiyai* : 'what could be said?', i.e. rhetorically 'how fine that would be!'.

[4] *tānasena nẽ kahī* : f. agreement is with *bāta* (understood); cf. 6 *desādhipati ke mana mẽ āī*, 10 *taba sunī*, etc.

[5] *jo* : most occurrences of *jo* in this text are as cj., typically after verbs of saying (cf. MSH *ki*).

[6] *jinanẽ yaha kīrtana kiyau hai* : *kar-* in the sense 'to make, create' has largely been replaced by *banā-* (or more specific verbs according to context) in the modern language (though MSH does retain *kavitā karnā*). Cf. 115 *sāmagrī karata hatī* 'was preparing the food'.

[7] *śrīmathurājī* : the status of sacred towns calls for honorifics on the human model.

[8] *śrīnāthajī dvāra* : *dvāra* here stands for 'the house of', i.e. the Śrīnāthjī temple at Govardhan: cf. the later designation of the Rajasthan town Nathdwara (*nāthdvārā*), which grew up around the temple of Śrīnāthjī after the image was removed from Braj in Aurangzeb's reign.

[9] *unakau* : this is genitive (cf. MSH *unkā*).

सूरदासजी तुमने विष्नुपद बहौत किये हैं सो तुम मोकों कछु सुनावो । तब सूरदास नें अकबर बादशाह आगै यह पद गायौ । सो पद —

॥ राग परज ॥

मन रे, माधव सौं कर प्रीति ।
काम क्रोध मद लोभ मोह तू छाँड़ि सबै बिपरीति ॥[10] …

यह सुनि देसाधिपति बहौत प्रसन्न भयौ । पाछै देसाधिपति के मन में यह आई जो सूरदासजी की परीच्छा करिकै देखूँ । जो भगवान के आस्रय होयगौ [11] तौ ये मेरौ जस गावेगौ नाँहीं । सो यह बिचारि कै देसाधिपति नें सूरदास सों कही जो श्री भगवान [12] नें मोकों राज्य दियौ है । सो सगरे गुनीजन मेरौ जस गावत हैं सो तिनकों मैं अनेक द्रव्यादिक [13] देत हौं । तासों तुम हू गुनी हो सो तुम हू मेरौ कछु जस गावो । सो तिहारे मन में जो इच्छा होय सो माँगि लेहु । सो यह देसाधिपति नें कह्यौ । तब सूरदासजी नें यह पद गायौ ।[14]

॥ राग केदारौ ॥

नाहिंन रह्यौ मन में ठौर ।[15]
नंदनंदन अछत कैसै आनियै उर और ॥
चलत चितवत द्यौस जागत सपन सोवत राति ।
हृदय तैं वह मदन मूरति छिन न इत उत जाति ॥
कहत कथा अनेक ऊधौ लोक लोभ दिखाय ।
कहा कहौं चित प्रेम पूरन घट न सिंधु समाय ॥
स्याम गात सरोज आनन ललित अति मृदु हास ।
सूर ऐंसे दरस कों ये मरत लोचन प्यास ॥

10 'Oh my mind, have love for Mādhav; abandon thou lust, anger, intoxication, greed and infatuation, for all are contrary.' This is the opening of a long stanza of 26 couplets on the *vinay* theme. Its list of human weaknesses is conventional: cf. MP 14.3. (A section of *Bhāv-prakāś* commentary has been excised here.)

11 *jo bhagavāna ke āsraya hoyagau*: 'if he is in the refuge of the Lord'.

12 *śrī bhagavāna*: a rather vague epithet, appropriate to Akbar's diplomatically ecumenical attitude.

13 *dravyādika*: (*dravya* + *ādika*), 'money and so forth'.

14 This allegorical narrative with the formula 'reluctant prodigy performs for celebrated patron' has parallels in e.g. the encounters between Svāmī Haridās and Akbar (P.D.Mītal 1968:445), between the Lucknow musician Haideri Khan and Ghazi-ud-din Haider (J. Kippen 1988:19), and between the nineteenth-century singer Inayat Hussein Khan and the Sufi saint Kahlil Mian of Sitapur (Peter Manuel 1989:20n).

15 'There is no room left in my heart': for translation of this stanza (with slightly variant text) see SS 38. In typical fashion, the *vārtā* has here appropriated a standard piece of devotional rhetoric to its own narrative purpose, making the stanza appear to be directed specifically at Akbar. Cf. a parallel example in the *vārtā* of Kṛṣṇadās, where a reference within a devotional poem becomes part and parcel of the *vārtā* narrative.

सो यह पद सुनिकै देसाधिपति नें अपने मन में विचारचौ जो ये मेरौ जस काहे कों गावेंगे। जो इनकों कछु लैवे कौ लालच होय तौ ये मेरौ जस गावैं। ये तौ परमेश्वर के जन हैं सो ये तौ ईश्वर कौ जस गावेंगे।

सो सूरदासजी या कीर्तन में पिछले चरन में कहे हैं [16] जो सूर ऐसे दरस कों ये मरत लोचन प्यास[17]। सो देसाधिपति नें सूरदास सों कह्यौ जो सूरदास तुम्हारे तौ नेत्र हैं नाँहीं[18] सो प्यासे कैसे मरत हैं ? सो यह तुम कहा कहे ? तब सूरदास नें कही जो या बात की तुमकों कहा खबर है। जो ये लोचन तौ सबके हैं [19] परंतु भगवान के दरसन की प्यास काहू कों है। जो श्री भगवान के दरसन के जो प्यासे नेत्र हैं सो तौ सदा भगवान के पास ही रहत हैं। सो स्वरूपानंद कौ रसपान छिन छिन में करत हैं और सदा प्यासे मरत हैं।

यह सुनि अकबर बादशाह नें कही जो इनके नेत्र तो परमेश्वर के पास हैं। सो परमेश्वर कों देखत हैं, और कों देखत नाँहीं। तब बादशाह नें सूरदास के समाधान की इच्छा कीनी। दोय चारि गाँम तथा द्रव्य बहौत दैन लाग्यौ सो सूरदास नें कछू नाँहीं लियौ। तब अकबर बादसाह सूरदासजी सों कहे जो बाबा साहिब कछू तौ मोकों आज्ञा करियै। तब सूरदासजी नें कही जो आज पाछै हमकों कबहू फेर मत बुलाइयो और मोसों कबहू मिलियो मत [20]।

> सो अकबर बादसाह विवेकी हतौ [21]। सो काहे तें। जो ये योगभ्रष्ट तें [22] म्लेच्छ भयौ है। सो पहले जनम में यह बालमुकंद [23]ब्रह्मचारी हतौ सो एक दिन यह बिना छानैं दूध पान कियौ तामैं एक गाय कौ रोम पेट में गयौ। सो ता अपराध तें यह म्लेच्छ भयौ है।

सो सूरदास कों दंडवत करिकै समाधान करिकै बिदा किये।

* * *

16 *sūradāsajī...kahe haĩ*: an example of a usage common in VV, where a transitive verb in a perfective tense shows concord with its logical subject (here honorific pl. *sūradāsajī*). See I.5.5.

17 'Sūr, these eyes thirst for such a vision': Akbar relates this line to Sūr's own blindness.

18 *tumhāre tau netra haĩ nā̃hī̃*: verb precedes negative for emphasis — 'you don't even *have* any eyes!'. An earlier part of the *vārtā* describes Sūrdās as being born 'without even the shapes of eyes'.

19 *ye locana ...kāhū kõ hai*: 'everybody has these [ordinary] eyes, but few thirst for a vision of God'.

20 *mata bulāiyo...miliyo mata*: note the increased assertiveness in the re-ordering of negative and verb in the second imperative. The forthright and rather gruff manner of Sūrdās as described here is very much of a piece with his characterization throughout the *vārtā.*

21 *so akabara bādasāha vivekī hatau*: the commentator finds it extraordinary that Akbar, a Muslim, should be sufficiently discriminating to appreciate Sūr's qualities, so he tries to explain the anomaly away.

22 *yogabhraṣṭa tẽ*: 'through a corruption of religious practice', i.e. through a ritual fault.

23 *bālamukanda* (= °*mukunda*) : a name of the child Kṛṣṇa (with a pun on *bāla* as 'hair'?).

और सूरदासजी के पास एक ब्रजवासी कौ लरिका हतौ सो सब काम काज सूरदासजी कौ करतौ । ताकौ नाम गोपाल [24] हतौ । सो एक दिन सूरदासजी महाप्रसाद [25] लैन कों बैठे तब वा गोपाल सों सूरदासजी कहे जो मोकूँ तू लोटी में जल भर दीजो । तब गोपाल ब्रजवासी नें कह्यौ जो तुम महाप्रसाद लैन कों बैठो जो मैं जल भरि देऊँगौ । सो यह कहिकै गोपाल तौ गोबर लैन कों गयौ । सो तहाँ दोय चार वैष्णव हते सो तिनसों बात करन लाग्यौ । तब सूरदास कों जल दैनौ भूल गयौ । और सूरदासजी तौ महाप्रसाद लैन बैठे सो गरे में कौर अटक्यौ । तब बाँये हाथ सों लोटा इत उत देखन लागे [26] सो पायौ नाँहीं । तब गरे में कौर अटक्यौ सो बोल्यौ न जाय । तब सूरदास व्याकुल भये । सो इतने में श्रीनाथजी [27] सूरदासजी के पास आयकै अपनी झारी [28] धरि आये । सूरदासजी नें झारी में तें जल पीयौ ।

तब गोपाल ब्रजवासी कों सुधि आई जो सूरदासजी कों मैं जल नाँहीं भरि आयौ । सो दौरचौ आयौ । इतने में सूरदास महाप्रसाद लैकै आये । तब गोपाल ब्रजवासी नें आयकै सूरदास सों कह्यौ जो सूरदासजी तुम महाप्रसाद लै उठे सो तुमने जल कहाँ तें पीयौ । जो मैं तौ गोबर लैन गयौ हतौ सो वैष्णव के संग बात करत में भूलि गयौ । तासों अब मैं दौरचौ आयौ हूँ । तब सूरदास ने ब्रजवासी सों कह्यौ जो तैंने गोपाल नाम काहे कों धरायौ । जो गोपाल तौ एक श्रीनाथजी हैं । सो तासों आज मेरी रक्षा करी । नातर [29] गरे में ऐसौ कौर अटक्यौ हतौ सो जल बिना बोल निकसै नाँहीं । तब मैं व्याकुल भयौ तब हाथ में जल की झारी आई सो मैं जल पान कियौ । तासों मैंनें जान्यौ [30] जो तैंनें धरचौ होयगौ । और अब तू कहत है जो मैं नाँहीं हतौ । सो तातें मंदिर वारौ गोपाल होयगौ[31] । जो देख तौ झारी कैसी है ।

24 *gopāla* : the fact that Sūr's servant shares a name with Kṛṣṇa is essential to the story.

25 *mahāprasāda* : food which has been consecrated by being placed before the deity. In a temple community, all food would be consecrated in this way.

26 *dekhana lāge* : Hindi shares with English the extended sense of 'to look for, search for' — ironic here, in the context of Sūr's blindness.

27 *śrīnāthajī* : the deity himself, who commonly takes a part in the action of the *vārtā* stories.

28 *jhārī* : the golden pitcher used in temple *sevā*, as opposed to Sūr's humble waterpot (*loṭā*).

29 *nātara* : 'otherwise' (cf. MSH *nahī̃ to*), rather than 'dry' (Pers. *nā-tar*).

30 *maĩnẽ jānyau* : *jān-* here has the sense of 'to assume, think (wrongly)'.

31 *maṁdira vārau gopāla hoyagau* : 'it must be the temple Gopāl' — i.e. Śrīnāthjī.

तब गोपाल ब्रजवासी जहाँ सूरदासजी महाप्रसाद लिए हते तहाँ आयकै देखै तो सौने की झारी है [32]। सो उठाय कै गोपाल सूरदासजी के पास आयकै कह्यौ जो यह झारी तौ मंदिर की है । सो तब सूरदास नें वा गोपाल ब्रजवासी सों कह्यौ जो तैंने बहौत बुरौ काम कियौ जो श्रीठाकुरजी [33] कों इतनौ स्रम करवायौ । जो मेरे लिएँ झारी लैकै श्रीठाकुरजी कों आनौ परचौ । सो या प्रकार सूरदासजी नें गोपाल सों कहचौ जो यह झारी तू जतन सों राखियो । और जब श्री गुसाईं जी [34] आपु पौढिकै उठें तब उनकों सौंप आइयो । तब गोपाल नें झारी लैकै श्रीगुसाईं जी पास आय दंडौत कर आगै राखी । तब श्रीगुसाईं जी आपु कहे यह झारी तेरे पास कैसै आई । जो यह झारी तौ श्रीगोवर्धनधर की है । तब गोपाल नें श्री गुसाईं जी सों बिनती कीनी जो महाराज यह अपराध मोसों परचौ है । पाछै सब बात कही ।

तब यह बात सुनिकै श्रीगुसाईं जी आप तत्काल स्नान करिकै [35] झारी कों मँजवाय दूसरौ वस्त्र लपेटिकै मंदिर में बेगि ही झारी लैकै पधारे । पाछै श्री गोवर्धनधर कूँ जल पान करायकै कहे[36] जो आज तौ सूरदास की बड़ी रक्षा कीनी । सो तुम बिन कौन वैष्णव की रक्षा करै । तब श्रीनाथजी नें कही जो सूरदास के गरे में कौर अटक्यौ सो व्याकुल भये तासों झारी धरि आयौ ।

> सो काहे तें । जो सूरदास व्याकुल भये सो मैं ही व्याकुल भयौ । जो भगवदीय मेरौ स्वरूप है ।

ता पाछै उत्थापन के किंवाड़ खोले ।[37] सो सूरदासजी आयकै उत्थापन के दरसन किये । सो उत्थापन समै कौ भोग श्री गुसाईं जी श्रीनाथजी कों धरि सूरदास के पास आयकै कहे जो आज गोपाल नें तिहारे ऊपर बड़ी कृपा करी है। तब सूरदासजी नें कह्यौ जो महाराज यह सब आपकी कृपा है । नाहिं तौ श्रीनाथजी मो सरीखे पतितन कों [38] कहा जानैं । जो सब श्री आचार्यजी की कानि तें अंगीकार करत हैं । तब श्री गुसाईं जी आपु कहे

32 *tahā̃ āyakai dekhai to saune kī jhārī hai* : the narrative slips into historic present tense for this sentence.

33 *śrīṭhākurajī* : *ṭhākura* is a name used for a temple deity — here, Śrīnāthjī.

34 *śrī gusāī̃ jī* : the title given in this text to Vallabha's son Viṭṭhalnāth.

35 *snāna karikai* : a ritual bath is essential before handling the sacred temple pitcher.

36 Here Viṭṭhalnāth addresses 'Govardhandhar' — an epithet of Kṛṣṇa as 'Mountain-holder'.

37 *utthāpana ke kī̃vāra khole* : '[Viṭṭhalnāth] opened the doors for the *utthāpan darśan*'. In Vallabhite temples the daily worship is divided into eight successive ritual periods (*aṣṭayām*), in each of which the doors may be opened for the devotees to take *darśan* of the deity after he has received food offerings etc. See Ambalal 1987:21-25; and for a modern account of *darśan* in the Śrīnāthjī temple see A.-M.Gaston 1991.

38 *mo sarīkhe patitana kõ* : 'sinners like me'.

जो तुम बड़े भगवदीय हौ । जो भगवदीय बिना ऐसी दैन्यता कहाँ मिले । सो सूरदास जी श्री आचार्य जी के ऐसे कृपापात्र भगवदीय हते [39]।

२. कृष्णदास (८४ वैष्णवन की वार्ता)

और एक समय श्रीगोवर्द्धननाथजी के मन्दिर में सामग्री चहियत हती, सो तब कृष्णदास गाड़ा लिवाय आपु रथ पर असवार होयके[40] श्रीगोवर्द्धन सों आगरे आये । सो जब आगरे के बजार में गये, तहां एक वेस्या अपनी छोरी कों नृत्य सिखावत हती । सो वह छोरी परम सुन्दर बरस बारह की हती, कण्ठ हू परम सुन्दर हतो । सो गान नृत्य में चतुर बहोत हती । सो वह वेस्या ख्याल टप्पा गावत हती । सो वा छोरी को गान कृष्णदास के कान में परचो हतो । सो कृष्णदास के मन में बैठि गयो, सो प्रसन्न होय गये । तब कृष्णदास ने तहां अपनो रथ ठाड़ो कियो । सो भीड़ सरकायके वे छोरी को रूप देखें, सो तहाँ गान सुनिके मोहित होय गये ।

> तहाँ यह संदेह होय, जो कृष्णदास श्रीआचार्यजी महाप्रभुन [41] के कृपापात्र सेवक वेस्या के गान पर मोहित क्यों भये । जो ये तो श्रीठाकुरजी के ऊपर मोहित हैं ।...[42] ये कृष्णदास वेस्या के ऊपर क्यों रीझे । यह सन्देह होय तहाँ कहत हैं जो यहाँ कारन और है [43] । जो यह वेस्या की छोरी लीला संबंधी दैवी जीव ललिताजी की सखी हैं[44], सो लीला में इनको नाम बहुभाषिनी है । सो एक दिन ललिताजी श्री ठाकुरजी के लिये सामग्री करत हती तब ललिताजी ने बहुभाषिनी सों कही जो तू मिश्री पीसि के ले आउ । सो बहुभाषिनी मिश्री को डबरा भरिके चली । सो दूसरी सखी सों बात करते करते छांटा उडचो, सो मिश्री में परचो । सो बहुभाषिनी कों खबरि नाहीं । पाछे मिश्री को डबरा लेके ललिताजी के पास आई, तब ललिताजी परम चतुर हती, सो जानि गई । पाछे बहुभाषिनी सों कही जो यह सामग्री छुइ गई, [45] जो तेरे मुख तें

39 *so sūradāsa jī...*: the episode closes with a formula which recurs throughout the *vārtā* texts.

40 *gāṛā livāya āpu ratha para asavāra hoyake*: 'had a waggon brought, while himself mounting a cart'.

41 *śrī ācārya mahāprabhuna*: i.e. Vallabha. Note the obl.pl. *-na* termination, honorific pl. being treated here like numerical pl.

42 A short section of the *Bhāv-prakāś* commentary, discussing a *śloka* by Vallabha, has been excised here.

43 *yahā̃ kārana aura hai*: 'here the reason is different [from that expected]'.

44 *yaha vesyā kī chorī līlā saṁbaṁdhī daivī jīva lalitājī kī sakhī hai*: 'this prostitute's lass is a divine soul, a friend of Lalitā [first amongst the eight companions of Rādhā], in the context of the divine sport'. See III.2.2 for an explanation of *līlā*; the purpose of the present section of *Bhāv-prakāś* commentary is to explain that Kṛṣṇadās's interest in the dancing girl is grounded in the fact that she belongs to the circle of 'divine souls' who, though temporarily born in mortal form, participate in the transcendental and eternal sport of Kṛṣṇa.

45 *yaha sāmagrī chui gaī*: 'this food has been touched', i.e. defiled by another person's spittle.

छांटा परचो है । सो भगवद् इच्छा होनहार [46] । तब बहुभाषिनी ने कही जो तुम झूठ कहत हों छांटा तो नाहीं परचो । और श्रीठाकुरजी सखामंडली में सबकी जूठनि हू लेत हैं । सो तब ललिताजी ने कह्यो जो प्रभुन की लीला तू कहा जाने । प्रभु प्रसन्न होय चाहे सो करें सोई छाजे [47] । जो अपने मन तें कछू हीन क्रिया करे सोई भ्रष्ट ।[48] तासों तू हीन ठिकाने जनमेगी [49] । तब बहुभाषिनी ने कही जो तुमहू शूद्र के घर जनम लेके मेरो उद्धार करो । जो तुमकों छोड़िके मैं कहाँ जाऊँ । सो या प्रकार परस्पर शाप भयो । तब कृष्णदास शूद्र के घर जन्मे और बहुभाषिनी को जनम वेस्या के घर मात्र भयो, सो लौकिक पुरुष को मुंह नाहीं देख्यो [50]। सो कृष्णदास कों श्रीगोवर्द्धनधर प्रेरिके आगरे में वा वेस्या के अंगीकार के लिये पठाये । तासों कृष्णदास के हृदय में वेस्या को गान प्रिय लग्यो ।

सो ठाड़े होयके गान नृत्य सुनिके मन में विचारे जो यह सामग्री तो अति उत्तम है [51] और दैवी जीव है सो श्रीगोवर्द्धननाथजी के लायक है । तासों श्रीगोवर्द्धननाथजी आपु वाकों अंगीकार करें तो आछो है । सो यह कृष्णदासजी अपने मन में बिचार करिके दस रुपैया वा वेस्या कों देके कहे जो हमारे डेरान पर [52] रात्रि कों आइयो । यह कहिके कृष्णदासजी जहाँ हवेली में हमेस उतरते ताही हवेली में उतरे [53] और सामग्री जो लेनी हती सो गाड़ा लदाय दिये । तो पाछें रात्रि प्रहर एक गई [54] तब वह वेस्या समाज सहित [55] आई सो तब नृत्य गान कियो । सो कृष्णदास बहोत प्रसन्न भये । तब वा वेस्या कों रुपैया १००) सौ दिये । और वा वेस्या सों कहे जो तेरो रूप गान नृत्य सब आछे हैं । तासों सवारे हम श्रीगोवर्द्धन जायंगे और हमारो सेठ तो उहाँ हैं [56] जो तेरो मन होय तो तू चलियो । तब वा वेस्या ने कही जो हमकों तो यही चहिये । पाछें वह वेस्या अपने मन में बहोत प्रसन्न

[46] *bhagavad icchā honahāra*: 'God's will will be done'.

[47] *cāhe so karẽ soī chāje*: 'whatever one may do is acceptable [to him]'.

[48] 'He alone is depraved [corrupt], who does some low deed wilfully'.

[49] *tū hīna ṭhikāne janamegī*: 'you will be born in a low place' — i.e. with low social (caste) status.

[50] *so laukika puruṣa ko mũha nāhī̃ dekhyo*: 'she did not see [even] the face of a wordly man' — i.e. the *daivī jīva* was not corrupted by her temporary earthly status.

[51] *yaha sāmagrī ati uttama hai*: 'this product is most excellent' — i.e. 'here's a nice piece of stuff!'.

[52] *hamāre ḍerāna para*: pl. number of *ḍerāna* is unexplained.

[53] *kṛṣṇadāsajī jahā̃ havelī mẽ hamesa utarate tāhī havelī mẽ utare*: 'Kṛṣṇadās stayed [lit. 'alighted'] at the *havelī* where he always stayed. A *havelī* is a large mansion; in the Vallabha sect, the term is used as 'temple'.

[54] *rātri prahara eka gaī*: 'when night had passed the first watch'. The first watch of night begins at about 6 p.m. and lasts three hours.

[55] *samāja sahita*: 'with her retinue [of accompanists etc.]'.

[56] *hamāro seṭha to uhā̃ haĩ*: Kṛṣṇadās lures the prostitute to Govardhan by implying that his patron (a member of the merchant classes who form the bulk of the Vallabhite following) will reward her further.

भई जो ये इतने रुपया दिये तो सेठ न जाने कहा देयगो [57] । सो तब वेस्या ने घर आयके अपनी गाड़ी सिद्ध कराई सो गायबे को साज सब आछे बनाय गाड़ी ऊपर धरि राख्यो । तब सवारे भये [58] कृष्णदास के पास आई । पाछें कृष्णदास वा वेस्या कों लिवाय के ले चले सो मथुरा आय रहे । तब दूसरे दिन मथुरा तें चले सो मध्यान्ह समय गोपालपुर में आये । पाछें वा वेस्या कों न्हवाय के नवीन वस्त्र पहेरवे को दियो सो वाने पहरचो । तब कृष्णदास अपने मन में विचारे जो यह ख्याल टप्पा गायगी [59] सो श्रीगोवर्द्धनधर सुनेंगे । तासों मैं याकों एक पद सिखाऊं । तब कृष्णदास ने वा वेस्या कों एक पद सिखायौ । और कह्यो जो ये पद तू पूरबी राग में गाइयो । सो पद —

॥ राग पूर्वी [60] ॥

मेरो मन गिरिधर छबि पर अटक्यो ।
ललित त्रिभंगी अंगन ऊपर चलि गयो तहाँ ही ठठक्यो ॥ १ ॥
सजल स्यामघन नील बरन है फिरि चित्त अनत न भटक्यो ।
कृष्णदास कियो प्रान न्योछावरि यह तन जग सिर पटक्यो ॥ २ ॥

यह पद कृष्णदास ने वा वेस्या कों सिखायो । ता पाछें उत्थापन के दरसन होय चुके तब भोग के दरसन के समय वा वेस्या कों समाज सहित कृष्णदास परवत के ऊपर [61] ले गये ।...[62] पाछें भोग के किवाड़ खुले । तब वा वेस्या ने पहले नृत्य कियो ता पाछें गान करन लागी । सो कृष्णदास ने पद करिके सिखायो सो हतो गायो । सो गावत २ [63] जब छेली तुक आई जो 'कृष्णदास कियो प्रान न्योछावरि यह तन जग सिर पटक्यो' या पद

57 *ye itane rupayā diye to seṭha na jāne kahā deyago*: 'he [Kṛṣṇadās] gave me so much money, the Seṭh will give goodness knows what!'.

58 *savāre bhaye*: 'when morning came'.

59 *ye khyāla ṭappā gāyagī... eka pada sikhāū̃*: 'she will sing *khyāl* and *ṭappā*... I should teach her a *pada*'. The singing styles *khyāl* and *ṭappā* are basically secular, and therefore less appropriate for singing in the temple than the devotional *pada*.

60 *rāga pūrvī*: the *rāga* name, which appears in its semi-tatsama spelling in the previous line, has been Sanskritized in this more formal context of a verse heading. (Note too that numerals designate the couplet, and not the individual line, as the basic unit of the stanza.) The stanza itself can be translated:

> My mind is ensnared in the beauty of the Mountain-holder;
> it has gone over to his lovely limbs of thrice-bent pose, and remains caught up there.
> The dark rain-cloud [Kṛṣṇa] is of blue colour: my mind will turn and stray nowhere else;
> Kṛṣṇadās has offered up his life, dashing down this body, this world, this head!

61 *paravata ke ūpara*: i.e. to the top of Govardhan hill, where the Śrīnāth temple was situated. Cf. 161 *nīce le jāyake* 'taking them down again'.

62 A brief paragraph of *Bhāv-prakāś* commentary, explaining that many devotees were regularly 'accepted' by Śrīnāthjī at this particular time, has been excised here.

63 *gāvata 2*: the numeral indicates a repeat of the preceding word, thus *gāvata gāvata*.

को गान करत ही[64] वा वेस्या की देह छूटि गई सो दिव्य देह होय लीला में प्राप्त भई [65] सो तब सगरे समाजी तथा वा वेस्या की माता रोवन लागी । जो हम यासों कमाय खाते [66], अब हम कहा करेंगे । तब कृष्णदास ने उनकों नीचे ले जायके कह्यो जो अब तो भई सो भई, जो याकी इतनी आरबल हती ।[67] सो या बात को कोऊ कहा करे । अब तुम कहो सो तुमकों देऊँ । तब उन कही जो हजार रुपैया देऊ जो कछुक दिन खायं । पाछें जो होनहार होयगी सो सही । तब कृष्णदास ने हजार रुपैया देके उन सबन कों बिदा किये । सो या प्रकार वा वेस्या की छोरी कों श्रीगोवर्द्धननाथजी कृष्णदास की कानि तें आपु अङ्गीकार किये ।...[68] सो वे कृष्णदास ऐसे भगवदीय हते । जो वेस्या कों अङ्गीकार करायो ।

३. **रसखान** (२५२ वैष्णवन की वार्ता)

सो वह रसखान दिल्ली में रहत हतो । सो वह एक साहुकार के बेटा के ऊपर बोहोत आसक्त भयो । सो वाकों अहर्निस देखे । और वह छोरा कछू खातो तो वाकी जूंठनि लेई । और पानी पीवतो तो हू वाकौ झूठो पीवे । सो ऐसो आसक्त भयो । सो रसखान की जाति के जो हते [69] सो रसखान के ऊपर बोहोत ईर्षा करते और कहते जो तू हिन्दु कौ जूठौ क्यों खात है । अब तू काफर भयो है । तब रसखान ने कही जो हों जैसो हूं ऐसो हौं [70] परि अब तुम मोसों कछु बोलोगे तो मैं ठौर मारूंगो । तब इनसों सब डरपत रहते । सो ऐसो आसक्त हतो । तब ऐसें करत बहोत दिन बीते ।

तब बहोरि एक दिन दो वैष्णव आपस में बतरात हुते । सो कहत हुते जो भाई देखो आसक्ति होंई तो ऐसी होंई [71] जैसी या रसखान की वा बनिया के छोरा पर है । सो वाके पाछें डोलत है । लोक लाज, जाति डर सब कछू छूट्यो । ऐसी प्रभुन में होंई तो कहा

[64] *yā pada ko gāna karata hī* : *pada* is here 'line, *tuk*' rather than 'stanza, poem'.

[65] *so divya deha hoya līlā mẽ prāpta bhaī* : 'became a divine body and was admitted to the eternal sport', i.e. returned to the transcendental state it had held before its present incarnation.

[66] *hama yāsõ kamāya khāte* : 'we earn our daily bread through her'.

[67] *bhaī so bhaī, jo yākī itanī ārabala hatī* : 'what's happened has happened, this much was her allotted lifespan'. (The f. subject of *bhaī* is the implicit *bāta*.)

[68] A lengthy paragraph of *Bhāv-prakāś* commentary, discussing sectarian initiation, has been excised here.

[69] *rasakhāna kī jāti ke jo hate* : 'those who were of Raskhān's community', i.e. the Muslims.

[70] *hõ jaiso hū̃ aiso haũ* : 'I am as I am'.

[71] *āsakti hōī to aisī hōī* : 'if one is to have attachment, then it should be of this kind'.

चहिए [72]। ता समै रसखान नेक दूरि उन्मत्त सो [73] ठाढ़ो हुतो । सो इन की ऐसी अवस्था देखि कै दूसरे वैष्णव ने दूरि तें इन कों देखि कै माथौ धुनायो । और नाक चढ़ाई । तब रसखान ने जान्यो जो याने मेरे ऊपर माथो धुनायो है । तब रसखान ने वासों पूछ्यो जो तेंने मेरे पर माथो क्यों धुनायो है । तब वा वैष्णव ने डरपि कै कही जो मैंनें तोकों देखि माथो नहीं धुनायो है । हम तो आपुस में बतरात हुते । तब रसखान ने कही जो तू साँच कहि मैं तोकों छोरि देउंगो । नहीं तो ठौर मारूंगो । तब ऐसे कहि कै खडग उठाय लियो । तब वह वैष्णव डरप्यो । और वासों कह्यो जो तेरो मन वा छोरा में आसक्त है तैसो मन प्रभुन में लगावे तो तेरो काम होंइ जाय [74]। तब रसखान ने कही जो प्रभु तू कौन सों कहत है । मैं तो कछू जानत नाहीं । [75] तब वा वैष्णव ने कही जो प्रभु वासों कहियत है जिन कौ यह सारो जगत विभूति है । तब रसखान ने कही जो यह सगरौ उन की विभूति है तो मैं उनकों कैसे जानों [76]। तब वा वैष्णव की पाग में श्रीनाथजी कौ चित्र हतो । तामें मुकुट काछनी कौ सिंगार हतो [77]। सो काढ़ि कै रसखान कों दिखायो । तब चित्र देखत ही रसखान कौ मन फिरि गयो । और आंखिनि में जल कौ प्रवाह चल्यो । सो वा छोरा में स्नेह हतो सो तो मिटि गयो ।

> यह कहि यह जनाए जो आसक्ति भगवद्धर्म है तातें लौकिक में होंई तोऊ अंत में जीव कों प्रभुन की ओर ले जात है [78] तातें आसक्ति साँची चाहिए । सो या रसखान की आसक्ति वा छोरा में सांची हती तो वाकौ मन प्रभु ने फेर्‍यो । सो वा छोरा में तें स्नेह मिटि कै प्रभुन में भयो ।

तब वा वैष्णव सों कही जो यह महबूब [79] कहां रहत है । तब वा वैष्णव ने कही यह महबूब तो ब्रज में रहत है । तब रसखान ने कही जो यह मूरति हम कों देउ । मति कहुं भूलि

[72] *kahā cahie*: 'what [more] could be desired?'.

[73] *unmatta so*: 'as if intoxicated', i.e. in a swoon-like state.

[74] *tero kāma hõi jāya*: 'your purpose would be achieved, you would win through'.

[75] *maĩ to kachū jānata nāhī̃*: the *vārtā* consistently emphasizes and lampoons Raskhān's ignorance and boorishness, even when relating his conversion.

[76] *yaha sagarau...kaise jānõ*: a clear example of the way in which a protagonist in the *vārtā* is typically given the rôle of 'straight man' to the didactic purpose of the text. Thus the theological question 'If God is omnipresent, how is he to be recognized?' is set up in order to be answered 'In the form of Śrīnāthjī'.

[77] *tāmẽ mukuṭa kāchanī kau siṁgāra hato*: 'He [Kṛṣṇa in the portrait] was adorned in crown and loin-cloth' (i.e. he was substantially unclothed, as would be usual in the summer *śṛṅgār*).

[78] *āsakti...le jāta hai*: 'attachment is of divine nature, and so though it be for worldly things, even so in the end it leads the soul towards the Lord'.

[79] *mahabūba*: Raskhān's Islamic background determines his choice of such nomenclature, incongruous in this Hindu setting. The 'Vaiṣṇava' takes it up sarcastically in the following sentence.

जाउं ।[80] तब वैष्णव ने बिचार्‍यो जो यह जीव तो दैवी दीसत है[81]। जो यह दैवी जीव न होतो तो याकौ मन ऐसो फिरतो नाहीं । सो यह बिचारि कै वह चित्र रसखान कों दियो । तब रसखानि चित्र लेत ही ब्रज कों उठि चल्यो । सो मार्ग में जहां देवालय आवे तहां दरसन करतो फिरे। सो दरसन करि कै वा चित्र के दर्सन करे । परि वा चित्र समान स्वरूप कहूं दीसे नाहीं [82]। तब ऐसे करत ब्रज में आयो । सो श्रीवृंदावन तथा मथुराजी तथा और हू सब ठिकाने दरसन किये । परि ऐसो स्वरूप कहूं दीसे नाहीं । तब फिरत फिरत एक दिन गोवर्द्धन पर्वत पैं यह चढ्यो । सो ता समै श्रीनाथजी की माला बोली हती । तब सब वैष्णव पर्वत ऊपर चढन लागे । तब यह रसखान हू दौरि कै मंदिर में जान लाग्यो । तब सिंघपोरि पैं पोरिया ब्रजबासी हतो । सो वाने रसखानि कों धक्का मारि कै बाहिर काढि दीनो ।[83] तब रसखान गोविंदकुंड पें जाय बैठ्यो । और मन में बिचारी जो जितने हिंदु के देवालय में गयो हतो सो कहूँ मोकों काहूने धक्का मार्‍यो नाहीं । और यहां मोकों धक्का दिए । सो ऐसे जानिये जो जहां ऐसे महबूब रहत हैं तहां ऐसी करड़ी चौकी रहत होगी । सो ऐसें बिचारि कै रसखान गोविंदकुंड ऊपर जाय बैठ्यो । और श्रीनाथजी के मंदिर सों टकटकी लगाइ दीनी। और मुख सों ऐसें कह्यो करे[84] जो या घर में महबूब रहत हैं । तिनके दरसन किए बिना कहुँ न जाउंगो । सो ऐसें निश्चय करि कै बैठ्यो रह्यो । भूख प्यास की कछू सूधि नाहीं रही ।

सो ऐसें बैठे बैठे दिन दोइ होइ गए । फेरि तीसरे दिन राजभोग आर्ति होय चुकी । अनोसर होय चुके । तब श्रीनाथजी मन में बिचारे जो रसखान कों तो कछु देहानुसंधान[85] है नाहीं । तीनि दिन याकों भूखे होइ गए है । सो याके भूखे प्रान निकसि जाइंगे । सो यह दसा देखि कै श्रीनाथजी कों मन में दया आई । तब वाही समै श्रीगोवर्द्धननाथजी ने अपनो

80 *mati kahū̃ bhūla jāū̃*: 'lest I should happen to forget it'.

81 *yaha jīva to daivī dīsata hai*: 'this soul appears to be divine', i.e. Raskhan appears to be the incarnation of one of Kṛṣṇa's *sakhās,* his companions who participate with him in the eternal *līlā.*

82 *pari vā citra samāna svarūpa kahū̃ dīse nāhī̃*: 'But nowhere was an image similar to that picture to be seen'. The iconography of Śrīnāthjī is very distinctive, having a stylized *govardhana-dhāraṇ* pose, and is quite unlike the conventional images of Kṛṣṇa found in the majority of Vaiṣṇava temples.

83 The temple of Śrīnāthjī is to this day very strict about access, and its doors are policed by armed guards. See A.-M.Gaston 1991 for a vivid description from the present day.

84 *kahyo kare*: as in MSH (*kahā kar-*), the construction of perf.ptc. plus *kar-* emphasizes the repetitiveness (or habitualness) of an action.

85 *dehānusaṁdhāna*: (*deha* + *anu*°) 'awareness of body'.

सिंगार हतो सो बडो करके [86] जैसो सिंगार वा चित्र में हतो तैसेई वस्त्र आभूषन अपने श्रीहस्त सों [87] धारन किये । गाय ग्वाल सखा सब साथ ले कै आप पधारे । सो श्रीगिरिराज की सिखिर पर चढि कै वेणुनाद किये । तब यह वेणुनाद सुनत ही रसखान कों यह निश्चै भयो [88] जो मूरति में महबूब देखे हैं सोइ महबूब ये हैं । सो ऐसो निरधार करिकै श्रीनाथजी कों पकरन कों दोरयो [89]। तब श्रीनाथजी तो ताही समय अंतर्धान होइ गए । सो श्रीगोकुल पधारे । सो ता समै श्रीगुसांईजी आप भोजन करिकै पोढे हते । सो श्रीनाथजी ने श्रीगसांईजी के केस पर श्रीहस्त फेरिकै जगाए । तब श्रीगुसांईजी जागिकै श्रीनाथजी के दरसन किये । सो श्रीमुख पर हाथ फेरिकै कह्यो जो भक्तताप-निवारकायनमः [90]। तब श्रीगुसांईजी सों श्रीनाथजी ने कही जो एक दैवी जीव है परि वाकौ जन्म बड़ी जाति [91] में है । और या प्रकार सों वह आयो है । सो प्रकार सब कहे [92] और तीन दिन कौ भूखो बैठो है । सो आज मैंने उनकों दरसन दीनो है । परि वह मोकों पकरन कों आयो । तब मैं उहां सों आयो हूं । सो अब तुम श्रीगोवर्द्धन पर्वत के ऊपर पधारो और वाकों नाम देउ [93] । तब मैं वाकों अंगीकार करूंगो । तब श्रीगुसांईजी ने श्रीनाथजी सों कही जो तुम उहां सों भाजि काहेकों आए हो । तब श्रीनाथजी ने कही जो मोकों स्पर्स करिवे कों दोरयो । तब मैं उहां सों भाजि आयो हूं । सो मेरे तो यह प्रतिज्ञा है जो जा जीव कों तुम ब्रह्मसंबंध [94] करावोगे तिनसों हों बोलूंगो (१) [95]। तथा तिनही के अंग सों अपनो अंग स्पर्स करूंगो (२) । और तिनही के हाथ कौ आरोगुंगो (३) । सो ये तीन बस्तु तिहारे संबंध बिना काहूकों सिद्ध न होइगी ।

86 *apano siṁgāra hato so baḍo karake* : 'augmenting the livery that he had on'. Kṛṣṇa makes his appearance tally with that in Raskhān's portrait of him — a concession with implications for the theology of divine grace, which directs that the deity's appearance should accommodate the expectations of the devotee.

87 *apane śrīhasta sõ* : 'with his holy hand' — cf. 224 *śrīmukha.*

88 *rasakhāna kõ yaha niścai bhayo* : 'Raskhān became convinced, certain'.

89 *śrīnāthajī kõ pakarana kõ doryo* : 'ran to grab Śrīnāthjī' — an example of the impetuousness which characterizes Raskhān's devotion in this story.

90 *bhakta-tāpa-nivārakāya-namaḥ* : 'salutation to the remover [*nivāraka*] of the suffering of devotees'.

91 *baṛī jāti* : an unconventional allusion to the Muslim community; Mr Simon Digby notes, in a private communication, that the expression was current (in a Vaiṣṇava family of Benares) in the early 1900s.

92 *so prakāra saba kahe* : 'he told him all about how it happened' — a narrative parenthesis interposed into Kṛṣṇa's speech, which continues with the following phrase.

93 *vākõ nāma deu* : 'give him the name', i.e. 'initiate him' (see following note).

94 *brahmasaṁbaṁdha* : 'connexion with God' — initiation into the Vallabha *sampradāya* through the imparting of a sacred formula revealed to Vallabha by Kṛṣṇa.

95 Following the conventional system of numbering used in text verses etc., the three elements of Kṛṣṇa's pledge are followed (rather than preceded) by their respective numerals. Note how the pledge further buttresses the importance of the guru's role as intermediary between devotee and deity.

तब यह बचन सुनि कै श्रीगुसांईजी बोहोत हरखे । और तहां तें बेगि उठि कै श्रीयमुनाजी के तट आये । सो आप नाव में बैठि कै श्रीयमुनाजी के पार उतरि कै घोड़ा ऊपर असवार होंई कै तहां तें बेगि ही श्रीनाथजीद्वार पधारे । सो सूधे गोविंदकुंड जाइ उतरे । तब रसखान ने श्रीगुसांईजी के दरसन किये ।और मन में बिचारी जो ये घोड़ा पे तें उतरे हैं सो तो महबूब के मित्र दीसत हैं । तब श्रीगुसांईजी के पास आय बिनती करी जो साहिब या घर में महबूब रहत हैं । तासों मेरो मन बोहोत आसक्त भयो है । सो मैं जानत हूं जो यह तुम्हारो मित्र है । सो अब तुम मोकों मिलाय देऊ तो बोहोत आछौ है । तब श्रीगुसांईजी वासों बोहोत प्रसन्न होंय कै पूछे जो तेंने हमारी मित्रता कैसें जानी । तब रसखान ने कही जो तुम आए हो ताही समय तें तुम्हारी आंखि याही घर की ओर लागी है । तब श्रीगुसांईजी बोहोत प्रसन्न होंइ कै रसखान सों कहे जो तू न्हाइ आउ [96]। तब वह रसखान न्हाय कै श्रीगुसांईजी के आगें आय कै ठाढ़ो भयो । तब श्रीगुसांईजी ने कृपा करिकै वाकों नाम सुनायो । पाछें खवास सों कही जो इनकों मंदिर में ले आइयो । तब श्रीगुसांईजी ने मंदिर में जाय कै संखनाद करवाय कै श्रीनाथजी कों उत्थापन भोग धरचो । तब समय भए [97] भोग सरायो । सो ता समय खवास याकों मंदिर में ले आयो । तब रसखान ने श्रीनाथजी के दरसन किये सो बहोत प्रसन्न भयो । पाछें वह रसखान बाहिर जाइबे लाग्यो [98]। तब श्रीजी [99] ने वाकी बाँह पकरि कै कह्यो जो अरे सारे [100] अब कहां जात है । सो ता दिन तें श्रीजी गोचारन कों पधारते तब रसखान कों संग ले पधारते । सो जहां जा लीला के दरसन करते तहां ता लीला के कवित्त दोहा चोपाई सवैया करते । सो इन कों गोपीभाव सिद्ध भयो [101]।

सो वे रसखान श्रीगुसांईजी के ऐसे परम कृपापात्र भगवदीय हते इन की वार्ता कहां तांई कहिए ।

96 *tū nhāi āu* : as in MSH, the sequence 'bathe and come [back]' corresponds to English 'go and bathe'. Cf. RN 3 *choṛi āyau*, and note.

97 *samaya bhae* : 'when the time came'.

98 *jāibe lāgyo* : an unusual use of the *-ibo* inf. in composition with *lāg-* (see I.5.11).

99 *śrījī* : an honorific applied to the deity (as here, to Śrīnāthjī) or to revered holy personages.

100 *are sāre* : 'hey you old sod!'. *sāre*, from *sālā* 'brother-in-law' is a very common term of abuse, its derogatory implication being 'you are my "brother-in-law" because I have slept with your sister'. An extreme illustration of the familiarity of discourse existing between deity and devotee!

101 *ina kō gopībhāva siddha bhayo* : 'he attained the sentimental attitude of a gopi', i.e. based his devotional stance on a gopi's attitude towards Kṛṣṇa.

सूरसागर

सूरदास

चरन कमल बंदौं हरि राइ ।
जाकी कृपा पंगु गिरि लंघै, अंधे कौं सब कछु दरसाइ ॥
बहिरौ सुनै गूँग पुनि बोलै, रंक चलै सिर छत्र धराइ ।
सूरदास स्वामी करुनामय, बार बार बंदौं तिहिं पाइ ॥ १ ॥

सब तजि भजिऐ नंदकुमार ।
और भजे तैं काम सरै नहिं, मिटै न भव जंजार ॥
जिहिं जिहिं जोनि जन्म धारयौ बहु जोरयौ अघ कौ भार ।
तिहिं काटन कौं समरथ हरि कौ तीछन नाम कुठार ॥
बेद पुरान भागवत गीता, सब कौ यह मत सार ।
भव समुद्र हरि पद नौका बिनु, कोउ न उतारै पार ॥
यह जिय जानि इहीं छिन भजि दिन बीते जात असार ।
सूर पाइ यह समौ लाहु लहि, दुर्लभ फिरि संसार ॥ २ ॥

अब तौ यहै बात मन मानी ।
छाड़ौ नाहिं स्याम स्यामा की बृंदाबन रजधानी ॥
भ्रम्यौ बहुत लघु धाम बिलोकत छनभंगुर दुख-दानी ।
सर्वोपरि आनंद अखंडित सूर मरम लपिटानी ॥ ३ ॥

अब कैं नाथ मोहिं उधारि ।
मगन हौं भव अंबुनिधि मैं, कृपासिंधु मुरारि ॥
नीर अति गंभीर माया, लोभ लहरि तरंग ।
लिए जात अगाध जल कौं गहे ग्राह अनंग ॥
मीन इंद्री तनहिं काटत, मोट अघ सिर भार ।
पग न इत उत धरन पावत, उरझि मोह सिवार ॥
क्रोध दंभ गुमान तृष्ना पवन अति झकझोर ।
नाहिं चितवन देत सुत तिय, नाम नौका ओर ॥
थक्यौ बीच बिहाल बिहवल, सुनौ करुना मूल ।
स्याम भुज गहि काढ़ि लीजै, सूर ब्रज कैं कूल ॥ ४॥

Sūr-sāgar

Sūrdās

1 I salute the lotus feet of Hari, the king,
through whose mercy the lame may cross a mountain, the blind may all things see;
the deaf hear, the dumb speak again, the pauper go with a canopy held above his head;
Sūrdās' lord is composed of compassion, again and again I salute his feet.

2 Give up everything, and worship Nandkumār;
through other worship you achieve nothing, nor are the cares of the world removed.
In all the lives in which you have taken birth, you amassed a great burden of sin;
the sharp axe of Hari's name is capable of cutting that away.
Veda, Purāṇa, Bhāgavata, Gītā — this doctrine is the essence of all of them:
nothing but the ferry of Hari's feet will get you across the ocean of worldliness.
Knowing this in your heart, worship him this very moment, the days slip by in vain;
having found this chance, Sūr, profit from it — it is rare when wandering the world.

3 Now this alone is my heart's pleasure:
I shall not leave Vṛndāvan, Śyām and Śyāmā's royal domain.
I have wandered much, seeing lesser abodes — transient and grievous;
[but now] Sūr has embraced the inner truth of undivided and supreme bliss.

4 Lord, save me at this time;
I am sunk in a sea of worldliness, O Murāri, ocean of pity!
The waters of illusion are very deep, and ripple with waves of greed;
Anaṅga the crocodile seizes me and takes me down into the fathomless water.
The fish of the senses nibble at my body, a bundle of sin is a weight on my head;
nowhere can I set my feet, entangled in the waterweeds of infatuation.
Most turbulent are the winds of anger, vanity, pride and longing;
wife and son do not let me look toward the boat of the Name.
I am worn out, half-way across, distressed and afflicted: hear me, root of mercy:
Śyām, seize this arm, and pull Sūr out onto the bank of Braj!

2.2 *bhaje* : the perf.part. of *bhaj-*, used nominally.

2.4 *kāṭana* : an inf. used as a verbal noun, 'for the cutting of'.

2.5 *purāna bhāgavata* : The *Bhāgavata* is separated out from the other *Purāṇas* because of its elevated status in Vaiṣṇavism.

2.8 *phiri saṁsāra* : i.e. wandering through a succession of rebirths in the world.

4.4 *grāha* : a crocodile or sea-monster (also called *makara, magara*), a symbol of Kāmdev (called *Anaṅga* , 'incorporeal', because Śiva destroyed his body in anger at being aroused with desire for Pārvatī).

4.8 *suta tiya* : i.e. worldly domestic ties.

मेरौ मन मतिहीन गुसाईं ।
सब सुख निधि पद कमल छाँड़ि, स्रम करत स्वान की नाईं ॥
फिरत बृथा भाजन अवलोकत, सूनैं सदन अजान ।
तिहिं लालच कबहूँ कैसैं हूँ, तृप्ति न पावत प्रान ॥
कौर कौर कारन कुबुद्धि जड़, किते सहत अपमान ।
जहँ जहँ जात तहीं तहिं त्रासत अस्म लकुट पद-त्रान ॥
तुम सर्वज्ञ सबै बिधि पूरन, अखिल भुवन निज नाथ ।
तिन्हैं छाँड़ि यह सूर महा सठ, भ्रमत भ्रमनि कैं साथ ॥ ५ ॥

हरि हौं सब पतितनि पतितेस ।
और न सरि करिबे कौं दूजौ, महामोह मम देस ॥
आसा कैं सिंहासन बैठ्यौ, दंभ छत्र सिर तान्यौ ।
अपजस अति नकीब कहि टेर्‌यौ, सब सिर आयसु मान्यौ ॥
मंत्री काम क्रोध निज दोऊ अपनी अपनी रीति ।
दुबिधा दुंद रहै निसि बासर, उपजावत बिपरीति ॥
मोदी लोभ खवास मोह के, द्वारपाल अहँकार ।
पाट बिरध ममता है मेरैं, माया कौ अधिकार ॥
दासी तृष्ना भ्रमत टहल हित, लहत न छिन बिश्राम ।
अनाचार सेवक सौं मिलिकै, करत चबाइनि काम ॥
बाजि मनोरथ गर्व मत्त गज, असत कुमत रथ सूत ।
पायक मन बानैत अधीरज, सदा दुष्ट मति दूत ॥
गढ़वै भयौ नरकपति मोसौं, दीन्हे रहत किवार ।
सेना साथ बहुत भाँतिन की, कीन्हे पाप अपार ॥
निंदा जग उपहास करत मग बंदीजन जस गावत ।
हठ अन्याय अधर्म सूर नित नौबत द्वार बजावत ॥ ६ ॥

हरि हौं सब पतितनि कौ राजा ।
निंदा पर मुख पूरि रह्यौ जग निसान नित बाजा ॥
तृष्ना देसऽरु सुभट मनोरथ, इंद्री खड्ग हमारी ।
मंत्री काम कुमति दीबे कौं, क्रोध रहत प्रतिपारी ॥
गज अहँकार चढ्यौ दिग-बिजयी, लोभ छत्र करि सीस ।
फौज असत संगति की मेरैं, ऐसौ हौं मैं ईस ॥
मोह मया बंदी गुन गावत, मागध दोष अपार ।
सूर पाप कौ गढ़ दृढ़ कीन्हौ, महुकम लाइ किवार ॥ ७ ॥

5 My mind is devoid of understanding, O lord;
forsaking your lotus feet, treasury of all joys, it toils like a dog.
It wanders uselessly looking for pots [to lick] in an empty house, unknowing;
for that greed the soul could never, in any way, find satisfaction.
For the sake of each and every morsel the stupid dolt endures so many insults;
wherever it goes, stones, sticks and shoes terrorize it.
You are omniscient, complete in every way, eternal lord of all the world,
forsaking whom this Sūr is a great fool, wandering in the company of his delusions.

6 Hari, I am the king-sinner of all sinners;
there is no other to equal me: great infatuation is my homeland.
Seated on the throne of aspiration I have erected a canopy of pride above my head;
the herald of my great infamy has called out and all have heeded my command.
My two ministers are lust and anger, each has his own way;
dubiety and discord subsist night and day, creating discord.
Greed is my steward, my attendants are of infatuation, my doorkeepers vanity;
my seat is aged egoism, illusion holds sway.
The handmaidens of my desires dance service upon me, taking not a moment's rest;
joining the servants of indecorum they inform against me.
Fancies are my horses, pride my rutting elephant, untruth and folly my chariot and charioteer;
My mind is my courier, restlessness my archer, an evil mind is ever my messenger.
The lord of hell has become a fortress-holder, he keeps the door closed against me;
with me is an army of varied sort — the limitless sins that I have committed.
The world censures and mocks me, heralds on the road sing my praises;
obstinacy, tyranny, and iniquity, Sūr, constantly play a fanfare at my gate.

7 Hari, I am the prince of all the wicked;
I am full of calumny and censure and have ever trumpeted this in the world.
Craving is my country and desires are my noble warriors, my senses are my sword;
Lust is my minister for giving perverse counsel, anger is ever my gatekeeper.
I have mounted the elephant of vanity, all-conquering, greed's canopy above my head;
my army is the company of the false — such an overlord am I.
The heralds, infatuation and illusion, sing my praises, bards my limitless faults;
Sūr has made firm the fort of sin, shutting tight the door.

6.10 *karata cabāina kāma*: 'do the work of backbiters'.

6.13 *narakapati* : an epithet usually taken to refer to Yama (Yamrāj).

6.13 *dīnhe rahata kivāra*: 'remains with door closed'.

6.15 *bandījana*: *-jana* is a pluralizing suffix (cf. MSH *log*); the *bandī* are a caste of bards who extol the king and his army in battle — cf. 7.7 *māgadha*, another caste of bards.

7.2 *bājā*: a rhyme-form for *bājai*.

7.3 *desa 'ru*: *avagraha* (ऽ) indicates elision of initial *a-* after final *-a* of *desa*. Cf. 30.2 *dharama 'ru dhīra*.

7.4 *kumati dībe kaū* : 'for the giving of perversity'

7.5 *diga bijayī*: 'conquering [countries in all] directions'.

अब मैं नाच्यौ बहुत गुपाल ।
काम क्रोध कौ पहिरि चोलना, कंठ विषय की माल ॥
महामोह के नूपुर बाजत, निंदा सब्द रसाल ।
भ्रम भोयौ मन भयौ पखावज, चलत असंगत चाल ॥
तृष्ना नाद करति घट भीतर, नाना बिधि दै ताल ।
माया को कटि फेंटा बाँध्यौ, लोभ तिलक दियौ भाल ॥
कोटिक कला काछि दिखराई, जल थल सुध नहिं काल ।
सूरदास की सबै अबिद्या दूरि करौ नँदलाल ॥ ८ ॥

जैसें राखहु तैसें रहौं ।
जानत हौ दुख सुख सब जन के, मुख करि कहा कहौं ॥
कबहुँक भोजन लहौं कृपानिधि, कबहुँक भूख सहौं ।
कबहुँक चढ़ौं तुरंग महा गज, कबहुक भार बहौं ॥
कमल नयन घनस्याम मनोहर, अनुचर भयौ रहौं ।
सूरदास प्रभु भक्त कृपानिधि, तुम्हरे चरन गहौं ॥ ९ ॥

भक्त जमुने सुगम अगम औरैं ।
प्रात जो न्हात अघ जात ताके सकल, ताहि जमहू रहत हाथ जोरैं ॥
अनुभवी जानही बिना अनुभव कहा, प्रिया जाकौ नहीं चित्त चोरै ।
प्रेम के सिंधु कौ मर्म जान्यौ नहीं, सूर कहि कहा भयौ देह बोरैं ॥ १० ॥

भीतर तै बाहर लौं आवत ।
घर आँगन अति चलत सुगम भए देहरि अँटकावत ॥
गिरि गिरि परत जात नहिं उलँघी, अति स्रम होत न धावत ।
अहुँठ पैग बसुधा सब कीनौ, धाम अवधि बिरमावत ॥
मनहीं मन बलबीर कहत हैं, ऐसे रंग बनावत ।
सूरदास प्रभु अगनित महिमा भगतनि कैं मन भावत ॥ ११ ॥

जसुमति लै पलिका पौढ़ावति ।
मेरौ आजु अतिहिं बिरुझानौ, यह कहि कहि मधुरैं सुर गावति ॥
पौढ़ि गई हरुऐं करि आपुन, अंग मोरि तब हरि जँभुआने ।
कर सौं ठोंकि सुतहिं दुलरावति, चटपटाइ बैठे अतुराने ॥
पौढ़ौ लाल कथा इक कहिहौं, अति मीठी स्रवननि कौं प्यारी ।
यह सुनि सूर स्याम मन हरषे, पौढ़ि गए हँसि देत हुँकारी ॥ १२ ॥

8 Now I have danced enough, Gopāl,
wearing a tunic of lust and anger, a necklace of sensuality at my throat.
The anklets of grand delusion jingle with the sweet sound of rebuke;
my mind, engrossed in error, has become a drum and goes with incoherent beat.
Desire resounds within my body, giving rhythms of various kinds;
I have tied on the waist-band of illusion and put a *tilak* of greed on my brow.
I have acquired millions of skills and shown them off, heedless of place or time:
remove all Sūrdās' ignorance, O Nandlāl.

9 As you maintain me, so shall I remain;
you know the sorrows and joys of all people, what can *I* say?
Sometimes I shall take food, ocean of mercy, sometimes I shall suffer hunger;
sometimes I shall ride a horse or a great elephant, sometimes I shall bear burdens.
I have become, and remain, a follower of the lotus-eyed one, the captivating Ghanśyām;
lord of Sūrdās, ocean of mercy for the devotee, I grasp your feet.

10 O Yamuna! Accessible to the devotee, inaccessible to others;
he who bathes [in your waters] at dawn is cleansed of all sins, and even Yama stands before him with hands joined.
Only the experienced will comprehend — what is there without experience? He whose mind the beloved has not stolen
has not known the secret of the ocean of love: what matter, Sūr, if his [mere] body is immersed?

11 Out of the house he comes;
house and courtyard have become so easy for walking, [but] the threshold trips him.
He keeps falling, it can't be crossed; it is such hard work, and he can't run [over it];
In three and a half steps he covered all the world, but the house boundary stops him.
Balbīr says to himself, 'What a performance he makes of it!';
the incalculable greatness of Sūrdās' lord pleases the minds of his devotees.

12 Yaśodā takes [her son] and lays him in the cradle;
repeating 'Today my boy was very bad-tempered', she sings in a very sweet tone.
She lay herself down gently, then Hari stretched his limbs and yawned;
poking him with her hand she cossets her boy; he sits up, restless and disturbed.
'Lie down, Lāl, I'll tell you a story — a very sweet one you'll love to hear!'
Hearing this, Sūr's Śyām was delighted in his mind, and lay down smiling with a moan of approval.

8.5 *ghaṭa* : from the primary meaning 'pot, jar' derive the two senses 'body' and 'drum' intended here.

9.2 *mukha kari* : lit. 'with [my] mouth'.

10.2 *yamahū* : Yama, regent of death, is the brother of Yamunā.

11 The *bāl-līlā* poems begin here.

11.2 The line is deficient by two *mātrās*.

11.4 *ahūṭha paiga* : the 'three and a half steps' which Viṣṇu took in his dwarf incarnation.

12.5 *sravanani kaū pyārī* : lit. 'dear to the ears'.

सुनि सुत एक कथा कहौं प्यारी ।
कमल नैन मन आनँद उपज्यौ, चतुर सिरोमनि देत हुँकारी ॥
दसरथ नृपति हुतौ रघुबंसी, ताकैं प्रगट भए सुत चारी ।
तिन मैं मुख्य राम जो कहियत, जनकसुता ताकी बर नारी ॥
तात बचन लगि राज तज्यौ तिन, अनुज घरनि सँग गए बनचारी ।
धावत कनक मृगा के पाछैं, राजिव लोचन परम उदारी ॥
रावन हरन सिया कौ कीन्हौ, सुनि नँदनंदन नींद निवारी ।
चाप चाप करि उठे सूर प्रभु, लछिमनु देहु जननि भ्रम भारी ॥ १३ ॥

जेंवत स्याम नंद की कनिया ।
कछुक खात कछु धरनि गिरावत, छबि निरखति नँदरनियाँ ॥
बरी बरा बेसन बहु भाँतिनि, व्यंजन बिबिध अगनियाँ ।
डारत खात लेत अपनैं कर, रुचि मानत दधि दोनियाँ ॥
मिस्री दधि माखन मिस्रित करि, मुख नावत छबि धनियाँ ।
आपुन खात नंद मुख नावत, सो छबि कहत न बनियाँ ॥
जो रस नंद जसोदा बिलसत, सो नहिं तिहूँ भुवनियाँ ।
भोजन करि नँद अचमन लीन्हौ, माँगत सूर जुठनियाँ ॥ १४ ॥

प्रथम करी हरि माखन चोरी ।
ग्वालिनि मन इच्छा करि पूरन, आपु भजे ब्रज खोरी ॥
मन मैं यहै बिचार करत हरि, ब्रज घर घर सब जाउँ ।
गोकुल जनम लियौ सुख कारन, सबकैं माखन खाउँ ॥
बाल रूप जसुमति मोहिं जानै, गोपिनि मिलि सुख भोग ।
सूरदास प्रभु कहत प्रेम सौं, ये मेरे ब्रज लोग ॥ १५ ॥

देखि फिरे हरि ग्वाल दुवारैं ।
तब इक बुद्धि रची अपनैं मन, गए नाँघि पिछवारैं ॥
सूनैं भवन कहूँ कोउ नाहीं, मनु याही कौ राज ।
भाँड़े धरत उघारत मूँदत, दधि माखन कैं काज ॥
रैनि जमाइ धरचौ हो गोरस, परचौ स्याम कैं हाथ ।
लै लै खात अकेले आपुन, सखा नहीं कोउ साथ ॥
आहट सुनि जुबती घर आई, देख्यौ नंदकुमार ।
सूर स्याम मंदिर अँधियारैं, निरखति बारंबार ॥ १६ ॥

13 'Listen son, I'll tell you a favourite story';
joy grew in the mind of the lotus-eyed, the jewel of the wise moaning his approval.
'There was a King Daśrath in the clan of Raghu; to him were born four sons;
first amongst them was the one called Rāma, Janak's daughter his fine lady.
Adhering to his father's word he gave up the monarchy, and with his younger brother and wife went wandering in the forest;
the lotus-eyed one, most noble, ran after a golden deer.
Rāvaṇ abducted Sītā...' — hearing this, Nandanandan shook off sleep,
and calling 'My bow! My bow! Lakṣmaṇ, give it to me!', Sūr's lord jumped up, his mother in great confusion.

14 Śyām feeds in the lap of Nanda;
he eats some, he drops some to the ground, Nanda's wife beholding his beauty.
Various cooked foods of pulse and flour, countless delicacies of varied kinds:
he throws! He eats! He takes in his hand! The bowls of curd are his favourite.
He tosses into his mouth sugarcandy, curd and butter mixed in his hand, rich in splendour;
he feeds himself and he pops some into Nanda's mouth, his splendour past telling.
The joy in which Nanda and Yaśodā delight, is not to be found in the three worlds;
after eating, Nanda drank a sip of water, and Sūr begs for the leftovers.

15 Hari made his first butter-theft;
fulfilling the desire of the gopis' minds, he ran off down the lanes of Braj.
In his mind Hari thinks, 'I'll go to each and every home in Braj;
I have taken birth in Gokul for enjoyment, I'll eat butter in everyone's house!
Yaśodā knows me in child's form — [but] I'll enjoy pleasure with the gopis!'
Sūrdās' lord says affectionately, 'these are my Braj folk'.

16 Hari looked, and went back to the house of the cowherd;
then he thought up a ruse in his mind, and crossed over the back way.
An empty house, no-one anywhere about — as though it were his own kingdom;
taking the pots, he opens, closes, looking for curd and butter.
The soured milk, put out at night to set, fell into Śyam's hands;
he takes it and eats it all alone, no companion with him.
Hearing a noise, the young woman came into the house and saw Nandkumār;
continually she gazed on Sūr's Śyām in the dark house.

13 Yaśodā, only dimly aware of Kṛṣṇa's true identity, tells him the Rāmāyaṇ story; he becomes spontaneously involved in it because of his shared identity with Rāma.

13.2 *kamala naina*: 'lotus-eyed' (here Kṛṣṇa) anticipates the synonymous 13.6 *rājiva locana* (here Rāma).

13.5 *tāta bacana lagi*: i.e. honouring the terms of a boon promised by Daśrath to Bharat's mother Kaikeyī, who insisted that Bharat take the throne and Rāma be exiled.

14.1 *kaniyā* : this *-iyā* ending sets up a rhyme (nasalized in the remainder of the stanza) which has to be more or less contrived in all subsequent lines except 4, which has a regular f.pl.

14.6 *kahata na baniyā̃*: 'cannot be told' [MSH *kahte nahī̃ bantī*].

15.4 *sabakaī̃*: 'at everyone's place' [MSH *sabke (yahā̃)*].

16.3 *yāhī kau rāja*: a poetic irony, all of creation being part of Kṛṣṇa's 'kingdom'. Cf. 17.5.

स्याम कहा चाहत से डोलत ।
पूछे तैं तुम बदन दुरावत, सूधे बोल न बोलत ॥
पाए आइ अकेले घर मैं, दधि भाजन मैं हाथ ।
अब तुम काकौ नाउँ लेउगे, नाहिंन कोऊ साथ ॥
मैं जान्यौ यह मेरो घर है, ता धोखैं मैं आयो ।
देखत हौं गोरस मैं चींटी, काढ़न कौं कर नायौ ॥
सुनि मृदु बचन निरखि मुख सोभा, ग्वालिनि मुरि मुसुकानी ।
सूर स्याम तुम हौ अति नागर, बात तिहारी जानी ॥१७॥

जसुदा कहँ लौं कीजै कानि ।
दिनप्रति कैसैं सही परति है, दूध दही की हानि ॥
अपने या बालक की करनी, जौ तुम देखौ आनि ।
गोरस खाइ खवावै लरिकनि, भाजत भाजन भानि ॥
मैं अपने मंदिर के कोनें, राख्यौ माखन छानि ।
सोई जाइ तिहारैं ढोटा, लीन्हौ है पहिचानि ॥
बूझि ग्वाल निज गृह मैं आयौ, नैंकु न संका मानि ।
सूर स्याम यह उतर बनायौ, चींटी काढ़त पानि ॥ १८ ॥

कबहिं करन गयौ माखन चोरी ।
जानै कहा कटाच्छ तिहारे, कमल नैन मेरौ इतनक सो री ॥
दै दै दगा बुलाइ भवन मैं, भुज भरि भेंटति उरज कठोरी ।
उर नख चिन्ह दिखावत डोलति, कान्ह चतुर भए तू अति भोरी ॥
आवति नित प्रति उरहन कैं मिस, चितै रहति ज्यौं चंद चकोरी ।
सूर सनेह ग्वालि मन अँटक्यौ, अंतर प्रीति जाति नहिं तोरी ॥१९ ॥

कहा कहौं हरि के गुन तोसौं ।
सुनहु महरि अबहीं मेरें घर, जे रँग कीन्हे मो सौं ॥
मैं दधि मथति आपनैं मंदिर, गए तहाँ इहिं भाँति ।
मो सौं कह्यौ बात सुनु मेरी, मैं सुनि कै मुसुकाति ॥
बाँह पकरि चोली गहि फारी, भरि लीन्ही अँकवारि ।
कहत न बनै सकुच की बातैं, देखौ हृदय उघारि ॥
माखन खाइ निदरि नीकी बिधि, यह तेरे सुत की घात ।
सूरदास प्रभु तेरे आगैं, सकुचि तनक ह्वै जात ॥ २० ॥

17 'Śyām, what is your will as you roam about?
When asked, you hide your face and won't give a straight reply.
I came and found you alone in the house, your hand in the curd-pot;
who will you blame this time? There's no-one with you!'
'I thought this was my own house, because of that mistake I came in;
I saw an ant in the milk and I reached down with my hand to pull it out.'
Hearing his sweet words and seeing the beauty of his face, the gopi turned and smiled:
'Sūr's Śyām, you're very clever, but I've seen through your game!'.

18 Yaśodā, how long can I put up with it?
How can the daily loss of milk and curd be tolerated?
You come and see the deed of this son of yours;
he eats the curd, feeds it to the boys, and flees, breaking the pots!
I had strained the butter and put it in a corner of my house;
he noticed it, that son of yours, and went and took it.
Realizing that the cowherd had come back home, he wasn't at all alarmed —
Sūr's Śyām made up this reply: 'I was pulling out an ant with my hand!'.

19 When did he ever go stealing butter?
Who knows about *your* sidelong glances — my lotus-eyed one is just so-big!
You constantly trick him, call him into the house, take him in your arms and hug him to your hard breasts;
you parade about showing the nail-marks on your chest — has Kānha become so artful, and you so innocent?
You come here every day on the pretext of scolding him, gazing at him like a *cakorī* watching the moon;
your mind's ensnared in love, milkmaid, and the heart's affection cannot be broken.

20 What can I tell you of Hari's qualities?
Hear, Yaśodā, what revels he got up to just now in my house with me!
I was churning the curds in my house when he went in there just like that!
He said to me 'Listen to what I say'; I listened and smiled.
He grabbed my arm, seized and tore my blouse, and took me into an embrace;
I can't tell you how alarmed I was, open my heart and see.
He ate my butter and affronted me thoroughly — this is your son's ploy —
in front of you, Sūrdās' lord shrinks and becomes all small!

17 A gopi addresses Kṛṣṇa.

17.1 *cāhata* : not a ptc. but a f. noun, 'liking, desire'.

18.3 *apane ya bālaka kī karanī jau* : *jau* (*jo*) here picks up and emphasizes *karanī*, to which it relates.

19 Yaśodā addresses a gopi who has accused Kṛṣṇa of butter theft.

19.2 *itanaka so* : 'little, next-to-nothing' [MSH *itnā-sā*].

19.4 *kānha catura bhae* : Yaśodā sarcastically mocks the gopi's pretence that she is the innocent victim of Kṛṣṇa's amorous advances.

19.5 *jyaũ caṁda cakorī* : Yaśodā is sarcastic and mocking — 'Your eyes are out like organ-stops!'.

कत हो कान्ह काहु कैं जात ।
ये सब ढीठ गरब गोरस कैं, मुख सँभारि बोलतिं नहिं बात ॥
जोइ जोइ रुचै सोइ तुम मोपै माँगि लेहु किन तात ।
ज्यौं ज्यौं बचन सुनौं मुख अमृत, त्यौं त्यौं सुख पावत सब गात ॥
कैसी टेव परी इन गोपिनि, उरहन कैं मिस आवतिं प्रात ।
सूर सु कत हठि दोष लगावति, घरही कौ माखन नहिं खात ॥ २१ ॥

गए स्याम ग्वालिनि घर सूनैं ।
माखन खाइ डारि सब गोरस, बासन फारि किए सब चूनै ॥
बड़ौ माट इक बहुत दिननि कौ, ताहिं करचौ दस टूक ।
सोवत लरिकनि छिरकि मही सौं, हँसत चलै दै कूक ॥
आइ गई ग्वालिनि तिहिं औसर, निकसत हरि धरि पाए ।
देखे घर बासन सब फूटे, दूध दही ढरकाए ॥
दोउ भुज धरि गाढ़ैं करि लीन्हे, गई महरि के आगैं ।
सूरदास अब बसै कौन ह्याँ, पति रहिहै ब्रज त्यागैं ॥ २२ ॥

महरि तैं बड़ी कृपन है माई ।
दूध दही बहु बिधि कौ दीनौ, सुत सौं धरति छपाई ॥
बालक बहुत नहीं री तेरैं, एकै कुँवर कन्हाई ।
सोऊ तौ घरही घर डोलतु, माखन खात चोराई ॥
वृद्ध बयस पूरे पुन्यनि ते, तैं बहुतै निधि पाई ।
ताहू के खैबे पीबे कौं, कहा करति चतुराई ॥
सुनहु न बचन चतुर नागरि के, जसुमति नंद सुनाई ।
सूर स्याम कौं चोरी कैं मिस, देखन है यह आई ॥ २३ ॥

भाजि गयौ मेरे भाजन फोरि ।
लरिका सहस एक सँग लीन्हे, नाचत फिरत साँकरी खोरि ॥
मारग तौ कोउ चलन न पावत, धावत गोरस लेत अँजोरि ।
सकुच न करत फाग सी खेलत, तारी देत हँसत मुख मोरि ॥
बात कहौं तेरे ढोटा की, सब ब्रज बाँध्यो प्रेम की डोरि ।
टोना सौ पढ़ि नावत सिर पर, जो भावत सो लेत है छोरि ॥
आपु खाइ सो सब हम मानैं, औरनि देत सिकहरैं तोरि ।
सूर सुतहिं बरजौ नँदरानी, अब तोरत चोली बँद डोरी ॥ २४ ॥

21 Why, Kānha, do you go to anyone else's house?
They are all brazen with pride at their cows' milk, they do not speak nicely.
Whatever you fancy, why don't you just ask me for it, son?
As I hear the nectar of speech from your mouth, I feel bliss throughout my body.
What has come over these gopis — they come every morning pretending to scold you;
Sūr: why do they insist on blaming you, even at home you don't eat butter!

22 Śyām went into the milkmaids' empty house;
he ate the butter, poured out all the milk, broke the pots and smashed them to bits.
One big earthen jar, ages old, he reduced to ten pieces;
sprinkling the sleeping boys with earth, he went off shrieking with laughter.
The milkmaid came at that moment and caught the absconding Hari;
she saw all the pots in the house broken, and the curds and yoghurt spilt.
She seized his two arms, took him firmly and went before Yaśodā:
(Sūr:) 'Who could live here now? Only by leaving Braj can one's honour survive!'.

23 'Yaśodā, you are very mean, my friend;
you have much milk and curd, given by God, but you keep it hidden from your son.
You don't have a host of children — there is only young Kanhāī;
and he wanders from house to house, stealing butter and eating it.
In old age, through accomplished past virtues, you received a great treasure indeed:
[yet] even in his food and drink do you resort to cunning?'
'Hear the crafty words of the clever woman', said Yaśodā to Nand:
'On the pretext of a theft she came to see Sūr's Śyām!'.

24 He broke my pots and ran away!
Taking some thousand boys with him, he wanders dancing in the narrow lane.
No-one can walk the path, he runs and snatches away the milk;
quite unbashful, he plays a game like Holi, clapping, laughing, looking away.
It's your lad I speak of, he has bound the whole of Braj in a thread of love;
casting a spell he leans over our heads, and snatches whatever appeals.
I'd put up with all he eats himself, but he breaks the pot-string and feeds the others;
restrain your son Yaśodā, for now he's breaking the drawstring on my blouse!

21 Yaśodā addresses Kṛṣṇa, ironically unaware of his involvement with the gopis.

21.2 *mukha sãbhāri bol-* : 'to speak with mouth restrained', i.e. inoffensively.

22.7 *dou bhuja* : a favourite irony of Sūr's, referring to the two arms of Kṛṣṇa who, as Viṣṇu, appears in a four-armed (*caturbhuj*) form.

23.1 *taĩ* : an irregular use of the agentive pr. in nominative case.

23.2 *bidhi kao dīnau* : 'given by God', the ptc. used nominally [MSH *vidhi kā diyā (huā)*].

24.2 *larikā sahasa eka sãga līnhe* : *eka* gives the sense 'about' — *sahasa eka*, 'a thousand or so' (rather than reading as *eka sãga* 'together'). Cf. 37.5 *bālaka sãga liyaĩ.*

24.4 *phāga sī* : [f. for *keli* or *līlā* (?), understood] i.e. the decadent games of Holi, in which social conventions are thrown to the wind and liquid substances (here, milk) are thrown over passers-by.

24.7-8 *sikaharaĩ tori...torata colī bãda ḍorī* : first he breaks the string net in which the butter-pots hang, then he progresses to breaking the string which supports other pitcher-like vessels.

मैया मैं नहिं माखन खायौ ।
ख्याल परैं ये सखा सबै मिलि, मेरैं मुख लपटायौ ॥
देखि तुही सींके पर भाजन, ऊँचै धरि लटकायौ ।
हौं जु कहत नान्हे कर अपनैं, मैं कैसैं करि पायौ ॥
मुख दधि पोंछि बुद्धि इक कीन्ही, दोना पीठि दुरायौ ।
डारि साँटि मुसुकाइ जसोदा, स्यामहिं कंठ लगायौ ॥
बाल बिनोद मोद मन मोह्यौ, भक्ति प्रताप दिखायौ ।
सूरदास जसुमति कौ यह सुख, सिव बिरंचि नहिं पायौ ॥ २५ ॥

जसोदा ऊखल बाँधे स्याम ।
मनमोहन बाहिर ही छाँड़े, आपु गई गृह काम ॥
दह्यौ मथति मुख तैं कछु बकरति, गारी दे लै नाम ।
घर घर डोलत माखन चोरत, षट-रस मेरैं धाम ॥
ब्रज के लरिकनि मारि भजत हैं, जाहु तुमहु बलराम ।
सूर स्याम ऊखल सों बाँधे, निरखहि ब्रज की बाम ॥ २६ ॥

पौढ़े स्याम जननि गुन गावत ।
आजु गयौ मेरौ गाइ चरावन, कहि कहि मन हुलसावत ॥
कौन पुन्य तप तैं मैं पायौ, ऐसौ सुंदर बाल ।
हरषि हरषि कै देति सुरनि कौं, सूर सुमन की माल ॥ २७॥

मुरली धुनि करी बलबीर ।
सरस निसि को इंदु पूरन, देखि जमुना तीर ॥
सुनत सो धुनि भई ब्याकुल, सकल घोष कुमारि ।
अंग अभरन उलटि साजे, रही कछु न सम्हारि ॥
गई सोरह सहस हरि पै, छाँड़ि सुत पति नेह ।
एक राखी रोकि कै पति, सो गई तजि देह ॥
दियौ तिहि निर्वान पद हरि, चितै लोचन कोर ।
सूर भजि गोविंद यौं जग मोह बंधन तोर ॥ २८ ॥

बसौ मेरे नैननि मैं यह जोरी ।
सुंदर स्याम कमल दल लोचन, सँग वृषभानु किसोरी ॥
मोर मुकुट मकराकृत कुंडल, पीतांबर झकझोरी ।
सूरदास प्रभु तुम्हरे दरस को, का बरनौं मति थोरी ॥ २९ ॥

25 'Mother, I didn't eat the butter!
On a whim, these friends joined forces and smeared my face.
See for yourself, the pot is in a string net, put hanging up high;
what I say is, my hands are small, how could I have got it?'
Wiping the curd from his face, he tried a trick, hiding the pot behind his back;
Yaśodā threw away her stick, and smiling, hugged Śyām close.
The joy of his childish sport charmed her heart, showing devotion's splendour;
Sūrdās, even Śiva and Brahma did not attain this joy of Yaśodā's.

26 Yaśodā tied Śyām to the mortar:
she left Kṛṣṇa right out in the open, and went about her household tasks.
Even as she churned the curd she muttered something, cursing and taking his name:
'He wanders from house to house stealing butter, but there are delicacies at home.
He beats the boys of Braj and runs away — off with you too, Balrām.'
And the women of Braj watch Sūr's Śyām, tied to the mortar.

27 His mother sings in praise of the sleeping Śyām;
'Today my one went grazing the cows' — repeating this she delights her mind.
'Through what merit or penance did I receive such a beautiful child?'
In constant delight she offers to the gods, Sūr, a garland of flowers.

28 Kṛṣṇa sounded his flute:
behold the full moon of this sweet night on Yamuna's bank!
Hearing that sound, all the cowherds' young womenfolk became aroused;
the ornaments on their bodies put on crooked, they were quite beside themselves.
Sixteen thousand of them went to Hari, abandoning love of sons and husbands;
one was stopped and held back by her husband — she went without her body.
To her Hari gave the state of salvation with a glance from the corner of his eye;
Sūr, adore Govind thus, breaking the bond of worldly infatuation.

29 May this couple dwell in my eyes:
beautiful Śyām, lotus-petal-eyed, and with him, Vṛṣabhānu's daughter.
His peacock crown, his crocodile-shaped earrings, his flowing yellow sash:
lord of Sūrdās — with my small intellect, how can I describe your appearance?

26.3 *dahyau*: i.e. *dahi* + emphatic *-u*.

26.3 *mukha taĩ*: lit. 'from her mouth', a pleonasm of a kind common with verbs of speech.

26.3 *lai nāma*: ironically suggesting the usual devotional sense of 'taking the name of God'.

26.4 *ṣaṭa-rasa*: '[food] of all six flavours' — i.e. sweet, sour, salt, bitter, acrid, astringent.

28.4 *soraha sahasa*: the traditional number of Kṛṣṇa's wives in the Dwarka period of his life, here transposed to the *rāsa* context.

28.6-8 The story of the gopi prevented by her husband from attending the *rāsa* dance is an important subplot in the *Bhāgavata Purāṇa*, where it represents the merit of complete abandonment in the cause of *bhakti*.

इहिं बँसुरी सखि सबै चुरायौ, हरि तो चुरायौ इकलौ चीर ।
मनहि चोरि चित बितहिं चुरायौ, गई लाज कुल धरम ऽरु धीर ॥
तब तैं भई फिरति हाँ व्याकुल, अति आकुलता भई अधीर ।
सूरदास प्रभु निठुर निठुर वह, नहिं जानत पर-हिरदै पीर ॥ ३० ॥

मुरली हरि कौं नाच नचावति ।
एते पर यह बाँस बँसुरिया, नंदनँदन कौं भावति ॥
ठाढ़े रहत बस्य ऐसें ह्वै, सकुचत बोलत बात ।
वह निदरे आज्ञा करवावति, नैकुँहुँ नाहिं लजात ॥
जब जानति आधीन भए हैं, देखति ग्रीव नवावत ।
पौढ़ति अधर चलित कर पल्लव, रंध्र चरन पलुटावत ॥
हम पर रिस करि करि अवलोकत, नासापुट फरकावत ।
सूर स्याम जब जब रीझत हैं, तब तब सीस डुलावत ॥ ३१ ॥

नटवर वेष धरे ब्रज आवत ।
मोर मुकुट मकराकृत कुंडल, कुटिल अलक मुख पर छबि पावत ॥
भ्रकुटी बिकट नैन अति चंचल, इहिं छबि पर उपमा इक धावत ।
धनुष देखि खंजन बिबि डरपत, उडि न सकत उड़िबै अकुलावत ॥
अधर अनूप मुरलि सुर पूरत, गौरी राग अलापि बजावत ।
सुरभी बृंद गोप बालक सँग गावत अति आनंद बढ़ावत ॥
कनक मेखला कटि पीतांबर, निर्तत मंद मंद सुर गावत ।
सूर स्याम प्रति अंग माधुरी, निरखत ब्रज जन कैं मन भावत ॥ ३२ ॥

आवत मोहन धेनु चराए ।
मोर मुकुट सिर उर बनमाला, हाथ लकुट गोरज लपटाए ॥
कटि कछनी किंकिन धुनि बाजति, चरन चलत नूपुर रव लाए ।
ग्वाल मंडली मध्य स्यामघन, पीत बसन दामिनिहिं लजाए ॥
गोप सखा आवत गुन गावत, मध्य स्याम हलधर छबि छाए ।
सूरदास प्रभु असुर सँहारे, ब्रज आवत मन हरष बढ़ाए ॥ ३३ ॥

30 This flute, friend, has stolen everything — all Hari stole was our clothes;
she's stolen our hearts, stolen our minds' power; gone is our modesty, family duty and fortitude!
Ever since, we have become restless, roaming about here, agitated in great distress;
Sūrdās' lord is cruel, and cruel is she, knowing not the pain in another's heart.

31 The flute makes Hari dance a dance!
Even so, this bamboo flute appeals to Nandanandan.
He stands subjugated thus, afraid to say anything;
she disrespectfully issues him with orders, quite unabashed.
When she knows he has become subservient, she looks at him and makes him bend his neck;
lying on his lip, she makes his trembling blossom-hands press the feet of her holes.
She looks at us with constant anger and makes his nostrils flare;
and whenever Sūr's Śyām is pleased, she makes him shake his head.

32 He comes to Braj wearing the guise of a fine dancer;
with peacock crown and fish-shaped earrings, a curly lock finding splendour on his face.
Arched brow and such restless eyes — I pursue a simile for this beauty:
seeing a bow a pair of wagtails is alarmed, desperate to fly but afraid of flying!
His unequalled lips fill the flute with melody as he picks up a tune in Gaurī mode;
the herd of cows and the cowherd boys sing together and greatly augment their joy.
With golden belt at his waist, and yellow tunic, he dances, singing in mellow tone;
looking at the sweetness of Śyām's every limb delights the people of Braj.

33 Mohan comes, grazing the cows;
peacock-crown on his head, [wearing] a garland of wild flowers, a stick in his hand, smeared in dust from the cows' hooves.
His waist-girdle resounds with the sound of bells, the anklets at his feet bring a sound as he walks;
Ghanśyām is amidst the circle of cowherds, his yellow garb shaming the lightning.
His cowherd friends come singing praises, amidst them are Śyām and Balrām, their splendour spread around.
Sūrdās' lord has destroyed the demons; coming to Braj he increases our hearts' joy.

30.1 *curāyau...cīra* : an allusion to Kṛṣṇa's theft of the gopis' clothes as they bathed in the Yamuna.

30.2 *cori...curāyau* : a clear demonstration of the semantic equivalence of the verbs *cor-* and *curā-*.

31.6 The image is of the imperious flute, luxuriating on the soft bed of Kṛṣṇa's lower lip, making his fingers massage the note-apertures which represent her 'feet'.

31.8 *sīsa ḍulāvata* : shaking of the head indicates aesthetic pleasure in an Indian audience.

32.4 *khaṁjana* : the wagtail represents the eyes because of the flickering or 'wagging' motion of its tail.

उपमा हरि तनु देखि लजानी ।
कोउ जल मैं कोउ बननि रहीं दुरि, कोउ कोउ गगन समानी ॥
मुख निरखत ससि गयौ अंबर कौं, तड़ित दसन छबि हेरि ।
मीन कमल कर चरन नयन डर, जल मैं कियौ बसेरि ॥
भुजा देखि अहिराज लजाने, बिबरनि पैठे धाइ ।
कटि निरखत केहरि डर मान्यौ, बन बन रहे दुराइ ॥
गारी देहिं कबिनि कैं बरनत, श्रीअँग पटतर देत ।
सूरदास हमकौं सरमावत, नाउँ हमारौ लेत ॥ ३४ ॥

निसि दिन बरषत नैन हमारे ।
सदा रहति बरषा रितु हम पर, जब तैं स्याम सिधारे ॥
दृग अंजन न रहत निसि बासर, कर कपोल भए कारे ।
कंचुकि-पट सूखत नहिं कबहूँ, उर बिच बहत पनारे ॥
आँसू सलिल सबै भइ काया, पल न जात रिस टारे ।
सूरदास प्रभु यहै परेखौ, गोकुल काहैं बिसारे ॥ ३५ ॥

निरगुन कौन देस कौ बासी ।
मधुकर कहि समुझाइ सौंह दै, बूझति साँच न हाँसी ॥
को है जनक कौन है जननी, कौन नारि को दासी ।
कैसो बरन भेष है कैसो, किहिं रस मैं अभिलाषी ॥
पावैगौ पुनि कियौ आपनौ, जो रे करैगौ गाँसी ।
सुनत मौन ह्वै रह्यौ बावरौ, सूर सबै मति नासी ॥ ३६ ॥

फिरि फिरि कहा बनावत बात ।
प्रातकाल उठि खेलत ऊधौ, घर घर माखन खात ॥
जिनकी बात कहत तुम हमसौं, सो है हमसौं दूरि ।
ह्याँ हैं निकट जसोदानंदन, प्रान सजीवन मूरि ॥
बालक संग लिऐं दधि चोरत, खात खवावत डोलत ।
सूर सीस नीचौ कत नावत, अब काहैं नहिं बोलत ॥ ३७ ॥

34 Seeing Hari's body, the similes are ashamed;
one hides in the water, one in the woods, some few find refuge in the heavens.
Seeing his face, the moon went to the sky, [as did] the lightning on seeing the brilliance of his teeth;
fish and lotus, for fear of his hands, feet and eyes, made their abode in the water.
Seeing his arms, great serpents were put to shame, and hurried to enter their holes;
seeing his waist, the lion felt fear, and stayed hidden in the forests.
Giving comparisons to his sacred body abuses the poets' descriptions;
Sūrdās: you put us to shame, taking our name.

35 Night and day our eyes rain tears;
It has been a constant rainy season with us since Śyām went away.
The kohl in our eyes stays not night or day, our hands and cheeks are blackened;
the cloth of our blouses never dries, channels stream between our breasts.
Our bodies are all awash with tears, not for a moment is our suffering removed;
Sūrdās' lord, examine this: why did you forget Gokul?

36 'In which country dwells this "one without qualities"?
Explain and tell us, bee, on oath — we ask in good faith, we are not joking!
Who is his father? Who his mother? Who is his wife, who his maidservant?
What is his colour, how does he dress, in what sentiment does he take delight?
If you tell us false, you will reap the rewards of your deed!'
Hearing this, the crazy one fell silent and stayed that way, Sūr, all his wit destroyed.

37 What is this story you keep contriving?
He gets up at dawn to play, Uddhava, and eats butter in every house.
The one of whom you speak to us, is remote from us;
here, near at hand is Yaśodā's boy, the enlivening herb for our souls.
Taking the boys with him he steals the curds; eating, feeding them he roams;
Sūr: Why do you bend your head low? Why don't you speak now?

34.7 *baranata* and *deta* are used nominally here.

34.8 *hamārau* : refers to the (personified) similes listed in the earlier lines.

36 In this poem, and in the following four, the gopis address Uddhava (Braj *Ūdhau*), whom Kṛṣṇa sent as an emissary to the gopis when he left Braj for Mathura. Uddhava's mission was to console the gopis with *advaita* philosophy, according to which they should feel no separation from him because in reality the soul is not distinct from God. This teaching was received with scorn by the gopis, who compared his dry wisdom with the sweet delight of *saguṇa bhakti*. The gopis' conquest of Uddhava is complete in this vernacular treatment of the theme, but the BhP version is more circumspect and does not allow such a complete victory to the *saguṇa* argument.

36.2 *madhukara* : 'honey-maker, bee'. The gopis associate Uddhava with a bee who flies past as they speak to him — the bee being an image of fickleness, flying from flower to flower — and they transfer its epithet to him. Such songs are thus known as *bhramar gīt*, 'bee songs'.

36.5 *kiyau āpanau* : the perf. ptc. is used nominally.

मन मैं रह्यौ नाहिंन ठौर ।
नंदनंदन अछत कैसैं आनियै उर और ॥
चलत चितवत दिवस जागत, स्वप्न सोवत राति ।
हृदय तैं वह मदन मूरति छिन न इत उत जाति ॥
कहत कथा अनेक ऊधौ, लोक लोभ दिखाइ ।
कह करौं मन प्रेम पूरन, घट न सिंधु समाइ ॥
स्याम गात सरोज आनन, ललित मृदु मुख हास ।
सूर इनकैं दरस कारन, मरत लोचन प्यास ॥ ३८ ॥

ऊधौ जोग कहा है कीजतु ।
ओढ़ियत है कि बिछैयत है किधौं खैयत है किधौं पीजत ॥
कीधौं कछू खिलौना सुंदर, की कछु भूषन नीकौ ।
हमरे नंदनँदन जो चहियतु, मोहन जीवन जी कौ ॥
तुम जु कहत हरि निगुन निरंतर, निगम नेति है रीति ।
प्रगट रूप की रासि मनोहर, क्यौं छाँड़े परतीति ॥
गाइ चरावन गए घोष तैं, अबहीं है फिरि आवत ।
सोई सूर सहाइ हमारे, बेनु रसाल बजावत ॥ ३९ ॥

ऊधौ इतनी कहियौ जाइ ।
अति कृस-गात भई ये तुम बिनु, परम दुखारी गाइ ॥
जल समूह बरषतिं दोउ अँखियाँ, हूँकति लीन्हैं नाउँ ।
जहाँ जहाँ गो-दोहन कीन्हों, सूँघतिं सोई ठाउँ ॥
परतिं पछार खाइ छिन ही छिन, अति आतुर ह्वै दीन ।
मानहु सूर काढ़ि डारी हैं, बारि मध्य तैं मीन ॥ ४० ॥

रुकमिनि चलौ जन्मभूमि जाहिं ।
जद्यपि तुम्हरौ बिभव द्वारिका, मथुरा है सम नाहिं ॥
जमुना के तट गाइ चरावत, अमृत जल अँचवाहि ।
कुंज केलि अरु भुजा कंध धरि, सीतल द्रुम की छाँहि ॥
सुरस सुगंध मंद मलयानिल, बिहरत कुंजन माहिं ।
जो क्रीड़ा श्री बृंदावन मैं, तिहूँ लोक मैं नाहिं ॥
सुरभी ग्वाल नंद अरु जसुमति, मम चित तैं न टराहिं ।
सूरदास प्रभु चतुर सिरोमनि, तिनकी सेव कराहिं ॥ ४१ ॥

38 There is no room left in my heart;
while Nandanandan remains there, how can another be brought in?
Walking, looking, awake in the day and dreaming in slumber at night,
that intoxicating image strays from my heart not for a single moment.
You tell all kinds of stories, Uddhava, with a show of worldly greed;
what should I do? — my heart is full of love, and a pot cannot hold an ocean.
That dark body and lotus face, the charming, gentle-faced laugh:
for the sake of a vision of these, Sūr, my eyes die of thirst.

39 Uddhava, what is done with this 'yoga'?
Is it worn, or is it wrapped around one? Or is it rather eaten or drunk?
Is it then some beautiful toy, or some fine ornament?
Our Nandanandan is the one we want, Mohan is the life of our soul.
What you say is that Hari is without qualities, perpetual, the Vedic 'not this' is his way;
he is manifest as a charming mass of beauty — why abandon faith in him?
He has left the cattle station to graze the cows, he is coming back quite soon;
he, Sūr, is our support, playing the sweet flute.

40 Uddhava, go and say just this:
'Without you, these most doleful cows have grown very thin of body.
Their two eyes rain masses of tears, as they call out to you by name;
wherever you did the cow-milking, they sniff that very place.
They fall swooning at every moment, wretched in great distress,
as though, Sūr, they were fishes drawn from the water and cast down.'

41 Rukmiṇī, come! Let us go to my birthplace;
though your dominion abides in Dwarka, it is not equal to Mathura.
Grazing the cows on the Yamuna's bank, giving its ambrosial water to drink —
the bower sport, and arms placed around shoulders in the trees' cool shade.
A delectable, fragrant, gentle, sandal-scented breeze, wandering in the groves —
the sport that subsists in holy Vṛndāvan is not to be found in the three worlds.
The cattle, the cowherds, Nand and Yaśodā cannot be removed from my mind;
perform the service of the lord of Sūrdās, crown jewel of the wise!

38 In the narrative of the sectarian hagiology of Sūrdās, Sūr addresses this poem to Akbar in refutation of worldly fame: see VV 29-36.

39.2 The line is over-long: long vowels in *oṛhiyata* and in the first *kidhaũ* are perhaps to be read as short (or the first *kidhaũ* may be redundant, though excising it leaves only 15+12 *mātrās*).

39.2 *bichaiyata*: passive ptc. of the verb *bichā-* 'spread, cover'.

39.7 *abahĩ hai phiri āvata*: in this deliberately ironic reference (Kṛṣṇa actually does not return to the gopis once he has left for Mathura) the present tense has future reference [MSH *abhī āte haĩ*].

41 While ruling in Dwarka, Kṛṣṇa tells his queen of the joys of his previous days in Braj; the stanza asserts the superiority of Braj *bhakti*.

41.5 *malayānila* (*malaya* + *anila*): the breeze which blows from the mountain range called *malaya* — the Western Ghats — always associated in poetry with the sandal trees which grow there.

पदावली

मीरा

चालो मन गंगा जमना तीर।
गंगा जमना निरमल पाणी सीतल होत सरीर ।
बँसी बजावत गावत कान्हो, संग लियाँ बलवीर ।
मोर मुगट पीतांबर सोहै, कुंडल झलकत हीर ।
मीराँ के प्रभु गिरधर नागर चरण कमल पै सीर ॥ १ ॥

बसो मेरे नैनन में नँदलाल।
मोहनी मूरति साँवरी सूरति, नैणा बने बिसाल ।
अधर सुधारस मुरली राजति, उर बैजंती माल ।
छुद्र घंटिका कटि तट सोभित, नूपुर सबद रसाल ।
मीराँ प्रभु संतन सुखदाई, भक्त बछल गोपाल ॥ २ ॥

हरि तुम हरो जन की पीर।
द्रोपती की लाज राखी, तुरत बाढचौ चीर ।
भक्त कारण रूप नरहरि धरचौ आप सरीर ।
हिरणाकुश मारि लीन्ह, धरचौ नाहिंन धीर ।
बूड़तो गजराज राख्यौ, कियौ बाहर नीर ।
दासी मीराँ लाल गिरधर चरण कँवल पै सीर ॥ ३ ॥

मैं तो साँवरे के रँग राची।
साजि सिंगार बाँधि पग घूँघरु, लोक लाज तजि नाची ।
गई कुमति लई साधु की संगति, भगत रूप भई साँची ।
गाय गाय हरि के गुन निस दिन, काल-व्याल सूँ बाँची ।
उण बिन सब जग खारो लागत, और बात सब काँची ।
मीराँ श्री गिरधरनलाल सूँ भगति रसीली जाँची ॥ ४ ॥

पग घुँघरू बाँध मीराँ नाची रे।
मैं तो मेरे नारायण की आपहि हो गइ दासी रे ।
लोग कहैं मीराँ भई बावरी, न्यात कहैं कुल नासी रे ।
विष का प्याला राणाजी भेज्या, पीवत मीराँ हाँसी रे ।
मीराँ के प्रभु गिरधर नागर सहज मिले अबिनासी रे ॥ ५ ॥

Padāvalī

Mīrā

1 Come, my mind, to the bank of Ganges and Yamuna;
in the pure water of Ganges and Yamuna the body is cooled.
Kṛṣṇa plays the flute and sings, taking Balbīr with him;
his peacock crown and yellow sash shine, his earrings sparkle with diamonds.
Mīrā's head is at the lotus feet of her lord, the courtly Giridhar.

2 Dwell in my eyes, Nandalāl!
Your enchanting form, your dusky face, your eyes made wide!
The flute adorns your nectarous lip, on your heart a jewelled necklace.
With tiny bells are your hips resplendent, your anklets have a sweet sound;
Mīrā's lord is Gopāl, a giver of joy to the pious, loving to his devotees.

3 Hari, you remove the pain of mankind;
you protected Draupadī's honour, and immediately her clothing extended.
For the sake of a devotee you took incarnation in 'man-lion' form:
you slew Hiraṇyakaśipu, who held not his courage.
You saved the drowning elephant and brought him out of the water;
the maidservant Mīrā has her head at the lotus feet of beloved Giridhar.

4 As for me, I am dyed in the colour of the dark one;
decked out in ornament, tying anklets to my feet, forsaking public shame I danced.
Gone was wrong understanding as I took holy company, cast in devotee's form;
ever singing Hari's qualities night and day I escaped from the serpent of death.
Without him the whole world seems bitter, all other talk banal;
Mīrā has tested sweet devotion to lord Giridharlāl.

5 Mīrā tied bells to her feet and danced;
I have myself become the slavegirl of my Nārāyaṇ.
People say Mīrā has gone mad, kinsmen call her a destroyer of family;
Rāṇājī sent a poisoned cup, Mīrā laughed as she drank it.
Mīrā has readily found her lord, the courtly Giridhar, the eternal one.

1.1/2 *gaṁgā jamanā*: an unlikely collocation, given the entirely Braj-based context of the poem. Some texts (e.g. B.D. Tivārī 1974:148) read *vā jamunā,* or equivalent.

1.5 *mīrā̃ ke prabhu giradhara nāgara*: this formulaic *pāda* containing the *chāpa* is found in a large number of the poems, sometimes with variations. Cf. the unmetrical *mīrā̃ kahai/kahe...* in 6.5, 7.5, 11.6.

2.4 Cf. SS 8.3.

4.1 *rācī*: this usage conflates the two senses of *rāc-*, 'to be dyed', 'to be enamoured' (CDIAL 10583 and 10584 *rajyate*).

4.3 *sā̃cī*: alternatively adj. 'true' — 'became true [found truth] in the form of a devotee'.

5.4 *viṣa kā pyālā rāṇājī bhejyā*: an incident from the hagiography of Mīrā in which her husband's half-brother, from a rival faction in the royal house of Mewar, tried to poison Mīrā. See Alston 1980:3.

जोगी मत जा मत जा मत जा, पाँइ परूँ मैं चेरी तेरी हौं ।
प्रेम भगति को पैंड़ो ही न्यारा, हमकूँ गैल बता जा ।
अगर चँदण की चिता बणाऊँ, अपणे हाथ जला जा ।
जल बल भई भस्म की ढेरी, अपणे अंग लगा जा ।
मीराँ कहै प्रभु गिरधर नागर, जोत में जोत मिला जा ॥ ६ ॥

देखो सहियाँ हरि मन काठो कियो ।
आवन कह गयो अजूँ न आयो, करि करि बचन गयो ।
खान पान सुध बुध सब बिसरी, कैसे करि मैं जियो ।
बचन तुम्हारे तुमही बिसारे, मन मेरो हर लयो ।
मीराँ कहे प्रभु गिरधर नागर, तुम बिनि फटत हियो ॥ ७ ॥

मेरे तो गिरधर गोपाल, दूसरो न कोई ।
जाके सिर मोर मुकट, मेरे पति सोई ।
छांड़ि दई कुल की कानि, कहा करिहै कोई ।
संतन ढिक बैठि बैठि लोक लाज खोई ।
अँसुवन जल सींचि सींचि प्रेम बेलि बोई ।
अब तो बेल फैल गई, आणँद फल होई ।
भगति देखि राजी हुई, जगति देखि रोई ।
दासी मीराँ लाल गिरधर, तारो अब मोहीं ॥ ८ ॥

दरस बिन दूखण लागै नैण ।
जब के तुम बिछुरे प्रभु मोरे, कबहुँ न पायो चैन ।
सबद सुणत मेरी छतियाँ काँपै, मीठे मीठे बैन ।
बिरह कथा कासूँ कहूँ सजनी, बह गई करवत अैन ।
कल न परत तल हरि मग जोवत, भई छमासी रैण ।
मीराँ के प्रभु कब रे मिलोगे, दुख मेटण सुख दैण ॥ ९ ॥

मोहि लागी लगन गुरु चरनन की ।
चरन बिन कछुवै नाहिं भावै, जग माया सब सपनन की ।
भवसागर सब सूखि गयो है, फिकर नहीं मोहि तरनन की ।
मीराँ के प्रभु गिरधर नागर, आस वही गुरु सरनन की ॥ १० ॥

6 Yogi, do not go! Do not go! Do not go! I fall at your feet, I am your handmaiden.
The very path of loving devotion is unique, show me the way.
I shall make a pyre of aloe and sandalwood — light it with your own hand;
When I am burnt to a heap of ashes, smear them onto your body.
Says Mīrā, O lord, courtly Giridhar, merge your flame with mine.

7 See, friends, Hari has hardened his heart;
he spoke of returning, but still he has not come: he left, promising time and again.
Eating, drinking, sense, mind — all are forgotten; how have I stayed alive?
You it was who forgot your own words, mine was the mind you stole;
says Mīrā, O lord, courtly Giridhar, without you my heart is breaking.

8 My one is Giridhar Gopāl, there is no other;
he whose head bears a peacock crown, he alone is my lord.
I have abandoned family honour, what can anyone do?
Sitting with pious folk I have done away with worldly shame.
Constantly irrigating it with tears I have sown the creeper of love;
now the creeper has spread and the fruit of bliss has grown.
Seeing devotion I was gladdened, seeing the world, I wept;
[says] the handmaiden Mīrā — dear Giridhar, save me now!

9 Without a vision of you my eyes have begun suffering;
since you left, my lord, I have found no comfort.
Hearing his voice my heart trembles at those sweet, sweet words;
to whom can I tell the tale of my lovesickness, it has sliced me with a saw's motion.
I have no rest, watching from the roof for Hari, and the night has become a six-month;
Mīrā's lord, when will you meet me, to remove sorrow and to bring joy?

10 I have found a fondness for the feet of the guru;
nothing but his feet pleases, all the world is an illusion of dreams.
The ocean of worldliness has all dried up, I have no concern with crossings;
Mīrā's lord is the courtly Giridhar, her hopes lie with the refuge of that guru's feet.

6.1 The two *pādas* of this first line (*ṭek*) are transposed, and one metrically superfluous *mata jā* added.

6.1 *jogī*: in this verse, which combines ascetic references with a raw sensuality, the wandering ascetic is identified with Kṛṣṇa (just as the *guru* is identified with God).

6.3 *agara cãdaṇa*: costly kinds of fragrant wood, their value emphasizing Mīrā's dedication as she builds her own (metaphorical) pyre. The practice of *satī*, still a reality in Rajasthan, underlies the reference.

7.3 *jiyo*: for the convenience of the rhyme, Mīrā temporarily assumes m. gender.

10.3 *guru*: not any human teacher, but the *satguru*, the 'inner voice' (or God himself) referred to by the Sant tradition with which Mīrā was at least partially aligned. Cf. 11.1.

10.3 *taranana*: the obl.p. of *tarana* 'boat, crossing' — use of a pl. is rather contrived here, but is necessary for the rhyme. Cf. following note.

10.4 *saranana*: = *sarana*, again contrived to fit the *-anana* rhyme. (Abstract nouns are rarely 'countables' having pl. forms — though MSH does follow English usage in this respect. Cf. note to SR 5.1.)

री मेरे पार निकस गया, सतगुर मारचा तीर ।
बिरह भाल लगी उर अंतरि, ब्याकुल भया सरीर ।
इत उत चित चलै नहिं कबहूँ, डारी प्रेम जँजीर ।
कै जाणैं मेरो प्रीतम प्यारो, और न जाणै पीर ।
कहा करूँ मेरो बस नहिं सजनी, नैन झरत दोउ नीर ।
मीराँ कहै प्रभु तुम मिलियाँ बिनि प्राण धरत नहिं धीर ॥ ११ ॥

आली म्हाँने लागे बृन्दावन नीको ।
घर घर तुलसी ठाकुर पूजा, दरसण गोविंद जी को ।
निरमल नीर बहत जमना में, भोजन दूध दही को ।
रतन सिंघासण आप बिराजे, मुगट धरचो तुलसी को ।
कुंजन कुंजन फिरत राधिका, सबद सुणत मुरली को ।
मीराँ के प्रभु गिरधर नागर भजन बिना नर फीको ॥ १२ ॥

होरी खेलत हैं गिरधारी ।
मुरली चंग बजत डफ न्यारो, संग जुवति ब्रजनारी ।
चंदन केसर छिरकत मोहन अपने हाथ बिहारी ।
भरि भरि मूठि गुलाल लाल चहुँ देत सबन पै डारी ।
छैल छबीले नवल कान्ह संग, स्यामा प्राण पियारी ।
गावत चार धमार राग तहँ, दै दै कल करतारी ।
फाग जु खेलत रसिक साँवरो, बाढ़चो रस ब्रज भारी ।
मीराँ के प्रभु गिरधर नागर मोहन लाल बिहारी ॥ १३ ॥

राम नाम रस पीजै मनुआँ, राम नाम रस पीजै ।
तज कुसंग सतसंग बैठ नित, हरि चरचा सुण लीजै ।
काम क्रोध मद लोभ मोह कूँ चित से बहाय दीजै ।
मीराँ के प्रभु गिरधर नागर, ताहि के रंग में भीजै ॥ १४ ॥

11 O, the arrow shot by the *satguru* has passed right through me;
the spear of separation has struck within my heart, my body is in torment.
My mind can never move here or there, the fetters of love are cast about it;
none but my dear beloved knows my pain, no-one else.
What should I do? I have no control, friend, tears pour from my two eyes;
says Mīrā, without meeting you, lord, my soul holds no composure.

12 Friend, I love Vṛndāvan;
in every house there is worship of the deity and *tulsī*, and audience with Govind.
Pure waters flow in the Yamuna, food is of milk and curd;
He adorns a jewelled throne, wearing a *tulsī* crown.
Rādhikā wanders among the groves, hearing the sound of the flute;
without adoration for Mīrā's lord, the courtly Giridhar, man is dull.

13 Giridhārī plays Holi;
flute, mouth-harp and wondrous drum resound; with him are the young Braj maidens.
Mohan the sportive one scatters sandalwood and saffron with his own hand;
taking handful after handful, Lāl hurls the red powder on everyone all around.
With the dashing and handsome young Kānha is Rādhā, his heart's beloved;
they sing a lovely Holi song there, marking time with soft hand-clapping.
With the Holi that the dark lover plays, the joy of Braj grows greatly;
Mīrā's lord is the courtly Giridhar, Mohanlāl, the sportive one.

14 Drink the nectar of Rām's name, O mind, drink the nectar of Rām's name;
quit bad company, and sitting with the pious listen ever to accounts of Hari.
Wash away from your mind lust, anger, intoxication, greed and infatuation;
Mīrā's lord is the courtly dancer, drench yourself in the colour of his love.

11.4 *kai jāṇaī...aura na jāṇai* : 'either my dear beloved knows...[or] there is nobody who knows'.

11.5 *mero* : read as two short syllables for metre.

11.6 *miliyā̃* : = perf.ptc.

12.1 *mhā̃ne* : (a Rajasthani form), obl.pl. *mhā̃* + objective ppn. *ne* (cf. Braj *mohi*, MSH *mujhe*).

12.2 *tulasī* : the sacred basil plant, revered as an aspect of Viṣṇu and thus grown in Vaiṣṇava temples etc.

13.2 *caṁga* : the name of various instruments, including (locally) a small drum, and (across Northern India and the Middle East) the jew's harp.

13.4 *cahū̃* : 'in all four [directions]'.

13.4 *ḍārī* : the stem form *ḍāri* (used in comp. with *de-*) with final vowel lengthened for rhyme.

13.5 *chaila* and its doublet *chabīlo* (both < Skt. *chavi-*) differ slightly in sense: *chaila* 'dandy, wanton' (with an emphasis on a wilful projection of a foppish appearance) vs. *chabīlo* 'handsome, elegant' (with less implication of contrivance).

13.8 *bihārī* : repeating a rhyme-word (cf. line 3) is typical of the casual manner of composition in Mīrā's poetry.

सुजान रसखान

रसखान

मानुष हौं तो वही रसखानि बसौं ब्रज गोकुल गाँव के ग्वारन ।
जो पशु हौं तौ कहा बस मेरो चरौं नित नंद की धेनु मँझारन ॥
पाहन हौं तौ वही गिरि को जो धरचौ कर छत्र पुरंदर धारन ।
जो खग हौं तौ बसेरो करौं मिलि कालिंदी कूल कदंब की डारन ॥ १ ॥

गोरज बिराजै भाल लहलही बनमाल
आगे गैया पाछे ग्वाल गावै मृदु तान री ।
तैसी धुनि बाँसुरी की मधुर मधुर तैसी
बंक चितवनि मंद मंद मुसकानि री ॥
कदम विटप के निकट तटनी के तट
अटा चढ़ि चाहि पीत पट फहरानि री ।
रस बरसावै तन तपन बुझावै नैन
प्राननि रिझावै वह आवै रसखानि री ॥ २ ॥

मोर पखा सिर ऊपर राखिहौं गुंज की माल गरें पहिरौंगी ।
ओढ़ि पितंबर लै लकुटी बन गोधन ग्वारनि संग फिरौंगी ॥
भावतो वोहि मेरो रसखानि सों तेरे कहे सब स्वाँग करौंगी ।
या मुरली मुरलीधर की अधरान धरी अधरा न धरौंगी ॥ ३ ॥

छीर जो चाहत चीर गहैं ए जू लेउ न केतिक छीर अचैहौ ।
चाखन के मिस माखन माँगत खाहु न माखन केतिक खैहौ ॥
जानत हौं जिय की रसखानि सु काहे को एतिक बात बढ़ैहौ ।
गोरस के मिस जो रस चाहत सो रस कान्ह जू नेकु न पैहौ ॥ ४ ॥

Sujān-raskhān

Raskhān

1 Be I a man [in my next life], then [let me be] that same Raskhān
and dwell in Braj with the cowherds of Gokul village;
if I am a beast, then what power do I have [to alter my fate] ? —
let me graze eternally amongst Nanda's cows.
If I am a stone, then [let it be] of that very [Govardhan] mountain
which [Kṛṣṇa] held in his hand as an umbrella against Indra's torrents;
if I am a bird, then let me make my abode
in the boughs of a kadamba tree on Yamuna's bank.

2 Dust from cows' hooves adorns his brow, his forest garland is luxuriant;
ahead, the cows; behind, the cowherds sing sweet melodies.
As sweet as the sweet sound of his flute
is his crooked glance and slow, gentle smile;
on the river's bank near the kadamba tree —
climb to the rooftop and spy the fluttering of his yellow sash;
the eyes rain a nectar and extinguish the body's burning,
delighting the soul, he comes — Raskhān!

3 I shall place his peacock-feather [crown] on my head,
I shall wear his necklace of seeds around my neck;
wrapping on his yellow sash and taking his stick
I shall roam the woods with the cattle and cowherds.
He is my beloved, that Raskhān —
at your command I shall imitate him in every way;
[but] this flute of the flute-player's, which was held to his lips,
I shall not hold to my lips!

4 The milk that you want as you seize my dress,
well sir, take it, won't you — how much milk will you drink?
The butter you ask for on the pretext of tasting it,
eat it, won't you — how much butter will you eat?
I know what is in your mind, Raskhān,
so why should you beat about the bush?
The taste that you seek, pretending to want milk —
that taste, Kānha-jū, you will not get at all!

1 The poem considers various possible future births, each maintaining some connexion with Kṛṣṇa.

1.4 *mili* : this seems semantically superfluous here (though metrically correct).

2.1 *bhāla* : this reading (Bhāṭī 1977:180) preferred to *bhāga* (Amīr Siṁh 1947:22).

2.3 *taṭa* : this reading (Bhāṭī 1977:180) preferred to *āya* (Amīr Siṁh 1947:22).

4.1 *ketika chīra acaihau* : the question is rhetorical, implying 'you won't drink much, because that's not your real purpose'. Cf. 4.2 *mākhana ketika khaihau.*

ब्रह्म मै ढूँढ्यो पुरानन गानन बेद रिचा सुनि चौगुने चायन ।
देख्यो सुन्यो कबहूँ न कितूँ वह कैसे सरूप औ कैसे सुभायन ॥
टेरत हेरत हारि पर्‍यौ रसखानि बतायो न लोग लुगायन ।
देखो दुरो वह कुंज कुटीर मैं बैठौ पलोटत राधिका पायन ॥ ५ ॥

अबहीं गई खिरक गाइ के दुहाइबे कों
बावरी ह्वै आई डारि दोहनी यौं पानि की ।
कोऊ कहै छरी कोउ मौन परी डरी कोऊ
कोऊ कहै मरी गति हरी अँखियान की ॥
सास व्रत ठानै नंद बोलत सयाने धाइ
दौरि दौरि जानै मानो खोरि देवतानि की ।
सखी सब हँसैं मुरझानि पहिचानि कहूँ
देखी मुसकानि वा अहीर रसखानि की ॥ ६ ॥

आजु भटू इक गोपबधू भई बावरी नेकु न अंग सम्हारै ।
मात अघात न देवनि पूजत सासु सयानी सयानी पुकारै ॥
यों रसखानि घिर्‍यो सिगरो ब्रज कौन को कौन उपाय बिचारै ।
कोउ न कान्हर के कर तें वह बैरिनि बाँसुरिया गहि जारै ॥ ७ ॥

आवत लाल गुलाल लिए मग सूने मिली इक नार नवीनी ।
त्यों रसखानि लगाइ हिए भटू मौज कियो मन माहीं अधीनी ॥
सारी फटी सुकुमारी हटी अँगिया दरकी सरकी रँग भीनी ।
गाल गुलाल लगाइ लगाइकै अंक रिझाइ बिदा कर दीनी ॥ ८ ॥

5 I sought God in the songs of the *Purāṇas,*
listening to the Vedic hymns with fourfold zeal;
[yet] never did I ever see or hear
how was his form, or of what kind his nature.
Calling and searching I admitted defeat,
neither men nor women could show me Raskhān:
— [but] see him concealed in the hut in the grove,
sitting massaging the feet of Rādhikā!

6 Just now she went to the cowshed to milk the cow,
and came back crazy, just throwing down the milk-pail in her hand;
some say she's shamming, some that she's struck dumb, some that she's afraid,
some say she's dead or that she has lost the use of her eyes.
Mother-in-law takes a vow, sister-in-law hurries to call the exorcist,
they run about, thinking it as it were the mischief of the gods;
[but] the sakhis laugh, understanding her swooning — somewhere
she has seen the smile of that herdsman, Raskhān!

7 Today, sister, a cowherd's wife went crazy
and could not control her body at all;
her mother tired not from worshipping the gods,
her mother-in-law called constantly for the exorcist.
Thus has Raskhān girded the whole of Braj,
no-one at all could think of a remedy:
nobody will take from Kānha's hand
our enemy, that little flute, and burn it up.

8 Lāl came holding red powder in his hand
when on a deserted road he met a young lady;
there and then Raskhān embraced her to his heart, sister,
and had the pleasure he desired with that helpless one.
With sari torn the tender girl drew back,
with bodice rent she slipped away, drenched in (love's) colour;
Smearing the powder on her cheeks,
he ravished her in embrace and took his leave.

5.1 *caugune cāyana* : an allusion to the four books of the Veda. The rhyme-word initiates a sequence of nouns all obl. pl. but with different case: *cāyana* instrumental (a rather contrived pl., as is the next); *subhāyana* genitive ('of what natures?'); *lugāyana* ergative; *pāyana* accusative.

6.2 *gati harī ākhiyāna kī* : 'the movement of the eyes is lost'.

6.3 *sāsa vrata ṭhānai* : the taking of vows, promising particular service to a deity in return for intercession, is traditionally the duty of older women in the family.

7.3 *kauna ko kauna* : the repetition is rhetorical, 'who, but *who*?' — i.e. nobody at all.

8.1 *gulāla* : this reading (Bhāṭī 1977:275) preferred to *gupāla* (Amīr Siṁh 1947:31).

8.2 *adhīnī* : this reading (Bhāṭī 1977:275) preferred to *ajīnī* (Amīr Siṁh 1947:31).

सेस गनेस महेस दिनेस सुरेसहु जाहि निरंतर गावैं ।
जाहि अनादि अनंत अखंड अछेद अभेद सुबेद बतावैं ॥
नारद से सुक ब्यास रहैं पचि हारे तऊ पुनि पार न पावैं ।
ताहि अहीर की छोहरिया छछिया भरि छाछ पै नाच नचावैं ॥ ९ ॥

ए री आजु काल्हि सब लोक लाज त्यागि दोऊ
सीखे हैं सबै विधि सनेह सरसाइबो ।
यह रसखान दिना द्वै में बात फैलि जैहै
कहाँ लौं सयानी चंदा हाथन छिपाइबो ॥
आजु हौं निहारयो बीर निपट कलिंदी तीर
दोउन को दोउन सों मुरि मुसकाइबो ।
दोउ परै पैयाँ दोऊ लेत हैं बलैया इन्हें
भूलि गई गैयाँ उन्हें गागर उठाइबो ॥१० ॥

कान्ह भए बस बाँसुरी के अब कौन सखी हमकों चहिहै ।
निस द्योस रहै सँग साथ लगी यह सौतिन तापन क्यों सहिहै ॥
जिन मोहि लियो मनमोहन को रसखानि सदा हमकों दहिहै ।
मिलि आओ सबै सखी भाग चलैं अब तो ब्रज मैं बँसुरी रहिहै ॥ ११ ॥

कौन ठगौरी भरी हरि आजु बजाई है बाँसुरिया रँग भीनी ।
तान सुनी जिनही तिनहीं तबहीं तिन लाज बिदा कर दीनी ॥
घूमै घड़ी घड़ी नंद के द्वार नवीनी कहा कहूँ बाल प्रबीनी ।
या ब्रजमंडल में रसखानि सु कौन भटू जो लटू नहिं कीनी ॥ १२ ॥

9 He whom Śeṣa, Gaṇeś, Śiva, Sūrya and Indra
praise ceaselessly;
whom the holy Veda describes as
'without beginning or end, indivisible, impenetrable, not to be divided';
whom the likes of Nārad, Śuka and Vyās, though they labour in vain,
fail finally to fathom;
— that same one, the cowherds' daughters
set a-dancing for a cup of buttermilk!

10 Well, recently, abandoning all worldly shame the two of them
have learnt all the ways of furthering their love;
within a day or two, Raskhān, this news will spread around —
how far, wise one, can you hide the moon with your hands?
Today, friend, right by the Yamuna's bank I saw
the turning and smiling of each to the other;
both fell at the other's feet, both bestowed a blessing,
he has forgotten the cows, and she the carrying of the water-pot!

11 Kānha has fallen under the spell of the flute —
who will love us now, friend?
Night and day she remains attached to him,
who can bear the rival wives' anguish?
She who has charmed the charmer of the heart
will always make us burn [with jealousy], Raskhān;
come, let us all run away together, friend,
for now the flute will reside in Braj.

12 Filled with what magic is the little flute
drenched in joy, that Hari played today;
whosoever heard her tune, they at that very moment
bade farewell to modest shame.
They hover at every moment at Nanda's door
— should I call them maidens? — these *knowing* girls;
in this Braj district what woman is there
whom Raskhān has not dazzled with love?

9 Lines 1-3 are relative clauses picked up by the correlative of line 4: a favourite convention of Raskhān.

10.1 *sarasāibo* : this and the other three rhyme-words are inf. used as verbal nouns.

10.2 Syntax: *yaha...bāta.*

10.2 *sayānī* : here synonymous with *sakhī* (cf. 10.3 *bīra*) without the 'exorcist' sense of 6.3, 7.2.

10.3 *nipaṭa kalim̐dī tīra* : composition with adv. *nipaṭa* suggests that *tīra* may here be ppn. sense 'near'.

10.3 *douna ko...musakāibo* 'the turning of both of them'.

10.4 *inhaĩ bhūli gaĩ gaiyā̃* : the verb is intransitive, and its subject is *gaiyā̃* .

11.1 Line 1 is metrically distinct from 2-4, beginning / - ⏑ ⏑ / rather than / ⏑ ⏑ - /. See II.4.3.

11.2 *sautina* : the *sakhīs* see themselves as 'co-wives' of their rival, Kṛṣṇa's flute.

द्रौपदी औ गनिका गज गीध अजामिल सों कियो सो न निहारो ।
गौतम गेहिनी कैसी तरी प्रहलाद को कैसे हरचो दुख भारो ॥
काहे को सोच करै रसखानि कहा करिहैं रविनंद बिचारो ।
ता खन जा खन राखिए माखन चाखनहारो सो राखनहारो ॥ १३ ॥

गोकुल को ग्वाल काल्हि चौमुँह की ग्वालिन सों
चाँचर रचाइ एक धूमहिं मचाइ गो ।
हियो हुलसाय रसखानि तान गाइ बाँकी
सहज सुभाइ सब गाँव ललचाइ गो ॥
पिचका चलाइ और जुबती भिजाइ नेह
लोचन नचाइ मेरे अंगहि नचाइ गो ।
सासहिं नचाइ भोरी नंदहि नचाइ खोरी
बैरिन सचाइ गोरी मोहि सकुचाइ गो ॥ १४ ॥

संपति सों सकुचाइ कुबेरहिं रूप सों दीनी चिनौती अनंगहिं ।
भोग कै कै ललचाइ पुरंदर जोग कै गंग लई धरि मंगहिं ॥
ऐसे भए तो कहा रसखानि रसै रसना जो जु मुक्ति तरंगहिं ।
दै चित ताके न रंग रच्यो जु रह्यो रचि राधिका रानी के रंगहिं ॥ १५ ॥

धूर भरे अति शोभित स्याम जू तैसी बनी सिर सुंदर चोटी ।
खेलत खात फिरैं अँगना पग पैजनी बाजती पीरी कछोटी ॥
वा छबि को रसखानि बिलोकत वारत काम कला निज कोटी ।
काग के भाग बड़े सजनी हरि हाथ सों लै गयो माखन रोटी ॥ १६ ॥

13 You did not look [in judgement] on the deeds of
Draupadī and the harlot, the elephant, the vulture, and Ajāmil;
how was Gautam's wife saved,
how did you remove Prahlād's burden of suffering?
Why should one worry, Raskhān — what can poor Yama do
the moment when you accept a saviour like the butter-taster?

14 The cowherd of Braj yesterday with the gopis from all around
set going a Holi dance and created a stir;
singing a rakish tune he delighted their hearts,
with natural ease he aroused the whole village.
Squirting his syringe he drenched the other damsel with unctuous love,
with dancing eyes he set my body a-dancing;
mother-in-law and simple sister-in-law he has dancing in the lane,
he soaked my fair rivals, he filled me with shyness.

15 With your wealth you may intimidate Kuver,
with your beauty you have defied Kāmdev;
through constant enjoyment you may tantalize Indra,
and through yoga you may hold the Ganges on your head;
what of all this, Raskhān,
[even] if you relish the rapture of beatitude on your tongue,
if with all your heart, you are not dyed in the colour of him
who remains dyed in the colour of queen Rādhikā!

16 Covered with dust, Śyām jū is most resplendent,
decorated as he is with a lovely topknot on his head;
playing and eating he roams round the courtyard
clad in a yellow dhoti, the anklets on his feet resounding.
Seeing that beauty, Raskhān,
Kāmdev sacrifices myriads of his arts;
and great is the fortune of that crow, friend,
who has taken the bread and butter from Hari's hand!

13 The poem praises Kṛṣṇa/Viṣṇu for distributing grace without judging the recipient.

13.1 *nihāro*: probably to be read as perfective ptc., i.e. = *nihāryau*.

13.4 MSH: *us kṣaṇ, jis kṣaṇ makkhan-cakhnevāle jaisā rakhnevālā rakhā jāe.*

14.1 *macāi go*: in each line the verb comprises stem + perfective ptc. of *jā-*, and can be interpreted either as a compound (MSH *macā gayā* etc.) or as abs. + finite verb ('created a stir and left'). Cf. 21.4.

14.2 *bā̃kī*: two senses apply — both 'crooked' (i.e. the twists and turns of the *tāna* up and down the musical scale) and 'rakish' (the characteristic quality of Kṛṣṇa's wanton lovemaking).

14.3 *neha*: both 'love, affection' and 'fluid, unguent'. The latter sense is imbued with sexual symbolism.

14.3 *nacāi go*: this reading (Bhāṭī 1977:274) preferred to *bacāi go* (Amīr Siṁh 1947:32).

14.4 *bairina sacāi gorī*: the phrase is not wholly clear, but *sacāi* is perhaps for *sī̃cāi*.

15.3 *aise bhae to kahā*: 'if such things have happened, so what?'. (Cf. MSH *kyā huā*, 'so what?'.)

बेनु बजावत गोधन गावत ग्वालन के सँग गो मधि आयो ।
बाँसुरी मै उन मेरोई नाम सु ग्वालन के मिस टेरि सुनायो ॥
ए सजनी सुनि सास के त्रासनि नंद के पास उसास न आयो ।
कैसी करौं रसखानि नहीं हित चैन नहीं चित चोर चुरायो ॥ १७ ॥

कंचन के मंदिरनि दीठ ठहरात नाहिं
सदा दीपमाल लाल मानिक उजारे सौं ।
और प्रभुताई अब कहाँ लौं बखानौं प्रति-
हारन की भीर भूप टरत न द्वारे सौं ॥
गंगाजी में न्हाइ मुक्ताहल हू लुटाइ वेद
बीस बार गाइ ध्यान कीजत सवारे सौं ।
ऐसे ही भए तो नर कहा रसखानि जो पै
चित दै न कीनी प्रीत पीतपटवारे सौं ॥१८ ॥

बागन काहे को जाओ पिया घर बैठेही बाग लगाय दिखाऊँ ।
एड़ी अनार सी मौर रही बहियाँ दोउ चंपे सी डार नवाऊँ ॥
छातिन में रस के निबुआ अरु घूँघट खोलि कै दाख चखाऊँ ।
ढाँगन के रस के चसके रति फूलनि की रसखानि लुटाऊँ ॥ १९ ॥

अंगनि अंग मिलाय दोऊ रसखानि रहे लपटे तरु छाँहीं ।
संग निसंग अनंग को रंग सुरंग सनी पिय दै गल बाहीं ॥
बैन ज्यों मैन सु ऐन सनेह कों लूटि रहे रति अंतर जाहीं ।
नीबी गहै कुच कंचन कुंभ कहै बनिता पिय नाहीं जू नाहीं ॥ २० ॥

17 Playing his flute and singing a herding-song
he came with the cowherds amidst the cows;
through his flute he sounded my own name
on a pretext of [calling] the fine cowherd boys.
O friend! Hearing it, for fear of my mother-in-law,
even with sister-in-law nearby I could not catch my breath;
how should I act, Raskhān, I have no wellbeing,
no peace have I, for the stealer of hearts has stolen it.

18 One's sight cannot settle on those houses of gold,
ever with the brightness of rows of lamps, rubies and gems;
How further can I praise your supremacy now,
a crowd of gatekeepers and kings never leave your door.
Bathing in the Ganges and giving away pearls with abandon,
reciting the Veda a score of times, meditating from morning:
despite all this, what is man, Raskhān, if
he loves not with all his heart the one who wears the yellow sash.

19 Why go to the gardens, beloved —
sitting at home I shall plant a garden to show you;
my heels are like pomegranate flowers,
my two arms I shall bend over you like champak branches.
In my breasts [see] succulent limes,
and opening my veil I shall give you grapes to taste;
with cups of the nectar of my loins, Raskhān,
I shall give freely of the passion of my blooms!

20 Clinging limb to limb, the two, Raskhān,
remain embracing in the shade of a tree;
meeting in fearless union, steeped in Kāmdev's bright joy,
she has her arms round her lover's neck.
Their words are as it were Kāmdev's fine house of love —
they go inside and plunder its passion;
he grasps her drawstring (her breasts are golden jugs!) —
and the loving lady says to the lover, 'No sir! No!'.

17.2 *su gvālana*: prefixed *su-* is perhaps primarily for metre. Cf. 20.3 *su aina* and 22.1 *su gāina*.

17.3 *sāsa ke trāsana*: the mother-in-law perceives what the flute's call implies. (The pl. number of *trāsana* is another metrical convenience.)

19.1 *bāga dikhāū̃*: cf. the idiom noted by Platts (1930:123), '*sabz bāg dikhānā*, 'To excite desire and expectation by deceitful promises (*lit.* 'to exhibit a blooming garden, as by legerdemain')'.

19.4 *ḍhā̃gana*: perhaps < **ḍhākka-* 'back, waist' (CDIAL 5582), among whose derivatives are regional forms in *-g* and the sense 'hip'. But etymology and sense are both uncertain: cf. Bhāṭī's easier reading *ṭā̃gana* 'legs' (1977:301). Miśra (1953:40) assimilates to *ḍā̃ga* and glosses *chuhārā* ('date-palm').

19.4 *casake*: if not from *caṣaka* 'chalice', then *casakā* 'taste for, relish' (CDIAL 4727 *caṣati* 'eats'?).

20.1 *milāi*: the reading from Miśra (1953:40) and Bhāṭī (1977:298); Amīr Siṁha has *milāpa*.

20.4 *nībī*: a conventional play on 'drawstring' and 'capital, treasure' (as her priceless golden breasts).

आयो हुतो नियरें रसखानि कहा कहूँ तू न गई वह ठैंया ।
या ब्रज में सिगरी बनिता सब वारति प्रानिनि लेत बलैया ॥
कोऊ न काहू की कानि करै कछु चेटक सो जु करचो जदरैया ।
गाइ गो तान जमाइ गो नेह रिझाइ गो प्रान चराइ गो गैया ॥ २१ ॥

ग्वालन सँग जैबो बन ऐबो सु गाइन सँग
हेरि तान गैबो हाहा नैन फरकत हैं ।
ह्याँ के गजमोती माल वारौं गुंज मालन पै
कुंज सुधि आए हाय प्रान धरकत हैं ॥
गोबर को गारो सु तौ मोहि लगै प्यारौ
कहा भयो महल सोने को जटत मरकत हैं ।
मंदर ते ऊँचे यह मंदिर हैं द्वारिका के
ब्रज के खिरक मेरे हिय खरकत हैं ॥ २२ ॥

मोहन छबि रसखानि लखि, अब दृग अपने नाहिं ।
ऐंचे आवत धनुष से, छूटे सर से जाहिं ॥ २३ ॥

देख्यो रूप अपार, मोहन सुन्दर स्याम को ।
वह ब्रजराजकुमार हिय जिय नैननि मै बस्यो ॥ २४ ॥

या लकुटी अरु कामरिया पर राज तिहूँ पुर को तजि डारौं ।
आठहुँ सिद्धि नवो निधि को सुख नंद की गाइ चराइ बिसारौं ॥
रसखानि कबौं इन आँखिन सौं ब्रज के बन बाग तड़ाग निहारौं ।
कोटि करौ कलधौत के धाम करील के कुंजन ऊपर वारौं ॥ २५ ॥

21 Raskhān came up to me —
what can I tell you, you did not go to that place;
in this [land of] Braj, all the girls
offer their souls and extend him a blessing.
No-one has a care for others' thoughts,
it is some magic that the Yādav lord has wrought —
his sang a tune, he launched his love,
he delighted our souls, he grazed the cattle.

22 For his going to the woods with the cowherds, for his coming with the fine cows,
for his singing of tunes, glancing — ah! — my eyes yearn;
I would give up these garlands of great pearls for those garlands of seeds;
when the groves come to mind — alas! — my soul blazes.
That earthen plaster is what is dear to me,
what of this palace of gold, studded with emeralds?
Taller than Mandara mountain are these houses of Dvārkā,
[but] the cattle-pens of Braj chafe my heart.

23 Having seen the enchanting grace of Raskhān, my eyes are no longer my own;
they are drawn back like a bow, but fly off like an arrow.

24 I have seen the boundless beauty of the enchanting, beautiful Śyām;
that young king of Braj has settled in my heart, my soul, my eyes.

25 For the sake of this stick and blanket
I would give up sovereignty of all the three regions;
the joys of all the eight accomplishments and all the nine treasures
I would put out of mind, grazing Nanda's cows.
Raskhān, when shall I see with these eyes
the forests, gardens and pools of Braj?
Though you make ten million golden palaces,
I would sacrifice them for those thorny groves.

22 This stanza has the Dwarka Kṛṣṇa reminiscing nostalgically about the Braj episode of his life.

22.3 *gobara ko gāro* : the floors and walls of village houses are constantly refurbished by a smooth plaster wash of mud mixed with cowdung, said to have purifying properties.

22.3 *jaṭata marakata haĩ* : *jaṭata* = ptc.adj. *jaṭita*, thus *haĩ* is superfluous (but for rhyme).

22.4 *maṁdara* : the reading from Bhāṭī's edition (1977:315); cf. Amīr Siṁha's *maṁdira*.

23.2 The glance is hard to pull away from Kṛṣṇa, to see whom it constantly flies. The image is a conventional one, in which the 'bow' of the arched eyebrows shoots the 'arrow' of a glance.

25.1 *lakuṭī aru kāmariyā* : the cowherd's equipment, identifying Kṛṣṇa Gopāl as the subject of the poem. Some commentators regard the nostalgic context as parallel to that of SR 22, with Kṛṣṇa as speaker.

25.1 *tihũ pura* : i.e. the 'three worlds' — earth, heaven and hell.

25.2 *āṭhahũ ... navo* : these are aggregatives [MSH *āṭhõ, navõ*].

बरवै

रहीम

बन्दौं बिघन बिनासन, ऋधि सिधि ईस ।
निर्मल बुद्धि प्रकासन, सिसु ससि सीस ॥ १ ।

सुमिरौं मन दृढ़ करिकै नंदकुमार ।
जो वृषभान-कुँवरि कै प्रान अधार ॥ २ ॥

भजहु चराचर नायक, सूरज देव ।
दीन जनन सुखदायक, तारन एव ॥ ३ ॥

ध्यावौं सोच बिमोचन, गिरिजा ईस ।
नागर भरन त्रिलोचन, सुरसरि सीस ॥ ४ ॥

ध्यावौं बिपद बिदारन, सुवन समीर ।
खल दानव बन जारन, प्रिय रघुबीर ॥ ५ ॥

पुन पुन बन्दौं गुरु के पद जलजात ।
जिहि प्रताप तैं मनके तिमिर बलात ॥ ६ ॥

बरसत मेघ चहूँ दिसि, मूसरा धार ।
सावन आवन कीजत नंदकुमार ॥ ७ ॥

अजौं न आये सुधि कै सखि घनश्याम ।
राख लिये कहुँ बसिकै काहू बाम ॥ ८ ॥

कबलौं रहिहै सजनी मन में धीर ।
सावन हूँ नहिं आवन कित बलबीर ॥ ९ ॥

घन घुमड़े चहुँ ओरन, चमकत बीज ।
पिय प्यारी मिलि झूलत, सावन तीज ॥ १० ॥

मनमोहन बिन देखे, दिन न सुहाय ।
गुन न भूलिहौं सजनी, तनक मिलाय ॥ ११ ॥

Barvai

Rahīm

1 I salute the destroyer of obstacles, lord of success and attainment,
imparter of pure intellect, child of the one whose head bears a moon.

2 With steadfast mind I rehearse the name of Nandakumār,
the foundation of life for Vṛṣabhānu's daughter.

3 Worship the lord of animate and inanimate, the sun god,
giver of pleasure to afflicted folk, a very saviour.

4 I meditate upon the deliverer from grief, Girijā's lord [Śiva],
maintainer of the skilful, three-eyed, having the Ganges on his head.

5 I meditate upon [Hanumān], the breaker of adversity, son of the wind,
destroyer of the grove of the wicked demon, and dear to Raghubīr.

6 Again and again I salute the lotus feet of my preceptor,
through whose brilliance the darkness of my mind is removed.

7 The clouds pour rain on all sides in unceasing torrent,
the month of Sāvan comes, O Nandakumār.

8 Still Ghanaśyām has not remembered us and come, friend;
some woman has settled somewhere and kept him.

9 How long will patience remain in my heart, my friend?
Even in Sāvan he does not come — where is Balbīr?

10 Clouds gather all around, lightning flashes:
lover and beloved swing together in Sāvan's Tīj festival.

11 A day without seeing Manmohan has no charm;
I shall not forget his qualities, friend — just bring us together!

1 The first stanza is the traditional encomium to Gaṇeś, who as the remover of obstacles is invoked at the outset of any new undertaking: see III.3.1. Gaṇeś is the son of Śiva, whose head is adorned with a crescent moon. The eulogy sets a pattern for 1-6, praising respectively Gaṇeś, Kṛṣṇa, Sūrya, Śiva, Hanumān, and the guru.

1 *bināsana...prakāsana*: 'destroyer', 'illuminator' — see I.5.11.

7 Following the opening eulogistic references, the main substance of the poem begins here. The advent of the rains signifies the end of the season when travel is possible, and thus the beginning of a period of *virah* when the absent lover can no longer be expected to return.

8.1 *ghanaśyāma*: Kṛṣṇa's epithet 'dark rain-cloud' is ironic in the context of his absence in Śrāvaṇ.

8.2 *sajanī*: a vocative (synonymous with the ubiquitous *sakhī*) which frequently recurs at this point in the line: cf. 9.1, 11.2, 12.2, 13.2, etc.

10.2 *sāvana tīja*: the swing festival celebrated on the third day of the dark half of the month of Śrāvaṇ.

झूमि झूमि चहुँ ओरन, बरसत मेह ।
त्यों त्यों पिय बिन सजनी, तरसत देह ॥ १२ ॥

डोलत त्रिबिध मरुतवा, सुखद सुढार ।
हरि बिन लागत सजनी, जिमि तरवार ॥ १३ ॥

कहियो पथिक सँदेसवा, गहिके पाय ।
मोहन तुम बिन तनिकहु रह्यौ न जाय ॥ १४ ॥

लगत असाढ़ कहत हो चलन किसोर ।
घन घुमड़े चहुँ ओरन, नाचत मोर ॥ १५ ॥

बिरह बढ़्यौ सखि अंगन, बढ़्यौ चवाव ।
कर्‌यो निठुर नँदनंदन कौन कुदाव ॥ १६ ॥

भज रे मन नँदनंदन, बिपति बिदार ।
गोपी जन मन रंजन, परम उदार ॥ १७ ॥

बिरह बिथा तें लखियत मरिबौं झूरि ।
जो नहिं मिलिहै मोहन, जीवन मूरि ॥ १८ ॥

इन बातन कछु होत न कहो हजार ।
सबही तैं हँसि बोलत नन्दकुमार ॥ १९ ॥

कहा छलत हो ऊधौ, दै परतीति ।
सपनेहू नहिं बिसरै, मोहनि मीति ॥ २० ॥

घेर रह्यौ दिन रतियाँ बिरह बलाय ।
मोहन की वह बतियाँ, ऊधौ हाय ॥ २१ ॥

ज्यों चौरासी लख में मानुष देह ।
त्योंही दुर्लभ जग में सहज सनेह ॥ २२ ॥

अति अद्‌भुत छबि सागर मोहन गात ।
देखत ही सखि बूढ़त दृग जलजात ॥ २३ ॥

12 Surging from all sides, the rain pours down:
so too without my lover, friend, my body pines.

13 A breeze of threefold nature roams, pleasant and lovely;
in Hari's absence, friend, it seems like a sword.

14 O wayfarer! Deliver this message, grasping his feet:
'Mohan, without you I cannot survive for a moment'.

15 You spoke of coming, Kiśor, at the beginning of Asāṛh;
[but now] clouds gather on all sides, the peacock dances.

16 The love-sickness in my limbs has grown, friend; slander has grown —
what cruel trick is this you have done, Nandanandan?

17 O my heart, adore Nandanandan, remover of distress,
delighter of the hearts of the cowherd girls, most bountiful.

18 A withering death from the agony of separation is in prospect
if I do not meet Mohan, the root of life.

19 Saying these things has no effect, though one may repeat them a thousand times;
Nandakumār talks laughingly with one and all.

20 What trickery are you trying, Uddhav, with your show of conviction?
Not even in my dreams can Mohan the lover be forgotten.

21 Day and night I am surrounded by the affliction of separation,
Alas, Uddhav, for those words that Kṛṣṇa spoke!

22 Like a human body amongst the eighty-four lakhs [of births],
this natural love is rare in the world.

23 Most wondrous is the ocean of beauty of Mohan's body;
immediately on seeing it, my friend, the lotuses of my eyes are immersed.

13.1 *tribidha* : 'threefold, triple', hence 'of three constituent qualities'; formulaic use of the adj. refers to the wind as being 'gentle, cool and fragrant'.

13.1 *marutavā* : *-vā* is a definite nominal suff. used in Eastern dialects such as Avadhī, but also borrowed in Braj; cf. 14.1 *sā̃desavā*, 25.1 *mitavā*.

14.2 *rahyau na jāya* : the impersonal passive expressing incapacity — cf. MSH *(mujhse) rahā nahī̃ jātā.*

16.1 *cavāva* : the 'condemnation' is the criticism of Kṛṣṇa for breaking his promise of a return to Braj.

17 The abrupt change of tone intends no irony, but is simply part of the rhetoric of *bhakti.* Cf. RB 32.

18.1 *maribaũ* : inf. as verbal noun, the subject of passive *lakhiyata* , lit. 'a dying is being seen'.

18.2 *jīvana mūri* : may be interpreted also as 'restorative herb', with a (metaphorical) medical sense.

20 In this and the following stanza, the gopis address the *advaitin* Uddhav, whose mission is to teach them to perceive Kṛṣṇa as omnipresent. Cf. SS 36-40, and see Index of Epithets.

22 84 lakhs is the traditional reckoning of births to be lived through in a cycle of *saṁsāra*; to gain a human birth represents a rare achievement, attained only with difficulty.

23 The 'lotus eyes' have a natural place in the 'ocean' of Kṛṣṇa's beauty; but the gopis' tears of course contribute to the sense of 'drowning'.

बिन देखें कल नाहिन, यह अखियाँन ।
पल पल कटत कलप सों, अहो सुजान ॥ २४ ॥

जब तें बिछुरे मितवा, कह कस चैन ।
रहत भरयौ हिय साँसन, आँसुन नैन ॥ २५ ॥

गये हेरि हरि सजनी, हँसि कछूक ।
तबते लगनि अगनि की उठत भबूक ॥ २६ ॥

होरी पूजत सजनी, जुर नर नारि ।
हरि बिन जानहु जिय में, दई दवारि ॥ २७ ॥

जब ते मोहन बिछुरे, कछु सुधि नाहिं ।
रहे प्रान परि पलकनि, दृग मग माहिं ॥ २८ ॥

जब तें बिछुरे मोहन, भूख न प्यास ।
बेरि बेरि बढ़ि आवत बड़े उसास ॥ २९ ॥

अंतरगत हिय बेधत, छेदत प्रान ।
विष सम परम सबन तें लोचन बान ॥ ३० ॥

उझकि उझकि चित दिन दिन हेरत द्वार ।
जब ते बिछुरे सजनी नन्दकुमार ॥ ३१ ॥

रे मन भज निस बासर श्री बलबीर ।
जो बिन जाँचे टारत जन की पीर ॥ ३२ ॥

सबै कहत हरि बिछुरे, उर धर धीर ।
बौरी बाँझ न जानै ब्यावर पीर ॥ ३३ ॥

लखि मोहन की बंसी, बंसी जान ।
लागत मधुर प्रथम पै बेधत प्रान ॥ ३४ ॥

भजि नरहरि नारायन, तजि बकवाद ।
प्रगटि खंब ते राख्यो जिन प्रहलाद ॥ ३५ ॥

24 Without seeing him there is no repose for these eyes;
each and every moment passes like an age, O friend.

25 Since the lover departed, say, how can there be peace?
My heart is ever filled with sighs, with tears my eyes.

26 Hari went away with a glance, my friend, smiling slightly;
since then the fire of attachment has been rising in flames.

27 Men and women worship the Holi fire together, my friend;
without Hari, it is as though a conflagration were lit in my heart.

28 Since Mohan left, I have lost my senses;
my life lies on my eyelids and my eyes upon the road.

29 Since Mohan left, I have neither hunger no thirst;
at every moment my mighty sighs expand.

30 They pierce my inner heart and impale my soul,
poison-like, supreme amongst all, these eye-arrows.

31 Constantly my mind stands on tiptoe, ever watching the door —
ever since Nandakumār left, my friend.

32 O my heart, night and day worship lord Balbīr
who removes people's pain without appraising them.

33 All say 'Be strong of heart!', now Hari's gone away —
a stupid barren woman knows not the pain of childbirth.

34 Seeing Mohan's flute, I thought it a kinsman;
it seems sweet at first, but it pierces the soul.

35 Leave off idle chatter and worship Narhari Nārāyaṇ,
who became manifest from a pillar and saved Prahlād.

24.2 *sujāna* : another vocative, parallel in usage to *sakhī, sajanī* etc.

25.2 An effective but relatively rare use of the *alaṅkāra* called *dīpaka* ('zeugma' — see BhBh 44 and note), a figure of speech in which a single phrase (here the verb phrase *rahata bharyau*) completes two distinct subjects (here *hiya* and *naina*). The construction of the *barvai* line is fully exploited here, the second clause (*ā̃suna naina*) being completely contained by the second short *pāda*. Cf. 28.2, another such figure, in which the second phrase *dṛga maga māhī̃* similarly occupies the second *pāda*.

27 Like the celebrations of Tīj (RB 10), the rituals of Holi performed by other loving couples serve only to deepen the suffering of the *virahiṇī*.

32 *bina jā̃ce* : an essential characteristic of divine grace, often stressed in *bhakti* verse, is that it is bestowed unconditionally and without appraisal of the recipient. Cf. SR 13.

34.1 *baṁsī...baṁsī* : a conventional play on the two senses of the word as 'flute' and 'kinsman' respectively. The gopi thinks the flute a kinsman because it too is a beloved of Kṛṣṇa, but later perceives it to be a rival for his attentions. Cf. SS 30-31, SR 11, etc.

रसिक अनन्य माल (श्री नरवाहनजी की परचई)

भगवत मुदित

श्री हरिवंश चरण शिर नाऊं । नरवाहन की कथा सुनाऊं ॥ १ ॥
श्री हरिवंश रसिक मणि रास । शरणागत की पुजवत आस ॥ २ ॥

नरवाहन भैगाऊं निवासी । वारपार में एक मवासी ॥ ३ ॥
जाकी आज्ञा कोउ न टारै । जो टारै तिहिं चढ़ि करि मारै ॥ ४ ॥

बस करि लियौ सकल ब्रज देश । तासौं डरपैं बड़े नरेश ॥ ५ ॥
पातशाह के वचननि टारे । मन आवै तौ दगरौ मारै ॥ ६ ॥

जो कोऊ यापै चढ़ि आवै । अमल न देई मार भजावै ॥ ७ ॥
कबहुंक श्री वृंदावन आयौ । श्री हितजू कौ दरशन पायौ ॥ ८ ॥

चरचा होत नवल अरु आप । नरवाहन सब सुन्यौ अलाप ॥ ९ ॥
दरशन तैं मति शुद्ध जु भई । श्री हितजू की पद रज लई ॥ १० ॥

बचन सुनत उपज्यौ निरवेद । पिछले कृत कौ मान्यौ खेद ॥ ११ ॥
कहन लग्यौ हों सरनहिं आयौ । अपुनौं सब विरतांत सुनायौ ॥ १२ ॥

अब प्रभु मोहि आपुनौं करौ । सिर कर धरौ कुमति मम हरौ ॥ १३ ॥
बिना कपट कौ बचन सुनायौ । दिक्षा दे तब हित अपनायौ ॥ १४ ॥

बाट मारिबौ तुरत छुड़ायौ । पूरण भाग उदै ह्वै आयौ ॥ १५ ॥
इष्ट धाम कौ भेद बतायौ । नरवाहन त्यों ही मन लायौ ॥ १६ ॥

सेवा करन लग्यो मन लाई । करत भावना नाहिं अघाई ॥ १७ ॥
आयो एक बड़ौ व्यौपारी । लादैं नाव सौंज बहु भारी ॥ १८ ॥

देहि जगात न सबसों अरै । तुपक जमूरन सौं बहु लरै ॥ १९ ॥
येहू मागन लगे जगात । वह मद अंध सुनैं क्यों बात ॥ २० ॥

Rasik-ananya-māl (Śrī Narvāhanjī kī parcaī)

Bhagvat Mudit

1 I bow my head to Śrī Harivaṁś and relate the story of Narvāhan;
2 Śrī Harivaṁś, a gem among votaries in the *rāsa* dance, fulfils the hopes of followers.

3 Narvāhan, a resident of Bhaigā̃v, was a potentate of far and wide
4 whose command none rejected: any who did so, he attacked and killed.

5 He subjugated all of the Braj country, great monarchs feared him;
6 he rejected the declarations of the emperor, and pillaged travellers at will.

7 If anyone attacked him, he would grant no quarter but beat them off.
8 At some time he came to holy Vrindaban, and had an audience with Hit Harivaṁś.

9 Discussion was going on between him and Navaldās, and Narvāhan heard all their talk;
10 when through *darśan* his mind was purified, he took the dust of the feet of Harivaṁś.

11 Hearing the words [of Harivaṁś] he felt remorse and regretted his past deeds;
12 he began, 'I have come for refuge' and related his whole story.

13 'Accept me now, lord, put your hand on my head and remove my perversity.'
14 He spoke without guile, and then Hit Harivaṁś initiated him and adopted him.

15 Immediately he gave up his banditry, and his fortune flourished in fullness;
16 [Harivaṁś] showed him the mystery of the beloved domain, and Narvāhan forthwith fixed his mind upon it.

17 He began to perform service there with full attention, never satiated in sentiment.
18 A grand merchant came that way, his ship heavily laden with costly goods.

19 Paying no levy he opposed everyone, fighting much with mortar and cannon.
20 He [Narvāhan] too began demanding the levy, but how would he listen, greed-blinded?

1 *śrī harivaṁśa* : Hit Harivaṁś, c. 1502-52, the *bhakta* whose devotion for Rādhā and for Kṛṣṇa as 'lover of Rādhā' (*rādhāvallabh*), as expressed in his Braj and Sanskrit poetry, is the theological basis of the Rādhāvallabh *sampradāy*. 'Hit' (*hita*) signifies 'divine love' in Rādhāvallabhī doctrine, and is often adopted by Rādhāvallabhīs as part of their name: cf. lines 8 and 14.

4 *kou na ṭārai* : the historical present tense ('none resists') has not been followed in the translation.

6 *dagarau mārai* : 'attacks [on] the road', i.e. robs travelling merchants etc. — cf. 15 *bāṭa māribau.*

9 *navala* : Navaldās, a devout disciple of Harivaṁś from Raibari. His biography elsewhere in the RAM describes his persecution by the Hindu general Hemu, an unsuccessful contender for the throne of Hindustan after the death of the emperor Humayun.

10 *pada raja laī* : 'took the foot-dust [to his forehead]', an act of submission and veneration.

16 *iṣṭa dhāma* : Vrindaban, the location of Rādhā and Kṛṣṇa's *lila* and of the temple of Rādhāvallabh.

17 *lāī/aghāī* : *caupāī* rhymes often require original short vowels to be lengthened — thus *lāī* is for abs. *lāi*, *aghāī* for abs. or present-subjunctive *aghāi*.

हौ सरावगी धर्म विरोधी । हरि भक्तनि सों लरचौ किरोधी ॥ २१ ॥
तुपक सात सै वाके संग । दुहुं दिसि लागे लरन अभंग ॥ २२ ॥

तीन लाख मुद्रा कौ वित्तनि । लाये लूटि निवेद्यौ भृत्तनि ॥ २३ ॥
वाकौ बाँधि गांव में लाये । तुपक हथ्यार सबै धरवाये ॥ २४ ॥

कोठे मधि सौंज सब रखाई । गरैं तौंक पग बेरी नाई ॥ २५ ॥
इतनौई धन अवर मगावै । तब यह ह्यां तें छूटनि पावै ॥ २६ ॥

वाकौं बंधे बहुत दिन बीते । धन न मगावै मारौं जीते ॥ २७ ॥
बैठि सभा में यह ठहराई । सो घर की चेरी सुनि पाई ॥ २८ ॥

सुघर तरुण सुन्दर वह साह । देखन कौं चेरियै उमाह ॥ २९ ॥
दासी के जिय दया जु आई । सुनी जु त्यौं ही ताहि सुनाई ॥ ३० ॥

काल्हि तोहि मारैंगे राव । जीवन कौ नहिं कोउ उपाव ॥ ३१ ॥
तुहीं बचाइ ज्याइ जिय मेरौ । जन्म जन्म गुन मानौं तेरौ ॥ ३२ ॥

एक मंत्र हौं तोहि बताऊं । तातैं तेरौ प्राण बचाऊं ॥ ३३ ॥
अपुनौ दर्व फेरि सब पैहै । आदर सौं अपनैं घर जैहै ॥ ३४ ॥

भाल तिलक धरि कंठीमाला । मो पै सुनि लै नाउं रसाला ॥ ३५ ॥
(श्री) राधावल्लभ श्री हरिवंश । सुमिरत कटैं पाप जम फंस ॥ ३६ ॥

पिछली राति पुकारि पुकारि । कहियौ ऐसी भांति सुधारि ॥ ३७ ॥
इतनी सुनत आपु चलि आवैं । बेरी काटि तोहि बतरावैं ॥ ३८ ॥

तब कहियौ मैं उनकौ सेवक । भव तरिवै कों वेई खेवक ॥ ३९ ॥
यह सिखाइ रावर मैं आई । लागी टहल न काहु जनाई ॥ ४० ॥

भई प्रतीति बात मन मानी । पिछली रैनि वही धुनि ठानी ॥ ४१ ॥
धुनि सुनि उठि नरवाहन आयौ । गुरुभाई लखि पद लपटायौ ॥ ४२ ॥

महादीन ह्वै वचन सुनाये । बार बार अपराध छिमाये ॥ ४३ ॥
जैनी जानि लूटि हम लीन्हौ । यह गुरु भेद न किनहूं चीन्हौ ॥ ४४ ॥

21 He was an irreligious Jain, and fought furiously with Hari's devotees;
22 seven hundred guns had he with him; on both sides continuous fighting began.

23 [Narvāhan's] servants looted and brought in offering three lakhs in coin, and property;
24 they bound [the Jain] and brought him to the village, confiscating all guns and weapons.

25 They put all the freight in a store, cast an iron ring round his neck and fetters on his feet;
26 as much wealth again they demanded, [only] then might he be released from this place.

27 Many days passed with him tied up; 'If he does not send for money I'll kill him outright' —
28 Sitting in his court [Narvāhan] so resolved, and this was overheard by a housemaid.

29 Comely, young and handsome was that merchant, and the maid thrilled to behold him.
30 When pity came to the maid's heart she told him straightaway what she had heard.

31 'The king will kill you tomorrow! There is no way for you to live!'.
32 'You rescue me and save my life — I shall acknowledge your favour over many births.'

33 'I shall tell you one mantra and through that I shall save your life;
34 you will get back all your property, and will go to your home with honour.

35 'Wear a *tilak* on your brow and a bead necklace, and hear from me the sweet name:
36 "Rādhāvallabh, Śrī Harivaṁś" — thinking on this, Yama's noose of sin is cut.

37 'Call it out constantly in the coming night — say it thus, in polished fashion;
38 hearing it, he [Narvāhan] himself will come and cut your fetters and converse with you.

39 'Then say to him, "I am his [Harivaṃś'] servant; he alone is the boatman to ferry us across the world".'
40 Having thus instructed him she returned to the palace and resumed her work without letting anyone know.

41 He trusted her and accepted what she had said, and that night perfomed that very cry;
42 hearing the cry Narvāhan rose and came, and seeing a fellow-disciple clung to his feet.

43 Very meekly he spoke to him and repeatedly sought forgiveness for his offence:
44 'Thinking you a Jain I robbed you, no-one knew this secret matter of your guru.

21 *hau* = *hatau* (MSH *thā*). See I.5.2.

25 *nāī* : unless somehow for *pahanāī*, which sense seems to require, perhaps for adv. *nāī̃*, 'like', i.e. 'put an iron ring round his neck, and fetters on his feet likewise' ?

26 *itanauī dhana avara magāvai* : i.e. Narvāhan or his men demanded a ransom equal to the amount already looted from the merchant.

26 *chūṭani pāvai* : 'may be able to leave' — cf. 28 *suni pāvai*, where *pā-* follows the verb stem (as is increasingly common in MSH) rather than the obl. inf.

27 *māraū̃ jīte* : lit. 'I shall kill him as he lives'.

30 *sunī...sunāī* : f. agreement is with an unstated *bāta*. Cf. 38 *itanī sunata*.

35 *bhāla tilaka...kaṁṭhīmālā* : the two emblems of sectarian allegiance or membership — a forehead mark of the sectarian pattern (each *sampradāy* has its own design: see A.W. Entwistle 1982) and a necklace of seeds which is first worn after initiation into the sect.

36 (*śrī*) *rādhāvallabha* : piety dictates the addition of a metrically superfluous honorific to the sectarian mantra, but the *caupaī* line should be of only 15 *mātrās* : see II.2.5.

37 *pichalī rāti* : the following night, the night coming. For the past/future usages of *āge*, *pīche* and related words see M. Shapiro 1986.

गुरु कौ नाम लेत मैं जानी । दासी नैं तब रीति बखानी ॥ ४५ ॥
मेटौ चूक जु मोते भई । कछु इच्छा प्रभु यों ही ठई ॥ ४६ ॥

भोर होत स्नान कराये । उज्ज्वल पट भूषण पहिराये ॥ ४७ ॥
सिगरौ दर्ब फेरि कर दियौ । रती न मन में लालच कियौ ॥ ४८ ॥

श्री गुरु कौ विश्वास सुहायौ । सेवा करि चरणनि सिर नायौ ॥ ४९ ॥
करि दंडवत बिदा जब कीने । पहुंचावन सेवक बहु दीने ॥ ५० ॥

देखि साह कैं भक्ति जु आई । सिष्य हौन कौं मति ललचाई ॥ ५१ ॥
जिनकौ छल सौं नाम उचारयौ । तानैं तन धन प्राण उबारयौ ॥ ५२ ॥

अब तौ उनकौ दरशन करौं । सर्वसु उनके आगे धरौं ॥ ५३ ॥
यों कहि बनिक वृंदावन आयौ । पसरि दंडवत करि सिर नायौ ॥ ५४ ॥

अपनी सकल विवस्था कही । तातें आइ शरण मैं गही ॥ ५५ ॥
मरत जियौ सो तुम्हरी दया । यह सब धन तुमहीं तैं भया ॥ ५६ ॥

साठ बासनी मुहरन भरी । लै हित जू के आगें धरी ॥ ५७ ॥
गरुनि कही धन तुमहीं राखौ । हरि हरिजन भजिकैं रस चाखौ ॥ ५८ ॥

श्रद्धा लखि कैं नाम सुनायौ । रीति धर्म सब कहि समुझायौ ॥ ५९ ॥
वह धन हाथन हूँ नहिं छियौ । यौं कहि बनिक बिदा कर दियौ ॥ ६० ॥

ता पाछै नरवाहन आयौ । पूछैं तैं विरतांत सुनायौ ॥ ६१ ॥
कृपा सु करकें निकट बुलायौ । गुरु भक्ता लखि हृदय लगायौ ॥ ६२ ॥

गुन समूह औगुन लघु चीन्हौ । हितजी ने फिरि सिच्छित कीन्हौ ॥ ६३ ॥
गुरु प्रसन्न ह्वै द्वै पद गाये । नरवाहन के भोग लगाये ॥ ६४ ॥

सब सेवक में नरवाहन मुख । गुरु धर्मी लखि होत परम सुख ॥ ६५ ॥

भगवत नरवाहन रसिक परम अनन्य उदार ।
कपटी मुख गुरु नाम सुनि अर्प्यो तन भंडार ॥ ६६ ॥

45 'On your taking the guru's name I understood, then the servant explained the affair.
46 'Wipe out the error that occurred through me; the will of the lord was so ordained'.

47 When dawn broke he had him bathe and dressed him in radiant clothes and jewels;
48 he gave back all his wealth, having not a jot of greed in his mind.

49 That trust in the guru pleased him, and he bowed his head in service to [the Jain's] feet;
50 prostrating himself and bidding him farewell, [Narvāhan] gave many servants to escort him

51 Seeing the devotion that came to him, the merchant longed to become a disciple:
52 'He whose name I fraudulently recited has freed my body, my wealth, my life.

53 'Now I should take his *darśan* and place my all before him'.
54 So saying the merchant came to Vrindaban, and falling in prostration, bowed his head.

55 He explained his whole state [to Harivaṁś] — 'Thus have I come and sought refuge.
56 Dying, I lived, and that is through your grace; all this wealth is through you alone'.

57 Taking sixty jars filled with gold coins he placed them before Hit jī;
58 the guru said, 'You keep the money; and taste the relish of worshipping Hari and his devotees'.

59 Seeing his faith [Harivaṁś] initiated him, and explained all about the [sectarian] ways.
60 'I did not even touch that money with my hands' — so saying the merchant took his leave.

61 After that, Narvāhan came; on being asked, he told the tale.
62 Through his grace [Harivaṁś] called him near, and recognising a loyal devotee, held him to his heart.

63 Seeing his virtues to be a mass and his faults to be minor, Hit jī again instructed him;
64 well pleased, the guru sang two hymns, putting Narvāhan's signature into them.

65 Narvāhan is foremost among all devotees; seeing a faithful disciple gives great joy.

66 Bhagvat, Narvāhan was a devotee supremely single-minded and noble;
even hearing the name spoken falsely he dedicated to it his body and his storehouse.

46 *meṭau cūka ju mote bhaī* : the impersonal construction (having *cūka* as subject) helps to mitigate the speaker's guilt — 'this mistake has occurred', rather than 'I have made this mistake'.

56 *bhayā* : the characteristically Khaṛī Bolī *-ā* termination here provides a convenient rhyme.

58 *guruni kahī* : this honorific pl. is treated like a numerical pl. — cf. VV 110 and note. (The alternative, with 'gurus' as a numerical pl., seems unlikely in this sectarian context where Hit Harivaṁś is the sole guru and is never mentioned alongside equals.)

58 *harijana* : there is of course absolutely no implication of the euphemistic sense 'untouchable' for which this term was to be appropriated by Gandhi in the twentieth century.

59 *nāma sunāyau* : i.e. gave him the sectarian mantra.

64 This line refers to two stanzas in the *Caurāsī-pad* (also known as *Hit-caurāsī*) of Hit Harivaṁś: stanzas 11 and 12 bear the *chāp* (or *bhog*) of Narvāhan, and it is presumed that they were 'dedicated' to him by their author. See R. Snell 1991a.

65 *saba sevaka mẽ* : obl.p. *-na* termination is dropped (for metrical convenience ?).

सतसई

बिहारीलाल

अपने अँग के जानि कै, जोबन-नृपति प्रबीन ।
स्तन मन नैन नितंब कौ बड़ौ इजाफा कीन ॥ १ ॥

जुवति जोन्ह मैं मिलि गई, नैंक न होति लखाइ ।
सौंधे कैं डोरैं लगी, अली चली सँग जाइ ॥ २ ॥

डारे ठोड़ी-गाड़ गहि नैन-बटोही मारि ।
चिलक-चौंध मैं रूप-ठग हाँसी-फाँसी डारि ॥ ३ ॥

पलनु पीक अंजनु अधर, धरे महावरु भाल ।
आजु मिले सु भली करी, भले बने हौ लाल ॥ ४ ॥

कुच-गिरि चढ़ि अति थकित ह्वै, चली डीठि मुँह-चाड़ ।
फिरि न टरी परियै रही, गिरी चिबुक की गाड़ ॥ ५ ॥

नहिं परागु नहिं मधुर मधु, नहिं विकासु इहिं काल ।
अली कली ही सौं बँध्यौ, आगैं कौन हवाल ॥ ६ ॥

कहा भयौ जौ बीछुरे मो मनु तो मन साथ ।
उड़ी जाउ कित हूँ तऊ गुड़ी उड़ाइक हाथ ॥ ७ ॥

छुटी न सिसुता की झलक, झलक्यौ जोबनु अंग ।
दीपति देह दुहून मिलि दिपति ताफता रंग ॥ ८ ॥

पत्रा हीं तिथि पाइयै, वा घर कैं चहुँ पास ।
नितप्रति पून्यौई रहै आनन ओप उजास ॥ ९ ॥

चलन न पावतु निगम मगु, जगु उपज्यौ अति त्रासु ।
कुच उतंग गिरिबर गह्यौ मैना मैनु मवासु ॥ १० ॥

Satsaī

Bihārīlāl

1 Knowing them to be his private members, skilful King Youth
gave a big rise to breasts, hearts, eyes and buttocks.

2 The young girl merged into the moonlight and could not be seen at all;
but following the threads of her fragrance, the sakhi-bee accompanied her.

3 In the dazzlement of her brilliance, the Thug of her beauty casts the noose of a smile,
striking and seizing my wayfarer-eyes, and casting them into her chin's hollow!

4 Betel-juice on your eyelids, kohl on your lips, lac placed on your brow:
You've done well in today's encounter — you are well got-up, Lāl!

5 Wearied after climbing her breast-mountains, my glance went on, desiring her mouth;
but couldn't move again, just lay there fallen into the cleft of her chin.

6 No pollen, no sweet nectar, no blossoming yet;
if the bee is caught up with the bud even, what will happen later [when it blooms]?

7 What matter if my heart lose the company of yours?
Wherever it may fly, still the kite is in its flyer's hand.

8 The sparkle of childhood has not yet gone, yet youth glows in her limbs;
with both together, the brilliance of taffeta shines in her body.

9 Only from the almanac can the date be found, all around that house:
it remains ever full-moon night in the brightness of her face's lustre.

10 One cannot tread the righteous path, great dread is born in the world:
that bandit Madan has taken the lofty peaks of her breasts as his fortress.

1 At the onset of maturity, Youth personified causes the advancement of its own attributes; the image rests on the ambiguity of 'members' (*aṁga*) as both 'faction in court' and 'limbs'.

2 The heroine's fair complexion hides her on her moonlit tryst; but her fragrance gives her away.

3 The *ṭhag* is a highwayman who garrottes travellers into whose party he has insinuated himself. The lover's wandering gaze is ensnared by the heroine's beauty and is left lying helpless in the dimple on her chin.

4 The betel-juice should be on the lips, the kohl on the eyes, the lac on the feet: their displacement is the result of love-making, as the couplet cryptically observes.

4.1 *dhare mahāvaru bhāla* : i.e. MSH *bhāl par mahāvar dhare (hue) haĩ.*

5.1 *thakita* : an adj. having the form of a Skt ptc. adj., but based on Braj *thak-* (< **sthakk-*).

6 According to a legend cited by Lallūlāl in his *Satsaī* commentary (G.A.Grierson 1896:4), this couplet was addressed by Bihārī to his patron Jai Singh, who was besotted with a young girl.

6.2 *havāla* : < Arabic *aḥwāl*, the 'broken plural' (one formed by a re-patterning of the radical letters of an Arabic word) of *ḥāl*, 'state, condition, situation'.

9.1 *tithi* : the date by the lunar calendar, which can usually be estimated by the moon's phase; but when the moon is itself outshone by the heroine's face, an almanac becomes necessary.

10.1 *nigama maga* : the path prescribed by the Vedas, now made impassable by Madan, god of love.

या अनुरागी चित्त की गति समुझै नहिं कोइ ।
ज्यौं ज्यौं बूड़ै स्याम रँग, त्यौं त्यौं उज्ञलु होइ ॥ ११ ॥

भौ यह ऐसोई समौ, जहाँ सुखद दुखु देत ।
चैत चाँद की चाँदनी डारति किए अचेत ॥ १२ ॥

कर समेट कच भुज उलटि, खएँ सीस पटु टारि ।
काकौ मनु बाँधै न यह जूरा बाँधनहारि ॥ १३ ॥

सोहत ओढ़ैं पीतु पटु स्याम सलौनैं गात ।
मनौ नीलमनि-सैल पर आतपु परचौ प्रभात ॥ १४ ॥

अजौं न आए सहज रँग, बिरह दूबरैं गात ।
अब हीं कहा चलाइयति ललन चलन की बात ॥ १५ ॥

जोन्ह नहीं यह तमु वहै किए जु जगत निकेतु ।
होत उदै ससि के भयौ मानहु ससहरि सेतु ॥ १६ ॥

जिन दिन देखे वे कुसुम, गई सु बीति बहार ।
अब अलि रही गुलाब मैं अपत कँटीली डार ॥ १७ ॥

मोहूँ दीजै मोषु, ज्यौं अनेक अधमनु दियौ ।
जौ बाँधैं ही तोषु, तौ बाँधौ अपनैं गुननु ॥ १८ ॥

चितु तरसतु मिलत न बनतु, बसि परोस कैं बास ।
छाती फाटी जाति सुनि टाटी-ओट उसास ॥ १९ ॥

मैं तपाइ त्रयताप सौं, राख्यौ हियौ हमामु ।
मति कबहुँक आएँ यहाँ पुलकि पसीजै स्यामु ॥ २० ॥

सुनत पथिक मुँह माह निसि चलति लुवैं उहिं गाम ।
बिनु बूझैं बिनु हीं कहैं, जियति बिचारी बाम ॥ २१ ॥

11 None can understand the state of this lovelorn heart;
the more it is steeped in Śyām's dark hue, the brighter it becomes!

12 Such a time has come when pleasurable things give pain;
the light of the Caitra moon strikes me, rendering me senseless.

13 Gathering her tresses with her hands, arms back, veil thrown back on shoulder —
whose heart would she not bind, she who binds her hair?

14 Wrapped round his dusky, lovely body the yellow sash shines
like sunshine fallen on a sapphire mountain at dawn.

15 A natural colour has not yet come to this body, emaciated by separation:
can talk of going, O lover, be coming already?

16 No moonlight, this — it is that darkness, which has made the world its home;
at the rising of the moon, it seems, it has turned white through fear.

17 The days in which you saw those blooms — that springtime has passed away;
and now all that is left of the rose, O bee, is the leafless, thorny bough.

18 Grant salvation to me too, as you have granted to many a wretch;
or if only binding appeals, bind me in the strands of your qualities.

19 My heart yearns, but no meeting is possible, dwelling in the neighbouring house;
my breast is burst apart as I hear her sighs through the bamboo screen.

20 Heating it with the 'three fires', I have kept my heart as a Turkish bath —
lest Śyām pass this way, feel a thrill, and melt a little.

21 Hearing from a traveller's mouth that in a January night, summer winds blow in that village, without asking, without his saying, [I know] the poor lady lives.

11 The conceit rests on the dual sense of *syāma* as both 'Kṛṣṇa' and 'dark', as contrasted with *ujjalu* 'bright, radiant, passionate'; and on *rāga* as both 'colour' and 'love, delight'.

12.1 *bhau* = *bhayau* (MSH *huā*).

13.1 *khaaī*: obl.sg. of *khavā* m. 'shoulder'.

15.2 Syntax: *calana kī bāta calāiyati*, 'talking of going is set in motion'.

16.2 *sasahari* : the conceit rests on the sense 'to be afraid', but seems also to involve a play with *sasihara* (< Skt. śaśidhara) 'moon'.

17.1 *gaī su bīti bahāra* : syntax *su bahāra bīti gaī.*

18.2 *jo bā̃dhaī hī toṣu* : 'if satisfaction is only through binding', i.e. 'if you are pleased only by keeping me tied [to you, to the world]'.

18.2 *gunanu* : a conventional play on the senses of 'qualities, attributes' and 'strands'. Cf. NS 17.

19.1 *milata na banatu* : 'meeting is not managed' [MSH *milte nahī̃ bantā*].

19.2 *chātī phāṭī jāti* : the alliteration is strengthened by the long vowels of an analytic passive (I.5.8b).

20.1 *trayatāpa* : the conventional trinity of afflictions — extrinsic (caused by the outer world), intrinsic (caused by disorders of the mind or body), and supernatural.

20.2 *pasīj-* the two senses 'become soft-hearted in compassion' and 'perspire' are complementary.

21.1 *luvaī*: p. of *lū* (f.), 'hot summer wind'. The unseasonal heatwave in the winter month of Māgh is caused by the sighings of the *virahiṇī*.

स्याम सुरति करि राधिका तकति तरनिजा तीरु ।
अँसुवनु करति तरौंस कौ खिनकु खरौंहौं नीरु ॥ २२ ॥

कन दैबौ सौंप्यौ ससुर, बहू थुरहथी जानि ।
रूप रहचटैं लगि लग्यौ माँगन सबु जगु आनि ॥ २३ ॥

भृकुटी मटकनि पीतपट चटक लटकती चाल ।
चलचख चितवनि चोरि चितु लियौ बिहारी लाल ॥ २४ ॥

संगति-दोषु लगै सबनु, कहे ति साँचे बैन ।
कुटिल बंक भ्रुव सँग भए कुटिल बंक-गति नैन ॥ २५ ॥

गहिली गरबु न कीजियै, समै सुहागहिं पाइ ।
जिय की जीवनि जेठ सो माह न छाँह सुहाइ ॥ २६ ॥

तीज परब सौतिनु सजे भूषन बसन सरीर ।
सबै मरगजे-मुँह करीं, इहीं मरगजैं चीर ॥ २७ ॥

भूषन भारु सँभारिहै क्यौं इहिं तन सुकुमार ।
सूधे पाइ न धर परैं, सोभा हीं कैं भार ॥ २८ ॥

छुटन न पैयतु छिनकु बसि, नेह नगर यह चाल ।
मारचौ फिरि फिरि मारियै, खूनी फिरै खुस्याल ॥ २९ ॥

डीठि न परतु समान दुति कनकु कनक सैं गात ।
भूषन कर करकस लगत, परसि पिछाने जात ॥ ३० ॥

रह न सकी सब जगत में, सिसिर सीत कैं त्रास ।
गरम भाजि गढ़वै भई, तिय कुच अचल मवास ॥ ३१ ॥

तिय कित कमनैती पढ़ी, बिनु जिहि भौंह-कमान ।
चलचित बेझैं चुकति नहिं बंक बिलोकनि बान ॥ ३२ ॥

22 Remembering Śyām, Rādhikā gazes at the Yamuna's bank;
and with her tears she makes the shore's water saltish for a moment.

23 Considering the lass meagre of hand, father-in-law entrusted her with alms-giving:
but stricken by desire for her beauty, all the world came and started begging.

24 The bending of his eyebrow! The splendour of his yellow sash! His wayward walk!
With nimble glances, Bihārīlāl has stolen my heart away.

25 'Detriment of association applies to all' — these words are spoken full true;
being with arched and raked brows, arch and rakish is the motion of the eyes.

26 Proud one! Do not boast, finding a temporary wedded bliss:
that shade which saves the soul in June has no appeal in January.

27 At the Tīj festival, the co-wives adorned their bodies with jewels and garments;
but with these crumpled clothes she has crumpled their faces, every one.

28 How will she bear the weight of her ornaments with this delicate frame?
Even with the burden of her beauty, her feet do not fall steadily on the ground.

29 This is the way of the city of love — once settled for a moment, you cannot leave;
the stricken one is struck wherever he turns, the assassin wanders at will.

30 Being of equal radiance, gold cannot be seen on her gold-like body;
the ornaments feel rough to the hand, identified by touch [alone].

31 For fear of winter's cold, it could not live in all the world;
warmth fled and became a ward in the mountain refuge of a lady's breasts.

32 Woman, where did you study archery? — with the stringless bow of your brow,
in striking the moving mind, the arrows of your crooked glances never miss.

22.1 *surati* : behind the sense 'memory' is commonly to be inferred the tatsama sense 'great [sexual] pleasure' (*su-rati*).

22.1 *taranijā tīra* : the bank of the Yamuna ('daughter of the sun'), the site of Kṛṣṇa's *līlā* with Rādhā.

22.2 Syntax: *taraũsa kau ...nīra* , 'the water of the riverbank'.

23 A miserly householder plans economies by appointing the delicate-handed young daughter-in-law as doler-out of alms; but the scheme backfires as her daintiness has an unforeseen effect.

25.1 *ti* : = *ati*, with initial vowel dropped through elision with preceding -*e*.

26.1 *samai suhāga* : 'a temporary state of marital happiness', while current favourite among the co-wives.

26.2 The subject of the line is *so...chā̃ha*.

27 Evidence of their rival's conquest (of their shared husband) deprive the co-wives of all the joy of the Tīj festival, at which married women celebrate their marital status.

28.2 *sūdhai pāi na dhara paraĩ* : an uneven gait is a giveaway sign of a night spent without sleep, and is thus part of the conventional description of the so-called *suratānta chavi*, 'post-coital splendour'.

29.2 *māryau* : ptc. used nominally, 'he who is struck'.

29.2 *phirai* : the diphthong *ai* must be read as two short vowels to accommodate the boundary between the 6-*mātrā* and 4-*mātrā gaṇas* of this quarter-verse (*khūnī phira/ -i khusyā̃/ -la*).

31.2 *garama* : for f. noun *garamī*.

32.2 *calacita bejhaĩ cukati nahĩ* : 'you do not miss the mark in striking the moving mind' — a secular conceit, but one having a spiritual aspect, suggesting the power of divine beauty to still the mind.

तौ लगु या मन-सदन मैं हरि आवैं किहिं बाट ।
बिकट जटे जौ लगु निपट खुटैं न कपट-कपाट ॥ ३३ ॥

नहिं नचाइ चितवति दृगनु, नहिं बोलति मुसकाइ ।
ज्यौं ज्यौं रूखी रुख करति, त्यौं त्यौं चितु चिकनाइ ॥ ३४ ॥

उड़ति गुड़ी लखि ललन की अँगना अँगना माँह ।
बौरी लौं दौरी फिरति, छुबति छबीली छाँह ॥ ३५ ॥

पतवारी-माला पकरि, और न कछू उपाउ ।
तरि संसार-पयोधि कौं, हरि नावैं करि नाउ ॥ ३६ ॥

क्यौं बसियै क्यौं निबहियै, नीति नेह पुर नाँहि ।
लगालगी लोइन करैं, नाहक मन बँधि जाँहि ॥ ३७ ॥

मानहु बिधि तन अच्छ छबि स्वच्छ राखिबैं काज ।
दृग-पग पोंछन कौं करे भूषन-पायंदाज ॥ ३८ ॥

देखौं जागत वैसियै साँकर लगी कपाट ।
कित ह्वै आवतु जातु भजि, को जानै किहिं बाट ॥ ३९ ॥

सुनि पग धुनि चितई इतै, न्हाति दियैं हीं पीठि ।
चकी झुकी सकुची डरी, हँसी लजी सी डीठि ॥ ४० ॥

को कहि सकै बड़ेनु सौं, लखैं बड़ीयौ भूल ।
दीने दई गुलाब की इन डारनु वे फूल ॥ ४१ ॥

इहीं आस अटक्यौ रहतु अलि गुलाब कैं मूल ।
ह्वैहैं फेरि बसंत ऋतु इन डारनु वे फूल ॥ ४२ ॥

कुटिल अलक छुटि परत मुख बढ़ि गौ इतौ उदोतु ।
बंक बकारी देत ज्यौं दामु रुपैया होतु ॥ ४३ ॥

33 By what route will Hari enter this heart-dwelling
unless the tightly-jammed door of falsehood opens?

34 Neither do you glance with dancing eyes, nor do you speak with a smile:
the more you adopt this harsh aspect, the more unctuous you make my mind!

35 Seeing the lover's flying kite, the lady in the courtyard
runs about like a lunatic, touching its lovely shadow.

36 Grasp the rosary as a rudder — there is no other way —
and cross the ocean of worldly existence, with Hari's name itself as a boat.

37 How can one dwell or survive in the city of love? There is no propriety there;
the eyes it is which ensnare, yet hearts are caught unjustly.

38 It is as though the Creator, in order to keep pure her body's bright lustre,
made her ornaments as a doormat for the wiping of the eye-feet.

39 I see on waking that just as before, the chain is fastened on the door:
which way does he come and go away again, who knows, by what path?

40 Hearing a footfall she looked hither while bathing, and with back still turned,
startled, she bent over, shrank back alarmed — and laughed with bashful glance.

41 Who dare say anything to the great, seeing even a major fault?
God it was who gave, to these rose stems, those [tender] blooms.

42 In this hope alone, the bee remains attached to the root of the rose-bush:
that in the spring will be once more, on these stems, those blooms.

43 With that winding curl falling freed across it, her face's splendour has increased
just as by writing a curved line a 'penny' becomes a 'shilling'.

33.2 Syntax: *jau lagu nipaṭa bikaṭa jaṭe kapaṭa-kapāṭa na khuṭaĩ*; cf. correlative *tau lagu* in previous line. *jau lagu... tau lagu,* lit. 'until...' is here translated more clearly as 'unless'.

34.2 *rūkhī* and *cikanāi* are double antonyms: 'dry/harsh' vs. 'making oily/loving'.

35.1 *āganā* is both 'woman' (Skt *aṅganā-*) and 'courtyard' (Skt *aṅgana-*).

37 The eyes are the criminals, loitering with intent, while innocent hearts are the ones who get caught. (Cf. 29.) The word order stresses the subject, *loina* — 'it is the eyes which do the ensnaring'; cf. 41.2 *dīne daī* 'God it was who gave...'.

38 The ornaments are inferior to the natural beauty of the body they are meant to beautify; cf. 30,73.

39.1 *jāgata*: 'on waking', implying 'after a dream (of love-making)'.

39.2 *hvai*: the 'via' sense of MSH *(se) hokar*.

41.1 *sakai*: the diphthong *ai* is to be scanned as two short syllables.

41.1 *baṛenu*: obl.pl. from *baṛau.*

43 In Indian currency, a curved line marks off the rupee from the coin of smaller value, just as in British pre-metric currency, '3/6d' stood for 'three shillings and sixpence'. In Bihārī's time the rupee was sub-divided into (40?) *dām*, such that the amount 'twelve rupees and twenty *dām*' would be written '१२)२०'. (This would represent 'twelve rupees and 20 *paise*' in decimal currency.) In the same way the dangling curl on the heroine's face revalues her beauty.

43.1 *gau* = *gayau.*

बाढ़तु तो उर उरज भरु, भरि तरुनई बिकास ।
बोझनु सौतिनु कैं हियैं आवति रूँधि उसास ॥ ४४ ॥

अरी खरी सटपट परी, बिधु आधैं मग हेरि ।
संग लगैं मधुपनु लई भागनु गली अँधेरि ॥ ४५ ॥

इक भीजैं चहलैं परैं, बूड़ैं बहैं हजार ।
किते न औगुन जग करैं, बै-नै चढ़ती बार ॥ ४६ ॥

दीप उजेरैं हू पतिहिं हरत बसनु रति काज ।
रही लपटि छबि की छटनु, नैंकौ छुटी न लाज ॥ ४७॥

लखि दौरत पिय कर-कटकु बास छुड़ावन काज ।
बरुनी-वन गाढ़ैं दृगनु रही गुढ़ौ करि लाज ॥ ४८ ॥

सकुचि सुरत आरंभ हीं, बिछुरी लाज लजाइ ।
ढरकि ढार ढुरि ढिग भई ढीठि ढिठाई आइ ॥ ४९ ॥

नाचि अचानक हीं उठे बिनु पावस बन मोर ।
जानति हौं नंदित करी यह दिसि नंदकिसोर ॥ ५० ॥

रही लटू ह्वै लाल हौं, लखि वह बाल अनूप ।
कितौ मिठास दयौ दई, इतैं सलोनैं रूप ॥ ५१ ॥

दिसि दिसि कुसुमित देखियत उपबन बिपिन समाज ।
मनहुँ बियोगिनु कौं कियौ सर पंजर रितुराज ॥ ५२ ॥

नाहिंन ए पावक प्रबल लुवैं चलैं चहुँ पास ।
मानहु बिरह बसंत कैं ग्रीषम लेत उसास ॥ ५३ ॥

कहा कुसुम कह कौमुदी, कितक आरसी जोति ।
जाकी उजराई लखैं आँखि ऊजरी होति ॥ ५४ ॥

44 The weight of the breasts on your bosom grows, filled with youth's blooming;
with those burdens on their hearts, the co-wives can barely breathe.

45 Friend, panic really struck when, halfway [to the tryst], I saw the moon;
but the bees accompanying me made the lane, luckily, dark!

46 One is drenched, [or] falls in the mire; a thousand are drowned and washed away:
how many misdeeds the rising river of age commits in the world!

47 Even in the lamplight, at her husband's removing of her clothes for lovemaking,
she remains clad in the lustre of beauty, modesty not compromised at all.

48 Seeing the army of her lover's hands running to strip her of cover,
modesty made her eyes a refuge, and remained in the dense thicket of her lashes.

49 Abashed at the very outset of lovemaking, shame felt shy and took its leave;
slipping slyly and smoothly closer, drawing close, bold boldness came.

50 Peacocks in the wood suddenly broke into a dance, out of season;
and thus I know, Nandkiśor has gladdened this region.

51 I am all in a whirl, Lāl, seeing that peerless girl;
how much sweetness has God given her, and in such savoury form!

52 All around, groups of woods and groves are seen blossoming,
as though spring, king of seasons, had made an arrow-cage for separated lovers.

53 These are not the fire-fierce winds blowing all around:
it seems they are the sighs of summer in the pain of spring's parting.

54 What is a flower, what the moonlight; how lustrous is a looking-glass?
When one sees *her* brilliance, the eye brightens.

44 The co-wives (*sauti*) are oppressed by the appearance of budding maturity in the body of their rival, the new young bride.

45 A heroine going to a clandestine tryst is saved from discovery in the waxing moonlight by a black-out of bees swarming to her fragrance: a variation of the conceit in 2.

45.2 *bhāganu* : obl.pl. of *bhāga* '(good) fortune', used adverbially — 'fortunately'.

46.2 *kite na auguna...karaī* : the negative is rhetorical, 'how many misdeeds does the river of age not do?'.

46.2 *caṛhatī bāra* : 'at the time of rising'.

48.2 Syntax: *lāja, dṛganu guṛhau kari, gāṛhaī barunī-vana [mẽ] rahī.*

49.2 *ḍhīṭhi* = *ḍhīṭha* (a well-attested variant in this line).

50.1 *binu pāvasa* : 'without the rainy season' (when peacocks usually perform their courting display).

51.1 *rahī* : f. gender defines the context — the sakhi speaks to the hero of the heroine's beauty.

51.2 *salonaī* : the literal sense (< Skt *sa-lavaṇa* , 'salty, tasty') is essential to the conceit. Cf. MSH (< Pers.) *namkīn*, 'salty, savoury, tasty, beautiful, racy'.

52.2 *sara paṁjara* : an 'iron maiden' or cage fitted with inward-pointing spikes. Here the blossoming of spring, reviving memories of past pleasures, becomes a torture-chamber for separated lovers.

कारे बरन डरावने कत आवत इहिं गेह ।
कैवा लखी सखी लखैं लगै थरथरी देह ॥ ५५ ॥

छ्वै छिगुनी पहुँचौ गिलत, अति दीनता दिखाइ ।
बलि बावन कौ ब्यौंतु सुनि, को बलि तुम्हैं पत्याइ ॥ ५६ ॥

छिप्यौ छबीलौ मुँहु लसै नीलै अंचर चीर ।
मनौ कलानिधि झलमलै कालिंदी कैं नीर ॥ ५७ ॥

मैं लखि नारी ज्ञानु करि राख्यौ निरधारु यह ।
वहई रोग निदानु, वहै बैदु औषधि वहै ॥ ५८ ॥

छुटे छुटावत जगत तैं सटकारे सुकुमार ।
मनु बाँधत बेनी बँधे नील छबीले बार ॥ ५९ ॥

चित पितमारक जोगु गनि भयौ भयैं सुत सोगु ।
फिरि हुलस्यौ जिय जोइसी, समुझै जारज जोगु ॥ ६०॥

चमचमात चंचल नयन, बिच घूँघट पट झीन ।
मानहुँ सुरसरिता बिमल जल उछरत जुग मीन ॥ ६१ ॥

डिगत पानि डिगुलात गिरि, लखि सब ब्रज बेहाल ।
कंपि किसोरी दरसि कै, खरैं लजाने लाल ॥ ६२ ॥

कीनैं हूँ कोरिक जतन अब कहि काढ़ै कौनु ।
भो मन मोहन रूपु मिलि पानी मैं कौ लौनु ॥ ६३ ॥

कर लै चूमि चढ़ाइ सिर उर लगाइ भुज भेटि ।
लहि पाती पिय की लखति बाँचति धरति समेटि ॥ ६४॥

चाह भरीं अति रस भरीं बिरह भरीं सब बात ।
कोरि सँदेसे दुहुनु के चले पौरि लौं जात ॥ ६५ ॥

55 Why does the dark-hued terrifying one come to this house?
Often I have seen, friend, that seeing him brings a trembling to your body.

56 Touching the little finger, you swallow the wrist — pretending such humility!
After hearing the story of Bali and the dwarf, who, pray, would trust you?

57 Hidden, her lovely face shines through the blue border of her veil
as though the moon were twinkling in the waters of the Yamuna.

58 After examining, with a knowledge of woman's vein, I diagnose with certainty:
he is the cause of the disease, *he* the physician, *he* the healing herb.

59 Free, your silken tresses free me from this world;
tied in a braid, your lustrous black hair ties up my heart.

60 A son being born, the astrologer was pained to read a horoscope of patricide;
but then, delight in his heart, he cast a bastard birth.

61 Her playful eyes flash through the fine cloth of her veil
like a pair of fishes leaping in the pure waters of the Ganges.

62 Shaking the mountain with shaking hand, and seeing all Braj afraid,
trembling as he viewed the maiden, thoroughly ashamed was Lāl!

63 Say now, who could extract it, even by ten million efforts? —
My mind has become blended with Mohan's beauty as salt in water.

64 She takes it in her hand, kisses it, touches it to her head, hugs it in her arm;
receiving her lover's letter she looks at it, reads it, folds it, stores it away.

65 Filled with longing, brimful with love, filled with love's pain all their talk:
millions of messages flew between them as they walked to the door.

55.1 *kāre barana* : the dark stranger is Kṛṣṇa; and the trembling is from sentiments other than fear.

56 The myth of Bali and the dwarf (see 'Bali' in the Index of Epithets) teaches that conceding an initial modest demand may open the door to unlooked-for implications later; here, the reference advises caution in dealing with an encroaching suitor, whose modest initial advance — touching the heroine's wrist — may conceal a larger ambition.

58.1 *nārī jñānu* : a pun, nearly accommodated in translation, on *nārī* 'woman' vs. *nārī/nāṛī* 'vein, artery'.

60.1 The syntax, which allows exceptional economy of narrative, is: *bhayaĩ suta, pitamāraka jogu gani, cita [mẽ] sogu bhayau.*

61.2 The point of the comparison is that the Ganges is regarded as being fair in colour; cf. the Yamuna's 'blueness' implicit in 57, and the note to 75.

62 A decadent variation on the 'lifting of Govardhan hill' motif: the sight of Rādhā makes Kṛṣṇa tremble, and he nearly drops the hill on the Braj people.

63.1 *kīnaĩ hū̃* : 'even on doing'.

63.2 *mohana rūpu* : as typically, *mohana* can be read either as a name of Kṛṣṇa or as the adj. 'charming'.

63.2 *pānī maĩ kau launu* : the double ppn. gives the sense 'the salt which is in water' [MSH *pānī mẽ kā lavaṇ* ; cf. MSH phrases of the type *mez par kī kitāb* 'the book [which is] on the table', etc.]. (The 'saline' image is defective: salt is easily separated from water by distillation!)

64.1 *caṛhāi sira* : touching to the forehead an object (such as a book or anything containing writing) indicates reverence to it.

करौ कुबत जगु कुटिलता तजौं न दीनदयाल ।
दुखी होहुगे सरल हिय बसत त्रिभंगी लाल ॥ ६६ ॥

दूरचौ खरे समीप कौ लेत मानि मन मोदु ।
होत दुहुनु के दृगनु हीं बतरसु हँसी बिनोदु ॥ ६७ ॥

नीठि नीठि उठि बैठि हूँ प्यौ प्यारी परभात ।
दोऊ नींद भरैं खरैं गरैं लागि गिरि जात ॥ ६८ ॥

यौं दलमलियतु निरदई दई कुसुम सौ गातु ॥
करु धरि देखौ धरधरा उर कौ अजौं न जातु ॥ ६९ ॥

पलनु प्रगटि बरुनीनु बढ़ि, नहिं कपोल ठहरात ।
अँसुवा परि छतिया छिनकु छनछनाइ छिपि जात ॥ ७० ॥

कोरि जतन कोऊ करौ, तन की तपनि न जाइ ।
जौ लौं भीजे चीर लौं रहै न प्यौ लपटाइ ॥ ७१ ॥

मिलि परछाँहीं जोन्ह सौं रहे दुहुन के गात ।
हरि राधा इक संग हीं चले गली महिं जात ॥ ७२ ॥

अंग अंग प्रतिबिंब परि दरपन सैं सब गात ।
दुहरे तिहरे चौहरे भूषन जाने जात ॥ ७३ ॥

डीठि-बरत बाँधी अटनु, चढ़ि धावत न डरात ।
इतहिं उतहिं चित दुहुनु के नट लौं आवत जात ॥ ७४ ॥

तजि तीरथ हरि राधिका तन दुति करि अनुरागु ।
जिहिं ब्रज केलि निकुंज मग, पग पग होत प्रयागु ॥ ७५ ॥

तौ बलियै भलियै बनी, नागर नंदकिसोर ।
जौ तुम नीकैं कै लख्यौ मो करनी की ओर ॥ ७६ ॥

66 Though the world reprove, I shall not give up my rakishness, Dīndayāl:
you'd be discomforted, dwelling in a straightened heart, O Lāl of the three curves.

67 Standing far apart, in their hearts they enjoy [a feeling of] being close:
in the very eyes of both is the mirth and merriment of sweet talk.

68 Somehow managing to sit up, lover and beloved at dawn
both quite overcome with sleep, embrace — and fall back again.

69 It is so crushed, merciless one — God! — her flower-like body;
place your hand on her and see, still the throbbing of her heart does not leave.

70 Born from her eyelids, passing her lashes — nor do her cheeks stop them —
the tears fall onto her breast, sizzle for a moment, and are gone.

71 Though one make scores of efforts, the burning of her body will not go
until her lover clings to her like a drenched garment.

72 The bodies of the two are merged with shadow and with moonlight [respectively]:
Hari and Rādhā walk together, going along the lane.

73 Reflections of all her limbs fall in the mirror of her whole body;
twofold, threefold, fourfold her jewels seem to be.

74 They mount a tightrope of glances tied between the rooftops and fear not to run:
to and fro the hearts of the two, like acrobats, come and go.

75 Leave pilgrimage places, and have love for the bodily splendour of Hari and Rādhikā,
through whose Braj sports every step along the arbour path becomes a Prayāg.

76 Well, skilful Nandkiśor, it is well done I swear,
if you look kindly toward my deed.

66 The couplet plays on the literal and metaphorical senses of *kuṭilatā*, 'crookedness, perversity', having both the literal sense picked up by *tribhaṁgī* ('thrice bent', describing Kṛṣṇa in his fluting pose with jauntily bent neck, waist and knee) and the metaphorical image of the unconventional *bhakta*, for whom the rules of normative behaviour have no meaning.

70.2 *chipa jāta* : the sense of 'hiding' is subsidiary to the alliterative sequence of *ch* sounds which suggest the spluttering of tears on the *virahiṇī's* burning breast.

71 The image of diaphanously clinging wet clothes (revealing more than they conceal) is as striking to Bihārī as it is to the makers of modern Hindi films, for whom this continues to be a stock image.

71.2 *jau laū ...cīra laū* : the ppn. is used in two distinct senses, 'until' and 'like' respectively.

72 Dark Kṛṣṇa is invisible in the shadows: and fair Rādhā in the moonlight.

73 The heroine's body is more lustrous than the jewels which are supposed to lend it lustre.

75 The couplet subsumes the traditional places of pilgrimage — including even Prayāg, the greatest *tīrtha* — under the groves of Rādhā and Kṛṣṇa's sport in Braj, thereby implicitly subsuming *smārta* Hinduism under *bhakti*. Ratnākar's typically creative commentary suggests that the fair and dark bodies of Rādhā and Kṛṣṇa respectively represent the Ganges and Yamuna whose confluence at Prayāg makes it the *tīrtharāja* or 'king of pilgrimage places', the mythical third river, Sarasvati, being represented by the devotee's *anurāga*.

भाषा-भूषण

जसवंत सिंह

बिघनहरन तुम हौ सदा, गनपति होहु सहाइ ।
बिनती कर जोरें करौं, दीजै ग्रंथ बनाइ ॥ १ ॥

जिहिं कीनो परपंच सब अपनी इच्छा पाइ ।
ताकों हौं बंदन करौं, हाथ जोरि सिर नाइ ॥ २ ॥

करुना करि पोसत सदा सकल सृष्टि के प्रान ।
ऐसे ईस्वर को हिये रहौ रैन दिन ध्यान ॥ ३ ॥

मेरे मन में तुम बसौ, ऐसी क्यों कहि जाइ ।
तातें यह मन आप सों लीजै क्यों न लगाइ ॥ ४ ॥

रागी मन मिलि स्याम सों भयो न गहिरो लाल ।
यह अचरज उज्जल भयो, तज्यो मैल तिहि काल ॥ ५ ॥

* * *

इहि बिधि सब समता मिलै, उपमा सोई जानि ।
ससि सो उज्जल तिय बदन, पल्लव से मृदु पानि ॥ ६ ॥

बाचक धर्म ऽरु बर्ननिय, है चौथो उपमान ।
इक बिन द्वै बिन तीनि बिन, लुप्तोपमा प्रमान ॥ ७ ॥

बिजुरी सी पंकज-मुखी, कनकलता तिय लेखि ।
बनिता रस सिंगार की कारन-मूरति पेखि ॥ ८ ॥

उपमे ही उपमान जब कहत अनन्वय ताहि ।
तेरे मुख की जोर कौं तेरो ही मुख आहि ॥ ९ ॥

उपमा लागे परसपर, सो उपमा-उपमेय ।
खंजन हैं तुव नैन से, तुव दृग खंजन-सेय ॥ १० ॥

Bhāṣā-bhūṣaṇ

Jasvant Siṁh

1 You are ever the remover of obstacles — Gaṇapati, be my help;
with folded hands I pray to you: complete this book.

2 He who made all this visible world through his own will [alone];
him I salute, with hands folded and head bowed.

3 Compassionately he ever nourishes the life-breath of all creation;
may contemplation of such a lord remain in my heart night and day.

4 'You dwell in my heart' — why should such a thing be said?
Then why not embrace this soul to yourself?

5 When the impassioned mind unites with Śyām, it is not more deeply infused;
a wonder, this — it has become pure, and immediately has lost its uncleanness.

* * *

6 In this way when all equivalence is present, know this to be a 'simile':
"bright as the moon is the woman's face, soft as blossom her hands".

7 'Signifier', 'property', 'subject described', fourth is 'object of comparison' —
lacking one, two or three [of these], an 'incomplete simile' is attested:

8 "The lotus-faced one is like lightning"; "behold, the woman is a jasmine";
"lo, the lady is the causal image of the erotic sentiment".

9 When the subject itself is the object, it is called a 'simile without connexion':
"as a match for your face there is only your face".

10 If a simile applies reciprocally, it is a 'reciprocal comparison':
"the wagtails are like your eyes, and your eyes are like wagtails".

[NB: double quotation marks (" ") in the translation indicate an example of a particular figure of speech.]

3.2 Syntax: *aise īsvara ko dhyāna*, 'contemplation of such a lord' (*ko* being genitive).

4.2 *aisī kyõ kahi jāi* : f. agreement is with *bāta* (understood).

5 The couplet rests on untranslatable word-plays: *rāgī*, both 'impassioned' and 'red'; *syāma*, both 'Kṛṣṇa' and 'dark'; *lāla*, both 'dear Kṛṣṇa' and 'red'; *ujjala*, both 'pure' and 'white'; finally *maila* ('pollution, discolourant') connects the two sets of meanings. The conceit has a close parallel in BS 11; and the concept of the sanctification of passion is reflected in VV 191-194.

6.1 *ihi bidhi* : this may refer to a previous couplet, absent here but given by Grierson, defining the simile.

7.1 [a] *bācaka* : the word implying comparison, e.g. (in 6.2) *so* ; [b] *dharma*, the shared quality, e.g. 'brightness'; [c] *barnaniya*, the subject of comparison, or *upameya*, e.g. 'the woman's face' [d] *upamāna*, the object of comparison, e.g. 'the moon'. (In what follows, the words 'subject' and 'object' are to be understood in these technical senses.)

8 The three examples of 'incomplete similes' lack [b], [a] [b], and [a] [b] [d] respectively.

8.2 The implicit comparison is indicated by Grierson's translation: 'Lo, the lady (is) [fair] [as] [love itself], (for she) is the causal image of the erotic sentiment'. Alternatively, the moon may be meant.

9.1 *kahata* : the impersonal usage familiar from MSH, e.g. *ise kyā kahte haĩ?* 'What is this called?'.

10.2 *seya* : apparently a forced rhyme-form for *se*.

सो प्रतीप उपमेय कों कीजै जब उपमान ।
लोयन से अंबुज बने, मुख सो चंद बखान ॥ ११ ॥

उपमे को उपमान तें आदर जबै न होइ ।
गरब करत मुख को कहा, चंदहि नीकें जोइ ॥ १२ ॥

अन-आदर उपमेय तें जब पावै उपमान ।
तीछन नैनकटाक्ष तें मंद काम के बान ॥ १३ ॥

उपमे कों उपमान जब समता लायक नाहिं ।
अति उज्जल दृग मीन से, कहे कौन पै जाहिं ॥ १४ ॥

ब्यर्थ होइ उपमान जब बर्ननीय लखि सार ।
दृग आगें मृग कछु न ये पंच प्रतीप प्रकार ॥ १५ ॥

है रूपक द्वै भाँति को, मिलि तद्रूप अभेद ।
अधिक न्यून सम दुहुँन के, तीनि तीनि ये भेद ॥ १६ ॥

मुखससि वा ससि तें अधिक उदित जोति दिन राति ।
सागर तें उपजी न यह कमला अपर सुहाति ॥ १७ ॥

नैन कमल ये ऐन हैं, और कमल किहिं काम ।
गवन करत नीकी लगति, कनकलता यह बाम ॥ १८ ॥

अति सोभित बिद्रुम अधर, नहिं समुद्र उतपन्न ।
तुव मुख पंकज बिमल अति सरस सुबास प्रसन्न ॥ १९ ॥

करै क्रिया उपमान ह्वै, बर्ननीय परिनाम ।
लोचनकंज बिसाल तें देखत देखौ बाम ॥ २० ॥

सो उल्लेख जु एक कों बहु समझैं बहु रीति ।
अर्थिनि सुरतरु तिय मदन, अरि कौं काल प्रतीति ॥ २१ ॥

11 It is an 'inverse simile' when the object is made into the subject:
"the lotuses look lovely like your eyes"; the moon is described as "like your face".

12 [A second type is] when the subject receives no honour by [comparison with] the object: "Are you proud of your face? Look well at the moon!".

13 [Thirdly] when the object is slighted by the subject:
"compared with the piercing glances of her eyes, blunt are Kāmdev's arrows".

14 [Fourthly] when the object is not worthy of equivalence to the subject:
"Who would compare her utterly bright eyes to the fish?".

15 [And finally] when the object is useless, seeing the excellence of the subject:
"before her eyes, the deer['s] are nothing" — these are the five kinds of 'converse simile'.

16 Metaphor is of two kinds; together, [these are] 'equivalent' and 'identical';
'superior', 'inferior', 'equal' — these are the three varieties of each.

17 "Her moon-face is superior to *that* moon, shining in brilliance day and night";
"she was not born of the ocean, but is a different resplendent Lakṣmī".

18 "These eyes are lotuses indeed — what need is there of other lotuses?";
"This lady is a jasmine who looks nice when moving".

19 "Her coral lips are most resplendent, but were not born of the ocean";
"your lotus face is pure, so sweet, fragrant and joyful".

20 When a subject acts after becoming the object, it is a 'transference':
"look at the lady, she looks with those wide lotus-eyes!".

21 That is a 'representation', when various people perceive a thing in varied ways:
"to supplicants, he seems a wishing-tree; to women, Kāmdev; to an enemy, death".

11 Sub-categories of the 'inverse simile' are described in couplets 12-15.

14 *ujjala* : the variant reading *uttama* seems more apposite, since the 'fish' simile alludes primarily to the eyes' tapered shape and nimble movement, rather than their brightness. Thus Grierson (reading *uttama*): 'Who would compare to the (silvery darting) fish, her perfect eyes (floating in tears)'.

15.2 Syntax and metre do not coincide: *dṛga āgẽ mṛga kachu na, ye pañca pratīpa prakāra.*

16.2 *tīni tīni* : repetition indicates distribution — three varieties in each type.

17.1 An 'equivalent' (*tadrūpa*) metaphor of the 'greater' category.

17.2 An 'equivalent' metaphor of the 'lesser' category: the heroine shares Lakṣmī's beauty, but not her marine origin. (Lakṣmī 'sprang, like Aphrodite, from the froth of the ocean, in full beauty with a lotus in her hand, when it was churned by the gods and the Asuras' — Dowson 1982:176).

18.1 An 'equivalent' metaphor of the 'exactly equal' variety; *aina* is both 'indeed' and 'eyes'.

18.2 An 'identical' metaphor of the 'superior' variety — the heroine is not just an ordinary jasmine but a walking one (other senses of *gavana/gamana* apart). (The lady *is* a jasmine; whereas the 'eyes' in the previous line were merely equivalent in function to their parallel, the lotus.)

19.1 An 'identical' metaphor of the 'inferior' variety.

19.2 An 'identical' metaphor of the 'exactly equal' variety.

बहु बिधि बरनें एक कों बहु गुन सो उल्लेख ।
तूँ रन अरजुन तेज रबि, सुरगुरु बचन बिसेष ॥ २२ ॥

सुमिरन भ्रम संदेह ये लक्षन नाम प्रकास ।
सुधि आवति वा बदन की, देखें सुधानिवास ॥ २३ ॥

बदन सुधानिधि जानि ये तुव सँग फिरैं चकोर ।
बदन किधौं यह सीतकर, किधौं कमल भए भोर ॥ २४ ॥

धर्म दुरें आरोप तें, सुद्ध-अपन्हुति जानि ।
उर पर नाहिं उरोज ये कनकलता फल मानि ॥ २५ ॥

बस्तु दुरावै जुक्ति सों, हेत-अपन्हुति होइ ।
तीव्र चंद नहिं रैन रबि, बड़वानल ही जोइ ॥ २६ ॥

पर्जस्त जु गुन एक के, और बिषै आरोप ।
होइ सुधाधर नाहिं यह बदन सुधाधर ओप ॥ २७ ॥

भ्रांत-अपन्हुति बचन सों भ्रम जब पर को जोइ ।
ताप कंप है जर नहीं, ना सखि मदन सताइ ॥ २८ ॥

छेकापन्हुति जुक्ति करि पर सों बात दुराइ ।
करत अधर छत पिय नहीं, सखी सीतरितु बाइ ॥ २९ ॥

कैतवपन्हुति एक कों मिस करि बरनन आन ।
तीछन तीय कटाक्ष मिस, बरषत मन्मथ बान ॥ ३० ॥

उत्प्रेक्षा संभावना, बस्तु हेतु फल लेखि ।
नैन मनो अरबिंद हैं, सरस बिसाल बिसेखि ॥ ३१ ॥

मनो चली आँगन कठिन, तातें राते पाइ ।
तुव पद समता कौं कमल जल सेवत इक भाइ ॥ ३२ ॥

22 When one describes one thing in many ways because of its various qualities, that [too] is a 'representation': "in combat you are an Arjuna, in brilliance the sun, and a Bṛhaspati in the distinction of your speech".

23 'Recollection', 'mistake' and 'doubt' — these attributes are evident in their names: "reminiscence of that face comes when I see the nectarous moon".

24 "Thinking your face to be the nectarous moon, these partridges wander with you"; "is this her face, or is it the cool-rayed moon, or is it a lotus at the coming of dawn?"

25 When a quality is concealed by superimposition, know it to be 'entire denial': "these are not breasts on her chest — consider them jasmine fruits".

26 When one conceals a subject through artifice it is 'motivated denial': "neither is the moon hot, nor is there sun at night — see it as submarine fire indeed".

27 'Transposition' is when the quality of one thing is superimposed on another: "this is not the nectarous moon, but the brilliance of her nectarous face".

28 'Denial following error' is when another person's mistake is removed by words: "Your hot trembling is not from fever — no, dear, it is Kāmdev who inflames you".

29 'Artful denial' is when a thing is concealed from another person by contrivance: "It is not my lover who wounds my lip, dear, but the winter wind".

30 'Deceitful denial' is when one thing is described as another by pretence: "Pretending they are sharp female glances, Kāmdev rains down his arrows".

31 With regard to a 'thing', 'cause', or 'purpose', imagination [yields] an 'ascription': "her eyes are like lotuses — luscious and particularly broad".

32 "It seems she has walked in a rough courtyard, that is why her feet are red"; "for likeness to your feet, the lotus serves the water single-mindedly".

22 This figure involves the objective appraisal of the hero's various qualities, and is therefore distinct from that of 21, where perceptions of the hero's qualities are coloured by the subjective views of different individuals.

24.1,2 Examples of the 'mistake' and 'doubt' figures respectively.

24.2 *cakora*: the partridge, fabled to subsist on moonbeams, is an image of single-mindedness of devotion.

25.1 *suddha-apanhuti*: for Skt *śuddhāpahnuti.* (Cf. metathetical *-nh-* for *-hn-* in *cinha* < *cihna.*)

25.2 *kanakalatā phala*: cf. 8.1 and 18.2.

26.2 The 'concealed' subject is the burning pain of *viraha.* Grierson: 'The moon should quench her fever, as water quenches fire, but, instead, only increases it, as the ocean feeds the submarine fire at its bottom. The fierceness of the moon is the cause of the comparison'.

27 Another variety of the *apahnuti* figure.

32.1,2 Examples of 'ascriptions' based on 'cause' and 'purpose' respectively.

32.2 The lotus, a conventional *upamāna* for the foot, 'serves' the water (i.e. remains standing in it) in order to achieve a beauty like that of the heroine's feet (which have a natural rosy colour, or are decorated with lac).

अतिसयोक्ति रूपक जहाँ केवल ही उपमान ।
कनकलता पर चंद्रमा, धरे धनुष द्वै बान ॥ ३३ ॥

अतिनिन्हव गुन और को औरहि पर ठहराइ ।
सुधा भरचौ यह बदन तुव, चंद कहैं बौराइ ॥ ३४ ॥

अतिसयोक्ति भेदक सबै इहि बिधि बरनत जात ।
औरै हँसिबो देखिबो, औरै याकी बात ॥ ३५ ॥

संबंधातिसयोक्ति तब देत अजोगहि जोग ।
या पुर के मंदिर कहैं, ससि लौं ऊँचे लोग ॥ ३६ ॥

अतिसयोक्ति दूजी वहै जोग अजोग बखान ।
तो कर आगें कलपतरु क्यों पावै सनमान ॥ ३७ ॥

अतिसयोक्ति अक्रम जबै कारन कारज संग ।
तो सर लागत साथ ही धनुषहि अरु अरि अंग ॥ ३८ ॥

चपलातिसय जु हेत के होत नाम ही काज ।
कंकन ही भई मूँदरी, पीय गमन सुनि आज ॥ ३९ ॥

अत्यंतातिसयोक्ति सो, पूर्बापर क्रम नाहि ।
बान न पहुँचै अंग लौं, अरि पहिलें गिरि जाहि ॥ ४० ॥

तुल्यजोगिता तीनि ये लक्षन क्रम तें जानि ।
एक सब्द में हित अहित, बहु में एकै बानि ॥ ४१ ॥

बहु सों समता गुनन करि, इहि बिधि भिन्न प्रकार ।
गुननिधि नीकें देत तूँ तिय कौं अरि कौं हार ॥ ४२ ॥

नवल बधू की बदन दुति अरु सकुचित अरबिंद ।
तूँ ही श्रीनिधि धर्मनिधि, तुँही इंद्र अरु चंद ॥ ४३ ॥

33 The figure 'hyperbole' is where there is the object alone:
"there is a moon on a jasmine, holding a bow and two arrows".

34 In the 'obstinate denial' [hyperbole], the quality of a thing is predicated upon another:
"this face of yours is nectar-filled, only madmen say the moon [to be so]".

35 Hyperbole of 'distinction' are all described in this manner:
"quite other is her laughing and glancing, quite other her talk".

36 Hyperbole of 'relationship' bestows connexion on the unconnected:
"people say the buildings of this town are as high as the moon".

37 The second hyperbole [of 'relationship'] is that calling the connected unconnected:
"how could the wishing-tree attain honour in front of your hand?".

38 The 'non-sequential' hyperbole is whenever cause and effect are together:
"your arrows connect simultaneously to your bow and to your enemy's body".

39 'Rapidness' is that [hyperbole] whose effect follows the mere name of the cause:
"her ring became her very bracelet, hearing of her lover's leaving today".

40 The hyperbole of 'exaggeration' is that having no sequential order:
"before the arrow even reaches his body, the enemy falls".

41 These are the three [types of] 'equal pairing' — know their characteristics in order:
one word bears both good and bad; a single quality [exists] in several [words];

42 [and] when many [attributes] are one in their qualities — thus are the three varieties.
"O abode of virtues, well you give a garland to the lady, and defeat to the enemy".

43 "The lustre of the new bride's face and of the lotus is faded". "You alone are the abode of good fortune and of righteousness; you alone are Indra and the moon".

33.2 The four subjects of comparison — the heroine's face, body, eyebrows and glances — are omitted.

36.2 There is no actual parallel between the buildings' height and the moon, except rhetorically. Cf. a similar example from Carl Sandberg, quoted by Gerow (1971:22): 'They have yarns / of a skyscraper so tall they had to put hinges / on the two top stories so to let the moon go by'.

37.2 *kalapataru* : [Skt *kalpataru*], one of the five trees of Indra's heaven, which yields all desires. It thus represents the bountiful patron, this parallel being denied in the terms of the present figure.

39.2 The heroine became instantaneously emaciated through grief.

40.2 Lit. 'the arrow does not reach his body, the enemy first falls down'.

41.2 *bāni* : (< *varṇa*) 'quality, character, nature' (as opposed to *bāṇī* < *vāṇī* 'speech').

42.2 *gunanidhi* : i.e. God, the creator. The figure, which illustrates the 'good and bad' (or 'auspicious and inauspicious') implications of a single word, hinges on the two senses of *hāra* as (a) 'garland' and (b) 'defeat'. A further play on the multifarious senses of *guna* (e.g. 'garland' and 'bowstring') may also be involved.

43.1 The heroine's face and the lotus share the same characteristic: cf. 41.2.

43.2 Four distinct qualities — wealth, righteousness, majesty (like Indra's) and brilliance — are shared by the same person.

सो दीपक निज गुनन सों बर्न्य इतर इक भाइ ।
गज मद सों नृप तेज सों सोभा लहत बनाइ ॥ ४४ ॥

दीपक आबृति तीनि बिधि, आबृति पद की होइ ।
पुनि है आबृति अर्थ की दूजें कहिये सोइ ॥ ४५ ॥

पद अरु अर्थ दुहूँन की आबृति तीजें लेखि ।
घन बरखै है री सखी, निसि बरखै है देखि ॥ ४६ ॥

फूले बृक्ष कदंब के केतक बिकसे आहि ।
मत्त भए हैं मोर अरु चातक मत्त सराहि ॥ ४७ ॥

प्रतिबस्तूपम सो समझि, दोऊ वाक्य समान ।
आभा सूर प्रताप बर, सोभा सुरहि कमान ॥ ४८ ॥

अलंकार दृष्टांत सो लक्षन नाम प्रमान ।
कांतिमान ससि ही बन्यो, तूँ ही कीरतिमान ॥ ४९ ॥

* * *

आबृति बरन अनेक की, दोइ दोइ जब होइ ।
है छेकानुप्रास सुर समता बिनहू सोइ ॥ ५० ॥

अंजन लाग्यो है अधर, प्यारे नैनन पीक ।
मुक्तमाल उपटी प्रगट, कठिन हिये पर ठीक ॥ ५१ ॥

सो लाटानुप्रास जब पद की आबृति होइ ।
सब्द अर्थ के भेद सों भेद बिनाहू सोइ ॥ ५२ ॥

पीय निकट जाके नहीं, घाम चाँदनी ताहि ।
पीय निकट जाके सखी, घाम चाँदनी ताहि ॥ ५३ ॥

44 That is an 'illuminator' when the subject and another thing are described similarly
[but] according to their own qualities: "the elephant through his rut and the king
from his valour establish their fame".

45 The 'illuminator with repetition' is of three kinds: that having repetition of a word;
then, the second is described as that having a repetition of meaning;

46 [and] recognize the third 'repetition' as that of both word and meaning:
"the clouds pour rain, O friend see, the night is a year indeed".

47 "The kadamba trees are flowering and the ketaka is in bloom";
"excited are the peacocks, and excited the cuckoo — praise them".

48 Know that to be a 'counterpart simile' when there are two similar statements:
"the glory of the sun is from its fine brilliance, the glory of the hero is from his bow".

49 The characteristics of the figure 'exemplification' are known from its name:
"the moon alone was made lustrous, illustrious are you alone".

* * *

50 When there is a repetition of several syllables, two of each,
when there is not similarity of vowels, it is 'clever alliteration'.

51 "Kohl is smeared on the lips, beloved, and betel-juice on the eyes,
the impress of a pearl necklace is well apparent on your hard heart".

52 That is 'Gujarati alliteration' when a word is repeated
and there is a difference of meaning without any difference in the words:

53 "For she whose lover is not at hand, moonlight is like the sun's heat;
for she whose lover is at hand, friend, the sun's heat is like moonlight".

44 *dīpaka* : 'a construction wherein several parallel phrases are each completed by a single (unrepeated) word or phrase; zeugma' (Gerow 1971:193). Cf. RB 25 and 28.

46.2 With its play on *barakhai* 'pour rain' vs. *barakhai* 'year indeed' (*barakha* + *-i*), this is an illustration of the first kind of 'repetition', as defined in 45.1.

47.1 Both trees are described as blossoming, but the expressions are different: hence this is a 'repetition' of the second type (45.2).

47.2 Both the quality (excitement) and the descriptive word (*matta*) are shared: hence this is a 'repetition' of the third type (46.1). The shared excitement is at the coming of the rains — the mating season for the peacock, and the source of sustenance for the cuckoo (fabled to subsist on raindrops).

48 '*Prativastûpamā* involves the repetition of the common property; there need be no parallelism of terms within the two situations' (Gerow 1971:208). Here the figure hinges on the two distinct senses of *sūra* as both 'sun' and 'warrior, hero'.

49 *dṛṣṭānta* : 'the adjunction of a second situation which bears upon the same point as the first and where the purpose is entirely one of illustration' (Gerow 1971:208).

51 *adhara...pyāre; pyāre...pīka; muktamāla; upaṭī...pragaṭa*, etc. For a parallel context, cf. BS 4.

53.1,2 The second line, with *cā̃danī* as predicate of *ghāma*, is of course considerably less forced than the first.

जमक सब्द को फिरि श्रवन, अर्थ जुदैं सो जानि ।
सीतल चंदन चंद नहिं, अधिक अगिन तें मानि ॥ ५४ ॥

प्रति अक्षर आबृत्ति बहु, बृत्ति तीनि बिधि मानि ।
मधुर बरन जामें सबै, उपनागरिका जानि ॥ ५५ ॥

दूजें परुषा कहत सब, जामें बहुत समास ।
बिन समास बिन मधुरता, कहै कोमला तास ॥ ५६ ॥

अति कारी भारी घटा, प्यारी बारी बैस ।
पिय परदेस अँदेस यह, आवत नाहिं सँदेस ॥ ५७ ॥

कोकिल चातक भृंग कुल, केकी कठिन चकोर ।
सोर सुनें धरक्यो हियो, काम कटक अति जोर ॥ ५८ ॥

घन बरसै दामिनि लसै, दस दिसि नीर तरंग ।
दंपति हियें हुलास तें, अति सरसात अनंग ॥ ५९ ॥

अलंकार सब अर्थ के, कहे एक सौ आठ ।
किये प्रगट भाषा बिषै, देखि संसकृत पाठ ॥ ६० ॥

सब्दालंकृत बहुत हैं, अक्षर के संजोग ।
अनुप्रास षट बिधि कहे, जे हैं भाषा जोग ॥ ६१ ॥

ताही नर के हेत यह कीनो ग्रंथ नवीन ।
जो पंडित भाषा निपुन, कबिता बिषै प्रबीन ॥ ६२ ॥

लक्षन तिय अरु पुरुष के हावभाव रस धाम ।
अलंकार संजोग तें भाषाभूषन नाम ॥ ६३ ॥

भाषाभूषन ग्रंथ को जो देखै चित लाइ ।
बिबिधि अर्थ साहित्य रस समुझै सबै बनाइ ॥ ६४ ॥

54 Know that to be a 'pun', when on hearing a word again the meanings are different:
"sandalwood paste and the moon are not cooling, they seem hotter than fire".

55 When each character occurs often it is called 'repetition' — consider the three kinds:
know that in which all the syllables are melodious to be 'cultured';

56 the second is called 'harsh', in which there are many compounds;
that one without compounds and without melodiousness is called 'delicate'.

57 "Very dark and heavy are the clouds, the beloved is of tender years;
her lover is abroad, and the worry is this — that no message comes".

58 "Flocks of black cuckoos, pied cuckoos, shrikes, harsh peacocks and partridges:
hearing their din, my heart throbs — Kāmdev's army is so powerful!"

59 "Clouds pour rain, lightning flashes, all around are water-waves;
Kāmdev delights greatly through the gladness in the couple's hearts."

60 I have described all the one hundred and eight ornaments of meaning;
after seeing the Sanskrit texts I have rendered them in the vernacular.

61 There are many ornaments of sound, through the conjunction of characters;
I have described those six kinds of alliteration which are appropriate for the vernacular.

62 I have prepared this new book for the sake of that person
who is learned, conversant with the vernacular, and skilled in poetry.

63 [Here are] the characteristics of heroines and heroes, the blandishments wherein poetic flavour dwells; through the admixture of ornaments its name is 'The embellishment of language'.

64 One who peruses attentively the book *Bhāṣā-bhūṣaṇ*
will appreciate all the various meanings of the essence of poetry.

55 The 'difference of sense' is illustrated in *candana* vs. *canda na-*.

56.2 *tāsa*: pr. *tā* + ppn. *su*, in rhyme form.

57 The 'melodiousness' referred to in the definition of *upanāgarikā* (55.2) is illustrated through a succession of *-ā-* vowels in the first line, and *-esa* alliteration in the second.

58 The first line is of compounded nouns and, with its repeated *-k-* throughout, the couplet illustrates the 'harsh' variety of alliteration (56.1). ('Kāmdev's army', which so terrifies the lover, is the birds' spring chorus, the sound of which forewarns of the tribulations of love.)

59 Free of lengthy compounds and of the 'melodiousness' exemplified in 57, this couplet illustrates the 'delicate' variety of alliteration (56.2).

60 *alaṁkāra saba artha ke*: this is presumably to include both 'sound' and 'sense' ornaments: cf. Grierson's reading *alaṁkāra śabdārtha ke*, in which compounded *śabdārtha* implies 'literal meaning'.

60 *eka sau āṭha*: '108' is a sacred or auspicious number in metaphysics (and hence formulaic in literature and rhetoric).

61 *sabdālaṁkṛta*: for nominal °*ti* (Grierson's reading).

61 *ānuprāsa ṣaṭa bidhi*: i.e. those six varieties of alliteration defined and illustrated in couplets 50-59.

नीति-सतसई

वृन्द

नीकी पै फीकी लगै, बिनु अबसर की बात ।
जैसे बरनत युद्ध मैं, रस सिंगार न सुहात ॥ १ ॥

फीकी पै नीकी लगै, कहिए समय बिचारि ।
सब को मन हरषित करै ज्यौं बिबाह मैं गारि ॥ २ ॥

बिद्या धन उद्यम बिना कहौ जु पावै कौन ।
बिना डुलाए ना मिलै ज्यौं पंखा कौ पौन ॥ ३ ॥

सो ताके अबगुन कहै, जो जिहिं चाहै नांहि ।
तपत कलंकी बिस भर्‌यौ बिरहिन ससिहि कहाहि ॥ ४ ॥

मधुर बचन तैं जात मिट उत्तम जन अभिमान ।
तनिक सीतल जल सों मिटै जैसैं दूध उफान ॥ ५ ॥

सबै सहायक सबल के, कोउ न निबल सहाय ।
पबन जगाबत आग कौं, दीपहि देत बुझाय ॥ ६ ॥

जासों निबहै जीविका, करिए सो अभ्यास ।
बेस्या पालै सील तौ कैसैं पूरे आस ॥ ७ ॥

आडंबर तजि कीजिए गुन संग्रह चित चाय ।
छीर रहित गउ ना बिकै, आनिय घंट बँधाय ॥ ८ ॥

जैसौ गुन दीनौ दई, तैसौ रूप निबंध ।
ए दोऊ कहँ पाइयै, सोनौ और सुगंध ॥ ९ ॥

कोउ बिन देखे बिन सुनै कैसें कहै बिचार ।
कूप भेख जाने कहा सागर को बिस्तार ॥ १० ॥

Nīti-satsaī

Vṛnd

1 Though good, something said at an inappropriate time seems insipid,
just as in describing warfare, the amorous sentiment does not please.

2 Though insipid, something may seem good if said with consideration of the time,
just as abusive speech delights the hearts of all at a wedding.

3 Tell me sir, how could one attain the treasure of knowledge without effort?
— Just as you do not get a breeze from a fan without swinging it.

4 One talks of the faults of that thing which one does not like:
'burning, tainted, full of poison' says the lovelorn woman of the moon.

5 The pride of an excellent man is dispelled by sweet words,
just as the boiling-over of milk is stopped with a little cold water.

6 All are helpers of the strong, there is no help for the weak:
wind rouses the fire but puts out the lamp.

7 One should practise that by which one's livelihood is maintained:
if a whore observed modest conduct, how could she fulfil her desire?

8 Abandoning ostentation, accumulate pleasing qualities:
a milkless cow will not be sold by tying a bell to it.

9 As God has granted quality, so has he withheld beauty:
where are these two found [together] — gold and fragrance?

10 How could anyone utter an opinion without seeing, without hearing?
What will the well-frog know of the extent of the ocean?

1.1 *abasara* : this text often represents unstressed original *v* as *b*. Cf. 2.2 *bibāha*, 4.1 *abaguna* etc.

2.2 *bibāha maĩ gāri* : during a traditional wedding, women sing *gālīs* (abusive songs of explicit vulgarity) to taunt the bridegroom and his relatives.

3.2 *paṁkhā* : the large cloth fan suspended from the ceiling and swung to and fro by a string (with a *paṁkhāvālā* at the other end).

4.1 *so tāke...jo jihī* : such paired relative/correlatives are common in aphoristic couplets — cf. 31.

4.2 *tapata kalaṁkī bisa bharyau* : to the *virahiṇī*, all the traditional qualities of the moon — usually described as cooling, brilliant, and a source of nectar — are reversed.

8.1 The caesura is not a syntactic break: *āḍambara taji, kījie guna saṁgraha...*

9 Cf. the MSH idioms *sone mẽ sugandh*, *sonā-sugandh*, etc., 'gold and fragrance', i.e. two distinct and dissimilar qualities appearing together in one place.

10.2 *kūpa bhekha* : the 'frog in the well' [MSH *kuẽ kā mẽḍhak*] is a stock image for one with a limited knowledge of the world (but who croaks on regardless).

कुल बल जैसो होय सो तैसी करिहै बात ।
बनिक पुत्र जाने कहा गढ़ लैबे की घात ॥ ११ ॥

अति ही सरल न हूजियै, देखौ ज्यौं बनराय ।
सीधे सीधे छेदियै, बाँकौ तरु बच जाय ॥ १२ ॥

मिथ्या भाषी साँच हूँ कहै न मानै कोय ।
भाँड़ पुकारै पीर बस, मिस समुझौ सब लोय ॥ १३ ॥

काम समै पावै सु दुख, जे निबलन के संग ।
मरदन खंडन सहत हैं ज्यों अबला के अंग ॥ १४ ॥

छोटे नर तैं रहत हैं सोभायुत सिरताज ।
निरमल राखै चाँदनी जैसैं पायंदाज ॥ १५ ॥

बात प्रेम की राखिए अपने ही मन माँहि ।
जैसे छाया कूप की बाहर निकसै नाँहि ॥ १६ ॥

बाँके सीधे को मिलन निबहै नाँहि निदान ।
गुन ग्राही तौऊ तजत जैसे बान कमान ॥ १७ ॥

होय न कारज मो बिना, यह जु कहै सु अयान ।
जहाँ न कुक्कुट सबद तहँ होत न कहा बिहान ॥ १८ ॥

अपनी अपनी ठौर पर, सब कौं लागै दाव ।
जल में गाड़ी नाव पर, थल गाड़ी पर नाव ॥ १९ ॥

बुद्धि बिना बिद्या कहो कहा सिखावै कोइ ।
प्रथम गाँव ही नाहिं तौ सींब कहाँ ते होइ ॥ २० ॥

बहुत न बकिए कीजिए कारज औसर पाय ।
मौन गहे बक दाँब पर मछरी लेत उठाय ॥ २१ ॥

11 As are the strengths of one's family, so will one speak:
what would a merchant's son know of the stratagems for taking a fort?

12 Be not excessively straightforward: see the tree of the forest —
the completely straight ones are felled, the bent tree survives.

13 No-one believes a liar, even though he speak the truth:
when the buffoon cries out in pain, everyone thinks it a sham.

14 When it's time for work, they suffer who keep company with the weak:
just as the lady's limbs endure bruising and tearing.

15 Through [the efforts of] little men, the great maintain their splendour,
just as the doormat keeps the white floor-sheet spotless.

16 Keep matters of love within your heart,
just as the shadow of the well falls not outside.

17 A union of crooked and straight cannot endure in the end,
just as the fine arrow leaves the bow, though grasping its string.

18 'Nothing can be done without me' — he who says this is foolish:
is there no dawn there, where the cock does not crow?

19 All get a turn, each in his own place:
in the water, the cart is on the boat, on dry land, the boat on the cart.

20 Tell me, how could one teach knowledge without intelligence?
If there is no village to start with, how could there be a boundary?

21 Don't prattle overmuch, but act when you get the opportunity:
keeping silent, the heron catches the fish when its chance comes.

11.2 *banika* [= KhB *baniyā*]: the universal disdain reserved for the merchant classes doubtless had a particularly sharp edge in the context of the princely court, and is here compounded with a traditional emphasis on the restraints of individual *dharma*.

12 A rather more worldly-wise version of the conceit appearing in BS 66.

14 This conceit rests upon a pun on *kāma* as being both 'work' and 'passion' : a weak workmate means trouble, just as the limbs of the *abalā* ('frail woman, member of the weaker sex') may suffer during lovemaking.

17.1 *bā̃ke sīdhe* : antonyms referring metaphorically to qualities of character as respectively 'rakish, crooked' and 'simple, straightforward'. Cf. 12 and BS 66.

17.2 *guna grāhī* : based on a conventional pun with *guna* meaning both 'quality' and 'string', the phrase means both 'having qualities' and 'grasping the bowstring'. Cf. BS 18.

भजत निरंतर संत जन, हरि पद चित्त लगाय ।
जैसे नट दृढ़ दृस्टि करि धरत बरत पर पाँय ॥ २२ ॥

का रस में का रोष में, अरि ते जिनि पतियाय ।
जैसें सीतल तप्त जल डारत आगि बुझाय ॥ २३ ॥

अपनी प्रभुता को सबै बोलत झूठ बनाय ।
बेस्या बरस घटावही, जोगी बरस बढ़ाय ॥ २४ ॥

खाय न खरचै सूम धन, चोर सबै लै जाय ।
पीछे ज्यों मधुमच्छिका, हाथ मलै पछिताय ॥ २५ ॥

धन अरु गेंद जु खेल कौं, दोऊ एक सुभाय ।
कर में आबत छिनक में, छिन में कर तें जाय ॥ २६ ॥

धन अरु जोबन कौ गरब कबहूँ करिये नाँहि ।
देखत ही मिट जात हैं, ज्यों बादर की छाँहि ॥ २७ ॥

जोराबरहूँ कौं कियो बिधि बसकरन इलाज ।
दीप तमहिं अंकुस गजहिं, जलनिधि तरनि जहाज ॥ २८ ॥

भरत पेट नट निरत कै, डरत न करत उपाय ।
धरत बरत पर पाँय अरु परत बरत लपटाय ॥ २९ ॥

गहत तत्व ग्यानी पुरुष, बात बिचारि बिचारि ।
मथनिहार तजि छाछ कौं, माखन लेत निकारि ॥ ३० ॥

जो जिहिं कारज में कुसल, सो तिहि भेद प्रवीन ।
नद प्रवाह में गज बहै, चढ़ै उलट लघु मीन ॥ ३१ ॥

संवत ससि रस बार ससि, कातिक सुदि ससिबार ।
सातैं ढाका सहर में उपज्यौ इहै बिचार ॥ ३२ ॥

22 Pious folk worship continually, applying their minds to Hari's feet,
just as the acrobat, with steady gaze, sets his foot on the tightrope.

23 Whether in sentiment or in anger, do not trust your enemy;
just as throwing water — whether cold or hot — puts the fire out.

24 All speak falsely when talking of their eminence:
the whore diminishes her years, the yogi exaggerates his.

25 The miser neither consumes nor spends his wealth, and the thief takes it all away;
then, like a honey-bee, he rubs his hands in remorse.

26 These games of wealth and of ball are one in nature:
in a moment it comes into the hand, in a moment goes again.

27 Never be proud of wealth or youthfulness:
they disappear before your very eyes, like the shadow of a cloud.

28 Even for the powerful, the creator has made a means of subjugation:
a lamp for the darkness; an ankus for the elephant; and to cross the ocean, a ship.

29 Filling his belly by dancing, the acrobat fears not to do what he must:
he sets his foot on the rope, and falling, clings to the rope.

30 The learned man considers a matter thoroughly and grasps its essence;
the churner, rejecting the buttermilk, extracts the butter.

31 He who is skilled in a certain work is expert in its secrets:
the elephant is swept away by the river's flow, the minnow swims against the stream

32 On a Monday in the light half of Kārttika, in *samvat* 1761,
on the [fortnight's] seventh day in the city of Dhaka, was produced this [work]
with great thought.

22.2 *dharata barata para pā̃ya* : the elegant phrase seems to have pleased Vṛnd — cf. 29.2, where *ṭ* alliteration is again involved. An example of Vṛnd's tendency towards formulaic composition.

26.1 *dhana aru gẽda ju khela kaũ* : rel.pr. *ju* emphasizes the subject by restatement; *kaũ* governs *eka subhāya* [MSH *dhan aur yauvan ke jo khel haĩ, donõ kā ek hī svabhāv hai*]. See examples under I.4.4.

28.2 *jalanidhi tarani jahāja* : implicit in this phrase is the commonplace concept of the name of God as a boat to cross the ocean of worldly existence; cf. SS 4.8, RAM 39, etc.

29.1 *bharata peṭa* : i.e. earning his livelihood (which necessitates the risks described here).

31.2 *caṛhai ulaṭa* : lit. 'ascends contrarywise'. The context is a counter-example to 6.

32.1 *sasi rasa bāra sasi* : 'moon, flavour, day, moon' — symbols for the numbers '1,6,7,1', which are read in reverse order as a chronogram to yield the *samvat* date 1761 (= A.D. 1704). See III.3.3.

अष्टयाम

देव

प्रथम घरी चौथे पहर, बैठी गुरुजन ऐन ।
छिनु छिनु पल परवत भयो, काटे कठिन कटै न ॥ १ ॥

बैठी बधू गुरलोगनि मैं पिय के बिछुरे छिन भौन न भावै ।
पाछिलो जाम भयो जुग सो अब जामिनि क्यों करि भामिनि पावै ॥
चौंकि चितै रवि त्यों कवि देव सु बातन ही दबि द्यौस गंवावै ।
धाई सो बैन सखीन सो सैन सुनै नहि बैन सु नैन नचावै ॥ २ ॥

दुतिय घरी चौथे पहर, आवै महल सिंगार ।
रंग महल पठवै सखी, साजन सेज संवार ॥ ३ ॥

निपट उताहल सी अति उतसाह भरी
प्रेम मग मनोरथ चढ़ी अभिसार कै ।
गौरव सों गोरी गुरुजन की सभा ते उठी
लंक मैं लचनि परे कचनि के भार कै ॥
चंदन दै अगर कपूर दै पठाई सखी
सुख सेज सदन संवारन संवार कै ।
संग लिये दासी देव कहै देवता-सी आपु
सुंदरि हंसति आई मंदिर सिंगार कै ॥ ४ ॥

घरी तीसरी चतुर्थ जामु जु उबटि सरीर ।
सोधों लाइ अन्हाइ कै, पहिरो पीरो चीर ॥ ५ ॥

चोवा सों चुपरि केस केसर सुरंग अंग
केसर उबटि अन्हवाई है गुलाब सों ।
अतर तिलोछी आछे अंबर लै पोंछी ओछी
छतिया अंगोछी हंसि हंस रस भाव सों ॥

Aṣṭayām

Dev

1 In the first period of the fourth watch, sitting in the elders' place,
each minute and each moment has become a mountain, so difficult to traverse.

2 Sitting with the elder folk, separated from her lover,
the palace appeals to the bride not for a moment;
the next watch has become an aeon,
now how can the lady reach the night?
Startled from sleep, she watches the sun, and (the poet Dev likewise)
is oppressed by talk as she fritters away the daytime;
talking to her maidservant she signals to her friends
and she hears no words as she makes her eyes dance.

3 In the second period of the fourth watch comes the time for adornment;
to the pleasure palace she sends the sakhi to prepare and decorate the couch.

4 With exceeding impatience and filled with great zeal,
her desire ascended the path of love for the tryst;
grandly the fair one arose from the elders' assembly,
her waist bent with the burden of her tresses.
With sandalwood, aloes and camphor she sent the sakhi
to prepare and make ready the chamber of the pleasure-bed;
attended by a servant, and — declares Dev — herself like a goddess,
the beautiful one came smiling to the house of delight.

5 In the third period of the fourth watch she anointed her body,
applied a pomade and bathed, and put on a yellow garment.

6 Dressing her hair with pomade and anointing her saffron-bright body
with saffron, she bathed in rose-water;
oiled with attar and wiping herself with a fine fabric,
she dried her breasts, laughing a laugh of loving sentiment.

[stanza 6 continues...]

1 *gharī...pahara...chinu...pala* : the day is divided into eight 'watches' of three hours (*pahara* or *jāma*, Skt *prahara*, *yāma*) each of which is sub-divided into eight *gharīs*. A *chinu* (Skt *kṣaṇa*) is a period of four minutes, while a *pala* is one sixtieth of a *gharī*, i.e. a period of 24 seconds.

1.2 *kāṭe...kaṭai na* : 'cannot be traversed by traversing', i.e. 'cannot be passed despite trying'. Cf. SB 8.5.

2.4 *sunai nahi baina su naina nacāvai* : the heroine is deaf to her servant's smalltalk, and signals to her sakhis that she is anticipating the tryst. Note the alliterative sequence *sunai nahi...su naina na-* .

3.1 *mahala sĩgāra* : a compound of the Persian izafat type, in which the second element qualifies the first.

4.2 *kacani ke bhāra kai* : *kai* = *kari*, thus 'with the weight of her hair'. (A variant reading with *kucani*, 'breasts', is perhaps what is really intended, this being the conventional conceit.)

5.1 *ju* : a metrical filler, having no function in the sentence except perhaps a general demonstrative sense.

कटि मृगराज की सी मुख है मृगांकु मानो
तीखी देव द्रग गति सीखी मृग साव सों ।
पैन्हि पीरो चीर चारु चौकी पर ठाढ़ी भई
चांदनी सी प्यारी पै उज्यारी महताब सों ॥ ६ ॥

चौथि घरी चौथे पहर, सोंधे बसन मंगाइ ।
निरखे भूषन रतन मनि, पहिरै मन मनभाइ ॥ ७ ॥

अंबर अतर चोवा अंबर सों चुनि चुनि
लाइ सहचरी सोंधो जाति न्यारी न्यारी को ।
सुबरन संपुटनि आनी है रतन मनि
पुहुप समूह देव आन्यो बन क्यारी को ॥
मंद हांसी सुंदरि की भए सब मंद दुति
चंद हू ते उदित अमंद मुख प्यारी को ।
सूनो सो नखत जाल लूनो सो मसाल पुंज
सहज ही दूनो रूप पूनो की उज्यारी को ॥ ८ ॥

पांचि घरी चौथे पहर, पहिरति राते बास ।
करति अंग रचना बिबिध, भूषन भेष बिलास ॥ ९ ॥

पंकज सो पायनि झंवाइ रंग जावक, सु
धारे वर नेवर औ बिछिया सुभाइ के ।
पैन्ही फेरि ऊजरी वै गूजरी रतन जरी
बांधी कटि किंकिनी दमामे रतिराइ के ॥
बेंदी देखि दर्पन में कंचुकी रहिस कसी
बार गुहि पैन्हे हार देव चित्तचाइ के ।
अंजनु दै नैनन अतर मुख मंजनु कै
लीन्है उजराइ कर गजरा जराइ के ॥ १० ॥

छठी घरी चौथे पहर, कर गहि दर्पन देखि ।
रंग रंग भूषननि ते, सोहै अंग बिसेखि ॥ ११ ॥

[stanza 6 concluded:]

Her waist like a lion's, her face as it were a moon;
 and sharp, Dev, her glances learnt from a fawn;
wearing a yellow garment she stood on a pretty stool,
 her lunar loveliness bright as a moonbeam.

7 In the fourth period of the fourth watch, calling for fragrant clothes,
she looks at the ornaments, gems and jewels, and puts on whatever appeals.

8 Choosing variously from clothes of ambergris, attar and 'four-fold fragrance',
 the sakhi brought fragrances of various kinds;
in caskets of gold she brought gems and jewels,
 and brought a posy of blooms, Dev, from a wild flowerbed.
[Yet] all became faint in lustre before that beauty's faint smile,
 for brighter than the moon itself was the brilliant face of the beloved;
empty seemed the constellations' net; cropped, that stand of torches;
 easily she had twice the brilliance of the full-moon night.

9 In the fifth period of the fourth watch, she puts on red raiment,
and decorates her body in various ways, delighting in ornament and apparel.

10 Rubbing her lotus-like feet and [applying] lac colour,
 she puts on fine anklets and toe-rings with natural grace;
then donning a bright jewelled ankle-ring,
 she ties on waist-bells — the battle-drums of Kāmdev!
She looks at her brow-dot in the glass, joyfully draws tight her bodice,
 and braiding her hair, dons a necklace — Dev's desire;
putting kohl round her eyes and cleansing her face with attar,
 she takes to her fair hand a jewelled bracelet.

11 In the sixth period of the fourth watch she takes a mirror in her hand and sees
how splendidly her limbs gleam with the various colours of her ornaments.

6.4 *cā̃danī sī pyārī pai ujyārī mahatāba sõ* : the conceit, with two aspects of the moon put into opposition with *pai* 'but' is hard to render in English with its paucity of synonyms for 'moonlight'.

8.1 *aṁbara …aṁbara* : the first *aṁbara* means ambergris or 'grey amber', a costly substance with a sweet earthy odour used in perfumery (it is secreted from the intestines of the sperm whale and is found on the sea and seashore). The second *aṁbara* means 'clothing'.

8.1 *atara* : a variant reading preferred to *antara.*

8.2 *deva ānyo* : the poet suggests himself as the logical subject of the verb here — cf. next note.

10.3 *deva cittacāi ke* : 'appealing to Dev/to the gods' — the play on the poet's name cannot be accommodated by the translation.

सोनो से सुरंग सब वैसे ही लसत अंग
जगमग्यो जोबन जवाहिर सो संग तासु ।
रूप तरु कंद काम कंदुक से सोहैं कुच
चन्द्रमा सो आनन अमंद दुति मंद हास ॥
सोभा की निकाई देव काई की निकाई ही तें
नीके भए भूषन भ्रमर भ्रमें आस पास ।
चौगुनी चटक तन चीर की चटक हू ते
सौगुनी सुगंध ते सरीर की सहज बास ॥१२ ॥

रह्यो द्यौस जब द्वै घरी, साजि सकल सिंगार ।
उद्दित ह्वै अभिसार को बैठी परम उदार ॥ १३ ॥

सरस सुजाति अति सुंदर बरन तन
बोलति मधुर महाकविन की बानी सी ।
तोरनि तिलक सों अलिक पौरि चिलकति
धुजा दृग मीन रतिराज रजधानी सी ॥
रंभा रु तिलोतमा सुकेसी मंजुघोषा संग
सदा उरबसी देव देवपति रानी सी ।
सकल सिंगार करि सोहै आजु सिंहोदरि
सिंहासन बैठी सिंहवाहिनी भवानी सी ॥१४ ॥

पच्छिम पूरब भानु ससि अथवत उदवत बार ।
रंग महल भामिनि चली, भली भांति अभिसार ॥ १५ ॥

माँग गुही मोतिन भुजंगम सी बेनी उर
उरज उतंग औ मतंग गति गौन की ।
अंगना अनंग की सी पहिरे सुरंग सारी
तरल तुरंग मृग चालि दृग दौन की ॥
रूपे की तरंगनि वरंगनि के अंगनि ते
सोंधे की अरंग लै तरंग उठै पौन की ।
सखी संग रंग सौं कुरंग नैनी आवै तौ लौं
कैयौ रंगमई भूमि भई रंग भौन की ॥१६ ॥

12 Bright as gold they shine on her limbs,
just as her youth glimmers like a jewel in gold brocade;
like galls from the tree of beauty, or balls for Kāmdev's [sport] her breasts shine,
her face like the moon, of great splendour her gentle smile.
The excellence of her lustre, Dev, is better even than her adornments
which look so well, and bees buzz all around her.
The brightness of her body is fourfold even that of her clothes,
a hundred times her scent is the innate fragrance of her body.

13 When two periods of the daytime remained she was fitted with all her finery,
and sat most illustrious, eager for the tryst.

14 Elegant, high-born, her body of most lovely hue,
she speaks sweetly as though with the great poets' tongue;
with her *tilak* as its decoration, her curls adorn the gateway of
Kāmdev's capital, and her fish-shaped eyes are its banner.
With the nymphs Rambhā and Tilottamā and Sukeśī and Mañjughoṣā,
like Indra's queen, ever dwelling on Dev's heart;
with all her finery, resplendent today the lion-waisted one
is seated on the lion-throne like lion-mounted Bhavānī.

15 At the time when sun and moon set and rise in West and East,
the passionate lady went to the pleasure palace, well set for the tryst.

16 Her parting braided with pearls, her plaited hair like a snake on her chest,
her breasts lofty, and her walking like an elephant's gait;
like Kāmdev's lady, wearing a red sari,
wanton and rapid the deer-movement of her two eyes.
From the river of silver of the lithe lady's limbs
ripples of breeze arise, carrying the fragrance of her scent;
while with her friends, joyfully, the deer-eyed lady comes,
in so many ways was the floor of the pleasure-palace coloured.

12.3 *sobhā...nikāī hī tẽ*: i.e. the lustre of her body is superior to that of the jewellery which is supposed to beautify it, just as a glimmer [of water] shines through scum (*kāī*) floating on its surface. Cf. 12.4.

12.3 *bhramara bhrame*: a variant reading preferred to *bhavara bhare*.

14.2 *torani...cilakati*: the image has her brow as a palace doorway, decorated with a *tilak* (often used as a decorative symbol of auspiciousness), and further adorned by her hanging locks (*alika*). The conceit (whose wording is hardly straightforward) is developed further with her fish-shaped eyes representing Kāmdev's banner, which bears a *makara*, a fabulous sea-beast symbolizing sensuality.

14.3 *devapati rānī* : 'queen of the lord of the gods', i.e. Indra's queen, the voluptuous Indrāṇi. The other allusions are to *apsaras* famed for their beauty — Rambhā, one of the treasures produced by the churning of the ocean; Tilottamā, made by Brahmā from a particle (*tila*) of each of the best (*uttama*) substances of the universe; Sukeśī, 'she of the beautiful hair'; Mañjughoṣā, 'she of sweet voice'; and Urvaśī, whose name 'heart-dweller' also signifies a jewel worn on the chest, and is involved in a pun here. The allusions to these nymphs add more to the general panegyric tone of the verse than to its narrative.

16.1 *mataṁga gati*: 'elephant's gait', i.e. a gentle sensually rolling motion, with a swaying of the hips.

रस-प्रबोध

रसलीन

बसंतऋतु

कहूँ लावति विकसत कुसुम, कहूँ डोलावति वाइ ।
कहूँ बिछावति चाँदनी, मधुरितु दासी आइ ॥ १ ॥

यह मधुरितु मैं कौन कै बढ़त न मोद अनंत ।
कोकिल गावत हैं कुहुकि, मधुप गुंजरत तंत ॥ २ ॥

औषधीस सँग पाइ अरु लहि बसंत अभिराम ।
मनो रोग जग हरन को भयो धनंतर काम ॥ ३ ॥

फूले कुंजन अलि भँवत, सीतल चलत समीर ।
मानि जात काको न मनु, जात भानुजा तीर ॥ ४ ॥

सरबर माहि अन्हाइ अरु बाग बाग भरमाइ ।
मंद मंद आवत पवन, राजहंस के भाइ ॥ ५ ॥

कल्पवृच्छ तें सरस तुव बाग द्रुमन कौं जानि ।
सागर निकसौ लखन कौ जल जंत्रन मिसि आनि ॥ ६ ॥

ग्रीष्मऋतु

धूप चटक करि चेट अरु फाँसी पवन चलाइ ।
मारत दुपहर बीच मैं यह ग्रीषम ठग आइ ॥ ७ ॥

छुटत न यै नल नीर जल, जल सजि छिति तें आइ ।
निरख निदाघ अनीति को चल्यौ भानु पै जाइ ॥ ८ ॥

कोउ उभकत उछरत कोऊ, कोउ जल मारत धाइ ।
लखि नारिन जल केलि छबि, पिय छकि रह्यौ लोभाइ ॥ ९ ॥

पिय छीटत यौं तियन कर, लहि जल केलि अनन्द ।
मनो कमल चहुँओर तें मुकुतन छोरत चंद ॥ १० ॥

Ras-prabodh

Raslīn

SPRING

1 Here she brings a flower in bloom, there she stirs the wind;
here she spreads a moonlight quilt, the handmaid Spring, as she comes.

2 Whose delight does not grow endlessly in this spring season?
Cuckoos sing in shrill tones, bumblebees hum like a lyre's string.

3 Having the elixir of the moon, and bringing lovely Spring,
it is as though Kāmdev were become Dhanvantari to remove the world's ills.

4 The bee roams in the flowered groves and cool blows the breeze;
whose heart would not yield on going to Yamuna's bank?

5 Bathing in a pool and wandering from grove to grove,
slowly, slowly the breeze approaches, like a royal swan.

6 Knowing the trees of your garden to be lovelier than the tree of paradise,
the ocean's waters come and pour forth — the fountains their excuse — to see them.

SUMMER

7 With the dazzling sunshine as servant, and whirling the wind as a noose,
the thug of summer strikes full at noonday's height.

8 No water flows from these fountains, the water burns up and leaves the earth in
finery: seeing the tyranny of the hot season it flees to the sun-king.

9 Some overflow with delight, some leap, some run and beat the water:
seeing the grace of the women's water-games the lover is satiated, yet wanting more!

10 The lover splashes the women thus with his hands, taking delight in the water-games,
as though from all around, the moon were raining pearls onto the lotus.

1.2 *cā̃danī*: 'moonlight' — but also 'white sheet, quilt' (with spring personified as a handmaiden).

1.2 *āi*: a convenient (though semantically redundant) rhyme: cf. 7.2, 8.1, 12.1, 16.2.

2.1 *taṁta*: the string of a musical instrument, or of Kāmdev's bee-strung bow.

3 Kāmdev is personified as Dhanvantari, the celestial physician who, with Spring as his nurse, and equipped with the 'lord of elixirs' — the nectarous moon — will cure the ailing world.

6 In this conceit the ocean enters the garden fountains just in order to admire the springtime trees, more beautiful than even the magical wish-granting tree which was produced from the ocean when it was churned by the gods and demons. The *jala jantra* 'water-engines' were a characteristic feature of Mughal and Rajput palace gardens, and included elaborate ducts, waterfalls, fountains and so forth.

7 The sun is worse than a *ṭhag* (cf. BS 3), because it attacks even in broad daylight.

8 Water, fleeing the iniquitous summer heat, burns in anger; decorating itself (an allusion to the shimmer of heatwaves ?) it seeks refuge with the sun (*bhānu*, both 'sun' and 'king').

9.1 *ubharata*: this variant reading is preferred to the text's *ubhakata*.

9 With a change of context from 8, this stanza describes the heroines' games in abundant water.

10 The conceit hinges on *kara*, 'hand'/'moonbeam': the lover is like the moon; his hands are the moonbeams which make the women/lotuses blossom with delight as he splashes nectar onto them.

पावसऋतु

पावस मैं सुरलोक तें जगत अधिक सुख जानि ।
इन्द्रबधू जिहि रितु सदा छिति बिहरति है आनि ॥ ११ ॥

सुमन सुगंधन सों सनी, मंद मंद चलि आइ ।
प्रौढ़ा लौं मन को हरति, हिय लगि बरषा बाइ ॥ १२ ॥

अरुन चीर तन मैं सजै, यों बिहरति है नारि ।
मानो आई है सुरी, बसुधा हरी निहारि ॥ १३ ॥

झूलि झूलि तिय सिखति है गगन चढ़न की रीति ।
आजु काल्हि मंह आइहैं सुर नारिन कों जीति ॥ १४ ॥

सरदऋतु

चंद्र छत्र धरि सीस पै, लहि अनंग उपदेस ।
कमल अस्त्र गहि जीति जग लीन्हौं सरद नरेस ॥ १५ ॥

चंद्र बदन चमकाइ अरु खंजन नैन चलाइ ।
सकल धरा को छलति यह सरद अपछरा आइ ॥ १६ ॥

दिन सोहित जल अमल मैं निरमल कमल अनूप ।
निसि सोहत ही बाद बदि, हिय मोहत ससिरूप ॥ १७ ॥

हेमंतऋतु

दिन निसि रबि ससि लहत है हेम-सीत के जोग ।
भरम चकोरन भोग है, कोकन भरम वियोग ॥ १८ ॥

हेम सीत के डरन तें, सकति न ऊपरि जाइ ।
रह्यौ अगिनि कौ पाइ कै धूम भूमि पै छाइ ॥ १९ ॥

सिसिरऋतु

प्रगट कहत या सिसिर मैं, रूख रूख के पात ।
बिछुर न को सीतहु धरे, सूखि जात हैं गात ॥ २० ॥

मान न काहू को रहत, ल्याइ दूतिका घात ।
मिलै देति या सिसिर की सीरी सीरी बात ॥ २१ ॥

MONSOON

11 In the rains, know the world's pleasure to be greater than heaven's,
in this season when the heavenly 'ladyfly' ever comes and roams the earth.

12 Filled with flower fragrances, slow and gentle blows the wind;
like an accomplished lover the monsoon wind enwraps the heart and steals the mind.

13 Red clothing adorning her body, the woman roams pleasurably
as though a goddess had conquered the earth with a glance.

14 Swaying on the swing, the lady learns the skill of ascending the skies;
soon she will come to the point of defeating the gods' womenfolk.

AUTUMN

15 With the moon an umbrella over his head, and taking a lesson from Kāmdev,
holding a lotus as his weapon, King Autumn has vanquished the earth.

16 With moon-bright face resplendent and wagtail eyes a-dancing
this nymph of Autumn beguiles the wide world.

17 In the daytime an unparalleled pure lotus radiates in clear water,
at night too, in rivalry, it charms the heart in a moon's form.

WINTER

18 Day takes the role of night, and the moon that of the sun, in the winter mist:
cakoras have an illusion of union, cuckoos an illusion of separation.

19 For fear of the winter cold it cannot rise —
finding the fire, the smoke remains spread low on the ground.

THE COOL SEASON

20 The leaves of each tree show it clearly in this winter season:
may no-one be separated and suffer cold, their bodies shrivelling [thus]!

21 No-one's aloofness abides when the go-between has done her work:
this cold cold wind of winter brings all together.

11.2 *indrabadhū* : alluding to the literal sense 'Indra's wife', the poet suggests that this monsoon visit shows the beauty of the earth in this season to be superior to that of heaven.

13.2 *surī*: both 'sun' (< *sūrya*) and, personified, 'goddess'. In the context of the first meaning, *harī* can be interpreted as 'green', descriptive of the earth's monsoon verdure.

14.1 *jhūli jhūli*: playing on a swing is a traditional monsoon pastime (with a genre of songs, *hiṇḍolā).*

15.1 *chatra* : the umbrella is a symbol of royalty, appropriate to 'Autumn' personified as a king.

17 The lotus and the moon are rivals for the same role, for which they both contend; the former is resplendent in the daytime, the latter in the night (when its reflection in the water imitates the lotus).

18 The winter mist makes day seem like night; thus *cakoras* (which live on moonlight) think they are united, and cuckoos (habitually separated from their mates at night) believe themselves separated.

19.1 The smoke clings to the ground when the air is cold, as though staying near the fire for warmth.

20.2 The published reading *bichurana ko* has been adapted here, but the meaning is perhaps not fully clear.

21.1 *lyāi dūtikā ghāta* : 'the go-between having brought about her stratagem', i.e. the contrivance of a meeting between lover and beloved. *bāta* has the additional sense '*dūtikā*'s words'.

अरिल्ल-पचीसी

नागरीदास

संग फिरत है काल भ्रमत नित सीस पर ।
यह तन अति छिन-भंग धुँवें को धौलहर ॥
यातैं दुर्लभ सांस न वृथा गमाइयैं ।
ब्रजनागर नँदलाल सु निस दिन गाइयैं ॥ १ ॥

चली जात है आयु जगत जंजाल मैं ।
कहत टेरिकैं घरी घरी घरियाल मैं ॥
समैं चूकि बेकाम न फिरि पछिताइयैं ।
ब्रजनागर नँदलाल सु निस दिन गाइयैं ॥ २ ॥

सुत मित पति तिय मोह महा दुख मूल है ।
जग मृगतृष्णा देखि रह्यो क्यौं भूल है ॥
स्वपन राज सुख पाय न मन ललचाइयैं ।
ब्रजनागर नँदलाल सु निस दिन गाइयैं ॥ ३ ॥

कलह कलपना काम कलेस निवारनौं ।
पर निंदा पर द्रोह न कबहुँ बिचारनौं ॥
जग प्रपंच चटसार न चित्त चढ़ाइयैं ।
ब्रजनागर नँदलाल सु निस दिन गाइयैं ॥ ४ ॥

अन्तर कुटिल कठोर भरे अभिमान सौं ।
तिनके गृह नहिं रहैं संत सनमान सौं ॥
उनकी संगति भूल न कबहूँ जाइयैं ।
ब्रजनागर नँदलाल सु निस दिन गाइयैं ॥ ५ ॥

कहूँ न कबहूँ चैन जगत दुख कूप है ।
हरि भक्तन कौं संग सदा सुख रूप है ॥
इनकैं ढिग आनंदित समैं बिताइयैं ।
ब्रजनागर नँदलाल सु निस दिन गाइयैं ॥ ६ ॥

Arill-pacīsī

Nāgarīdās

1 Death walks with you, ever hovering over your head;
this body is so transitory, a tower of cloud.
Do not therefore waste that breath so rare:
sing night and day of Nanda's dear son, the skilful one of Braj.

2 A lifetime slips by in the entanglements of the world,
calling out each and every hour on the gong.
Do not miss your chance uselessly, to repent later:
sing night and day of Nanda's dear son, the skilful one of Braj.

3 Infatuation for son, friend, husband or wife is a source of great grief;
why do you remain deceived, seeing the mirage of the world?
Do not tempt your mind with dreams of royal delights:
sing night and day of Nanda's dear son, the skilful one of Braj.

4 Ward off disputation, mental fancy, and the anguish of desire;
never contemplate malice or hostility to others.
Enrol not your mind in the world's school of illusion:
sing night and day of Nanda's dear son, the skilful one of Braj.

5 [Those whose] souls are perverse and harsh, and filled with pride,
the saintly do not reside with honour at their house.
Never even dream of consorting with them:
sing night and day of Nanda's dear son, the skilful one of Braj.

6 Nowhere is there ever repose, the world is a well of pain;
[yet] the company of god's votaries is ever blissful.
Spend your time with them, in a happy state:
sing night and day of Nanda's dear son, the skilful one of Braj.

1.3 *durlabha sā̃sa* : the soul wandering in *saṁsāra* attains human birth only with great difficulty, and hence this is seen as a valuable opportunity for true devotion to God.

3.1 *suta mita pati tiya moha* : i.e. all family and domestic relationships.

4.1 *kalaha kalapanā kāma kalesa* : as so often with such phrases, the compounded nouns can be resolved in a number of different ways.

4.1/2 *nivāranaũ/ bicāranaũ* : examples of the didactic or dictatorial imperative mood so often associated with the infinitive in Braj and MSH.

5.1 This line stands as a rel. clause, picked up by correlative *tinake* in the following line. A more elegant English translation would transpose the two phrases (cf. 7.1/2).

5.3 *bhūla na kabahū̃ jāiyaī̃* : *bhūla* is abs. '[even] by mistake' (MSH *bhūlkar bhī*). Cf. SB 2.1 & 3.

6.2 *sukha rūpa* : as the final member of a compound, *rūpa* means 'having the appearance or nature of, consisting of'. Thus 'comprised of bliss'.

कृष्ण भक्ति परिपूरन जिनकैं अंग हैं ।
दृगनि परम अनुराग जगमगैं रंग हैं ॥
उन संतन के सेवन दसधा पाइयैं ।
ब्रजनागर नँदलाल सु निस दिन गाइयैं ॥ ७ ॥

बृज बृंदावन स्याम पियारी भूमि है ।
तहँ फल फूलनि भार रहैं द्रुम झूमि हैं ॥
भुव दंपति पद अंकित लोटि लुटाइयैं ।
ब्रजनागर नँदलाल सु निस दिन गाइयैं ॥ ८ ॥

नंदीश्वर बरसानौं गोकुल गाँवरो ।
बंसीबट संकेत रमत तहँ साँवरो ॥
गोबर्द्धन राधाकुंड सु जमुना जाइयैं ।
ब्रजनागर नँदलाल सु निस दिन गाइयैं ॥ ९ ॥

नंद जसोदा कीरति श्री वृषभान हैं ।
इनतैं बड़ो न कोऊ जग मैं आन है ॥
गो गोपी गोपादिक पद रज धाइयैं ।
ब्रजनागर नँदलाल सु निस दिन गाइयैं ॥ १० ॥

बँधे उलूखल लाल दमोदर हारिकैं ।
विश्व दिखायो बदन बृच्छ दये तारिकैं ॥
लीला ललित अनेक पार कित पाइयैं ।
ब्रजनागर नँदलाल सु निस दिन गाइयैं ॥ ११ ॥

मेटि महोछो इंद्र कुपित कीन्हो महा ।
जब बरस्यो जल प्रलय करन कहिए कहा ॥
गिरधर करी सहाय सरन जिहिं जाइयैं ।
ब्रजनागर नँदलाल सु निस दिन गाइयैं ॥ १२ ॥

7 Those whose limbs are brimful with adoration for Kṛṣṇa,
the hue of supreme love glows in their eyes.
Through serving such saintly folk, tenfold devotion is achieved:
sing night and day of Nanda's dear son, the skilful one of Braj.

8 Braj and Vrindaban are Śyām's beloved domain;
there the trees are ever bent with the burden of fruits and flowers.
Roll with me there on the ground marked by the couple's feet:
sing night and day of Nanda's dear son, the skilful one of Braj.

9 In Nandīśvar, Barsānā, and Gokul village,
at the fluting-tree, and at Sanket, there roams the dark one.
Go to Govardhan, to Rādhākuṇḍ, to the sweet Yamuna:
sing night and day of Nanda's dear son, the skilful one of Braj.

10 Nanda, Yaśodā, Kīrti and Vṛṣabhānu —
there is no other in the world greater than these.
Worship the dust of the feet of the cows, milkmaids, herdsmen and others:
sing night and day of Nanda's dear son, the skilful one of Braj.

11 Defeated, dear Dāmodar was bound to a mortar;
he showed the universe in his mouth, and he liberated trees.
His wanton sports are many — how could one encompass them all?
Sing night and day of Nanda's dear son, the skilful one of Braj.

12 He abolished Indra's great feast, and angered him greatly;
what can one say of that time when the rains of dissolution fell?
Giridhar saved those who came to him for refuge:
sing night and day of Nanda's dear son, the skilful one of Braj.

7.3 *dasadhā*: 'tenfold', glossed by Gupta (1975:169) as meaning '*navadhā bhakti* (ninefold devotion) plus *premā bhakti* (loving devotion)'. 'Ninefold devotion' conventionally comprises the following: *śravaṇa* (listening to sacred texts), *kīrtana* (singing God's praises), *smaraṇa* (meditating on God), *pādasevana* (worship of the deity's feet), *arcana* (worshipful homage), *vandanā* (praise), *sākhya* (intimate friendship), *dāsya* (humble servilitude) and *ātmanivedana* (surrender of self).

8. 1 *bṛja*: a common spelling in both early and modern texts for *braja*; here it suggests an assimilation to the following *bṛṁdāvana*, whose *ṛ* is etymological.

8.3 *loṭi luṭaiyai*: 'roll on the ground [in ecstasy], and make me do so'.

9. 1,2 *naṁdīśvara barasānau gokula ...saṁketa*: the names of villages in Braj. Nandīśvar is an old name for Nandagā̃v or 'Nanda's village'; its meaning of 'Lord of Nandī' suggests that the place had associations with Śiva before it became established as a place of Kṛṣṇaite pilgrimage. Barsānā is the neighbouring village, traditionally identified as the hometown of Rādhā's father Vṛṣabhānu. Gokul is an important centre of the Vallabha sect, to which Nāgarīdās belonged. Saṅket, 'the tryst', is a village near Barsānā associated with Kṛṣṇa and Rādhā's assignations. See Entwistle 1988: chapter 8.

9.3 *su* is superfluous both metrically and semantically, and perhaps represents a mis-copying from 9.4.

10 For episodes described in this and subsequent verses, see Index of Epithets and Motifs.

बकी बकासुर आदिक असुर अभावनैं ।
हते सदगते किए स्याम मन भावनैं ॥
रक्षिक घोष गुपाल सु नहिं बिसराइयैं ।
ब्रजनागर नँदलाल सु निस दिन गाइयैं ॥ १३ ॥

निरविष जमुना करी दवानल कौं पियो ।
नंद त्रास अहि हरी सबन कौं सुख दियो ।
आरति घोष निवारन सौं मन लाइयैं ।
ब्रजनागर नँदलाल सु निस दिन गाइयैं ॥ १४ ॥

मंडल गोप समाज स्याम तिन माँहिं हैं ।
हँसि हँसि जेंवत छाक ढाक की छाँहिं हैं ॥
विधि मोहन कौतूहल ध्यान समाइयैं ।
ब्रजनागर नँदलाल सु निस दिन गाइयैं ॥ १५ ॥

मोर पच्छ धर गुंज धात तन लावहीं ।
गोप बेस गो चारि सहित बल गाँवहीं ॥
रज मंडित मुख ध्यान परम सचु पाइयैं ।
ब्रजनागर नँदलाल सु निस दिन गाइयैं ॥ १६ ॥

टोकत गैल गुपाल दान मिस लैं छरी ।
गहबर बन अँधियार हार तिय हैं करी ॥
नैन बैन तन उरझन मन उरझाइयैं ।
ब्रजनागर नँदलाल सु निस दिन गाइयैं ॥ १७ ॥

तिय मन माखन हरत जु धरत दुराइकैं ।
देवी पूजत लीन्हैं चीर चुराइकैं ॥
इहीं चोर कौं चाहि चित्त चुरवाइयैं ।
ब्रजनागर नँदलाल सु निस दिन गाइयैं ॥ १८ ॥

13 Śyām, the heart's delight, dispatched to salvation
Pūtanā, the heron demon, and other malevolent demons.
He is guardian of the cattle-station and the cowherds, do not forget him:
sing night and day of Nanda's dear son, the skilful one of Braj.

14 He cleansed the Yamuna of [Kāliya's] poison, and drank the forest fire;
he overcame Nanda's dread, the serpent, and gave joy to all.
Set your heart on the banisher of the cowherds' pains:
sing night and day of Nanda's dear son, the skilful one of Braj.

15 The cowherds' band — Śyām is among them —
merrily they eat their workday food in the *ḍhāk* tree's shade.
Let the attention be filled with his charming ways and pranks:
sing night and day of Nanda's dear son, the skilful one of Braj.

16 Wearing peacock feathers and a seed necklace, he smears his body with pigments,
in cowherd's garb grazing the cows with Balrām near the village.
Through contemplation of that dust-adorned face, find the highest joy:
sing night and day of Nanda's dear son, the skilful one of Braj.

17 Gopāl obstructs the road on the pretext of a toll, bearing a staff;
in deep forest and on dark common he has taken a woman.
Entangle your mind in those entanglements of eyes, words and bodies;
sing night and day of Nanda's dear son, the skilful one of Braj.

18 He plunders butter and women's hearts, which they kept hidden;
he stealthily steals their clothes while they worship the goddess.
Look on this thief, and have your mind stolen by him:
sing night and day of Nanda's dear son, the skilful one of Braj.

13.2 Even demons defeated by Kṛṣṇa achieve salvation, through the mere fact of having come into contact with him.

14.1 *davānala* : on two separate occasions when the cowherds and cattle were threatened by forest fires, Kṛṣṇa drank the flames (BhP X.17.20-25, X.19).

15.2 *haĩ* at the end of the line is auxiliary to the ptc. *jĕvata.*

16.1 *mora paccha dhara* : 'with peacock feathers on his trunk'. In *Rāslīlā* performances, Kṛṣṇa performs a 'peacock dance', and wears appropriately elaborate costume. This description may have its origin here.

17.1 *laĩ charī* : 'having a staff [in his hand]' (MSH *charī lekar*). The staff is an emblem of rank in this *dān-līlā* context, wherein Kṛṣṇa takes on the guise of a tax official and extorts a toll from the gopis.

18.2 While they were bathing in the Yamuna in preparation for worship of the Goddess, Kṛṣṇa stole the gopis' clothes and climbed into a tree on the riverbank, insisting that each of them in turn must come forward in her nakedness (as the human soul must approach God) to retrieve them.

सुनि मुरली ब्रज बधू भई बस काम हैं ।
थिर चर गति बिपरीत बिबस सुर बाम हैं ॥
मादिक धुनि सुमिरत मन मादिक छाइयैं ।
ब्रजनागर नँदलाल सु निस दिन गाइयैं ॥ १६ ॥

सरद निसा सुख रच्यो रास बिसतारि हैं ।
गत-समाधि चल-चित्त भये त्रिपुरारि हैं ॥
रसानंद आवेस सुमिरि सरसाइयैं ।
ब्रजनागर नँदलाल सु निस दिन गाइयैं ॥ २० ॥

अन्यो-अन्य संकुलित बाहु मृदु पद चलैं ।
मंडित चन्द्राकार हार कुंडल हलैं ॥
विस्मै देव कुतूहल क्यौं बिसराइयैं ।
ब्रजनागर नँदलाल सु निस दिन गाइयैं ॥ २१ ॥

गुन सागर संगीत गतन अति छबि बढ़ी ।
बोल मधुर थेइ थेइ लोल भृकुटी चढ़ी ॥
काम बिजै लीला रस प्रान भिजाइयैं ।
ब्रजनागर नँदलाल सु निस दिन गाइयैं ॥ २२ ॥

नृत्त स्वेद रस भसे धँसे जमुना तबैं ।
बिहरत जनु गज संग जूथ करनी सबैं ॥
छबि छीटैं छिरकन की सुमिरि सिहाइयैं ।
ब्रजनागर नँदलाल सु निस दिन गाइयैं ॥ २३ ॥

राधा हित ब्रज तजत नहीं पल साँवरो ।
नागर नित्त बिहार करत मन भावरो ॥
राधा ब्रज मिश्रित जस रसनि रसाइयैं ।
ब्रजनागर नँदलाल सु निस दिन गाइयैं ॥ २४ ॥

ब्रज रस लीला सुनत न कबहुँ अघावनौं ।
ब्रज भक्तनि सत संगति प्रान पगावनौं ॥
नागरिया ब्रज बास कृपा फल पाइयैं ।
ब्रजनागर नँदलाल सु निस दिन गाइयैं ॥ २५ ॥

19 Hearing his flute, the woman of Braj have fallen into passion's grip;
inanimate and animate change roles, celestial women are compelled.
Remembering that intoxicating tune, let the intoxicant infuse your mind:
sing night and day of Nanda's dear son, the skilful one of Braj.

20 On an autumn night he unfolded the *rāsa* dance and created joy;
Śiva lost his concentration and his mind began to roam.
Remembering the frenzy of that blissful sentiment, delight your mind:
sing night and day of Nanda's dear son, the skilful one of Braj.

21 Holding each other's arms they move in sweet steps;
their jewelled crescent-shaped necklaces and their ear-rings tremble.
The wonder of the gods at this sport — how could it be forgotten?
Sing night and day of Nanda's dear son, the skilful one of Braj.

22 The splendour of that Ocean of Qualities increased greatly with the musical airs,
with sweet cries of '*thei! thei!*' as a wanton eyebrow arched.
Drench your soul in the spirit of that sport, the defeat of Kāmdev:
sing night and day of Nanda's dear son, the skilful one of Braj.

23 Drowning in perspiration from the dance, he plunges then into the Yamuna,
playing like an elephant with his whole retinue of females.
Remembering the splendour of that splashing and sprinkling, be charmed:
sing night and day of Nanda's dear son, the skilful one of Braj.

24 For Rādhā's sake, the dark one leaves Braj not for a moment;
the skilful one performs that eternal sport which pleases the mind.
Taste with your tongue the blended glory of Braj and Rādhā:
sing night and day of Nanda's dear son, the skilful one of Braj.

25 Hearing of the joyous sport of Braj never cloys;
steep your soul in the holy company of the Braj devotees.
May 'Nāgariyā' attain residence in Braj as the fruit of grace;
sing night and day of Nanda's dear son, the skilful one of Braj.

19.2 *sura bāma* : 'women of the gods', i.e. the gods' wives, or heavenly nymphs, Apsarases.

20.2 *gata samādhi cala-citta* : 'bereft of concentration, unsteady of mind'. Kṛṣṇa's disturbance of Śiva reflects the myth in which Śiva's meditation was disturbed by Kāmdev, who sowed seeds of desire for Pārvatī in his mind.

22.2 *thei-thei* : a *bol* or rhythmic mnemonic called out by dancers, and on which is based improvization and counter-improvization by dancer and drummer. As is usually the case with this phrase, -*e*- vowels are to be scanned as short.

24.1 *braja tajata nahī̃ pala* : Nāgarīdās here follows that tradition in which Kṛṣṇa is seen as residing permanently in Vrindavan with Rādhā; the concept of Kṛṣṇa as an incarnation of Viṣṇu with the purpose of going to Mathura to overcome Kansa is played down in favour of a concentration upon Kṛṣṇa and Rādhā's 'eternal sport' (*nitya vihāra* — cf. 24.2).

सभा-बिलास

लल्लूलाल

चिंता ज्वाल शरीर बन दावा लगि लगि जाय ।
प्रगट धुआं नहिं देखियै उर अंतर धुंधुवाय ॥
उर अंतर धुंधुवाय जरै जौं कांच की भट्टी ।
जर गौ लोहू मास रह् गई हाड़ की टट्टी ॥
कह् गिरधर कविराय सुनौ हो मेरे मिंता ।
वे नर कैसे जियैं जाहि तन ब्यापै चिंता ॥ १ ॥

साई अपने चित्त की भूल न कहियै कोय ।
तब लग मन में राखियै जब लग कारज होय ॥
जब लग कारज होय भूल कबहूं नहिं कहियै ।
दुरजन तातौ होय आप सीरे ह्वै रहियै ॥
कह् गिरधर कविराय बात चतुरन के ताई ।
करतूती कहि देति आप कहियै नहिं साई ॥ २ ॥

साई पुर पाला परचौ आसमान तें आय ।
पंगुहि आंधे छोड़िकै पुरजन चले पराय ॥
पुरजन चले पराय अंध एक मतौ बिचारचौ ।
पंगु कंध कै लियौ दृष्ट वा की पग धारचौ ॥
कह् गिरधर कविराय मते ह्वै चलियै भाई ।
बिना मते कौ राज गयौ रावन कौ साई ॥ ३ ॥

सोना लेने पी गये सूनौ कर गये देस ।
सोना मिल्यौ न पी फिरे रूपा हो गये केस ॥
रूपा हो गये केस रूप सब रोय गँवायौ ।
घर बैठी पछताय कंत अजहूं नहिं आयौ ॥
कह् गिरधर कविराय लौन बिन सबै अलोना ।
जब यौवन ढल जाय कहा लै करियै सोना ॥ ४ ॥

Sabhā-bilās

Lallūlāl

1 Care is a flame, the body a forest which keeps catching fire;
no smoke is seen openly, [but] the heart within is filled with fumes.
The heart within is filled with fumes, and burns like a glass-furnace;
blood and flesh are burnt up, a frame of bones remains.
Says Giridhar, prince of poets: hear me, O my friend —
how can those men live, whose bodies are pervaded by care?

2 Sir, no-one should ever dream of saying what is in his thoughts;
it should be kept in the mind as long as a motive remains.
As long as a motive remains, never dream of speaking;
if a wicked person becomes heated, you yourself stay cool.
Says Giridhar, prince of poets: to the wise,
actions speak for themselves, [so] do not you speak, sir.

3 Sir, snow fell on a town, coming from the skies;
leaving a blind man and a cripple, the townsfolk ran off.
The townsfolk ran off, and the blind man pondered a plan;
he took the cripple on his shoulder, and [relying on] his sight, set forth.
Says Giridhar, prince of poets: proceed in agreement, brother;
without agreement, Rāvaṇ lost his kingdom, sir.

4 In search of gold, her lover left, leaving homeland deserted;
neither gold was gained nor did the lover come home — silver became her hair.
Silver became her hair, all her beauty she wept away,
sitting at home regretting 'My husband still hasn't returned'.
Says Giridhar, prince of poets: without savoury beauty, all is insipid;
when youth declines, what is the use of gold?

1.4 *gau* = *gayau.*

2.1 *sāī̃* : Giridhar often uses this vocative to fulfil the requirement that the *Kuṇḍaliyā* stanza begin and end with same word — cf. verses 3 and 6. It is perhaps surprising that the acknowledged master of this verse form should have recourse to such an ingenuous device; cf. Edward Lear's fondness for completing a limerick with a repeat or paraphrase of its own first line.

2.1,3 *bhūla* : the abs. (cf. MSH *bhūlkar bhī*), 'even by mistake'. Cf. AP 5.3.

2.4 *hvai rahiyai* : lit. 'be and remain'.

2.5-6 Syntax: *karatūtī...bāta kahi deta.*

3.3 *eka matau* : here 'an idea', rather than adj. 'of one mind, unanimous'.

4.5 *launa bina* : lit. 'without salt'. Underlying this phrase is the metaphorical sense of *launa* (and its Skt etymon *lavaṇa*, and adj. derivates of both) as 'piquancy, beauty': cf. BS 51 etc.

4.6 *kahā lai kariyai sonā* : the syntax is *sonā lai kahā kariyai* (for *lai* cf. MSH *lekar* in this usage).

मोती लेने पी गये खार समुन्दर तीर ।
मोती मिले न पी मिले नैननि टपकत नीर ॥
नैननि टपकत नीर पीर अब का सों कहियै ।
बीते बारह मास पिया बिन घर ही रहियै ॥
कह गिरधर कविराय सांझ डारत सगनौती ।
जर जाओ वह सिंधु जहां उपजत है मोती ॥ ५ ॥

साई एकै गिरि धर्‍यौ गिरिधर गिरिधर होय ।
हनूमान बहु गिरि धरे गिरिधर कहै न कोय ॥
गिरिधर कहै न कोय हनू दौलागिरि लायौ ।
ता कौ किनका टूट पर्‍यौ सो कृष्ण उठायौ ॥
कह गिरधर कविराय बड़ेन की बड़ी बड़ाई ।
थोड़े ही जस होय यसी पुरुषन कौं साई ॥ ६ ॥

पानी बाढ़्यौ नाव में घर में बाढ़्यौ दाम ।
दोऊ हाथ उलीचियै यही सयानौ काम ॥
यही सयानौ काम नाम ईश्वर कौ लीजै ।
पर-स्वारथ के काज सीस आगै धरि दीजै ॥
कह गिरधर कविराय बड़ेन की यही है बानी ।
चलियै चाल सुचाल राखियौ अपनौ पानी ॥ ७ ॥

बिना बिचारै जो करै सो पाछैं पछिताय ।
काम बिगारे आपनौ जग में होत हँसाय ॥
जग में होत हँसाय चित्त में चैन न पावै ।
खान पान सनमान राग रंग मनहि न आवै ॥
कह गिरधर कविराय दु:ख कछु टरत न टारे ।
खटकत है जिय माहिं कियौ जो बिना बिचारे ॥ ८ ॥

हुक्का बांध्यौ फैंट में नै गहि लीनी हाथ ।
चले राह में जात है बंधी तमाकू साथ ॥
बंधी तमाकू साथ गैल कौ धंधा भूल्यौ ।
गई सब चिंता दूर आग देखत मन फूल्यौ ॥
कह गिरधर कविराय जु जम कौ आयौ रुक्का ।
जीव लै गयौ काल हाथ में रह गयौ हुक्का ॥ ९ ॥

5 In search of pearls, her lover went to the shore of the salty sea;
neither pearls nor her lover did she get, as tears dripped from her eyes.
Tears dripped from her eyes — whom could she tell now of her sorrow?
Twelve months passed as she stayed at home without her dear one.
Says Giridhar, prince of poets: in the evening she casts an omen;
may that ocean burn up where are produced those pearls!

6 Sir, by holding just one mountain, Giridhar became 'the mountain-holder';
Hanumān held many mountains, but no-one calls him 'mountain-holder'!
No-one calls him 'mountain-holder', Hanū who brought the snowy mountain;
a piece of it broke off and fell, which is what Kṛṣṇa lifted up.
Says Giridhar, prince of poets: grand is the aggrandizement of grandees;
small indeed is the glory of the glorified, sir.

7 If water gathers in the boat or money gathers in the home,
bale it out with both hands — this is the wise course of action.
This is the wise course of action: take the name of God,
and for another's self-interest, lay your head before him.
Says Giridhar, prince of poets, this is the nature of the great:
proceed with proper propriety, and maintain your reputation.

8 He who acts without thinking, later feels remorse;
he spoils his purpose and is ridiculed in the world.
He is ridiculed in the world and knows no peace of mind;
eating and drinking, honour, fun and frolic — nothing pleases.
Says Giridhar, prince of poets, that grief is not avoided by evasion;
the deed done without thinking rankles in the heart.

9 He tied a hookah in his waist-band, taking its mouthpiece in his hand,
and wended his way along the road, tobacco tied to his side.
Tobacco tied to his side, he forgot the purpose of his journey;
all cares went far away, his mind blossomed at the sight of fire.
Says Giridhar, prince of poets: when came a note from Yama,
Death took his life away — and in his hands remained his hookah.

5.6 *saganautī*: lit. 'good omen', but here evidently closer to 'curse'.

6.3 Hanumān's unrewarded mountain-holding was an episode in the Rāmāyaṇa war: despatched to the Himalayas for herbs to cure the wounded, he brought the whole mountain on which they grew.

7.1 *bāṛhyau...bāṛhyau*: perfective tense suggests resolution as a conditional clause.

7.6. *pānī*: the sense is distinct from that which started the stanza.

9.1 *tamākū*: 'tobacco' (cf. MSH *tambākū*). Giridhar's verse is amongst the first of its kind to show the first indications of the European presence in India, and this word (a loan from Portuguese, after Spanish *tabaco*, ultimately from Haitian) is the only word in this reader to be borrowed from (or via) a European language.

अर्द्ध निस वह आयौ भौन ।
सुन्दरता बरनै कहि कौन ॥
निरखत ही मन भयौ अनंद ।
क्यों सखि सज्जन ना सखी चंद ॥ १० ॥

दासी दे मैं मोल मँगायौ ।
अंग अंग सब खोल दिखायौ ॥
वा सों मेरौ भयौ जु मेल ।
क्यौं सखि सज्जन ना सखी तेल ॥ ११ ॥

रात दिना जा कौ है गौंन ।
खुले द्वार आवै मेरे भौंन ॥
वा कौ हर्ष बताऊँ कौन ।
क्यौं सखि सज्जन ना सखी पौन ॥ १२ ॥

आठ पहर मेरे ढिग रहै ।
मीठी प्यारी बातें कहै ॥
स्याम बरन अरु राते नैना ।
क्यौं सखि सज्जन ना सखी मैना ॥ १३ ॥

देखन में वह गांठ गंठीला ।
चाखन में वह अधिक रसीला ॥
मुख चूमौ तौ रस का भांड़ा ।
क्यौं सखि सज्जन ना सखी गांड़ा ॥ १४ ॥

निस दिन मेरे उर पर रहै ।
दोऊ कुच लै गाढ़े गहै ॥
उतरत चढ़त करत झकझोली ।
क्यौं सखि सज्जन ना सखी चोली ॥ १५ ॥

मो कौं तो हाथी कौ भावै ।
घट बढ़ होय तौ नाहिं सुहावै ॥
ढूंढ़ ढाँढ़कै ल्याई पूरा।
क्यौं सखि सज्जन ना सखी चूरा ॥ १६ ॥

हरित रंग मोहिं लागत नीकौ ।
वा बिन सब जग लागत फीकौ ॥
उतरत चढ़त मरोरत अंग ।
क्यौं सखि सज्जन ना सखी भंग ॥ १७॥

लंबी लंबी डगों जु आवै ।
सारे दिन की हौस बुझावै ॥
उठकै चला तो पकड़ा खूंट ।
क्यौं सखि सज्जन ना सखी ऊंट ॥ १८ ॥

छोटा मोटा अधिक सुहाना ।
जो देखे सो होय दिवाना ॥
कबहूं बाहर कबहूं अंदर ।
क्यौं सखि सज्जन ना सखी बंदर ॥ १९ ॥

अति सुरंग है रंग रँगीलौ ।
है गुनवंत बहुत चटकीलौ ॥
राम भजन बिन कभी न सोता ।
क्यौं सखि सज्जन ना सखी तोता ॥२०॥

धमक चढ़ै सुध बुध बिसरावै ।
दाबत जांघ बहुत सुख पावै ॥
अति बलवंत दिननि कौ थोरा ।
क्यौं सखि सज्जन ना सखी घोड़ा ॥ २१ ॥

10 At midnight he came to my house;
say, who could describe his beauty?
On seeing him my mind was thrilled —
Who, dear, your lover? No, dear, the moon.

11 I procured him through a servant girl;
I showed him all my naked limbs.
With him I have enjoyed union —
Who, dear, your lover? No, dear, oil.

12 He who comes both night and day
enters my house through my open door.
Whom can I tell of the joy he gives me? —
Who, dear, your lover? No, dear, the wind.

13 The whole day long he's by my side,
he says such sweet and lovely things.
Dusky is his body and reddish his eyes —
Who, dear, your lover? No, dear, my mynah.

14 To look at, he is knotty and stocky;
to taste, very sweet!
Kiss him on the mouth, a jar of nectar —
Who, dear, your lover? No, dear, sugarcane.

15 Night and day he dwells on my breast,
holding tight my two breasts.
Riding up and down he tosses and trembles.
Who, dear, your lover? No, dear, my bodice.

16 As for me, I prefer an elephant's:
smaller or bigger just doesn't please.
I seek it out and make it all fit —
Who, dear, your lover? No, dear, my bracelet.

17 His fresh colour pleases me greatly;
without him the whole world seems dull.
Mounting and dismounting he twists my limbs —
Who, dear, your lover? No, dear, *bhang*.

18 With great long strides he comes,
quenching his day-long appetite.
When he gets up to leave I grab his knob —
Who, dear, your lover? No, dear, my camel.

19 Small, stout, and very charming,
anyone who sees him goes quite crazy.
Sometimes he's in, sometimes he's out —
Who, dear, your lover? No, dear, my monkey.

20 He's a lovely colour, gaudy and gay,
full of qualities, a brilliant fellow.
He never sleeps without hymning Rām —
Who, dear, your lover? No, dear, my parrot.

21 Throbbing when mounting, losing his wits;
he finds great pleasure in squeezing thighs.
He's very strong, though tender of years —
Who, dear, your lover? No, dear, my horse.

11.1 *dāsī de*: 'giving [money] to the servant-girl'. Gilbertson notes the variant *te* for *de*.

14.1/2 *gaṁṭhīlā/rasīlā*: Kharī Bolī *-ā* endings in this stanza typify the mixed language of the *Mukrī* texts.

16.1 *hāthī kau*: 'an elephant's' — i.e. (in the more innocent meaning) the decorative metal band worn on an elephant's tusk, or a bracelet made of ivory; alternatively, 'jumbo size'.

18.3 *khū̃ṭa*: i.e. (again, in the innocent meaning) the pommel of the camel's saddle. Gilbertson, taking the other sense as 'shoulder', does not include this verse in the group described as 'too suggestive of the vulgar to be translated into literal English' (though our verses 15 and 16 are so designated).

19.1 *choṭā moṭā*: these two adjectives here maintain their distinct senses, 'small and stout', as opposed to the idiomatic compounded sense of 'trifling, insignificant'.

19.2 *jo dekhe*: the object 'him', necessary in English, spoils the joke (read 'him/it').

19.3 Gilbertson translates 'He is sometimes inside (the house), sometimes outside', and annotates his parenthesis with 'There is also, of course, the other meaning'.

20.3 Gilbertson: 'Natives often teach their parrots to say, "Ráma," "Shiva," etc. '.

Epilogue: Two Ṭhumrīs.

The *ṭhumrī,* usually classified musically as a 'light classical' song, is one of the most popular styles of Hindustani music. It is a love song, characterized by tender romanticism, and often describes the bittersweet emotion of *virah,* the pain of love in separation. *Ṭhumrīs* are often in Braj, though the language may be mixed with Khaṛī Bolī or Avadhī. The same songs may be used for either *ṭhumrī* performance and for the more 'classical' style of *khyāl,* in which the development of the rāga is followed more strictly. In terms of metre and rhyme the texts are usually rather free; the examples below have a *pāda* length of approximately 18 *mātrās.*

लट उलझी सुलझा जा रे बालम,
हाथन मोरे मेहँदी लगी है ।
माथे की बिंदिया बिखर गई रे
अपने हाथ लगा जा, रे बालम ॥ १ ॥

1 Untangle my tangled locks, O beloved,
for I have henna on my hands.
The dot on my forehead is disarranged;
put it right with your own hand, O beloved.

का करूँ सजनी, आए न बालम ।
तड़पत बीती मोरी उन बिन रतियाँ ॥
रोवत रोवत कल नाहीं आवे, तड़प तड़प मोहे कल न आवे ।
निस दिन मोहे बिरहा सताए, याद आवत जब उनकी बतियाँ ॥ २ ॥

2 What can I do, friend, my beloved has not come;
without him I spent the whole night writhing.
Weeping and weeping I find no rest, writhing and writhing no peace comes;
night and day lovesickness torments me whenever I think of his words.

1 The version given here is based on L. Garg 1981:75 and P.Manuel 1989:12; a recent recording (as a *khyāl* in Behāg) is by Ustad Munawar Ali Khan in *Homage to Bade Ghulam Ali Khan* (Audiorec ACCD 1003-S).

1.2 The *nāyikā* has decorated her hands with patterns of henna, and uses this as an excuse to give her beloved an imperious command. The disarray of her hair and her *bindī* are of course the result of lovemaking, but in typical *ṭhumrī* fashion this is alluded to only indirectly.

2 The text is from L. Garg 1981:74, and also appears in the recording noted above.

Index of Epithets and Motifs

(This index is intended to clarify narrative and descriptive allusions not covered in the notes or the glossary, and to cross-reference certain terms such as patronymics. Entries follow English alphabet order. The spelling conventions used here are those followed in the translations. Epithets of Kṛṣṇa are listed within the 'Kṛṣṇa' entry.)

Ajāmil: a Brahmin of Kanauj, who married a prostitute and lived a sinful life. On his deathbed he called out to his youngest son, named 'Nārāyaṇ': and by unwittingly taking this name of Viṣṇu, he was saved. See BhP. VI.1.26-68.

Arjun: third and most heroic of the five Pāṇḍu princes, Kṛṣṇa's charioteer in the Mahābhārata war, and his interlocutor in the *Bhagavad Gītā.*

Baka: the demonic brother of Pūtanā (q.v.); he tried to avenge her defeat by assuming the form of a giant stork and taking Kṛṣṇa in his beak, but Kṛṣṇa escaped by making his own body unbearably hot, and then tearing Baka in half. See BhP. X.11.47-53.

Baldev: son of Nanda and Rohiṇī, and half-brother of Kṛṣṇa.

Bali: a Daitya (demon) king who won control over the three worlds. Viṣṇu appeared before him in the form of a dwarf (Skt *vāmana,* Braj *bāvana*) and asked for as much land as he could cover in three strides; when the trifling request was granted, Viṣṇu assumed his universal form, and measured out the three worlds with his three steps, thus vanquishing Bali (who was allowed sovereignty of Pātāl, the infernal regions).

Balrām: a name of Baldev.

Bhavānī: a name of Pārvatī, wife of Śiva; her vehicle is the tiger (or lion).

Bṛhaspati: priest of the gods, later known as the deity of wisdom and eloquence.

Crane demon: see Baka.

Daśrath: king of Ayodhyā, descendant of Raghu and father of the four princes Rāma, Bharat, Lakṣmaṇ and Śatrughna. He granted two boons to Bharat's mother Kaikeyī after being tended by her after a battle: she used them to promote Bharat as heir to the throne and to have Rāma exiled — events which set in motion the Rāmāyaṇa narrative.

Draupadī: wife of the five Pāṇḍav brothers. The eldest of the five, Yudhiśthir, lost Draupadī together with all his possessions in a gambling match played against his cousins, the Kauravas. Duryodhan, the Kaurava prince, tried to dishonour her by stripping her of her clothing, but Viṣṇu miraculously lengthened her sari into an endless piece of cloth.

Elephant: the 'Gaj-rāj' or 'Gajendra', a 'royal elephant', saved by Viṣṇu on uttering the name 'Nārāyaṇ' when attacked by a crocodile. Like that of Ajāmil, the myth symbolizes the redemptive power of the divine name. See BhP. VIII.2.27-33 and VIII.3.

Gaṇeś: the elephant-headed son of Śiva and Pārvatī. He is the god of wisdom, and the scribe of the gods, who transcribed the *Mahābhārata* from the dictation of Vyāsa. As 'lord of obstacles' (Vighna-haraṇ etc.) he is invoked at the beginning of any new undertaking. His names Gaṇeś and Gaṇapati derive from his position as lord of the *gaṇas*, minor deities who wait on Śiva.

Gautam's wife: Ahalyā, wife of the sage Gautam, turned to stone by her husband after being seduced by Indra. She was restored to her human state by the touch of Rāma.

Girijā: 'daughter of the mountain', a patronymic of (synonymous) Pārvatī, born of the Himalaya mountain (*giri, parvata*). In RB her husband Śiva is called 'Girijā-īs'.

Gusāī̃ (Skt *gosvāmī*): 'master of sense faculties/master of cows', a religious title applied to Vallabha in VV, and also adopted as a hereditary title by his descendants and the dynastic priests of parallel Vaiṣṇava *sampradāys*. The term is also applied to God (SS 5.1 etc).

Haldhar: 'plough-holder', an epithet of Kṛṣṇa's half-brother Baldev, who carries (or rather is armed with) a ploughshare.

Hanumān: the monkey god, son of the wind, faithful servant of Rāma — and hence the ideal model of the 'servile' (*dāsya*) devotional attitude. When he was captured by Rāvaṇ's forces his tail was set on fire: but he put this to his advantage, ran amok, and burned down the city of Lanka. Flying through the air, he brought from the Himalaya a mountain on which grew herbs to restore those wounded in the battle with Rāvaṇ. He is referred to by various patronymics such as Mārutsut, Suvansamīr (from *māruta, samīra,* 'wind').

Harlot: see Piṅgalā.

Hiraṇyakaśipu: father of Prahlād, q.v.

Indra: lord of the gods in the Vedic pantheon, but reduced to a lower status in later Hinduism. As lord of the skies he has the rainclouds at his command. The Govardhan myth (q.v. under 'Kṛṣṇa' below), in which Indra is humbled by Kṛṣṇa, illustrates this change of status vis-à-vis Kṛṣṇa/Viṣṇu.

Indrāṇī: the wife of Indra.

Janak: king of Videha and father of Sītā, who is given the patronymic 'Jānakī'.

Jasumati (Skt *yaśumatī*), Jasodā: see Yaśodā.

Jaṭāyu: king of vultures, son of Viṣṇu's vehicle Garuḍa. Jaṭāyu was an ally of Rāma in the Rāmāyaṇa war, and fought to defend Sītā from Rāvaṇ; mortally wounded, he achieved salvation through Rāma's intercession.

Kālindī: a patronymic of Yamuna as 'daughter of the sun' (Kalinda).

Kāliya: a five- (or multi-) headed venomous serpent which inhabited a pool in the Yamuna, polluting the water and terrorizing the district. The child Kṛṣṇa jumped fearlessly into Kāliya's coils and vanquished him in a fierce struggle, to emerge dancing triumphantly on the serpent's heads. At the intercession of Kāliya's wives, Kṛṣṇa spared him but banished him to the ocean. See BhP. X.16; and cf. the *Śrīkṛṣṇakīrtana* version (M.H. Klaiman 1984:189-195).

Kāmdev: god of love; love and desire personified, and the epitome of physical beauty. The Indian Cupid, he bears a bow of sugarcane strung with humming bees and armed with blossom-arrows; Vasant (Spring) is his companion-cum-general. His symbol is the *makar*, a mythological fish or crocodile. He is also called Anaṅga, 'bodiless', from the occasion when he disturbed Śiva's meditation with thoughts of lust for Pārvatī, at which Śiva opened his third eye and burned him to ashes; Kāmdev's wife Rati ('lust') begged Śiva to resuscitate him, which he did — but without restoring his physical form. Amongst his other names are Ratipati and Madan.

Kṛṣṇa: 'the dark/black one', son of Vasudev and Devakī and adoptive son of Nanda and Yaśodā. He is more frequently referred to in devotional texts by patronymics, by pet names indicating endearment, or by epithets implying identity with Viṣṇu: the name 'Kṛṣṇa' itself is generally restricted to formulaic or technical uses (such as *kṛṣṇa-bhakti*, AP 7.1). The following names and epithets of Kṛṣṇa appear in this book:

Balbīr: 'mighty hero';

Brajnāgar: 'skilful one of Braj';

Brajrājkumār: 'prince of Braj';

Dāmodar: 'having a string round the belly'. Yaśodā, tiring of Kṛṣṇa's pranks, one day tied him by the waist to a heavy mortar: but Krishna dragged the mortar along, demolishing two trees and thereby releasing two Gandharvas who had been reduced to this form by a curse. (This episode is used to explain the epithet as deriving from Skt *dāma* 'string' + *udara* 'waist'.) In vernacular treatments of the theme, the incident forms the basis of the gopis' complaint at Yaśodā's mistreatment of her child. See BhP. X.9-10. In a related incident, Yaśodā rebuked Kṛṣṇa for eating earth: when she made him 'open wide' to show what he was eating, she had a temporary vision of the entire cosmos inside Kṛṣṇa's mouth; see BhP. X.8.32-45.

Ghanśyām: 'dark blue-black, cloud-dark';

Giridhar, Giridhārī: 'mountain-holder' — see Govardhandhar;

Gopāl: 'cowherd';

Govardhandhar, °nāth: 'holder/Lord of Govardhan'. In the famous Puranic episode, Kṛṣṇa persuaded the people of Braj to abandon their traditional annual tribute to Indra, lord of the heavens and of the rain-giving clouds, and to make offerings instead to Govardhan hill, while at the same time honouring their cattle. Kṛṣṇa then assumed the identity of the hill itself, appeared seated on its peak, and conferred his protection upon the Braj cowherds. When the incensed Indra attempted to wash away the whole of Braj with storm and flood, Kṛṣṇa lifted Govardhan as a protective umbrella, humiliating Indra. See BhP. X.24-25.

Govind: a name of Viṣṇu/Kṛṣṇa;

Hari: a name of Viṣṇu/Kṛṣṇa;

Jadurai (Skt *yadu*, + *rāi* < *rājan-*): lord of the lunar Yādav dynasty (descended from Yadu);

Kānha, Kānho, Kānhar, Kanhāī: derivatives of the name 'Kṛṣṇa';

Lāl: 'dear one, darling son' (often suffixed to other names, e.g. Mohanlāl);

Mādhav: 'descendant of Madhu', a figure in the Raghu dynasty;

Manmohan: 'heart's delight';

Manohar: 'charming' (may often be interpreted as adjective rather than epithet);

Muralīdhar: 'flute-holder';

['**Kṛṣṇa**' continued:]

Murārī: Viṣṇu/Kṛṣṇa as 'enemy of Mura' — a demon who, along with his seven thousand sons, was slain by Kṛṣṇa;

Mohan: 'enchanter';

Nanda-kiśor, °-nandan, °-lāl: 'son of Nanda';

Nārāyaṇ: a name of Viṣṇu/Kṛṣṇa;

Rādhāvallabh: 'lover of Rādhā', especially in the *svarūp* of that name worshipped by Hit Harivaṁś (1502-1552) and his followers;

Raskhāni, °na: 'mine of amorous sentiment' (and also name of a poet);

Sā̃varau (Skt *śyāmala-*): 'dark one, dusky one';

Śrīnāth: the *svarūp* of Kṛṣṇa worshipped by Vallabha, and principal deity of the Vallabha sect. In 1669, Śrīnāth was taken from the temple at Govardhan to escape the iconoclasm of Aurangzeb, and was eventually established in a new temple in Rajasthan; the temple formed the nucleus of the town of Nathdwara. (The name 'Śrīnāth', though existing independently as an epithet of Viṣṇu as 'lord of Śrī/Lakṣmī', is popularly regarded as a contraction of 'Śrīgovardhannāth'.)

Śyām: 'the dark one';

Tribhaṅgīlāl: 'having three curves' — Kṛṣṇa in his jaunty fluting pose, with bends at the knee, waist and neck.

Kuver: 'the ugly one', god of wealth and master of the obscure 'nine treasures', and chief of the Yakṣas.

Lakṣmaṇ: younger brother and staunch companion of Rāma; he is depicted as a bowman.

Lalitā: foremost of the eight sakhis of Rādhā, the eight often being referred to en masse by the formula *lalitādi*, 'Lalitā and the others'.

Madan: 'the intoxicating one', Kāmdev.

Maheś: 'great god', Śiva. He broke the fall of the Ganges, when it fell from heaven to earth, by catching it in his matted locks. Amongst his numerous epithets are Girijā-īsa 'Lord of Pārvatī', and Trilocana 'Three-eyed'.

Nanda: husband of Yaśodā and of Rohiṇī, and foster-father of Kṛṣṇa. The name is the base for various patronymics applied to Kṛṣṇa: Nandanandan, Nandalāl, etc. Nanda was on one occasion rescued by his adoptive son: he was set upon by a serpent which nobody could drive off, but Kṛṣṇa approached and touched the serpent with his foot, at which it turned into the musician Sudarśan, cursed to have the form of a snake until such time as he should receive Kṛṣṇa's touch. See BhP. X.34.1-18.

Nandarānī: 'Nanda's queen', a name of Yaśodā.

Narahari: the avatar of Viṣṇu as 'man-lion' — see Prahlād.

Piṅgalā: a prostitute who, despite her profession, was the recipient of Viṣṇu's grace because of her piety. See BhP. XI.8.22-44.

Prahlād: a staunch devotee of Viṣṇu, persecuted by his demonic father Hiraṇyakaśipu (who is portrayed as a Śaiva in some versions of this well-known myth). Hiraṇyakaśipu was protected by a boon of safety, granted by the gods, which ensured that he could not be killed by man or beast, by hands or weapons, by day or by night, inside or outside the house, etc. etc. — the details of the boon are elaborated variously, at great length in some versions of the myth. Secure in this apparently watertight guarantee, he persecuted his Vaiṣṇava son Prahlād, who nevertheless insisted on worshipping Viṣṇu. Hiraṇyakaśipu mocked Prahlād's claim that Viṣṇu was omnipresent, at which Viṣṇu manifested himself out of a pillar and appeared in the form of a man-lion (neither man nor beast), seized Hiraṇyakaśipu and sat on the threshold (neither inside nor out) and disembowelled him with his claws (neither hands nor weapons), the time being dusk (neither daytime nor night), thereby circumventing all the conditions of the boon. Prahlād is the archetypal devotee and recipient of Viṣṇu's grace. See BhP. VII.5-8.

Purandar: 'city-destroyer', an epithet of Indra.

Pūtanā: among the demons who tried to overcome Kṛṣṇa was Pūtanā, also called Bakī 'brother of Baka' (q.v.). She was a giant demoness who assumed the form of a beautiful woman and attempted to kill Kṛṣṇa by suckling him from poisoned nipples, but was herself killed when he sucked the life out of her. See BhP. X.6.2-18.

Rādhā, Rādhikā: a gopi, daughter of Vṛṣabhānu and lover of Kṛṣṇa; she becomes his consort in the later tradition. She is often referred to by such patronymics as 'Vṛṣabhānukiśorī', and also as 'Śyāmā' (in the sense 'Śyām's beloved').

Raghu: hero of the solar dynasty, and ancestor of Rāma (who is thus designated by the patronymic 'Rāghav' and the titles 'Raghubīr' and 'Raghupati' — 'hero/lord of the Raghus').

Rāsa: the climax of Kṛṣṇa's *līlās* is the great *rāsa* dance, performed under the autumn moon on the Yamuna's bank; Kṛṣṇa's fluting is an irresistable summons for the gopis, who join him in the dance which entrances the whole of creation. The *rāsa* is described in five chapters (the so-called *rāsapañcādhyāyī*) of the BhP. (X.29-33); cf. the Braj version of Nanddās (R.S.McGregor 1973).

Rāvaṇ: the demonic king of Lanka, 'villain' of the Rāmāyaṇa story, who abducted Sītā and was later vanquished by Rāma.

Ravinanda: see Yama.

Rukmiṇī: the queen of Kṛṣṇa during his reign as king of Dwarka.

Serpent: see Nanda; and see Kāliya.

Sītā: the daughter of Janak and wife of Rāma. Her name means 'furrow': in the Rāmāyaṇa she sprang from the furrow being ploughed by Janak, who reared her as his adoptive daughter.

Śiva: see Maheś.

Śyāmā: 'beloved/consort of Śyām', an epithet of Rādhā — though in non-Kṛṣṇaite contexts the name means 'the dark one' and designates Kālī.

Trilocan: see Maheś.

Uddhav: a companion of Kṛṣṇa who attempts (unsuccessfully) to persuade the gopis to a realization of Kṛṣṇa as the abstract *nirguṇ* godhead. The confrontation between Uddhav and the lovelorn gopis allows an airing of the *saguṇ/nirguṇ* dichotomy; for the *bhakti* poets, however, the triumph of the gopis' point of view is a foregone conclusion, and Uddhav is little more than a stooge for their *saguṇ* devotional rhetoric.

The gopis identify Uddhav — and his bumbling arguments — with a black bee which flies past as they speak: hence the genre of 'bee songs' (*bhramar-gīt*) which treats of this theme. See BhP. X.46-47; and cf. the Braj version of Nanddās (R.S. McGregor 1973).

Vulture: see Jaṭāyu.

Yama: king of the dead (whom he snares with a noose), son of the sun, and twin of the goddess Yamunā. The patronymic Ravinanda is applied to him; and from his capacity as judge of the dead he is called Dharmarāj.

Yamuna: the river Jumna; sister of Yama and daughter of the sun; she is often designated by patronymics such as Kālindī, Kalindanandinī, Taranijā, etc. Her waters are characteristically dark, or dark blue, in contradistinction to the fair or white waters of the Ganges.

Yaśodā: wife of Nanda and foster-mother of Kṛṣṇa; also called Jasumati (Yaśumati). The name is the base for the metronymic 'Yaśodānandan'.

GLOSSARY

Glossary

Most headwords fall into one of three categories: tatsama words, marked '[S]'; semi-tatsamas, for which tatsama spellings are indicated thus—'अपजस...[S *apayaśas*]'; tadbhavas, where a numerical reference indicates a CDIAL headword (e.g. 'बावरौ...[11504 *vātula*-]'. Where there is no CDIAL entry, 'S' precedes a suggested etymology. Etymologies relate to headwords only, and not necessarily to other forms within the entry.

The following conventions have been followed in the glossary:

(i) Verbs are listed as roots with a short dash (e.g. कर-, जा-); they are preceded in alphabetical order by any homonyms (thus कर m. 'hand' precedes कर- v.t. 'to do').

(ii) When no direct sg. form of a noun or adj. occurs in the text, its stem form is given with a long dash, followed by occurring forms in parenthesis, e.g. डोर— (डोरैं).

(iii) *Anusvār* and *candrabindu* are not distinguished etymologically or metrically but follow textual usage. When both graphs appear in the texts (as in अंग and अँग), the former only is listed.

(iv) When both tatsama and semi-tatsama forms of a word occur in the texts, the former is normally listed first, even though this may not be the usual vernacular form: 'कारण, °न'. Tadbhavas are listed separately as headwords in their own right.

(v) Cross-referenced words within an entry appear in Nagari.

(vi) Compound ppn. are listed under their second element.

(vii) Uncertain genders are bracketed: '(m.)', '(f.)'.

The following studies comprise or include etymological glossaries which have been referred to in compiling this glossary: A.W.Entwistle 1983; R.Mathur 1974; R.S. McGregor 1968; C.Shackle 1981 and 1984; J.D.Smith 1976; M.Thiel-Horstmann 1983.

SIGNS USED IN THE GLOSSARY:

*	hypothetical form
°	except for letters following or preceding this sign, the word is the same as the headword
×	contaminated or affected by
+	extended by, used with
=	is etymological doublet of
~	the headword as part of phrase or compound

अंक m. embrace [S]

अँकवारि f. embrace, bosom [103 *aṅkapāli-*]

अंकित adj. marked [S]

अंकुस m. elephant-driver's hook, ankus [111 *aṅkuśa-*]

अँख— (अँखियाँ, pl.) see आँख

अंग m. body, limb [114 *aṅga-*]

अंगना¹ f. woman [S]

अँगना² m. courtyard [118 *aṅgana-*]

अँगिया f. bodice, blouse [132 *aṅgikā-*]

अंगीकार m. embracing, acceptance [S]

अंगोछ- vt. to wipe dry [139 *aṅgoñcha-*]

अँचर, आँचर m. border, hem [168 *añcala-*]

अँचा- , अचा- vt. to drink, sip [1069 *ācāmati*]

अंजन m. collyrium, kohl [S]

अँजोर- vt. to snatch [?]

अँटक- , अटक- vi. to be caught, stuck, entangled, attached, enamoured, engrossed [182 **aṭṭakk-*]

अँटका- vt. to obstruct, impede [182 **aṭṭakk-*]

अंडकोष m. testicle; scrotum [S]

अंत m. end [S]

अंतर m. & adv. heart, soul, interior; within [357 *antara-*]

अंतरगत adj. innermost, inner [S *antargata-*]

अंतर्धान m. disappearance, vanishing [S]

अंदर adv. inside [Pers. *andar*]

अँदेस m. anxiety, concern [Pers. *andesh*]

अंध, adj. & m., अंध— (अंधे) adj. blind; blind person [385 *andha-*]

अँधियार, °र— (°रैं) adj. dark [386 **andhĭkāra-*]

अँधेर— (°रि) adj. dark [386 **andhĭkāra-*]

अंबर m. clothing, garment; sky; ambergris, grey amber [573 *ambara-*]

अंबुज m. lotus [S]

अंबुनिधि (f.) ocean [S]

अँसु, अँसुवा see आँसू

अकबर m. Akbar [Ar.]

अकुला- vi. to be agitated [1012 *ākula-*]

अकेले adv. alone [2506 **ekkalla-*]

अक्रम adj. not in sequence, simultaneous; a hyperbole in which cause and effect are simultaneous [S]

अक्षर m. character, letter of syllabary [S]

अखंड adj. indivisible, unbroken [S]

अखंडित adj. unbroken, continuous [S]

अखिल adj. whole, entire [S]

अगनि see अग्नि

अगनित adj. incalculable [S *agaṇita-*]

अगनियाँ (rh.) adj. incalculable [S *agaṇya-*]

अगम adj. inaccessible [S *agamya-*]

अगर m. fragrant aloe-wood; aloes, sap from the aloe used as skin emollient [49 *agaru-*]

अगाध adj. unfathomable [S]

अग्नि, अगनि, अगिन, अगिनि f. fire [S]

अघ m. sin [S]

अघा- vi. to be satiated [1062 *āghrāpayati*]

अचमन m. sipping water from the hand, rinsing of the mouth after eating [1065 *ācamana-*]

अचरज m. surprise [S *āścarya-*]

अचल m. mountain [S]

अचा- see अँचा-

अचानक adj. suddenly, unexpectedly [**ajāna(ka)-* ??]

अचेत adj. unconscious, senseless [S *acetas-*]

अच्छ adj. pure, clear, bright [S]

अछ- vi. to remain, exist, be [1031 *ākṣeti*]

अछेद adj. indivisible [*a* + *ched*]

अज(हूँ) see आजु

अजान, अयान adj. unknowing [157 *ajānant-*]

अजामिल m. Ajāmil, a sinner saved by Viṣṇu [S]

अजी interj. Oh! [5240 *jīva*]

अजूँ, अजौं see आजु

अजोग adj. unconnected [*a-* +*jog* (S *yoga-*)]

अट— (pl. अटनु) see अटा

अटक- see अँटक-

अटा (pl. अटनु) f. open upper storey, open roof [180 *aṭṭa-*]

अतर m. attar, rose-oil [Ar. *'iṯr*]

अति adj. & adv. great; very [S]

अतिनिन्हव m. 'utter denial', a trope in which an attribute shared by both subject and object of comparison is denied the latter [S °*hn*°]

अतिसयोक्ति f. hyperbole [S °*ś*°]

अतुरा- vi. to be disturbed, distressed [S *ātura*]

अत्यंतातिसयोक्ति f. 'extreme exaggeration', a hyperbole in which effect precedes cause [S °*ś*°]

अथ(व)- vi. to set (of sun) [976 *astam eti*]

अद्भुत adj. wondrous [S]

अधम adj. & m. vile, low; wretch [S]

अधर, अधरा m. lip, lower lip [S]

अधर्म m. unrighteousness, iniquity [S]

अधार m. basis, support, foundation [S °*ā*-]

अधिक adv. very, much [S]

अधिकार m. right, authority [S]

अधीनी (rh.) adj. helpless [S *adhīna-*]

अधीर adj. restless, distracted [S]

अधीरज m. impatience, lack of restraint [S *adhīra* + *ya*]

अन pref. with negative sense [S]

अनंग m. 'bodiless', name of Kāmdev [S]

अनंत adj. & adv. endless; endlessly [286 *ananta-*]

अनंद see आनंद

अनत adv. elsewhere [401 *anyatra*]

अनन्य adj. & m. single-minded (devotee) [S]

अनन्वय m. 'simile expressing uniqueness' (in which subject of comparison doubles as object) [S]

अनर्थ m. nonsense, absurdity, bad thing [S]

अनाचार m. indecorum, neglect of proper conduct [S]

अनादि adj. without beginning [S]

अनार m. pomegranate [Pers.]

अनीति f. injustice, tyranny [S]

अनुचर m. follower [S]

अनुज m. younger brother [S]

अनुभव m. perception, understanding, (spiritual) experience; °वी m. one who has this [S]

अनुराग m. love, attachment [S]

अनुरागी adj. impassioned, lovelorn [*anurāgin-*]

अनूप adj. unparalleled [irregular derivative from S *anupama-*]

अनेक adj. several, many, much [S]

अनोसर m. time at which a Vaiṣṇava temple deity is prepared for sleep (and when shrine is closed to public gaze) [S *anavasara-*]

अन्याय m. injustice, iniquity [S]

अनयो-अन्य adj. & adv. mutual(ly) [S *anyo-'nya-*]

अन्ह(व)ा- vi. to bathe [13786 *snāti*]

अपछरा f. apsaras, nymph, a class of celestial divinities who visit the earth [S *apsaras-*]

अपण— see अपन—

अपजस m. infamy [S *apayaśas-*]

अपत adj. leafless [S **apatra-*]

अपन—, अपण— (अपने, अपनी, अपणे) poss.pr. own [1135 **ātmanaka-*]

अपना- vt. to accept, adopt [1135 **ātmanaka-*]

अपन्हुति f. 'denial', a class of trope in which an object of comparison is affirmed in place of its subject [S *°hn°*]

अपमान m. disgrace, abuse [S]

अपर adj. different [S]

अपराध m. offence, fault [S]

अपार adj. unbounded, limitless [S]

अब adv. now; ~कैं now, at this time [Add[2] 2528 *evam eva* × *a-*]

अबगुन m. defect, fault [S *avaguṇa-*]

अबला f. woman [S]

अबसर, औसर m. moment [S *avasara-*]

अबिद्या f. ignorance, illusion [S *avidyā-*]

अबिनासी adj. & m. imperishable, immortal [S *avināśin-*]

अभंग adj. continuous [S *a-* + *bhaṅga-*]

अभरन m. adornment, jewellery [S *ābharaṇa-*]

अभावन— (°नैं) adj. malevolent, odious [S]

अभिमान m. pride [S]

अभिराम adj. lovely, delightful [S]

अभिलासी adj. & m. desirous, covetous [S *abhilāṣin*]

अभिसार m. meeting, tryst [S]

अभेद adj. indivisible; 'identical'—a metaphor whose subject shares all the qualities of its object [*a-* +*bheda-*]

अभ्यास m. practice, exercise [S]

अमंद adj. not dull, bright [S]

अमल[1] adj. pure, unsullied [559 *amala-*]

अमल[2] m. jurisdiction, authority; ~दे- vt. to yield authority [Ar. *'amal*]

अमृत m. nectar, ambrosia [S]

अयान see अजान

अर- vi. to oppose, be stubborn [187 **aḍ-*]

अरंग m. perfume, fragrance [?]

अरजुन m. Arjun [S *arjuna-*]

अरबिंद m. lotus [S *°v°*]

अरि m. enemy [S]

अरिल्ल m. a metre (see II.2.4) [S *aṭhillā-*]

अरी see अली[2]

अरु, रु cj. and (= MSH और) [434 *aparam*]

अरुन adj. red, reddish-brown [616 *aruṇa-*]

अरे interj. 'hey!' [621 *are*]

अर्थ m. meaning [S]

अर्थी m. supplicant [S *arthin-*]

अर्द्ध adj. half; ~निस f. midnight [S]

अर्बुद m. name of a mountain, Mt Abu [S]

अर्प- vt. to make an offering [S *arpayati*]

अलंकार m. ornament; figure of speech [S]

अलक f. lock of hair, ringlet [S]

अलग adj. separate [700 *alagna-*]

अलाप m. speech, talk [S *ā°*]

अलाप- vt. to catch a tune, run over the notes of a tune [S *ālāpa-*]

अलि see आली

अलिक f. lock of hair, ringlet [S *alaka-*]

अली[1] m. bumble bee [S *alin-*]

अली[2], अरी see आली

अलौना (rh.) adj. saltless, insipid [707 *alavaṇa-*]

अवधि f. term, limit (of space or time) [S]

अवर (= और) adj. other [434 *aparam-*]

अवलोक- vt. to look [S *avalok-*]

अवस्था f. condition [S]

अष्टयाम m. the 8 watches making up the 24-hour period [S]

असंगत adj. unharmonious, incoherent [S]

असत m. untruth [S]

असवार adj. mounted [926 *aśvavāra-*]

असार[1] adj. & adv. vain; in vain [968 *asāra-*]

असार[2] m. the month Āṣāṛh, June-July [1473 *āṣāḍha-*]

असुर m. demon [S]

अस्त्र m. weapon [S]

अस्म m. stone [S *aśman-*]

अहंकार m. vanity, egotism [S]

अहर्निस adv. night and day [S *°śa*]

अहार m. food, meal [1544 *āhāra-*]

अहि m. snake; ~ राज 'king of snakes', large snake [S]

अहित adj. & m. inimical; harm, injury [S]

अहीर; °री m.; f. member of herdsman caste [1232 *ābhīra-*]

अहुँठ num. three and a half [649 *ardhacaturtha-*]

अहो interj. O, ah! [996 *aho*]

आँख f. eye (pl. अँखियाँ) [43 *akṣi-*]

आँगन m. courtyard [118 *aṅgana-*]

आंध— (°धे) adj. & m. blind; blind man [385 *andha-*]

आँसू, अँसु, अँसुवा m. tear [919 *aśru-*]

आ-, आन- vi. to come [1200 *āpayati*]

आकुलता f. perplexity [S]

आग, आगि f. fire [55 *agni-*]

आगरा m. Agra [?]

आगें, आगैं, आगै adv. ahead, in front, further, before; later [68 *agra-*]

आचार्य m. title for religious teacher (designating Vallabha in VV) [S]

आछो, आछौ adj. good [142 *accha-*]

आजु, आज adv. today; आज काल्हि adv. recently, soon; अजूँ, अजौं, अजहूँ (emph.) still, even now [242 *adya-*]

आज्ञा f. order, command [S]

आठ num. eight [941 *aṣṭā*]

आडंबर m. ostentation, bombast [S]

आणंद see आनंद

आतप, °पु m. sunshine [S]

आतुर adj. distressed, pained [S]

आदर m. respect, honour [S]

आदिक adj. etc., and other such [S]

आध— (आधे) adj. & m. half [644 *ardha-*]

आधीन adj. dependent, subservient [S]

आन adj. other [399 *anya-*]

आन- vt. to bring (for 'come' sense see आ-) [1174 *ānayati*]

आनंद, आणंद, अनंद m. joy, bliss [1172 *ānanda-*]

आनंदित adj. delighted, happy [S]

आनन m. face, countenance [S]

आप, आपु, आपुन pr. oneself [1135 *ātman-*]

आपस, आपुस m. & pr. fellowship; one another; ~ में amongst themselves [1135 *ātman-*]

आपुनौं pr. one's own [1135 **ātmanaka-*]

आवृत्ति, °त्ति f. repetition; a trope with repetition of word or meaning [S *āvṛtti-*]

आभा f. splendour, light [S]

आभूषन m. ornament, decoration [S °*ṇa*]

आयसु m. command, order [1157 *ādeśa-*]

आयु f. age, lifespan [1292 *āyuṣ-*]

आरंभ m. commencement, outset [1307 *ārambha-*]

आरति f. pain, suffering [S *ārti-*]

आरबल f. lifespan, allotted period of life [S **āyurbala-*]

आरसी f. mirror [1143 *ādarśa-*]

आरोग- vt. to eat [1330 *ārogyayati*]

आरोप m. superimposition [S]

आर्ति f. temple ritual in which the deity is worshipped with lamps moved in a circular motion [1315 *ārātrika-*]

आली, अली, अरी f. woman's female friend [1380 *ālĭ̄-*]

आवेस m. intentness, frenzy [S °*śa-*]

आस, आसा f. hope, desire [1456 *āśas-*]

आसक्त adj. attached, engrossed [S]

आसक्ति f. attachment [S]

आस-पास adv. nearby, around [आस echo-word: see पास]

आसमान m. sky [Pers. *āsmān-*]

आस्रय m. refuge [S *āśraya-*]

आहट f. footfall, sound [1054 *āghaṭṭayati*]

इंदु m. the moon [1570 *indu-*]

इंद्र m. Indra [S]

इंद्रबधू f. the 'red-velvet' insect (which proliferates in the monsoon), MSH बीरबहूटी [S °*va*°]

इंद्री f. (any of) the senses [1581 *indriya-*]

इक see एक

इकलौ adj. alone [2506 **ekkalla-*]

इच्छा f. desire, wish [S]

इजाफा m. rise, increase, augmentation [Pers. *izāfa*]

इत adv. hither, here; इतहिं उतहिं adv. to and fro; इतै (emph.) right here [**itra*, cf. 228 *atra* ; base also for उत, कित, जित, (M. Thiel-Horstmann 1983:155), and for कत]

इतनक adj. so little [1589 *iyattaka-*]

इतनौ, इतौ adj. this much; इतने में adv. meanwhile, at that moment [1589 *iyattaka-* (इतनौ, etc. also model for जेत-, तेत-, etc.)]

इतर adj. & m. other; another [S]

इतौ see इतनौ

इन्हैं see यह

इलाज m. means, remedy [Pers. *'ilāj*]

इष्ट adj. chosen, desired [S]

इह, इहिं, इहीं see यह

ईर्षा f. jealousy, envy [S *īrṣyā-*]

ईश्वर, ईस्वर m. God, the Lord [S]

ईस m. lord, master [1617 *īśa-*]

उघार- vt. to open [1968 *udghāṭayati*]

उचार- vt. to pronounce, utter [1641 *uccārayati*]

उछर- vi. to leap, spring [1843 *ucchalati*]

उछाह see उतसाह

उजराई f. brilliance, brightness [1670 *ujjvala-*]

उजार— (°रे) m. brightness [1673 **ujjvālaka-*]

उजास m. brightness [1678 **ujjhāṣa-*]

उजेर— (°रैं) m. light [1673 **ujjvālaka-*]

उजयार— (°री) adj. bright; उज्यारी f. brightness [1673 **ujjvālaka-*]

उज्ञल, °लु adj. bright [1670 *ujjvala-*]

उझक vi. to stand on tip-toe, peep [1679 **ujjhukkati* ?]

उठ- vi. to rise; (as aux., e.g. नाचि उठ-) to begin to [1900 **ut-sthāti*]

उठा- vt. to lift, raise [1903 **ut-sthāpayati*]

उड-, उड़- vi. to fly [1697 *uḍḍayate*]

उड़ाइक m. flyer, one who makes fly [*uḍā-* < 1697 *uḍḍāpayati*]

उढ़ा- to wrap, cover [2547 **oḍḍha-*]

उण see उन

उत adv. thither, there [see इत]

उतंग adj. high, lofty [1794 *uttuṅga-*]

उतपन्न adj. produced, born [S *utpanna-*]

उतर m. reply [1767 *uttara-*]

उतर- vi. to encamp, stay; to cross; to alight; to come down; to decline (of intoxication, etc.) [1770 *uttarati*]

उतसाह, उछाह m. zeal, excitement [1882 *utsāha-*]

उतार- vt. to take down; to take across, ferry over [1770 *uttārayati*]

उताहल m. haste, impatience [1788 **uttāpala-* (*-h-* ?)]

उत्तम adj. superior, supreme [S]

उत्थापन m. 'arousal'—a temple rite in which the deity is aroused from sleep and worshipped [S]

उत्प्रेक्षा f. 'ascription', a class of trope in which a property is ascribed metaphorically to a subject, such that the subject behaves like the object of comparison [S]

उद(व)- vi. to rise (of moon) [S *udayati*]

उदार, °री (rh.) adj. noble, generous, illustrious [S]

उदित, उद्दित adj. risen, shining, bright [S]

उदै m. rise, rising [S *udaya-*]

उदोत m. light, splendour [S *uddyota-*]

उद्दित see उदित

उद्धार m. liberation, salvation [S]

उद्यम m. effort, exertion, labour [S]

उधार- vt. to save, rescue [2009 *uddhārayati*]

उन see वह

उनमत्त adj. drunk, intoxicated [S *°nm°*]

उन्हें see वह

उपज- vi. to be produced, to arise [1814 *utpadyate*]

उपजा- vt. to produce [1814 *utpadyate*]

उपट- vi. to run over, be excessive; to be marked, show an impression [1809 **utpaṭyati*]

उपदेस m. lesson, instruction [S *°śa-*]

उपनागरिका f. 'cultured', alliteration showing sequences of soft sounds [S]

उपबन m. grove, wood [S *°va°*]

उपमा f. simile, comparison; ~ उपमेय (for *upameyopamā*) reciprocal simile (in which subject and object define each other) [S]

उपमान m. object of comparison, thing to which a subject is compared (e.g. 'moon' in 'her moon-like face') [S]

उपमेय, उपमे m. subject of comparison (e.g. 'face' in 'her moon-like face') [S]

उपहास m. mockery, ridicule [S]

उपाय, उपाउ, उपाव m. way, means [S]

उफान m. boiling up [1838 **utphāna-*]

उबट- vt. to anoint, rub [2071 *udvartayati*]

उबार- vt. to liberate [2082 **udvārayati*]

उभर- vi. to overflow, run over, become (sexually) excited [2038 *udbharati*]

उमाह् m. rapture, ecstasy [2120 *unmātha-*]

उर m. chest, heart [2350 *uras-*]

उरज m. female breast, bosom [S]

उरझ- vi. to become entangled [2221 *uparudhyate*]

उरझा- vt. to entangle [2221 *uparudhyate*]

उरबसी f. Urvaśī, a nymph; a chest-ornament [S *urvaśī-*]

उरह्- vt. to reproach [2312 *upālabhate*]

उरोज m. female breast [S]

उलंघ- to traverse [2366 *ullaṅghayati*]

उलट adj. contrary, reversed [2368 **ullaṭyate*]

उलट- vi. to turn over, be in disorder, topsy-turvy [2368 **ullaṭyate*]

उलीच- vt. to bale out [2061 *udricyate*]

उलूखल m. wooden mortar [S]

उल्लेख m. 'representation', a trope in which the qualities of a subject are differently represented in different contexts [S]

उसास m. sigh, breathing; *~ā-* vi. to breathe, catch one's breath [1868 **ut-śvāsa-*, 1866 **ut-śvāsayati*]

उहाँ adv. there [see यहाँ]

उहिं see वह

ऊंच— (ऊंचै) adj. high, tall; ऊंचै adv. high up [1634 *ucca-*]

ऊंट m. camel [2387 *uṣṭra-*]

ऊखल (m.) mortar [2360 **udukkhala-*]

ऊजर— (°री) adj. bright [1670 *ujjvala-*]

ऊधौ m. Uddhav, *advaitin* friend of Kṛṣṇa [S *uddhava-*]

ऊपर adv. & ppn. above, on; for; about [2333 **uppari*]

ऋतु, रितु f. season; ~ राज m. 'king of seasons', spring [S]

ऋधि f. wealth, prosperity, accomplishment, supernatural power [S *ṛddhi-*]

ए¹ see यह

ए² interj. Oh! Listen! [S]

एक, इक num. one; (suffixed to noun) about, approximately; एक संग adv. together; इक भाइ adv. in one manner, single-mindedly, devotedly [2462 **ekka-*]

एड़ी f. heel [191 **eḍḍi-* or **eḍi-*]

एत— (एते), एतिक adj. so much; *ete para* even so [1589 *iyattaka-*]

एव adv. indeed, verily [S]

ऐंच- vt. to pull, draw [210 **atiyañcati*]

ऐन¹ m. motion; abode; [S *ayana-*]

ऐन² m. & adj. eye; the choice, the best, very essence; very, just, exact [Ar. *'ain*]

ऐसौ adj. & adv. such, of such a kind; thus [1611 *īdṛśaka-*]

ओंछ- see पोंछ-

ओट f. screen, shelter [2544 **oṭṭā-*]

ओढ़- vt. to wrap, wear [2547 **oḍḍh-*]

ओप f. lustre, beauty [2556 **opp-*]

ओर f. direction, side; ppn. towards [812 *avarā-*]

औ (= और) cj. and [434 *aparam*]

औगुन m. misdeed, transgression, fault [S *avaguṇa-*]

और cj. & adj. and; other [434 *apara-*]

औषधि f. herb, medicinal plant [S]

औषधीस m. 'lord of elixir', moon [S °*śa-*]

औसर see अबसर

कंकन m. bracelet [2597 *kaṅkaṇa-*]

कंचन m. gold [3013 *kāñcana-*]

कंचुकि f. bodice, blouse [S °*kī-*]

कंज m. lotus [S]

कँटील— (°ली) adj. thorny [2679 *kaṇṭin-*]

कंठ m. throat, neck; voice; ~ लगा- vt. to embrace [2680 *kaṇṭha-*]

कंठी (-माला) f. short necklace [2681 *kaṇṭhakā-*]

कंत m. husband, lover [3029 *kānta-*]

कंद m. bulbous root, bulb, gall [S]

कंदरा f. cave [S]

कंदुक m. ball [S]

कंध m. shoulder [13627 *skandha-*]

कंप m. trembling, shaking [S]

कंप- see कांप-

कँवल m. lotus [2764 *kamala-*]

कच m. hair [S]

कछनी f. loincloth, girdle [2592 *kakṣyā-*]

कछु, कछू, कछुक, कछूक indef.pr. any, anything [3144 *kiṁcid-*]

कछोटी f. dhoti [2590 **kakṣapaṭṭa-*]

कट- vi. to be cut; to pass (of time) [2854 *kartati*]

कटक m. army, legion [S]

कटाक्ष, °च्छ m. sidelong glance [S]

कटि f. waist [S]

कठिन adj. hard, difficult, harsh [S]

कठोर— (°री, in उरज कठोरी, 'hard-breasted one') adj. hard, firm [S *kaṭhora-*]

कत adv. why? [see इत]

कथा f. story, tale [S]

कदंब, कदम m. a flowering tree [S]

कन m. grain, corn, crumb, morsel [2661 *kaṇa-*]

कनक m. gold [S]

कनकलता f. 'golden vine', jasmine [S]

कनिया f. lap [2849 *karṇikā-*]

कन्हाई see कान्ह

कपट m. deceit, falsehood [S]

कपटी adj. deceitful [S]

कपाट m. door, door-leaf [S]

कपूर m. camphor [2880 *karpūra-*]

कपोल m. cheek [S]

कब adv. when?; ~ हुँक , ~ हूँ, ~ हू adv. ever, whenever (cf. MSH *kabhī*) [Add^2 2528 *evam eva* × *ka-*]

कबहुँक, कबहूँ कबहू see कब

कबि m. poet [S *kavi-*]

कबिता f. poetry [S *kavita-*]

कमनैती f. archery [Pers. *kamān* + *aitī* (1286 *āyatta-*) (cf. बानैत)]

कमल m. lotus; ~ नैन, ~ नयन 'lotus-eyed one', Kṛṣṇa [S]

कमला f. Lakṣmī [S]

कमा- vt. to earn [2897 **karmāpayati*]

कमान f. archer's bow [Pers.]

कर m. hand [S]

कर- vt. to do, make, compose, prepare; to utter [2814 *karoti*]

करकस adj. rough, hard [S *karkaśa-*]

करड़ी adj. firm, strict, severe [2657 *kaḍḍ-*]

करतारी f. marking time with claps [S °*lī*-]

करतूती f. deed, action [for S *kartavyatā*-]

करन adj. & m. doing, effecting [2790 *karaṇa*-]

करनी[1] f. action, deed [2791 *karaṇīya*-]

करनी[2] f. she-elephant [S *kariṇī*-]

करवत m. saw [2795 *karapattra*-]

करवा- vt. to cause to be done [2814 *karoti*]

करा- vt. to bring about, perform, effect, cause to be done [2814 *karoti*]

कराला f. 'dreadful', a bawd in RN [S]

करील m. a thorny shrub [2805 *karīra*-]

करुना f. compassion, pity; ~ मय adj. compassionate [S *karuṇā*-]

कर्म m. fate (as determined by deeds in past lives) [S *karman*-]

कल[1] adj. soft, gentle, melodious [S]

कल[2] m. ease, peace [2948 *kalya*]

कलंकी adj. stained, tainted [S *kalaṅkin*-]

कलधौत m. gold [S]

कलप, कलपतरु see कल्प

कलपना f. mental fabrication [S *kalpanā*-]

कलह m. strife, quarrel, contention [S]

कला f. practical art, skill [S]

कलानिधि m. moon [S]

कलिंदी see कालिंदी

कली f. bud, unblown flower [2934 *kali*-]

कलेस m. distress, pain [3627 *kleśa*-]

कल्प, कलप m. aeon, age; ~ तरु, ~ वृच्छ m. wishing-tree, one of the five wish-granting trees of Indra's heaven [S]

कवि m. poet [S]

कवित्त m. a Hindi verse-form [S *kavitva*-]

कस adv. how? [3197 *kīdṛśa*-]

कस- vt. to draw tight [2908 *karṣati*]

कहँ adv. where?; ~ लौं how far? [2574 *ka*-]

कह see कहा

कह- vt. to say, call [2703 *kathayati*]

कहा, कह, का pr., adv. & cj. what? who? how? why?; whether, either (see I.4.6) काहे (कों) adv. why?; कहा भयौ so what?, no matter [2574 *ka*-]

कहा- vt. & vi. to call, designate; to be called [2703 *kathayati*]

कहँ, कहूँ adv. anywhere, somewhere, in one place; somehow [कहँ + emph.]

का see कहा

कांच m. glass [3007 **kācca*-]

काँच— (°ची) rude, unfinished, insubstantial, MSH कच्चा [2613 **kacca*-]

कांति f. lustre; ~ मान adj. lustrous [S]

कांध— (°धे) m. shoulder [13627 *skandha*-]

कांप-, कंप- vi. to tremble [2767 *kampate*]

काई f. scum, water-moss [3109 **kāvikā*-]

काग m. crow [2993 *kāka*-]

काछ- vt. to tie on, gird [2592 *kakṣya*-]

काछनी f. loin-cloth, cloth worn over the dhoti [2592 *kakṣya*-]

काज m. & ppn. work; for the sake of [3078 *kārya*-]

काट- vt. to cut, bite; to pass (time) [2854 *kartati*]

काठ m. wood, timber [3120 *kāṣṭha*-]

काठो adj. hard (-hearted) [2978 *kaṣṭa*- (cf. Gujarati *kāṭhũ*)]

काढ़- vt. to extract [2660 **kaḍḍhati*]

कातिक m. the month Kārttik (October-November) [S *kārttika*-]

कान m. ear [2830 *karṇa*-]

कानि f. shame, honour, prestige; convention; forbearance [2830 *karṇa-* ? or 2705 *kathānaka* ? (see J.D. Smith 1976:109)]

कान्हो, कान्ह(र), कन्हाई m. Kṛṣṇa [3451 *kṛṣṇa-*]

काफर m. infidel, non-Muslim [Ar. *kāfir*]

काम[1] m. desire, lust; Kāmdev, god of love; कामांध adj. lust-blinded [S]

काम[2] m. work, action, purpose [2892 *karman-*]

कामरी, °रिया f. blanket [2771 *kambala-*]

कामांध see काम[1]

कायथ m. kayasth, man of the writer caste [3051 *kāyastha-*]

काया f. body [S *kāya-*]

कार— (°रे, °री) adj. black [3083 *kāla-*]

कारज m. work, business [S *kārya-*]

कारण, °न, m. & ppn. reason, cause; for the sake of [S]

काल m. time, death, fate; ~ बस adj. (ill-) fated, in the grip of fate [S]

कालिंदी, क° f. the river Yamuna [S]

काल्हि m. & adv. yesterday; tomorrow [3104 *kalya-*]

काहु, काहू see कोइ

काहे, काहें see कहा

किंकिन, °नी f. small bell [3152 *kiṅkiṇī-*]

किंवाड़ see किवार

कित adv. where?; ~हूँ, कितूँ anywhere [see इत]

कितक, कितेक, कितौ interr.pr. how much/ many? [3167 **kiyatta-*]

किधौं, कीधौं cj. or, or then, or rather [*ki* < 3164 *kim*, + *dhaũ* < 6892 *dhruva* ? (R.S. McGregor 1968:196)]

किन adv. why not? [3164 *kim* +*na* ?]

किनका m. piece, particle [2665 *kaṇika-*]

किरोधी adj. angry, passionate [S *krodhin-*]

किवार, किंवाड़, किवाड़ m. door [2963 *kavāṭa-*]

किसोर; °री m.; f. youth, boy; girl [3190 *kiśora-*]

किहिं see को[1]

की cj. or [3164 *kim*]

कीधौं see किधौं

कीरति f. fame, renown; Kīrti, Rādhā's mother; ~ मान adj. illustrious [S *kīrti*]

कीर्तन m. hymn, song of praise [S]

कील f. peg, wedge [3202 *kīla-*]

कुंज m. grove, bower, arbour [S]

कुंडल m. ear-ring [S]

कुंभ m. jug, jar, pitcher [S]

कुँवर m. boy, prince [3303 *kumāra-*]

कुकर्म m. wicked deed (as determinant of fate) [S °*karman-*]

कुक्कुट m. cock, rooster [S]

कुच m. female breast, bosom [S]

कुटनी f. bawd, pimp, procuress [3240 *kuṭṭanī-*]

कुटिल adj. curly; crooked, devious; कुटिलता f. crookedness [S]

कुटीर m. hut, bothy [S]

कुठार m. axe [S]

कुतूहल m. sport, spectacle [S]

कुदाव m. trick, dupery [*ku-* + *dāva*]

कुपित adj. angry, incensed [S]

कुबत f. slander, reprobation [S *ku-* +*bāta*]

कुबुद्धि adj. senseless [S]

कुबेर m. Kuber, god of wealth [S *kuvera-*]

कुमति, कुमत f. perversity, folly [S]

कुमारि f. young girl [3303 *kumāra-*]

कुरंग m. deer [S]

कुल m. family, dynasty, group; ~ वंती f. respectable woman, lady of high birth [S °*vatī*]

कुसंग m. bad company, association with the wicked (and worldly) [S]

कुसल adj. skilled, adept [3365 *kuśala-*]

कुसुम m. flower, blossom [S]

कुसुमित adj. in flower, blossoming [S]

कुहुक- vn. to call, cry (as bird) [33388 **kuharayati*]

कूँ see कौं

कूक f. cry, shriek [3390 **kūkkā-*]

कूकर, °रा m. dog [3329 *kurkura-*]

कूद- vi. to jump, leap [3412 *kūrdati*]

कूप m. well [S]

कूल m. bank, shore [S]

कृत m. deed, thing performed [S]

कृपन adj. mean [S *kṛpaṇa-*]

कृपा f. compassion, pity, grace; ~ निधि, ~ सिंधु, m. ocean of mercy; ~ पात्र, adj & m. favoured, recipient of grace; ~ फल, m. fruit of grace [S]

कृष्ण m. Kṛṣṇa [S]

कृष्णदास m. name of a devotee [S]

कृस adj. lean, thin [S *kṛśa-*]

केकी m. peacock [S]

केतक m. a flowering tree [S]

केतिक adj. how much? [3167 **kiyatta-*]

केदारौ m. name of a raga [S *kedāra-*]

केलि f. sport, amorous sport [S]

केवल adv. only [S]

केस m. hair [3471 *keśa-*]

केसर m. saffron (or its pollen) [3474 *kesara-*]

केहरि m. lion [3475 *kesarin-*]

कैं see कौ

कै¹ adj. how many? [2694 *kati*]

कै² cj. either, or [2574 *ka-*]

कैतवपन्हुति f. 'deceitful denial', a trope in which one affection appears in the guise of another [S *kaitavāpahnuti-*]

कैवा adv. several times [2696 *katipaya-*]

कैसैं adv. how?; ~ करि how? [3197 *kīdṛśa-*]

कैसौ adj. of what kind? [3197 *kīdṛśa-*]

को¹ interr.pr. who? which?; (see I.4.6) [2574 *ka, kaḥ*]

को² see कौ

कोइ, °ई, °य, °उ, °ऊ indef.pr. some, any, someone, anyone; obl. काहु, काहू (see I.4.7) [2967 *kaścid*]

कोक m. cuckoo; ruddy goose [S]

कोकिल m. black cuckoo [S]

कोटवार m. kotwal, chief constable [3501 *koṭṭapāla-*]

कोटि, कोटिक f. ten million, crore [S]

कोठ— (कोठें); °ठी m.; f. room, storeroom [3546 *koṣṭha-*]

कोन— (कोनें) m. corner [3504 *koṇa-*]

कोमला f. 'delicate', alliteration free of compounds and of constant repetition of particular sounds [S]

कोर f. corner, edge [3531 **korā-*]

कोरिक num. 20, a score [3503 **koḍi-*]

कौं, कूँ ppn. to [14342 *kakṣa-*]

कौ, को ppn. with genitive sense [2814 *karoti* >*kṛta* ? Cf. also Add² 8390 *paitrika-*]

कौतूहल m. desire; sport, prank [S]

कौन interr.pr. who? whom? what? which? (see I.4.6) [2575 *kaḥ punar*]

कौमुदी f. moonlight [S]

कौर m. morsel of food, mouthful [2960 *kavala-*]

कौसलधीस m. Rāma, lord of Kosala/Kośala (the district around Ayodhyā) [S °*lā*°]

क्यारी f. flowerbed [3463 *kedāra-*]

क्यों, क्यौं, adv. how? why?; ~ कि cj. because; ~ करि adv. how? [3164 *kim*]

क्रम m. sequence, order [S]

क्रिया f. action, deed [S]

क्रीड़ा f. sport, game [S]

क्रोध m. anger [S]

क्षुधा f. hunger, lust [S]

खंजन m. wagtail [S]

खंडन m. breaking, injuring [S]

खंभ m. pillar [13639 *skambha-*]

खग m. bird [S]

खटक- vi. to rankle, fester (cf. खरक-) [3771 *khaṭakhaṭāyate* ?]

खटिया f. bedstead [3781 *khaṭvā-*]

खड्ग, खडग f./m. sword [S]

खन m. moment [3642 *kṣaṇa-*]

खबर, खबरि f. news, intelligence, knowledge [Ar. *khabar*]

खर—1 (खरे) adj. standing [3784 *khaḍaka-*]

खर—2 (खरी, खरे) adj. real, genuine; खरैं adv. extremely [3819 *khara-*]

खरक- vi. to chafe, hurt (cf. खटक-) [3771 *khaṭakhaṭāyate* ?]

खरच- vt. to spend [Pers. *kharc*]

खरौंहौं adj. salty, brackish [3674 *kṣāra-* + ?]

खल adj. & m. low, wicked; wicked man [S]

खव— (खवा) m. shoulder [3852 **khavaka-*]

खवा- vt. to feed, cause to eat [3865 *khādayati*]

खवास m. attendant [Ar. *khawāṣṣ*]

खा- vt. to eat, consume; to undergo, suffer [3865 *khādati*]

खाट m. bedstead [3781 *khaṭvā-*]

खाती m. carpenter, wheelwright [3647 *kṣattṛ-*]

खान m. eating, food; ~ पान m. eating and drinking [3867 *khādana-*]

खार adj. & m. salty, salt [3674 *kṣāra-*]

खारो adj. bitter [3674 *kṣāra-*]

खिनकु adv. for a moment [S *kṣaṇika-*]

खिरक m. cowshed [3770 *khaṭakkikā-*]

खिलौना m. toy [3918 **khel-*]

खुट- vi. to open [3892 **khuṭati*, or for खुल- ?? (See note to BS 33.2)]

खुल- vi. to open [3945 **khull-*]

खुस्याल adj. happy, at ease [Pers. *khush-ḥāl* × *hush-yār* ?]

खूंट m. knob, pommel [3893 **khuṇṭa-*]

खूनी m. murderer, assassin [Pers. *khūnī*]

खेत m. field [3735 *kṣetra-*]

खेद m. regret, grief [S]

खेल m. game, sport [3918 **khel-*]

खेल- vi. to play, frolic [3918 **khel-*]

खेवक m. ferryman [3739 *kṣepaka-*]

खो- vt. to lose, do away with [3651 *kṣapayati*]

खोरि1, खोरी f. lane, alley [3943 **khora-*]

खोरि2 f. wickedness [3931 **khoṭi-*]

खोल- vt. to open; to untie [3945 **kholl-*]

ख्याल m. idea, whim; a style of Hindustani music [Ar. *khayāl*]

गंगा, गंग f. the river Ganga, Ganges [S]

गंठीला adj. knotty [4357 *granthila-*]

गंभीर adj. deep [S]

गँवा-, गमा- vt. to waste, squander, fritter away, lose [4028 *gamayati*]

गउ f. cow [4093 **gavu-*]

गगन m. sky [S]

गज m. elephant; ~ मोती m. large pearl (supposedly found in the projections of an elephant's forehead); ~ राज m. great or large elephant [S]

गजरा m. bracelet, or (carrot-shaped?) wrist-ornament [4140 *gārjara-*]

गढ़ m. fort [3986 **gaḍha-*]

गढ़वै m. commander of a fort; one who seeks asylum in a fortress [3987 *gaḍhapati-*]

गत¹ adj. gone, elapsed [S]

गत² f. tune, air; sequence of dance steps [S *gati-*]

गति f. motion; state, condition [S]

गदहा m., °ही f. donkey [4054 *gardabha-*]

गन- vt. to calculate [3993 *gaṇayati*]

गनपति m. Gaṇeś [S °*ṇ*°]

गनिका f. harlot, prostitute [S *gaṇikā-*]

गनेस m. Gaṇeś [S *gaṇeśa-*]

गमन m. going, moving, departure; sexual intercourse [S]

गमा- see गंवा-

गर— (गरे, गरैं) m. neck, throat [4070 *gala-*]

गरब see गर्व

गरम adj. hot, warm [Pers. *garm*]

गर्व, गरब m. pride [S]

गल m. neck [4070 *gala-*]

गली f. lane [4085 **galī-*]

गह- vt. to grasp, seize, take [4236 *grahati*]

गह्बर adj. & m. deep, impenetrable; bower, arbour [S *gahvara-*]

गहिरो adj. deep [4024 *gabhīra-*]

गहिल— (°ली) adj. & m./f. proud, stubborn (person) [4366 *grahila-*]

गांठ f. knot; ~ गँठीला adj. knotty, compact [4354 *granthi-*]

गांड़ा m. sugarcane [3998 *gaṇḍa-*]

गाँम, गाँव; गाँवरो (rh.) m. village [4368 *grāma-*]

गाँसी f. falsehood, trickery [4381 *grāsya-* ?]

गा- vt. to sing [4135 *gāyati*]

गाइ, गाय f. cow [4147 *gāvī-*]

गागर f. waterpot [4043 *gargara-*]

गाड़ m. ditch, hollow [3981 **gaḍḍa-*]

गाड़ा m. waggon [4116 **gāḍḍa-*]

गाड़ी f. cart [4116 **gāḍḍa-*]

गाढ़— (गाढ़ैं) adv. & adj. closely, tight; close, dense, firm [4118 *gāḍha-*]

गात m. limb, body [4124 *gātra-*]

गान m. song, singing [4130 *gāna-*]

गाम m. village [4368 *grāma-*]

गाय see गाइ

गारड़ू m. snake-charmer [4138 *gāruḍa-*]

गारी, गारि (rh.) f. abusive speech, insult [4145 *gāli-*]

गारो m. plaster mix of mud and cow-dung [4137 **gāra-*]

गाल m. cheek [4089 *galla-*]

गिर see गिरि

गिर- vi. to fall [4159 **girati*]

गिरधर see गिरि

गिरधारी see गिरि

गिरा- vt. to drop, let/make fall [4159 **girati*]

गिरि, गिर m. mountain; ~ धर(न), ~ धारी m. 'mountain-bearer', Kṛṣṇa; name of poet; ~ बर see बर; ~ राज m. Govardhan hill [S]

गिरिजा f. Pārvatī; ~ ईस m. Śiva [S]

गिल- vt. to swallow [4075 *gilati*]

गीता f. the *Bhagavad Gītā* [S]

गीध m. vulture [4233 *gṛdhra*-]

गुंज m. the seed of a shrub [4176 *guñjā*-]

गुंज- vi. to hum, buzz [4175 *guñjati*]

गुड़ी f. paper kite [4189 **guḍḍa*-]

गुढ़ौ m. hiding place, refuge [4223 *gūḍha*-]

गुन m. thread, strand; quality, attribute [S *guṇa*-]

गुनी adj. wise, virtuous [S *guṇin*-]

गुपाल see गोपाल

गुमान m. conceit, pride [Pers.]

गुरु, गुर m. spiritual guide, guru, master; elder, superior; God; ~ धर्मी m. one who respects his guru; ~ भाई m. co-religionist, fellow disciple [S]

गुलाब m. rose-water; rose [Pers.]

गुलाल m. red powder thrown during Holi festival [Pers. *gulāb* × *lāl* ?]

गुसाई m. 'owner of cows', a name of God; religious title (designating Viṭṭhalnāth in VV) [4342 *gosvāmin*-]

गुह- vt. to braid [4205 *guphati*]

गूँग adj. & m. dumb [4171 **guṅga*-]

गूजरी f. heavy anklet (as worn by Gūjar women) [4210 *gurjara*-]

गृह m. house, home [S]

गेंद f. ball [4248 *genduka*-]

गेह m. house [S]

गेहिनी f. wife [S]

गैया f. cow [4147 *gāvī*-]

गैल m. path, way [4009 *gati*-]

गो f. cow [S]

गोकुल m. place in Braj where Kṛṣṇa spent his youth [S]

गोचारन m. cow-grazing [S °*ṇa*]

गोदोहन m. cow-milking [S]

गोधन m. herd of cows; herding-song (?) [S]

गोप m. cowherd; ~ बधू f. cowherd's wife [S]

गोपाल, गुपाल 'cowherd', a name of Kṛṣṇa; ~ पुर m. a village in Braj [S]

गोपी f. cowherdess [S]

गोबर m. cowdung [4316 *gorvara*-]

गोबर्द्धन see गोवर्धन

गोरज m. dust from cows—i.e. dust kicked up by cows' hooves [S *gorajas*-]

गोरस m. (curdled) milk, buttermilk [S]

गोरी f. fair woman [4345 *gaura*-]

गोवर्धन, गोवर्द्धन, गोबर्द्धन m. a hill in Braj, held aloft by Kṛṣṇa to provide shelter from Indra's storm (and original location of the temple of Śrīnāthjī); ~ नाथ Kṛṣṇa in 'mountain-holding' pose, Śrīnāthjī [S]

गोवर्धनधर m. Kṛṣṇa [S]

गोविंद m. Kṛṣṇa; ~ कुंड m. a lake near Govardhan hill [S]

गौतम m. the sage Gautam, husband of Ahalyā [S]

गौतमारन्य m. name of a forest in RN [S °*ṇya*-]

गौरव m. grandeur, dignity [S]

गौरी f. name of a raga [S]

गौन, गौन m. going, moving; sexual intercourse [4027 *gamana*-]

ग्यानी adj. wise [S *jñānin*-]

ग्रंथ m. book [S]

ग्राह m. water creature, crocodile [S]

ग्राही adj. & m. holding, one who holds or possesses [S *grāhin-*]

ग्रीव (m.) neck [4387 *grīvā-*]

ग्रीष्म, ग्रीषम m. summer [S]

ग्वार see ग्वाल

ग्वाल, ग्वार m. cowherd [4293 *gopāla-*]

ग्वालि(नि) f. cowherdess, gopi [4293 *gopāla-*]

घंट m., घंटा f. bell; घंटाकरन m. 'bell-ears', name of a demon in RN [S]

घंटिका f. small bell [S]

घट m. pot, vessel; body [S]

घट- vi. to reduce, shrink; *ghaṭa-baṛha* adj. small(er) or great(er) [4415 **ghaṭṭati*]

घटा f. mass of cloud [S]

घटा- vt. to reduce [4415 **ghaṭṭati*]

घड़ी, घरी f. short period of time, moment; eighth part of a 'watch' (*yāma*); ~ घड़ी adv. at every moment [4406 *ghaṭī-*]

घन m. cloud [S]

घनस्याम m. 'cloud-dark', name of Kṛṣṇa [S °*śyā*°]

घर m. house [S]

घरनि f. wife [4442 *ghariṇī-*]

घरियाल m. gong [4413 **ghaṭītāḍa-*]

घरी see घड़ी

घात f. ploy, stratagem, intention, treachery [S *ghāta-*]

घाम m./f. heat, sunshine [4445 *gharma-*]

घिर- vi. to be surrounded [4474 **gher-*]

घुंघरू, घूं° m. ankle-bell [4477 **ghuṅghura-*]

घुमर- vi. to gather, circle [4485 **ghummati*]

घुसायन f. cowherd's wife [4528 *ghoṣa-*]

घूंघट m./f. veil [4484 **ghumbapaṭṭa-*]

घूंघरू see घुंघरू

घूम- vi. to roam, wander [4485 **ghummati*]

घेर- vt. to surround, beset [4474 **gher-*]

घोड़ा m. horse [4516 *ghoṭa-*]

घोष, घोस m. cowherd; station of herdsmen, cattle-station [S]

चंग m. Jew's harp, mouth-harp [Pers. *caṅg*]

चंचल adj. restless, fickle, capricious, quivering [S]

चंचलता f. fickleness [S]

चंद, चंदा m. moon [4661 *candra-*]

चंदन, °ण m. (salve of) sandalwood [S]

चंद्रमा m. moon [S]

चंद्राकार adj. crescent-shaped [S]

चंप— (°पे) m. champak tree, with yellow flowers [4678 *campa-*]

चक- vi. to be startled, bewildered [4537 **cakyate*]

चकोर, °री m., f. a partridge which allegedly subsists on the nectar of moonbeams (and epitomizes single-minded devotion) [S]

चख (in चलचख) m. eye [4560 *cakṣus-*]

चखा- vt. to give to taste [4557 **cakṣati*]

चटक f. lustre, dazzle [4570 **caṭa-*]

चटकीलौ adj. lustrous, gaudy [4570 **caṭa-*]

चटपटा- vi. to be agitated, in a flutter [4570 **caṭa-*]

चटसार f. school [5016 *chāttriśālā-* ?]

चढ़- vt. to mount, ascend, climb, rise, attack [4578 **caḍhati*]

चढ़ा- vt. to lift, raise, devote, offer up; to string (a bow) [4578 **caḍhati*]

चतुर adj. clever, skilful, artful [S]

चतुराई f. cunning, craftiness [S *catura-*]

चतुर्थ num. fourth [S]

चप- vi. to be pressed [4674 **capp-*]

चपलाई f. prank, frolic, play [S *capala-*]

चपलातिसय m. 'hyperbole of rapidity', in which an effect immediately follows the mere mention of the cause [S *°śaya-*]

चबाई m. backbiter, slanderer [4622 **caturvāda-*, or चबा- < 4711 *carvati* ?]

चमक- vi. to flash, shine [4676 **cammakka-*]

चमका- vt. to make shine; to display [4676 **cammakka-*]

चमचमा- vi. to glitter [4676 **cammakka-*]

चर adj. movable, mobile, animate [S]

चर- vi. to graze [4686 *carati*]

चरचा (f.) repetition, discussion, conversation, deliberation [S *carcā-*]

चरण, °न m. foot; segment of verse [S]

चरा- = चार-

चराचर adj. & m. movable and immovable, animate and inanimate, all of creation [S]

चल adj. unsteady, wavering, tremulous; ~ चख m. roving eye; ~ चित्त m. fickle or restless mind [S]

चल- vi. to walk, move, go, come, leave [4715 *calati*]

चला- vt. to set in motion, move, advance [4715 *calati*]

चलित adj. trembling [S]

चवाव m. rumour, slander [4622 **caturvāda-*]

चसक— (°के) m. cup, chalice [S *caṣaka-*]

चह- see चाह-

चहल— (°लैं) m. mud, mire [4784 **cakhalla-*]

चहुँ, चहूँ num. the four; ~ ओर(न), ~ दिसि, ~ पास adv. all around [S *catur-*]

चाँचर f. song and dance performed round a pole during Holi [4694 *carcarī-*]

चाँद m. moon [4661 *candra-*]

चांदी f. white patch [4669 *candrikā-*]

चांदनी, चांदिनी f. moonlight; white floor-sheet [4745 **cāndraṇa-*]

चाख- vt. to taste [4557 **cakṣati*]

चाड़ f. love, desire [4737 *cāṭu-*]

चातक m. pied cuckoo, said to live on raindrops alone [S]

चाप m. archer's bow [S]

चाम m. hide, skin [4701 *carman-*]

चाय, चाइ m. delight, zest [4775 **cāh-*]

चार[1], चारि, चारी num. four [4655 *catvāri*]

चार[2] see चारु

चार-, चरा- vt. to make graze, take grazing [4760 *cārayati*]

चारु, चार adj. lovely, pretty, elegant [S]

चाल, चालि f. gait, motion; way [4722 **calyā-*]

चाल- vi. to come along, go [4721 **calyati*]

चाह f. longing, desire [4775 **cāh-*]

चाह-, चह- vt. to look out for, spy; to want, love; चाहे cj. whether…or, whatever, though [4775 **cāh-*]

चाहत f. desire, wish [4775 **cāh-* (see C. Shackle 1981:96 *gaṇata* for f. nouns in *-ata*)]

चिंता f. anxiety, care [S]

चिंतित adj. alarmed, worried [S]

चिकना- vt. to make unctuous, smooth [4782 *cikkaṇa-*]

चित see चित्त

चित(व)- vt. to look at [4799 *citta-*]

चितवनि f. glance, stare [4799 *citta-*]

चिता f. funeral pyre [S]

चित्त, चित m. mind, heart, thought; चित-चाय, चित्तचाइ adj. pleasing, lovely [S]

चित्र m. picture, portrait [S]

चिनौती f. challenge, defiance [4814 *cinoti*]

चिन्ह m. mark [4833 *cihna-*]

चिबुक f. chin [S]

चिलक- vi. to shine, glisten; *cilaka* f. brilliance, glitter [4827 **cilla-*]

चींटी f. small ant [4822 **cimb-* ?? (See Platts 1968:471) But cf. also Tamil *ciṭṭu* 'anything small' (T.Burrow & M.B. Emeneau 1984:219, no. 2513); and S *cicciṭiṅga-* 'venomous insect' (Monier-Williams 1974:395)]

चीन्ह- vt. to know, recognize [4836 *cihnayati*]

चीर m. clothing, garment [S]

चीर- vt. to split, cleave [4844 **cīrayati*]

चुक- vi. to miss the mark; to be finished [4848 **cukk-*]

चुन- vt. to select, pick, set out, arrange [4814 *cinoti*]

चुप adj. silent [4864 **cuppa-*]

चुपर- vt. to anoint, oil [4865 **cuppa-*]

चुरवा- vt. to cause to be stolen [4933 *corayati*]

चुरा- see चोर-

चूक f. error [4848 **cukk-*]

चूक- vi. to miss, fail [4848 **cukk-*]

चून— (चूनै) m. (pl.) smithereens [4889 *cūrṇa-*]

चूम- vt. to kiss [4870 *cumbati*]

चूरा m. ring on elephant's tusk; bracelet [4884 *cūḍa-*]

चेट m. servant, slave [S]

चेटक m. magic, miracle [4913 *ceṣṭā-* ?]

चेरी f. maidservant [4902 *ceṭa-*]

चेष्टा f. effort, action, movement [S]

चैत m. the springtime month of Caitra [4915 *caitra-*]

चैन m. peace, rest, comfort [12323 *śayana-* ?]

चोटी f. peak; topknot, tuft of hair [4883 **coṭṭa-*]

चोर m. thief [4931 *cora-*]

चोर-, चोरा-, चुरा- vt. to steal [4933 *corayati*]

चोरा- = चोर-

चोरी f. theft [4937 *caurikā-*]

चोलना m. tunic, shirt [4923 *coḍa-*]

चोली f. bodice, blouse [4923 *coḍa-*]

चोवा m. pomade of four ingredients (e.g. sandalwood, eaglewood, saffron, musk) [4619 *caturvaya* ?]

चौंध f. dazzlement [4876 *culla-* × 385 *andha-* ?]

चौंक- vi. to be startled [4676 **camakka-*]

चौकी f. stool; watch, guard [4629 *catuṣka-*]

चौगुन— (°नी, °नै) adj. fourfold [4599 *caturguṇa-*]

चौथो num. fourth [4600 *caturtha-*]

चौपाई f. a quatrain metre [4646 *catuṣpādikā-*]

चौमुँह adv. all around [4617 *caturmukha-*]

चौरासी num. eighty-four [4597 *caturaśīti-*]

चौहर— (°रे) adj. quadruple, fourfold [4613 **caturdhāra-*]

छक- vi. to be satiated, delighted, astonished [4956 **chakka-*]

छगुन adj. sixfold [12795 *ṣaḍguṇa-*]

छछिया f. spoon [5012 **chācchī-*]

छट— (छटनु) see छटा

छटा, छट— (छटनु) f. light, lustre, ray [S]

छठ— (छठी) num. sixth [12808 *ṣaṣṭha-*]

छत adj. wounded [S *kṣata-*]

छतिया, °याँ f. chest, breast [5014 **chātti-*]

छत्र m. umbrella, parasol of royalty [S *chattra-*]

छनछना- vi. to sizzle [4990 **channa-*]

छनभंगुर; छिनभंग adj. momentary, transitory [S *kṣaṇabhaṅgura-*, *°bhaṅga-*]

छपा- vt. to hide [4994 **chapp-*]

छबि f. splendour, beauty [S *chavi-*]

छबीलौ, °लो adj. elegant, handsome, graceful [5006 *chavī-* or 5022 *chādmika-*]

छमासी f. period of six months [12802 *ṣaṇmāsika-*]

छर-, छल- vt. to deceive, beguile, pretend [5003 *chalayati*]

छरी f. stick, staff [4966 **chaṭa-*]

छल m. deceit, fraud [5001 *chala-*]

छल- see छर-

छाँटा m. spittle [4970 **chaṇṭ-* or 4998 *chardati*]

छाँड़-, छाड़- vt. to abandon, give up, leave [4998 *chardati*]

छाँह, छाह, छाँहि, छाँहीं (rh.) f. shade [5027 *chāyā-*]

छा- vt. to spread, pervade [5018 *chādayati*]

छाक m. packed food taken to work by labourers [4957 **chakka-*]

छाज- vi. to befit, be acceptable [4982 **chadyati*]

छाछ f. buttermilk [5012 **chācchī-*]

छाड़- see छाँड़-

छाती f. breast, heart [5014 **chātti-*]

छान- vt. to filter, strain [3643 **kṣāṇayati*]

छाया f. shade, shadow [S]

छाह see छाँह

छिगुनी f. little finger [?]

छिति f. earth, soil of the earth [S *kṣiti-*]

छिन m. moment; a period of four minutes [3642 *kṣaṇa-*]

छिनकु, छिनक m. & adv. moment; for a moment (= खिनकु) [*china + ek*]

छिनभंग see छनभंगुर

छिप- vi. to hide [4994 **chipp-*]

छिपा- vt. to hide [4994 **chipp-*]

छिमा- vt. to seek forgiveness, apologize [3657 *kṣamate* or *S kṣamate*]

छिरक- vt. to sprinkle [5035 **chiṭ-*]

छींट— (टें) m. sprinkling, splash [5035 **chiṭṭ-* or **chiṇṭ-*]

छीट- vt. to sprinkle, splash [5035 **chiṭṭ-*]

छी- vt. to touch [5055 *chupati*]

छीर m. milk [3696 *kṣīra-* (or S *kṣīra-*)]

छु- vt. to touch [5055 *chupati*]

छुट-, छूट- vi. to leave, be released [3707 **kṣuṭyate*]

छुटा- vt. to release [3707 **kṣuṭyate*]

छुड़ा- vt. to put aside, get rid of [3747 *kṣoṭayati*]

छुद्र adj. small, tiny [S *kṣudra-*]

छूट- see छुट-

छेकानुप्रास m. 'clever alliteration', having paired repeats of various consonants [S]

छेकापन्हुति f. 'artful denial', a trope in which an innocent cause is contrived to explain away an affection [S *°hnuti-*]

छेद- vt. to cut, pierce [5043 *chidra-*]

छेली f. lass, girl [5006 *chavī-*]

छैल adj. dashing, spruce, wanton [5006 *chavi-*]

छोटा adj. small, little [5071 **choṭṭa-*]

छोर-, छोड़- vt. to remove, snatch, leave, abandon [3747 *kṣoṭayati*]

छोरा; °री m. lad; f. lass [5070 **chokara-*]

छोहरा; °रिया m. boy; f. girl [5070 **chokhara-*]

जंजाल, °र m. worry, care, perplexity [5085 **jañjāla-*]

जँजीर f. chain, fetter [Pers. *zanjīr*]

जँभुआ- vi. to yawn [5265 *jṛmbhate*]

जग m. world [S]

जगत, °ति m. world [S *jagat-*]

जगमग-, °मगा- vi. to glitter, glimmer [5076 **jag-*]

जगा- vt. to awaken, arouse [5175 *jāgrati*]

जगात f. tax, octroi [Ar. *zakāt*]

जट- vi. to be stuck, jammed; जटित embossed, studded [5091 **jaḍati*]

जड़ adj. & m. stupid; fool [5090 *jaḍa-*]

जतन see यत्न

जद adv. when [see तद]

जदुरैया m. king of the Yadus, Kṛṣṇa [S *yadu* + राइ]

जद्यपि cj. although [S *yadyapi*]

जन m. person; mankind (and used as pluralizing suffix: cf. MSH लोग) [S]

जनक m. father [S]

जनकसुता f. patronymic of Sītā, daughter of Janak [S]

जननि f. mother [S *jananī-*]

जनम see जन्म

जनम- vi. to be born [S *janman-*]

जना- vt. to inform, tell, MSH जता-; vi. to seem, appear to be [5193 *jānāti*]

जनु cj. like, as if [< imperative from जान- ?; cf. जानहु; but also cf. मनु etc.]

जन्म, जनम m. birth, existence, life; ~भूमि f. birthplace [S *janman-*]

जब, जौ adv. when; ~लगि, लगु until [Add² 2528 *evam eva* × *ya-*]

जम m. Yama, god of the dead [S *yama-*]

जमक m. wordplay, paronomasia [S *y°*]

जमना see जमुना

जमा- vt. to set, make coagulate, implant, impress upon [10428 *yamyate*]

जमुना, जम° f. the river Yamuna [S *yamunā-*]

जमूर m. gun mounted on camel's back [Pers. *zambūr(a)*]

जर m. fever [5303 *jvara-*]

जर-¹ vt. to set (jewels), inlay [5091 **jaḍati*]

जर-² see जल-

जराइ f. inlay-work [5091 **jaḍati*]

जल m. water; ~जंत्र m. fountain; ~थल adv. on water and dry land, everywhere; ~निधि f. ocean [S]

जल-, जर- vi. to burn [5306 *jvalati*]

जलजात m. lotus [S]

जला- vt. to burn, set alight [5306 *jvalati*]

जव m. barley [10431 *yava-*]

जवाहिर m. jewel [Ar. pl. *jawāhir*, s. *jauhar*]

जस m. fame, renown [10443 *yaśas-*]

जसुदा see जसोदा

जसुमति f. Yaśodā, Kṛṣṇa's foster-mother [S *yaśomatī-*]

जसोदा f. Yaśodā, Kṛṣṇa's foster-mother; ~नंदन m. Kṛṣṇa [S *yaśodā-*]

जहँ, जहाँ adv. where; when; जहाँ तहाँ adv. here and there, everywhere [see यहाँ]

जहाज m. ship [Ar. *jahāz*]

जांघ m. thigh [5082 *jaṅghā-*]

जाँच- vt. to test, assay [10449 *yācyate*]

जा see जो¹

जा- vi. to go (and aux. uses) [10452 *yāti*]

जाग- vi. to wake up, be awake [5175 *jāgrati*]

जाति f. class, type, kind, caste, race [S]

जान- vt. to know, consider, assume; ~ *jā-* vi. to realize [5193 *jānāti*]

जाम m. watch, a three-hour period [S *y*°]

जामिनि f. night [S *yāminī-*]

जार m. paramour, lover [S]

जार- vt. to burn [5314 *jvālayati*]

जारज m. child by a paramour, bastard [S]

जारन adj. & m. burning; burner [5314 *jvālayati*]

जाल m. net [5213 *jāla-*]

जावक m. lac, lac-dye [S *yā*°]

जित adv. where [see इत]

जिन see जो¹

जिनि adv. not (in prohibitions) [10408 *yathā na*]

जिमि adv. like, as [formed by analogy with *ima* (2528 *evam eva*)]

जिय m. soul, heart, life [5239 *jīva-*]

जिहिं see जो¹

जिहि f. bowstring [Pers. *zeh, zah*]

जी¹ m. soul, heart [5239 *jīva-*]

जी² part. of respect [5240 *jīva*]

जी(व)- vi. to live, be alive [5241 *jīvati*]

जीत vt. to defeat [5224 *jita-*]

जीव m. life, soul, living being [S]

जीवन m. life [S]

जीवनी, °नि f. life-giver, restorative [S *jīvanī-*]

जीविका f. livelihood [S]

जु see जू

जुक्ति f. contrivance, artifice [S *y*°]

जुग¹ m. aeon, age, one of the four ages of creation [S *y*°]

जुग² m. pair, couple [10493 *yugma-*]

जुठन— see जूठो

जुद— (जुदें) adj. different, separate [Pers. *judā*]

जुबति see जुवति

जुर- vi. to be joined, united [10496 **yuṭati*]

जुवति, जुबति, जुबती adj. & f. young; young woman [S *yuvati-*]

जू, जु part. of assent 'yes Sir', 'Sir' [5240 *jīva-*]

जूठो, जूठौ, झूठो, m., जूठन— (जुठनियाँ) f. leftovers, leavings of food or drink [5255 *juṣṭa-*]

जूथ m. group, herd [S *yūtha-*]

जूरा m. woman's hair-knot, bun [5258 *jūṭa-*]

जेंव- vt. to eat [5267 *jemati*]

जेठ m. the month of Jeṭh (May-June) [5293 *jyaiṣṭha-*]

जेत— (जेते) adj. as much as [see इतनौ]

जैनी adj. & m. Jain [S *jaina-* + *ī*]

जैसो, जैसौ adj. as; जैसैं, जैसें adv. as, just as [10458 *yādṛśa-*]

जो¹ rel.pr. he who, etc.; (see I.4.4) [10391 *ya-*]

जो², जौ cj. if; ~ पै if [10401 *yataḥ*]

जो- see जोव-

जोइसी m. astrologer [5302 *jyautiṣika-*]

जोग[1] m. yoga, system of philosophy in which God is to be sought through mental abstraction; conjuncture caused by position of the planets; connexion [S *yoga-*]

जोग[2] adj. appropriate, fitting [10528 *yogya-*]

जोगी m. yogi, holy man, devotee [S *y°*]

जोत, °ति f. light, flame [S *jyotis-*]

जोनि f. womb, birth, station in life [S *yoni-*]

जोन्ह f. moonlight [5301 *jyotsnā-*]

जोबन m. youth, prime of youth [10537 *yauvana-*]

जोर[1] f. match, equal, like [10496 **yoṭa-*]

जोर[2] m. strength, power [Pers *zor*]

जोर- v.t. to amass, gather, join [10496 **yoṭayati*]

जोराबर adj. powerful, strong [Pers. *zor-āwar*]

जोरी f. pair, couple [10496 **yoṭa-*]

जो(व)- vt. to look at, watch [6612 *dyotate*]

जौं see ज्यों

जौ[1] see जो[2]

जौ[2] see जब

ज्ञान m. knowledge [S]

ज्या- vt. to give life to [5250 *jīvāpayati*]

ज्यों, ज्यौं, जौं adv. like [3164 *kim*, which is also base for क्यों etc.]

ज्वाल m. flame, blaze, fire [S]

झंवा- vt. to pumice [5366 *jhāmaka-*]

झकझोर adj. violent, turbulent [5316 **jhakk-* + 5414 **jhoṭati*]

झकझोर- vi. to tremble, shake, wave [5316 **jhakk-* + 5414 **jhoṭati*]

झकझोली, °री f. buffeting, shaking [5316 **jhakk-* + 5414 **jhoṭati*]

झर- vi. to fall, trickle, flow [5328 **jhaṭati*]

झलक f. sparkle, lustre [5352 **jhal-*]

झलक- vi. to sparkle, shine [5352 **jhal-*]

झलमल- vi. to shine, glow [5352 **jhal-*]

झारी f. pitcher, water jug [5377 **jhārikā-*]

झीन adj. fine, thin [5395 **jhīna* or 5397 **jhīrṇa-*]

झुंड m. bush [5400 **jhuṇṭa-*]

झुक- vi. to bend [5399 **jhukkati*]

झूठ m. lie, untruth [5407 **jhūṭṭha-*]

झूठो see जूठो

झूम- vi. to bend, sway [3726 **kṣumbhati* ?]

झूर- vi. to waste away [5409 **jhūrati*]

झूल- vi. to swing [5406 **jhulyati*]

टकटकी f. fixed look, stare [5716 *tarkayati*]

टट्टी f. frame [5990 **traṭṭa-*]

टपक- vi. to drop, drip [5444 **ṭapp-*]

टप्पा m. a style of song, with florid melisma and ornament (said to originate in a camel driver's song from Panjab) [5445 *ṭappa-* ?]

टर- vi. to move, stir, retire, be removed [5450 *ṭalati*]

टरा- vt. to remove [5450 *ṭalati*]

टहल f. menial service, attendance [5453 **ṭahall-*]

टाटी f. bamboo screen [5990 **traṭṭa-*]

टार- vt. to evade, remove, refute, draw back [5450 *ṭālayati*]

टारन m. remover, destroyer [5450 *ṭālayati*]

टूक m. small piece [5466 **ṭukka-*]

टूट- vi. to break [6065 *truṭyati*]

टेर- vt. to call, call out [5473 **ṭer-*]

टेव f. whim; habit, manner [5475 **ṭev-*]

टोक- vt. to impede, obstruct [5476 **ṭokk-*]

टोना m. spell, charm; ~पढ़ to cast a spell [5480 **ṭona-*]

ठ- see ठा-

ठग m. 'thug', highwayman who befriends travellers and then ritually murders them [5489 **ṭhagg-*]

ठगौरी f. trickery, spell [5489 **ṭhagg-*]

ठठक- vi. to stand amazed, stop dead [13771 *sthira-* ?]

ठहरा- vt. to stop, impede; to rest, impose, allege, determine, resolve [13680 **stabhira-*]

ठा-, ठ- vt. to establish, ordain [13756 *sthāpayati* (cf. *ṭhav-*, J.D.Smith 1976:310]

ठाउँ m.f. place [13760 *sthāman-*]

ठाकुर m. master; deity, idol, temple image [5488 *ṭhakkura-*]

ठाड़ो, ठाढ़ो adj. standing [13676 *stabdha-*]

ठान- vt. to perform, be set on [13753 **sthānya-*]

ठिकान— (°ने) m. place, station [5503 **ṭhīkka-*]

ठीक f. whereabouts, trace [5503 **ṭhīkka-*]

ठैंया (rh.) m. place [13760 *sthāman-*]

ठोंक- vt. to strike, pat, poke [5513 **ṭhokk-*]

ठोड़ी f. chin [5853 *tuṇḍa-*]

ठौर f. place, room; ~मार- vt. to beat to a standstill, knock out [13767 *sthāvara-*]

डग f. pace, step [5523 **ḍag-*]

डफ m. large tambourine, drum [Ar. > Pers. *daf*]

डबरा m. bowl [5528 **ḍabba-*]

डर m. fear [6186 *dara-*]

डर-, डरा- vi. to be afraid [6190 *darati*]

डरप- vi. to be afraid [6190 *darati*]

डरा- see डर-

डरावन— (°ने) adj. terrifying [6190 *darati*]

डार f. branch [5546 *ḍāla-*]

डार- vt. to throw, throw away, throw down, cast [5545 **ḍāl-* or **ḍār-*]

डिग- vi. to tremble, be shaken [5522 **ḍig-*]

डिगुला- vt. to shake, make wobble [5522 **ḍig-*]

डीठि f. glance, gaze, look; ~पर- vi. to be seen, be visible [6520 *dṛṣṭi-*]

डुला- vt. to cause to swing, shake, sway [6453 **dulati*]

डेरा m. lodgings, residence [5564 **ḍera-*]

डोर, डोरी f. thread, string [6225 *davara-*]

डोल- vi. to roam, wander [6585 *dolāyate*]

डोला- vt. to make move, stir [6585 *dolayati*]

ढरक- vi. to slip, slink [5581 **ḍhalati*]

ढरका- vt. to spill, pour [5581 **ḍhalati*]

ढल- vi. to decline [5581 **ḍhalati*]

ढाँग m. hip, loin (?? — see note to SR 19.4) [5582 **ḍhākka-*]

ढाँढ़- see ढूँढ-

ढाक m. a tree with blazing red foliage [6702 *dhakṣu-*]

ढाका m. Dhaka [S *ḍhakka-*]

ढार m. way, manner [5583 **ḍhālayati*]

ढिक, °ग adv. and ppn. near [5586 **ḍhigga-*]

ढिठाई f. boldness, temerity [6876 *dhṛṣṭi-*]

ढीठ adj. bold, impudent [6875 *dhṛṣṭa-*]

ढुर- vi. to move, slip [5593 **ḍhulati*]

ढूँढ़- vt. to seek; ढूँढ़-ढाढ़- vt. to seek and search [6839 **ḍhūṇḍh-*]

ढेरी f. heap, mound [5599 **ḍhera-*]

ढोटा m. boy, lad [5607 **ḍhoṭṭa-*]

तंत f. string, wire [5660 *tanti-*]

तऊ see तौ[2]

तक- vt. to gaze at, look [5716 *tarkayati*]

तज- vt. to give up, abandon, lose [S *tyajati*]

तट m. bank, shore; curved area (as pleonastically in कटि तट) [S]

तटनी f. river [S *taṭinī-*]

तड़ाग m. pond [S *taḍāga-*]

तड़ित f. lightning [S *taḍit-*]

तत्काल adv. immediately [S]

तत्व m. essence, reality [S *tattva-*]

तथा cj. and [S]

तद adv. then [5650 **taddivasam* ?? (See C.Shackle 1981:137 s.v. *tadi*)]

तद्रूप m. 'of the same quality'— a metaphor in which a subject shares the quality of an object in general terms, but not in every detail [S]

तन m. body [5656 *tanū-*]

तनिक, तनक adj. & adv. small, a little; just, MSH *zarā* [5654 *tanu-*]

तप m. religious penance, devout austerity [S *tapas-*]

तप- vi. to burn, feel pain; *tapani* f. burning, heat, distress [5684 *tapyati*]

तपन f. burning, heat, distress (5671 *tapati*)

तपा- vt. to heat [5684 *tapyati*]

तप्त adj. hot [S]

तब, तौ adv. then [Add[2] 2528 *evam eva* × *ta-*]

तम m. darkness [S *tamas-*]

तमाकू m. tobacco [Portuguese < Spanish 'tabaco']

तरंग f. wave; rapture, ecstasy [S]

तरंगनि f. river [S *°iṇī-*]

तर- vi. to cross over, ford, be saved [5702 *tarati*]

तरन m. boat, ferryboat [5700 *taraṇa-*]

तरनिजा f. the river Yamunā [S *taraṇijā-*]

तरल adj. tremulous, capricious [S]

तरवार f. sword [5706 *taravāri-*]

तरस- vi. to yearn, pine [5942 *tṛṣyati*]

तरा- vt. to take across, save [5702 *tarati*]

तरु m. tree [S]

तरुण adj. young [S]

तरुनई f. youth, pubescent maturity [5712 *taruṇa-*]

तरे, तरै ppn. beneath [5731 *tala-*]

तरौंस m. riverbank, water near bank [?]

तल m. flat roof [S]

तहँ, तहाँ see यहाँ

ताईं ppn. to, up to, until [5804 *tāvat*]

ता see सो[1]

तात m. son; father [S]

ताती adj. heated, hot [5679 *tapta-*]

तान f. tune, rapid run of notes [S]

तान- vt. to erect, extend [5762 *tānayati*]

तानसेन m. Tānsen, Akbar's chief court musician [S]

ताप m. heat, torment, suffering [S]

ताफ़ता m. taffeta, shot silk, cloth with a shimmering effect given by contrasted colours in warp and weft [Pers. *tāfta*]

तार- vt. to take across, save [5796 *tārayati*]

तारन adj. & m. carrying across; saviour [S °ṇa-]

तारी f. clapping the hands [5748 *tāḍa-*]

ताल m. rhythm, rhythmic cycle [S]

तासु m. cloth of gold, brocade [Pers. *tās*]

तित adv. there [see इत]

तिथि f. lunar day/date [S]

तिन see सो[1]

तिमिर m. darkness [S]

तिय, तीय f. woman, wife [13734 *strī-*]

तिलक m. forehead-mark [S]

तिलोछ- vt. to wipe with oil, make shiny [*tela* <5958 *taila-* + *och-* < *poch-och-* < 9011 *proñchati*]

तिलोतमा f. Tilottamā, a nymph [S *-tt-*]

तिहर— (°रे) adj. triple, threefold [6027 **tridhāra-*]

तिहारौ, तुम्हरौ, तुम्हारौ poss.pr. your, yours (see I.4.5b) [10511 *yuṣmad-*]

तिहि, तिहिं see सो (I.4.3)

तिहूँ num. three [5994 *trayaḥ*]

तीख— (°खे) adj. sharp [5839 *tīkṣṇa-*]

तीछन adj. sharp [S *tīkṣṇa-*]

तीज f. Tij, a festival held on the third day of the bright fortnight of Śrāvaṇ [5920 *tṛtīyā-*]

तीज— (°जे) num. third [5920 *tṛtīyā-*]

तीनि, तीन num. three [5994 *trīṇi*]

तीव्र adj. hot, intense [S *tīvra-*]

तीय see तिय

तीर[1], तीरु m. bank, shore [5842 *tīra-*]

तीर[2] m. arrow [Pers. *tīr*]

तीरथ m. place of pilgrimage [S *tīrtha-*]

तीसर— (°रे, °री) num. third [6018 **trihsara-*]

तुँ— see तू

तुक m. line of poem [5466 **ṭukka-* ?]

तुपक f. gun, cannon [Pers. *top, tupak*]

तुम pr. you (see I.4.5b) [10511 *yuṣmad-*]

तुम्हरौ, तुम्हारौ see तिहार-

तुरंग adj. & m. quick, nimble; horse [S]

तुरत adv. immediately [5879 *turant-*]

तुव poss.pr. your, yours (see I.4.5b) [5889 *tuvam*]

तुलसी f. basil shrub, sacred to Viṣṇu [S]

तुल्यजोगिता f. 'equal pairing', a trope imposing equivalence on various subjects having a shared property [S °y°]

तू , तूँ , तुँ— pr. you; agentive तैं (see I.4.5b) [5889 *tuvam*]

तृप्ति f. satisfaction [S]

तृष्ना f. thirst, desire [5941 *tṛṣṇā* -]

तें, ते see तैं[1]

तेज m. brilliance, glory, valour [S *tejas-*]

तेत— (तेते) adj. that much [see इतनौ]

तेर— (तेरी, तेरे, तेरैं) poss.pr. your, yours (see I.4.5b) [5889 *tuvam*]

तेल m. oil [5958 *taila-*]

तैं[1], तें, ते ppn. by, from; through, since [377 *antika-*]

तैं[2] pr. see तू (I.4.5a)

तैस— (तैसी) adj. such, of that kind; तैसें adv. so, in that way [5760 *tādṛśa-*]

तो[1] poss.pr. your, yours (see I.4.5b) [5889 *tuvam*]

तो[2], तौ cj. then; emph. indeed; तऊ , तौऊ even so [5639 *tatas*]

तोता m. parrot [Pers. *ṯoṯā*]

तोर- vt. to break [6079 *troṭayati*]

तोरनि m. festooned gateway [S °ṇa-]

तोष m. satisfaction, contentment [S]

तौ1 see तो2

तौ2 see तब

तौंक m. iron neck-ring [Ar. *ṯauq*]

त्याग- vt. to leave, abandon [S *tyāga-*]

त्यौं, त्यों adv. thus, in this way; just then, there and then, just like that [see ज्यौं]

त्रय num. three; ~ताप the three kinds of affliction (see note to BS 20.2) [S]

त्रास m. fear, alarm, dread [S]

त्रास- vt. to terrorize [S *trāsayati*]

त्रिपुरारि m. Śiva [S]

त्रिबिध adj. threefold (said of the wind, as 'gentle, cool, fragrant') [S °*v*°]

त्रिभंगी adj. & m. 'thrice-bent': having a bent knee, waist and neck—Kṛṣṇa's fluting posture [S]

त्रिलोचन m. Śiva [S]

थक- vi. to be tired; थकित ptc. adj. tired, worn out [13737 **sthakk-*]

थरथरी f. trembling [6092 **thar-*]

थल m. dry land [13744 *sthala-*]

थिर adj. immovable, inanimate; ~चर adj. & m. immobile and mobile, inanimate and animate, all of creation [13771 *sthira-*]

थुरहथी adj. & f. meagre-handed (woman) [13720 **stoka* + 14039 *hastin-*]

थेइ-थेइ f. keeping time; rhythmic syllables called out by dancer [S *thaithai*]

थोरा adj. small, little [13720 **stoka-*]

दंडवत , दंडौत m. prostration [S °*vat-*]

दंपति m. husband and wife, couple [S]

दंभ m. pride, arrogance, deceit [S]

दई m. God, destiny [6574 *daiviya-*]

दगरौ m. road; ~मार- vt. to hold up on the road, rob [5523 **dag-*]

दगा f. deceit, trick, artifice [Pers. *dagā*]

दधि m. thick sour milk, yoghurt [S]

दधिकरन m. 'sop-ears', name of a cat in RN [S °*karṇa-*]

दब- vi. to be oppressed, crushed [6173 **dabb-*]

दबक- vi. to hide [6173 **dabb-*]

दमाम— (°में) m. large kettledrum [Pers. *damāma*]

दमोदर m. Dāmodar, Kṛṣṇa [S *dā*°]

दया f. sympathy, compassion, mercy [S]

दरक- vi. to split, tear [6192 *darayati*]

दरपन m. mirror [S *darpaṇa-*]

दरशन see दर्सन

दरस m. vision, appearance, view [S *darśa-*]

दरस- vt. to see, have a sight of [S *darśa-*]

दरसा- vt. to cause to see [S *darśayati*]

दर्पन m. mirror [S °*ṇa-*]

दर्ब, दर्व see द्रव्य

दर्सन, दरसन, दरशन, दरसण m. vision, appearance, view [S *darśana*]

दल m. leaf, petal [S]

दलमल- vt. to crush [6213 *dala-* + 9870 **malati*]

दवानल m. forest fire [S]

दवारि f. forest fire [S]

दस num. ten [6227 *daśa*]

दसधा adj. tenfold [S °*ś*°]

दसन m. tooth [6231 *daśana-*]

दसरथ m. Daśrath, father of Rāma [S *daśaratha-*]

दसा f. condition, situation [S *daśā-*]

दह्- vt. (see note to SR 11.3) to burn, set alight [6245 *dahati*]

दही m. thick sour milk, yoghurt [6146 *dadhi*-]

दाँब see दाव

दाख f. grape [6628 *drākṣā*-]

दान m. offering, toll, gift [S]

दानव m. demon [S]

दानी m. giver [S *dānin*-]

दाब- vt. to press, squeeze [6173 **dabb*-]

दाम m. copper coin worth one twenty-fifth of a paisa (earlier one-fortieth of a rupee?); money [6622 *dramma*-]

दामिनि f. lightning [for S *saudamanī*-]

दाव, दाँब m. turn, opportunity, chance [6258 *dātu*-]

दावा m. forest fire [6311 *dāva*-]

दासी f. maidservant [S]

दिक्षा f. initiation [S *dī°*]

दिखरा- vt. to show, demonstrate [6507 **dekṣati*]

दिखा- vt. to show, demonstrate [6507 **dekṣati*]

दिग-बिजयी adj. conquering all directions, all-powerful [S *digvijayin*-]

दिन, दिना m. day; दिन-प्रति adv. daily [S]

दिनेस m. the sun god [S *°śa*-]

दिपति f. lustre, brilliance [S *dīpti*-]

दिल्ली f. Delhi [6559 *dehalī*- ?]

दिवस m. day [S]

दिवा- vt. to cause to be given [6141 *dadāti*]

दिवाना adj. crazy, ecstatic [Pers. *dīwāna*]

दिव्य adj. divine, spiritual [S]

दिसि f. direction, side; ~ दिसि adv. all around [6339 *diś*-]

दीठ f. glance, gaze, look [6520 *dṛṣṭi*-]

दीन adj. wretched, helpless, humble; ~ दयाल epithet of Kṛṣṇa; ~ बंधु m. friend of the poor [S]

दीनता f. humility [S]

दीप m. lamp, light; ~ माल f. row of lamps [S]

दीप- vi. to glow, shine [6362 *dīpyate*]

दीपक m. 'illuminator', zeugma, a trope in which separate descriptions are completed in parallel by a shared word or attribute [S]

दीस- vi. to appear, seem [6516 *dṛśyate*]

दुंद m. discord [6649 **duvaṁdva*-]

दुःख, दुख, दुखु m. grief, suffering [S & 6375 *duḥkha*-]

दुखार— (°री) adj. unhappy [6375 *duḥkha*-]

दुखी adj. unhappy [6380 *duḥkhita*-]

दुगुन— (°नी) adj. double [6390 **duguṇa*-]

दुति f. brightness, radiance [S *dyuti*-]

दुतिय num. second [S *dvitīya*-]

दुपहर f. noon [6648 *dvi*- + 8900 *prahara*-]

दुबिधा f. dubiety, wavering [S *dvidhā*-?]

दुर- vi. to hide, be hidden [6495 *dūra*-]

दुरजन m. bad person, villain [S *durjana*-]

दुरा- vt. to hide, conceal [6495 *dūra*-]

दुर्लभ adj. rare, hard to obtain [S]

दुलरा- vt. to fondle, cosset [*durlalita* × *lālana*-, *°ita*- ?]

दुवार- (दुवारैं) m. door, house [S *dvāra*-]

दुष्कर्मी adj. & m. evil-doing; sinner [S *°karman*-]

दुष्ट adj. & m. corrupt, wicked, evil; evil man, rogue [S]

दुष्टता f. wickedness [S]

दुहर— (°रे) adj. double, twofold [6407 **dudhāra*-]

दुहा- vt. to milk [6476 **duhati*]

दुहूँन, दुहून num. both, the two [6648 *dva-*]

दूख- vi. to hurt, be in pain [6376 *duḥkhati*]

दूजौ m. other, second [6402 **dutīya-*]

दूत m. messenger [S]

दूतिका f. messenger, go-between [S]

दूध m. milk [6391 *dugdha-*]

दूनो adj. double [6390 **duguṇa-*]

दूबर— (दूबरैं) adj. thin, weak [6438 *durbala-*]

दूरि adj. & adv. remote, far; + *kar-*, vt. to remove [6495 *dūra-*]

दूसरो adj. second, other [6676 **dviḥsara-*]

दृग, द्रग m. eye [S *dṛś-*]

दृढ़ adj. firm, strong, steady [S *dṛdha-*]

दृष्टांत m. 'exemplification', a trope involving a parallel (rather than qualitatively similar) example [S]

दृष्टि, दृष्ट f. sight, view [S]

दे- vt. to give; (as aux.) to allow to [6141 *dadāti*]

देख- vt. to see, look for [6507 *dekṣati*]

देव m. god, deity; name of a poet [S]

देवता m. god, deity; brahmin [S]

देवपति m. Indra [S]

देवालय m. temple [S]

देवी f. goddess [S]

देश, देस m. country, homeland [6547 *deśa-*]

देसाधिपति m. emperor, king [S *deś°*]

देह (f.) body [S]

देहरि f. threshold [6559 *dehalī-*]

देहानुसंधान m. awareness of body [S]

दैन्यता f. humility [S *dainya* + pleonastic *-tā* (on model of *dīnatā* ?)]

दैव m. fate, fortune; ~ *ke saṁjoga* adv. by the ordinance of fate [S]

दैवी adj. divine [S *daiva-*]

दोइ, दोय num. two; both [6648 *dva-*]

दोउ, दोऊ num. two; both (obl. *dauna*) [6648 *dva-*]

दोना m. leaf cup [6641 *droṇa-*]

दोनी f. small leaf-cup [6641 *droṇa-*]

दोय see दोउ

दोर- see दौर-

दोष m. blame, fault, detriment [S]

दोहनी f. milk-pail [S]

दोहा m. a couplet metre [S *dohaḍikā* - ?]

दौन m. subduing, taming [6177 *damana-*]

दौर-, दोर- vi. to run [6624 *dravati*]

दौलागिरि m. 'white mountain', a Himalayan peak [S *dhavalagiri-*]

द्योस, द्यौस m. day, daytime [6333 *divasa-*]

द्रग see दृग

द्रव्य, दर्व, दर्ब m. wealth, property [S]

द्रुम m. tree [S]

द्रोह m. malice, hostility [S]

द्रौपदी, द्रोपती f. Draupadī, wife of the five Pāṇḍu princes [S]

द्वार, द्वार— (°रे) m. door; residence [S]

द्वारपाल m. doorkeeper [S]

द्वारिका f. Dwarka, Kṛṣṇa's capital on the Gujarat coast [S *dvārakā-*]

द्वै num. two [6648 *dva-*]

धंधा m. task, work [6727 *dhandha-*]

धंस- vi. to enter, plunge in [6896 *dhvaṁsati*]

धक्का m. shove, push; ~ मार- vt. to shove, push [6701 *dhakk-]

धन m. wealth, property, treasure [S]

धनंतर m. Dhanvantari, physician of the gods, and inventor of medical science [S *dhanvantari-*]

धनियाँ (rh.) adj. rich [from next]

धनी m. master; husband [6722 *dhanin-*]

धनुष m. archer's bow [S]

धन्य adj. blessed, fortunate [S]

धमक- vi. to throb, beat, rush [6736 *dhammakka-]

धमार m. a Holi song (sung to 12-beat *dhamār tāl*) [6735 *dhamm- ?]

धर f. earth, ground [6748 *dharā-*]

धर-, धरा- vt. to place, hold, put on, assume [6747 *dharati*]

धरक- vi. to throb, blaze up [6711 *dhaḍ-]

धरधरा m. throbbing [6711 *dhaḍ-]

धरनि f. the earth, ground [6744 *dharaṇī-*]

धरवा- vt. to cause to be held, apprehended [6747 *dharati*]

धरा f. earth [S]

धरा- see धर-

धर्म m. usage, customary observance, law, duty, religious equity; property (in literary rhetoric); ~ निधि m. treasury of righteousness; ~ विरोधी adj. & m. impious, unlawful, (one) opposed to law [S]

धर्मारन्य m. 'forest of righteous conduct', name of a forest in RN [S °*ṇya-*]

धा-[1] vi. to run, rush [6802 *dhāvati*]

धा-[2] see ध्या(व)-

धाई f. wet-nurse, nanny, maidservant [6774 *dhātrī-*]

धात m. mineral, pigment (e.g. chalk, ochre) smeared on the body [S °*tu-*]

धाम m. abode, domain [S *dhāman-*]

धार m. heavy rainfall, torrent [6788 *dhāra-*]

धार- vt. to hold, place, have, take [6791 *dhārayati*]

धारन m. holding; ~ कर vt. to hold [S °*ṇa-*]

धीर m. patience, fortitude, courage [S]

धुंधुवा- vi. to fume, be filled with smoke [6858 *dhūmāndha-]

धुँवं— (धुँवं) m. smoke [6852 *dhūmara-]

धुआं m. smoke [6849 *dhūma-*]

धुजा f. flag, banner [S *dhvaja-*]

धुना- vt. to beat (in माथो ~) [6846 *dhunoti*]

धुनि f. sound, cry, tune [6823 *dhuni-*]

धुबिया see धोबी

धूम[1] m. smoke; mist [S]

धूम[2] f. stir, commotion [6824 *dhunman-]

धूर f. dust [6835 *dhūḍi-]

धेनु f. cow [S]

धोखा m. deceit, blunder [6894 *dhrokṣa-]

धोबी, धुबिया m. dhobi [6886 *dhauvati]

धौलहर m. tower [6768 *dhavalaghara-]

ध्या(व)-, धा- vt. to meditate on, worship [6812 *dhiyāyati*]

ध्यान m. attention, meditation [S]

न, ना neg.part. not; ना तौ cj. otherwise [6906 *na*]

नंद[1] m. Nanda, Kṛṣṇa's foster-father; ~ किसोर, ~ कुमार, ~ नंदन, ~ लाल 'son of Nanda', Kṛṣṇa ; ~ रनियाँ (rh.), ~ रानी 'wife of Nanda', Yaśodā [S]

नंद[2] f. husband's sister [6946 *nanāndṛ-*]

नंदित adj. gladdened, joyful [S]

नंदीश्वर m. a village in Braj [S]

नकीब m. herald, adjutant [Pers. *naqīb*]

नख m. nail (of finger or toe) [S]

नखत m. constellation, star [6913 *nakṣatra-*]

नगर m., °री f. town, city [S]

नचा- vt. to make dance [7583 *nṛtyati*]

नजर f. sight, view [Ar. *naẕar*]

नट m. dancer, acrobat; ~वर idem. [S]

नद f. river [S]

नयन, नैन, नैना, नैणा m. eye [S]

नर m. man, person, human [S]

नरक m. hell [S]

नरकपति m. 'lord of hell', Yama (?) [S]

नरवाहन m. Narvāhan, devotee of Hit Harivaṁś [S]

नरहरि m. 'man-lion' avatar of Viṣṇu [S]

नरेश, नरेस m. king [S]

नल m. pipe, conduit [6936 *naḍa-*]

नव num. nine [S]

नवल adj. & m. new, fresh, young; name of a disciple of Hit Harivaṁś [S]

नवा- vt. to cause to bend, lower [6956 *namayati*]

नवीन, °नी (rh.) adj. new [S]

नहिं, नाहिं , नाहि, नाहिंन, नाहीं neg.particle not [7035 *nahi*]

नाँघ- vt. to jump over [10905 *laṅghayati*]

ना see न

ना- see नाव-

नाई ppn. like, in the manner of [5284 **jñāyate-*]

नाउँ see नाम

नाउ see नाव2

नाक f. nose; ~चढ़ा- vt. to turn up the nose [6909 **nakka-*]

नागर adj. clever, urbane, sophisticated, courtly, elegant [S]

नागरि f. skilful woman [S *nāgarī-*]

नागरिया f. *chāp* (nom de plume) of poet 'Nāgarīdās' [for S *nāgarī-*]

नाच m. dance [7582 *nṛtya-*]

नाच- vi. to dance [7583 *nṛtyati*]

नातर cj. otherwise [5730 *tarhi*]

नाथ m. lord [S]

नाद m. sound [S]

नाना adj. various, diverse [S]

नान्हू— (नान्हे) adj. tiny [12732 *ślakṣṇa-*]

नाम, नाउँ, नाव m. name; ~दे-, सुना- vt. to initiate with a mantra [7067 *nāman-*]

नायक m. hero, lord, leader [S]

नार see नारि

नारद m. Nārad, legendary author of part of the Veda etc. [S]

नारायण, °न m. Nārāyaṇ,Viṣṇu [S]

नारि, नारी1, नार f. woman, wife [7078 *nāḍī-*]

नारी2 f. vein, pulse; ~ज्ञान m. pulse-taking [7047 *nāṛī-*]

नाव1, नाउ f. boat, ferryboat [7081 *nāvā-*]

नाव2 see नाम

ना(व)- vt. to bend, lower; to place (food into mouth etc.) [7068 *nāmayati*]

नास- vi. to be lost, destroyed; vt. to destroy [7027 *naśyati*; 7087 *nāśayati*]

नासापुट m. nostril [S]

नाहक adv. unjustly, without cause [Pers. *nā-ḥaq*]

नाहर m. tiger [6919 **nakhadara* or 6921 **nakharin-*]

नाहिं, नाहि, नाहिंन, नाहीं see नहिं

निंदा f. reproach, censure [S]

निकट adj. & adv. near, close by [S]

निकर- vi. to emerge [7478 *niṣkalati]

निकस- vi. to emerge, come/go out, pass, slip away [7479 *niṣkasati]

निकाई f. excellence [7150 nikta-]

निकार- vt. to take out, extract, expel [7484 niṣkālayati]

निकुंज m. grove, arbour [S]

निकेत, निकेतु m. abode, home [S]

निगम m. the Veda, scripture [S]

निगुन see निरगुन

निचतौ adj. free from care [7447 niścinta-]

निज adj. constant, eternal; pr. one's own, MSH अपना [S]

निठुर adj. cruel [7505 niṣṭhura-]

नित, नित्त adv. always, constantly; नित-प्रति always, constantly; नित्त-बिहार m. eternal sport, Kṛṣṇa's *līlā* [S nitya-]

नितंब m. buttocks, rump [S]

नित्त see नित

निदर- vt. to treat with contempt [7340 *nirdarati]

निदाघ m. heat, summer [S]

निदान m. & adv. cause; finally, ultimately, after all [S]

निधि f. treasury, store, treasure; the treasures of Kuber, god of wealth (nine in number, mostly being gems, but of uncertain description) [S]

निपट adv. extremely [7395 *nirvṛtta- (with nipaṭ-)]

निपुन adj. expert, conversant [S °ṇa-]

निबंध adj. & m. fixed; restraint [S (for *nibaddha* in adj. sense)]

निबल adj. weak [7356 nirbala-]

निबह- vi. to survive, get on, be maintained [7397 nirvahati]

निबुआ m. lime [7247 nimbū-]

निमित्त m. motive, purpose; के निमित्त ppn. for, for the purpose of [S]

नियरैं adv. near, nearby [7136 nikaṭam]

निरंतर adj. & adv. constant(ly) [S]

निरख- vt. to look at, stare at, admire [7280 nirīkṣate]

निरगुन, निगुन adj. & m. without attributes, unqualified (deity) [S & 7307 nirguṇa-]

निरत- see निर्त-

निरदई adj. pitiless [S nirdaya-]

निरधार m. certainty, ascertainment [S nirdhāra-]

निरमल see निर्मल

निरविष adj. free of poison [S nir- + viṣa-]

निरवेद m. despondency, indifference, loathing for worldly things [S nirveda-]

निर्त-, निरत- vi. to dance [S nṛtyati]

निर्मल adj. pure, unsullied [S]

निर्वान m. salvation, final emancipation [S nirvāṇa-]

निवार- vt. to ward off [7419 nivārayati]

निवारन m. removing, banishing; banisher [S °ṇa-]

निवासी m. resident [S]

निवेद्यौ adj. & m. to be offered; offering [S °dya-]

निश्चय, निश्चै m. conviction, certainty [S]

निसा, निस f. night [S or 7428 niśā-]

निसि f. night [7436 niśītha-]

निसंग adj. fearless [7106 niḥśaṅka-]

निसान m. kettledrum [7537 nisvāna-]

निहार- vt. to see, observe [7228 *nibhālayati* or **nibhārayati*]

नींद f. sleep [7200 *nidrā-*]

नीकौ, °को adj. good, beautiful; नीके, नीकें नीकैं, नीके करि adv. well [7150 *nikta-*]

नीचौ adj. low; नीचे adv. down [7540 *nīca-*]

नीठि adv. scarcely, barely [7503 *niṣṭhā-* ?]

नीति f. propriety, right conduct [S]

नीबी f. drawstring of skirt; capital, stock [S *nīvī-*]

नीर, नीरु m. water; tears [S]

नील, नील— (°लैं) adj. blue, dark, black [7563 *nīla-*]

नीलमनि m. sapphire [S *nīlamaṇi-*]

नूपुर m. anklet [S]

नृत्त m. dancing [S]

नृत्य m. dance, dancing [S]

नृप m. king [S]

नृपति m. king [S]

नें, ने ppn. of agentive case [derived from S instrumental termination]

नेक, नेकु see नैंक

नेति 'not this' (S *na* + *iti*)—the Upanishadic formula in which the ineffable nature of Brahman is defined only in negative terms [S]

नेत्र m. eye [S]

नेवर m. anklet [7577 *nūpura-*]

नेहृ m. love, affection, oiliness, unctuousness [13802 *sneha-*]

नैंक, नैंकु, नेक, नेकु adv. a little [S *na* + *eka-*]

नै[1] f. tube of a hookah [Pers.]

नै[2] f. river [6943 *nadī-*]

नैन, नैना, नैण, नैणा see नयन

नौका m. boat [S]

नौबत f. the playing of music (by shawm and drums) at a palace gateway, to mark the time of day [Pers.]

न्यात m. kinsman [S *jñāti-*]

न्यारो adj. unique, strange, wondrous [404 **anyākāra-*]

न्यून adj. less, deficient [S]

न्यौछावरि f. sacrifice, offering [Ar. *nisār* (× *niyama-* ??)]

न्हा- vi. to bathe [13786 *snāti*]

पंकज m. lotus; ~ मुखी adj. lotus-faced [S]

पंखा m. fan [7627 *pakṣa-*]

पंगु adj. & m. lame; cripple [S]

पंच num. five [S]

पंजर m. cage [S]

पंडित adj. & m. wise, learned; scholar [S]

पंथ m. way, road; ~ ले- vt. to set off, go one's way [S]

पकर-, पकड़- vt. to catch, seize, hold [7619 **pakkaḍ-*]

पकवान m. cooked food, delicacy [S *pakvānna-*]

पखा m. feather [7627 *pakṣa-*]

पखावज m. a barrel drum [7635 **pakṣātodya-*]

पग m. foot; step [7766 *padga-*]

पगा- vt. to steep, immerse [S *pragāhate* ? (C.Shackle 1984:99)]

पगार f. ridge around field, field-boundary [8464 **pragaḍḍa-* or 8914 *prākāra-*]

पच- vi. to be consumed, destroyed (in पचि हार- to toil and lose, to be defeated after great effort) [7654 *pacyate*]

पचीसी f. group of twenty-five [7672 *pañcaviṁśati-*]

पच्छ m. feather [S *pakṣa-*]

पश्चिम m. the West [S *paścima-*]

पछता-, पछि°- vi. to repent, be remorseful [8010 **paścottāpa-, paścāttāpa-*]

पछार f. (or abs. from पछार- vi.) swoon, faint [8493 **pracchāṭ-*]

पट m. cloth, garment [S]

पटक- vt. to throw down, dump [7691 *paṭ-*]

पटतर m. comparison [S *paṭutara* ??]

पठा- vt. to send [8607 *prasthāpayati*]

पढ़- vt. to study [7712 *paṭhati*]

पतवारी f. rudder, steering oar [S *pātrapāla-* or **-ikā*]

पति¹ m. husband, lord [S]

पति² f. good name, honour [8640 *pratyāyati* (C.Shackle 1981:180)]

पतित m. sinner [S]

पतितेस m. lord of sinners [S *patiteśa-*]

पत्या-, पतिया- vt. to trust [8640 *pratyāyayati*]

पत्रा f. almanac, ephemeris [S *patra-*]

पथिक m. wayfarer, traveller [S]

पद m. position, state, status; lyric hymn; word; line of poem; foot; ~ त्रान m. shoe [S]

पदावली f. collection of verses [S]

पधार- vi. to proceed, go [7768 **paddhārayati*]

पनार— (पनारे) m. channel, gutter [8673 *praṇāḍī-*]

पबन see पवन

पयोधि m. ocean [S]

पर¹ adj. prefix relating to another; ~ द्रोह m. malice; ~ निंदा f. calumny; ~ मुख adv. in/to the face of others [S]

पर², पै ppn. at, on [2333 **uppari*]

पर³, परि cj. but [S]

पर- vi. to fall, befall [7722 *patati*]

परंतु cj. but [S]

परचई f. story, biography [7809 *pariciti-*]

परछाँहीं f. shadow [8560 *praticchāyā-*]

परज f. name of a rāginī [8737 **prarajyate* ??]

परतीति f. trust, faith [8624 *pra°-*]

परदेस adv. abroad [S *°śa-*]

परपंच see प्रपंच

परब m. festival [S *parvan-*]

परभात m. & adv. (at) dawn [S *prabhāta-*]

परम adj. & adv. prime, supreme; most; ~ गति f. salvation, beatitude [S]

परमेश्वर m. God, the supreme Lord [S]

परवत see पर्वत

परस- vt. to touch [13811 *sparśayate*]

परस्पर, परसपर adj. reciprocal, mutual [S]

परा- vi. to flee, run away [7955 *palāyate*]

पराग m. pollen [S]

परि see पर³

परिनाम m. 'transference', a comparison in which a property of the subject is transferred to the object [S *°ṇāma-*]

परिपूरन adj. full, brimful [S *°pūrṇa-*]

परीक्षा, °च्छा f. test, examination [S]

परुषा adj. & f. harsh; alliteration with many compounded words [S]

परेख- vt. to examine, consider [7912 *parekṣate*]

परोस m. neighbourhood, neighbour's house [8598 *prativeśa-*]

पर्जस्त m. 'transposition', a trope of 'denial' (see अपन्हुति) in which a quality of the object of comparison is transposed to the subject [S *paryasta-*]

पर्वत, परवत m. hill, mountain [S]

पल f. eyelid [Pers. *palak*]

पल m. moment; one-sixtieth of a *ghaṛī* [S]

पलक f. eyelid; eyelash [Pers.]

पलिका (m.) bed, cot [7964 *palyaṅka*-]

पलुटा- vt. to cause to press, massage [8770 **pralortati*]

पलोट- vt. to massage [8770 **pralortati*]

पल्लव m. blossom, bud [S]

पवन, पबन m. wind [S]

पशु m. animal, beast [S]

पसर vi. to spread out, lie down [8825 *prasarati*]

पसीज- vi. to perspire, melt (with pity), soften, be touched [8896 **prasvidyati*]

पहर see प्रहर

पहर-, पहिर-, पहेर- vt. to wear, put on [7835 *paridadhāti*]

पहल-, पहिल— (°ले, °लें) adj. first; पहले adv. firstly [8652 **prathilla*-]

पहाड़ m. mountain, hill [8141 **pāhāḍa*-]

पहिचान-, पिछान- vt. to recognize, identify [8637 *pratyabhijānāti*]

पहिर—, पहेर— see पहर—

पहिरा- vt. to cause to don, dress [7835 *paridhāpayati*]

पहिल- (°लें) see पहल-

पहुँच- vi. to arrive, reach [8716 *prabhūta*-]

पहुँचा- vt. to escort [8716 *prabhūta*-]

पहुँचौ m. wrist, forearm [8018 **pahuñca*-]

पाँच num. five [7655 *pañca*]

पांचि num. fifth [7655 *pañca*]

पा- vt. to achieve, find, attain, get; (as aux.) to manage to [8943 *prāpayati*]

पाइ, पाँइ, पाय, पाँय, पैयाँ (rh.) m. foot [8056 *pāda*-]

पाग f. turban [7644 **paggā*-]

पाछिलो adj. last, previous [7990 **paśca*-]

पाछें, पाछैं, पीछे adv. behind, after, later [7990 **paśca*-]

पाट m. throne, seat [7699 *paṭṭa*-]

पाठ m. text, reading [S]

पाणी see पानी

पातशाह m. emperor [Pers. *pādshāh*]

पाताल m. one of the netherworlds, the abode of snakes [S]

पाती f. letter, note [7733 *pattra*-]

पान[1] m. drinking, drink [S]

पान[2] m. betel leaf, pan [7918 *parṇa*-]

पानि (m.) hand [S *pāṇi*-]

पानी, पाणी m. water; shine, lustre; character, honour [8082 *pānīya*-]

पाप m. sin [S]

पापी adj & m. wicked; sinner [S °*ina*-]

पाय see पाइ

पायंदाज m. doormat [Pers. *pā-andāz*]

पायक m. courier, footsoldier [8097 **pāyakka*-]

पार m. further bank; limit, extent; adv. across, through; ~पा- vt. to fathom [S]

पार- vt. to ascertain [8106 *pārayati*]

पाल- vt. to practise, maintain [8129 *pālayati*]

पाला m. snow, frost [8959 *prāleya*-]

पावक m. fire [S]

पावस f. the rainy season [8964 *prāvṛṣ*-]

पास adv. near [8118 *pārśvatas*]

पाहन m. stone [8138 *pāṣāṇa*-]

पाहुनौ m. guest [8973 *prāhuṇa*-]

पिचका (m.) syringe, squirter [8149 *piccayati*]

पिछ्ल– (°ले) adj. last; next [7990 *paśca-]

पिछवार– (पिछवारैं) m. rear (of house) [7994 *paścapāṭa-]

पिछान- see पहिचान-

पितंबर see पीतांबर

पितमारक m. patricide [S *pitṛmāraka-]

पिय, पीय m. lover, beloved [8974 priya-]

पिया f. lover, beloved [8974 priya-]

पियारी see प्यारी

पी m. lover [8974 priya-]

पी- vt. to drink [8209 pibati]

पीक f. juice of chewed betel [8144 *pikkā-]

पीछे see पाछें

पीठ, पीठि f. back; ~ दे- vt. to turn one's back [8370 pṛṣṭi-]

पीत adj. yellow; ~ पटवारे m. 'he of the yellow sash', Kṛṣṇa [S]

पीतांबर, पितंबर m. Kṛṣṇa's yellow sash [S]

पीय see पिय

पीर f. pain, suffering [8227 pīḍā-]

पीरो adj. yellow [8233 pītala-]

पीस- vt. to grind [8142 piṁśati]

पुंज m. mass, group, crop [S]

पुकार- vt. to call [8246 *pukkār-]

पुजव- see पूज-2

पुनि, पुन adv. & cj. again, still, further, furthermore [8273 punar]

पुन्य m. virtue, meritorious act; punyātmā adj. pure-souled, virtuous [S puṇya-]

पुर m. town; ~ जन m. townsfolk [S]

पुरंदर m. Indra [S]

पुरान m. the Purāṇa(s), sacred S texts ascribed to Vyāsa [S purāṇa]

पुरुष m. man, person [S]

पुलक- vi. to feel a thrill of delight (causing 'horripilation', bristling of the hairs of the body) [S pulaka-]

पुहुप m. flower [8303 puṣpa-]

पूछ- vt. to ask [8352 pṛcchati]

पूज-1 vt. to worship, adore [S pūjayati]

पूज-2 vi. (ptc. pujavata) to be fulfilled [8342 pūryate]

पूत m. son [8265 putra-]

पूनो, पून्यौ f. full-moon day/night [8340 pūrṇimā-]

पूरौ adj. full, complete, accomplished [8330 pūra-]

पूर- vt. to fill [8335 pūrayati]

पूरन, पूरण adj. full, complete, abundant, fulfilled, accomplished [S pūrṇa-]

पूरब m. the East [S pūrva-]

पूर्बापर adj. preceding and following, in sequence [S °v°]

पूर्वी, पूरबी f. name of a raga [S]

पेख- vt. to see, behold [8994 prekṣate]

पेट m. stomach [8376 *peṭṭa-]

पै1 ppn. to, for, by, from [Add2 8540 prati]

पै2 ppn. on, at [2333 *uppari-]

पै3 cj. but [8951 prāyeṇa]

पैंडा m. path, way [7753 *padadaṇḍa-]

पैग m. footstep [7750 *padagra-]

पैजनी f. ankle-bells worn by children [7747 pada- + 5333 *jhaṇikā-]

पैठ- vi. to enter [8803 praviṣṭa-]

पैन्ह- vt. to wear, put on [8198 *pinahati]

पैयाँ see पाइ

पोंछन m. wiping [9012 proñchana-]

पोंछ- vt. to wipe; पोंछ औछ- vt. to wipe [9011 proñchati]

पोढ- see पौढ़-

पोरिया m. gatekeeper [8632 **pratolika-* or 8666 **pradura*]

पोस- vt. to nourish, foster [8410 *poṣayati*]

पौंच- vt. to wipe, wipe off [9011 *proñchati*]

पौढ़-, पौढ-, पोढ- vi. to lie down, sleep [8789 *pravardhate*]

पौढ़ा- vt. to make lie down, put to sleep [8789 *pravardhate*]

पौन m. wind, breeze [7978 *pavana-*]

पौरि f. doorway [8633 *pratolī-* or 8666 **pradura*]

प्यारौ; °री, पियारी adj. & m./f. dear, beloved [8975 *priyakāra-*]

प्याला m. cup [Pers. *piyāla*]

प्यास f. thirst [8199 *pipāsā-*]

प्यास— (°से) adj. thirsty [8199 *pipāsā-*]

प्यौ adj. & m. beloved, lover [8974 *priya-*]

प्रकट, प्रगट adj. manifest, revealed; (of holy persons) born [S]

प्रकार m. type, variety, way, manner [S]

प्रकास adj. clear, apparent [S °*śa-*]

प्रगट see प्रकट

प्रगट- vi. to arise, be born [S *prakaṭa-*]

प्रताप m. splendour, glory, strength [S]

प्रति adj.pref. each, every [S]

प्रतिज्ञा f. vow, pledge [S]

प्रतिपारी m. guard, gatekeeper [S *pratipālin-*]

प्रतिबस्तूप f. 'counterpart simile', one in which the shared property is repeated [S *prativastūpamā-*]

प्रतिबिंब m. reflection [S]

प्रतिष्ठा f. rank, fame, celebrity [S]

प्रतिहार m. doorkeeper [S]

प्रतीति f. ascertainment, knowledge, trust, assurance [S]

प्रतीप m. inverse simile (one in which the object is compared to the subject, rather than vice versa) [S]

प्रथम adv. & adj. firstly; first [S]

प्रपंच, पर° m. the phenomenal universe; illusion, delusion [S]

प्रबल adj. powerful, strong [S]

प्रबीन (°नी (rh.)) adj. skilful, clever, knowing [S *pravīna-*]

प्रबोध m. awaking, manifestation [S]

प्रभु m. lord [S]

प्रभुता f. lordship, supremacy [S]

प्रमान m., ppn. & adv. evidence; of the measure of; (in RN) immediately on doing [S °*ṇa-*]

प्रयाग m. Prayag, sacred site of the confluence of the Ganges and Yamuna (modern Allahabad) [S]

प्रयोजन m. purpose, cause [S]

प्रलय m. dissolution, the destruction of the universe at the end of a *kalpa* [S]

प्रवाह m. flow, current [S]

प्रसन्न adj. pleased, happy [S]

प्रहर, पहर m. period of three hours, watch [S]

प्रह्लाद m. Prahlād, a pious Vaiṣṇava protected by Viṣṇu [S]

प्राण, °न m. soul, heart, spirit, life-breath, vitality; ~ पियारी f. heart's beloved [S]

प्रात ; प्रातकाल adv.& m. at dawn; dawn; [S *prātar-* ; *prātaḥkāla-*]

प्रान see प्राण

प्राप्त adj. arrived, admitted [S]

प्रिय adj. pleasing [S]

प्रिया f. beloved [S]

प्रीतम m. beloved [S]

प्रीति f. love [S]

प्रेम m. love [S]

प्रेर- vt. to send, despatch [9002 *prerayati*]

प्रौढ़ा adj. & f. mature; mature and experienced woman (esp. as heroine in literary rhetoric) [S]

फंस m. noose [13813 *spāśa-*]

फट- vi. to burst, tear [13825 **sphāṭyate*]

फरक- vi. to flutter; to yearn [13820 **spharati*]

फरका- vt. to cause to quiver, flare [13820 **spharati*]

फल m. fruit [9051 *phala-*]

फहरा- vi. to flutter [13820 **spharati* with reduplication?]

फाँसी f. noose [13813 *spāśa-*]

फाग m. the Holi festival [9062 *phalgu-*]

फाट- vt. (but see note to BS 19.2) to split, rend [13825 **sphāṭyate*]

फार- vt. to tear [13825 *sphāṭayati*]

फिकर f. concern, anxiety [Ar. *fikr*]

फिर- vi. to wander, roam, turn, return [9078 **phirati*]

फिरि, फेर, फेरि adv. again, then [9078 **phirati*]

फीको adj. dull, weak, bland [9037 **phikka-*]

फुर- see फूल-

फूट- vi. to break [13845 **sphuṭyati*]

फूल m. flower [9092 *phulla-*]

फूल-, फुर- vi. to bloom; to thrive; to swell with joy [9093 *phullati*]

फेंटा, फेंट m. waistband [9107 **pheṭṭa-*]

फेर, फेरि see फिरि

फेर- vt. to turn; to pass (the hand etc. over) [9078 **pherayati-*]

फैरि see फिरि

फैल- vi. to spread [8651 *prathita-*]

फोर- vt. to break [13857 *sphoṭayati*]

फौज f. army [Ar. *fauj*]

बंक adj. bent, crooked [11191 *vaṅka-*]

बंद adj. closed, cut off [Pers. *band*]

बंद- vt. to praise, revere, salute [11270 *vandate*]

बंदन m. salutation [S *va°*]

बंदर, °रा m. monkey [11515 *vānara-*]

बंदी m. bard, herald [S *vandin-*]

बँध m. tie, fastening [S]

बँध- vi. to be tied, bound, caught, ensnared [9139 *bandhati*]

बंधन m. bond, tether [S]

बँधा- vt. to tie [9139 *bandhati*]

बंसी 1 m. kinsman [S *vaṁśin-*]

बंसी 2 f. flute [11180 *vaṁśī-*]

बंसीबट m. 'flute banyan', the tree under which Kṛṣṇa fluted [S *vaṁśīvaṭa-*]

बँसुरी, बँसुरिया f. flute [11180 *vaṁśī-*]

बक m. heron [S]

बक-, बकर- vt. to gabble, mutter [9117 **bakk-*]

बकबाद f. idle talk [9118 **bakkavāda-* × S]

बकारी f. oblique bar or bracket separating denominations in a sum of money [perhaps connected to 11192/3 **vaṅkara-*, but cf. also Platts *bakār*]

बकासुर m. the heron demon [S]

बकी f. the demoness Pūtanā, sister of the heron demon Baka (Bakāsura) [S]

बखान- vt. to praise, describe [12188 *vyākhyāna-*]

बच- vi. to escape, be left [11208 *vañcati*]

बचन see **वचन**

बचा- vt. to save, rescue [11208 *vañcati*]

बछल adj. affectionate, loving, caring (in भक्त बछल) [11244 *vatsala-*]

बज- see **बाज-**

बजा- vt. to play (music) [11513 *vādyate*]

बजार m. market-place [Pers. *bāzār*]

बटोही m. traveller, wayfarer [11367 **vartmapathika-*]

बड़वानल m. submarine fire (*barvā*), said to emerge from a submarine cavity at the South Pole [S]

बड़ाई f. praise, magnifying [11225 *vaḍra-*]

बड़ौ, बडो adj. & adv. big, great; very (obl.pl. बड़ेन); बड़ी जाति f. Muslim community [11225 *vaḍra-*]

बढ़-, बाढ़- vi. to increase, grow, advance [11376 *vardhate*]

बढ़ई m. carpenter [11375 *vardhaki-*]

बढ़ा- vt. to augment, increase, extend [11383 *vardhāpayati*]

बणा- see **बना-**

बतरस m. the pleasure of conversation and gossip [*bāta* + *rasa*]

बतरा- vt. to talk, converse [11564 *vārtta-*]

बता- vt. to show, point out, identify, tell [11564 *vārtta-*]

बद- vt. to speak; to wager, stake [S *vadati*]

बदन m. face; mouth [S *vadana-*]

बधू f. wife, bride, woman [S *vadhū-*]

बन see **वन**

बन- vi. to be made, be managed, be adorned, look beautiful [11260 *vanati*]

बनखंड m. wood, forest, wild place [S *v°*]

बनचारी f. roaming or dwelling in the forest [S *vanacarya-*]

बनमाला, °माल f. garland of forest flowers [S *v°*]

बनराय m. tree [11265 *vanarājī-*]

बना- vt. to make, fabricate [11260 *vanati*]

बनिक m. merchant [S *v°*]

बनिता f. lady, loving woman [S *va°*]

बनिया m. merchant, trader [11231 *vaṇijaka-*]

बयस f. age, time of life [S *vayas-*]

बर adj. fine, best [11308 *vara-*]

बरख m. year [S *varṣa-*]

बरख- see **बरष-**

बरज- vt. to restrain, stop, check [S *varjayati*]

बरत f. tightrope [11320 *varatrā-*]

बरन m. colour; class, caste; consonant, syllable [S *varṇa-*]

बरन- vt. to describe [11342 *varṇayati*]

बरनन see **वर्णन**

बरव- (बरवै) m. a metre (see II.2.3) [?]

बरष-, बरख-, बरस- vi. & vt. to rain [11394 *varṣati*]

बरषा f. rain [S *varṣā-*]

बरस m. year [11392 *varṣa-*]

बरस- see **बरष-**

बरसा- vt. to rain down [11394 *varṣati*]

बरसानौं m. Barsānā, a village in Braj [11308 *vara-* + 13340 *sānu-* ? (see A.W. Entwistle 1988:370)]

बरा, बरी m., f. small cake of pulse flour, fried in ghee [11213 *vaṭa-*]

बरुनी f. eyelash [S *varaṇa-*, *°ṇaka-* ?]

बर्ननीय m. thing described, subject of comparison [S varṇanīya-]

बन्र्य adj. described, subject of description [S varṇya-]

बल1 m. strength, power [S]

बल2 m. Balrām, Kṛṣṇa's brother [S]

बल- vi. to burn [6654 *dvalati]

बलवीर, °बीर m. Kṛṣṇa; Balrām [S]

बलराम m. Balrām, Kṛṣṇa's brother [S]

बला- vi. to disappear, be removed [11906 vilīyate]

बलाय f. affliction, distress [Ar. balā]

बलि1 m. Bali, a demon-king defeated by Viṣṇu as Vāman [S]

बलि2 m. offering (hence rhetorical sense 'I offer myself', 'I ask on oath') [S]

बलैया f. misfortune, evil; ~ ले- vt. to take on the misfortunes of a person by passing one's hands over his/her head; to extend a blessing of protection [Ar. balā]

बसंत m. spring [S vasanta-]

बस m. power, control; ~ कर- vt. to subjugate, have power over [11430 vaśa-]

बस- vi. to dwell, inhabit [11435 vasati]

बसकरन m. subjugating [S vaśīkaraṇa-]

बसन m. garment, dress [11436 vasana-]

बसा- vt. to have power over, to influence, control [11431 vaśayati]

बसुधा f. earth [S vasudhā-]

बसेरि, °रो m. dwelling-place, nest [11594 *vāsakara-]

बस्तु f. thing, matter [S vastu-]

बस्य adj. subjugated, obedient to the will of another [S vaśya-]

बह- vt. & vi. to bear, carry; to flow, be washed away [11453 vahati]

बहा- vt. to wash away [11453 vahati]

बहार f. spring; flourishing state [Pers.]

बहिया f. arm [9229 bāhu-]

बहिरौ adj. & m. deaf; deaf person [9130 badhira-]

बहु1 f. son's wife, bride [11250 vadhū-]

बहु2 m. adj. great, much, many ; ~ भाषिनी f. name of a sakhi in VV [S]

बहुत, बहोत, बहौत, बोहोत adv. much; very [9190 bahutva-]

बहोरि adv. again, then [12192 *vyāghuṭati]

बाँकौ adj. crooked, winding; rakish, wanton, racy [11191 vaṅka-]

बाँच-1 vt. to read [11476 vācya-]

बाँच-2 vi. to escape [11208 vañcati]

बाँझ adj. barren [11275 vandhya-]

बाँध- vt. to tie, bind; बाँधनहारि f. 'one who ties', see -हार 4 [9139 bandhati]

बाँय—(ये) adj. left [11533 vāma-]

बाँस m. bamboo [11175 vaṁśa-]

बाँसुरी, °रिया f. flute [11180 vaṁśī-]

बाँह f. arm, upper arm [9229 bāhu-]

बाइ f. wind [11491 vāta-]

बाग m. garden [Pers. bāg]

बाघ m. tiger, lion [12193 vyāghra-]

बाचक m. signifier, expressive word [S vā°]

बाज-, बज- vi. to sound, play [11513 vādyate]

बाजि m. horse [S vājin-]

बाट f. way, path; ~ मार- vt. to hold up on the road, rob [11366 vartman-]

बाढ़- see बढ़-

बात f. matter, thing, thought, talk; ~ बढ़ा- vt. to prolong a matter, make a big thing of it [11564 vārtta-]

बाद speech; contention; ~ बद- vt. to contend, compete with [S *vāda-*]

बादर m. cloud [11567 *vārdala-*]

बादसाह see पातशाह

बान m. arrow [9203 *bāṇa-*]

बानर m. monkey [11515 *vānara-*]

बानि, °नी f. nature, character [11338 *varṇa-*]

बानैत m. archer (cf. कमनैती) [9203 *bāṇa-* + *aita* (1286 *āyatta-*) ?]

बाबा m. title of respect [9209 **bābba-*]

बाम f. woman [S *vāmā-*]

बारंबार adv. time and again, repeatedly [S *vāraṃvāram*]

बार[1] f. time, occasion; day of the week, a symbol for the number '7'; ~ बार adv. time and again, repeatedly [11547 *vāra-*]

बार[2] see बाल[2]

बार[3] m. door [6663 *dvāra-*]

बार—[1] (°रे) adj. suff. added to noun to indicate connexion (= MSH -वाला; cf. हारो) [8125 *-pālaka-*]

बार—[2] (°री) adj. young [9216 *bāla-*]

बारह num. twelve [6658 *dvādaśa*]

बारि m. water [S *vāri-*]

बाल[1] m. & f. child, young person [S]

बाल[2] m. hair [11572 *vāla-*]

बालक m. child [S]

बावन[1] num. fifty-two [6661 *dvāpañcāśat-*]

बावन[2] m. Vāman, the dwarf incarnation of Viṣṇu [11538 *vāmana-*]

बावरौ adj. mad, crazy [11504 *vātula-*]

बास[1] m. abode, dwelling [11591 *vāsa-*]

बास[2] f. fragrance [11592 *vāsa-*]

बास[3] m. clothing [11603 *vāsas-*]

बासन m. pot, dish [11599 *vāsana-*]

बासनी f. small pot [11599 *vāsana-*]

बासर m. day [S *vāsara-*]

बासी m. resident, inhabitant [11605 *vāsin-*]

बाहर, बाहिर adv. outside [9226 **bāhira-*]

बाहीं (rh.) f. arm [9229 *bāhu-*]

बिक- vi. to be sold [11642 *vikrīyate*]

बिकट adj. crooked; hard, formidable [S *vikaṭa-*]

बिकस- vi. to bloom, flower [S *vikasati*]

बिकास see विकास

बिगार- vt. to spoil, ruin [11673 **vighāṭayati*]

बिघन m. obstacle; ~ बिनासन, ~ हरन m. remover of obstacles, Gaṇeś [S *vighna-*]

बिच see बीच

बिचार m. thought, idea [S *vicāra-*]

बिचार- vt. to consider, think (of), ponder [S *vicārayati*]

बिचारो adj. wretched, helpless, pitiable [Pers. *be-cāra*]

बिछा- vt. to spread out (bedding etc.) [11692 **vicchādayati*]

बिछिया f. toe-ring (shaped like scorpion's sting) [12081 *vṛścika-*]

बिछुर-, (= बीछुर-) vi. to be parted, to leave [11651 **vikṣuṭati*]

बिजुरी f. lightning [11745 *vidyullatā-*]

बिजै m. conquest [S *vijaya-*]

बित m. power [11727 *vitta-*]

बिता- vt. to pass, spend (time) [12069 *vṛtta-*]

बिथरा- vt. to scatter, spread [12005 *vistarati*]

बिथा f. anguish, pain [S *vyathā-*]

बिदा f. departure, farewell; ~ कर- vt. to bid farewell [Ar. *widā'*]

बिद्या f. knowledge, learning [S *vidyā-*]

बिद्रुम m. coral [S °*vi-*]

बिधाता m. the creator [S *vi*°]

बिधि see विधि

बिधु m. moon [*vidhu-*]

बिनती f. entreaty, apology [S *vinati-*]

बिना see बिनु

बिना, बिनि, बिनु ppn./preposition but for, except, without [11772 *vinā*]

बिनोद m. pleasure, play, fun [S *vinoda-*]

बिपति f. adversity; ~ बिदार adj. & m. breaking/breaker of adversity [S *vipatti-*]

बिपद m. adversity; ~ बिदारन adj. & m. breaking/breaker of adversity [S *vipad-*]

बिपरीत, °ति adj. & f. inverted, contrary; contrariety, mischief, ruin [S *vi*°]

बिपिन m. wood, forest [S *vipina-*]

बिप्र m. brahmin [S *v*°]

बिबर m. snake-hole [S *vivara-*]

बिबस adj. powerless, compelled, deprived of will [S *vivaśa-*]

बिबाह m. marriage, wedding [S *vivāha-*]

बिबि num. two [6648 *dva-*]

बिबिध, °धि adj. various, diverse [S *vividha-*]

बिभचारिनी f. adultress [S *vyabhicāriṇī-*]

बिभव m. might, majesty, dominion [S *vibhava-*]

बिमल adj. pure [S *vimala-*]

बियोगी m. lover suffering separation from beloved [S *viyogin-*]

बिरंचि m. Brahmā [S *vi*°]

बिरध adj. aged [S *vṛddha-*]

बिरमा- vt. to stop, make stop [11846 **viramyati*]

बिरह m. the sorrow of separation, lovesickness [11851 *viraha-*]

बिरहिन f. woman suffering from separation [S *virahiṇī-*]

बिराज- vi. to adorn, shine forth [S *virāj-*]

बिरुझ- vi. to fret, quarrel [11866 *virudhyate*]

बिल m. hole of mouse or rat [9245 *bila-*]

बिलस- vi. to be delighted [11894 *vilasati*]

बिलाव m. cat [9237 *biḍāla-*]

बिलास m. delight, dalliance, voluptuous pleasure; name of a dhobi in RN [S *vi*°]

बिलोक- vt. to look at, observe, examine [S *vilokayati*]

बिलोकन m. the act of seeing [S *vi*°]

बिश्राम m. rest, repose [S *vi*°]

बिषै ppn. in, within [S *viṣaya-*]

बिस m. poison [11968 *viṣa-*]

बिसतार- vt. to spread out, develop [S *vistārayati*]

बिसर- vi. to forget, be forgotten [12021 *vismarati*]

बिसरा- see बिसार-

बिसार-, बिसरा- vt. to forget, efface from the memory, put out of mind [12023 *vismārayati*]

बिसाल adj. large, great [S *viśāla-*]

बिसेख, °खि (rh.) adj. & adv. special, particular; especially [S *viseṣa-*]

बिस्तार m. extent, spread [S *vi*°]

बिहर- vi. to sport, take pleasure, roam [12029 *viharati*]

बिह्वल adj. agitated [S *vihvala-*]

बिहान m. dawn [11813 **vibhāna-*]

बिहार m. sport, roving, pleasure [S *v*°]

बिहारी m. name of Kṛṣṇa, and of a poet; ~लाल idem. [S vihārin-]

बिहाल see बेहाल

बीच, बिच m. middle; adv., ppn. & preposition in the middle, through [12042 *vīcya-]

बीछुर- (= बिछुर-) vt. to be separated [11651 *vikṣuṭati]

बीज f. lightning [11742 vidyut-]

बीत- vi. to pass (of time) [12069 vṛtta-]

बीर f. sister (vocative: cf. भटू in similar usage) [12056 vīra-]

बीस num. twenty [11616 viṁśati-]

बुझा- vt. to extinguish, quench [11703 *vijjhāpāyati]

बुद्धि, बुद्ध, बुध f. wisdom, sense; clever idea, trick [S]

बुरौ adj. bad; ~मान- vt. to take amiss, be angered [9289 *bura-]

बुला- vt. to call, summon [9321 *boll-]

बूझ- vt. to understand, perceive, observe, ascertain, inquire [9279 budhyate]

बूड़-, बूढ़- vi. to drown, be immersed [9272 *buḍyati]

बृंद m. multitude, herd [S vṛnda-]

बृंदाबन, बृंदावन, बृ° m. Vrindaban, location of Kṛṣṇa's līlā [S vṛndāvana-]

बृक्ष, बृच्छ m. tree [S vṛkṣa-]

बृच्छ see बृक्ष

बृज see ब्रज

बृत्ति f. occurrence (of a word) [S v°]

बृथा see वृथा

बेंदी f. brow-dot [9240 bindu-]

बेकाम adv. uselessly, in vain [Pers. be- + kāma < 2892 karman-]

बेगि adv. quickly [S vega-]

बेझ- vt. to pierce, strike [11759 vidhyati]

बेटा m. son, boy [9238 *beṭṭa-]

बेद see वेद

बेध- vt. to pierce, wound [11739 viddha-]

बेनी f. braided hair, plait [12093 veṇi-]

बेनु m. flute, pipe [12096 veṇu-]

बेरि f. time [12115 velā-]

बेरी f. fetter [12130 veṣṭa-]

बेल, बेलि f. creeper, vine [12123 velli-]

बेला f. time [S v°]

बेस m. dress, guise [12129 veṣa-]

बेसन m. pulse flour [12133 vesana-]

बेस्या f. prostitute [S veśyā-]

बेहाल, बिहाल adj. worn out, ruined [Pers. be-ḥāl]

बै f. age [11305 vayas-]

बैजंती f. ensign of Viṣṇu; ~माल f. necklace of Kṛṣṇa/Viṣṇu (of sapphire, pearl, ruby, topaz and diamond, from the five elements earth, water, fire, air, ether respectively) [S vaijayantī]

बैठ- vi. to sit, be seated [2245 upaviśati]

बैद m. physician [S vaidya-]

बैन m. word, speech, saying [11199 vacana-]

बैरी m. enemy, rival [S vairin-]

बैरिनि f. enemy, rival [S vairiṇī-]

बैस f. age [S vayas-]

बो- vt. to sow [11282 vapati]

बोक, बोकरा m. goat [9312 *bokka-]

बोझ m. burden, load [11465 vahya-]

बोर- vt. to drown [9272 *boḍayati]

बोल m. talk, speech; drumming mnemonic [9321 *boll-]

बोल- vt. to speak, call, say; to pledge, offer up [9321 *boll-]

बोहोत see बहुत

बौरा/°री adj. & m./f. mad; lunatic [11504 *vātula*-]

ब्यर्थ adj. useless, vain [S *vyartha*-]

ब्याकुल see व्याकुल

ब्याप- vi. to spread, pervade [S *vyāp*-]

ब्यावर m. childbirth [11701 *vijāyate*]

ब्यास m. Vyās, legendary compiler of the Veda and the *Purāṇas* [S *vyāsa*-]

ब्यौंत m. scheme, contrivance, manner [11830 **viyavakartati*]

ब्रज m. 'cattle-station', the homeland of Kṛṣṇa's youth; ~नागर, m. skilful one of Braj, Kṛṣṇa; ~बासी, ~वासी m. inhabitant of Braj; ~मंडल m. district of Braj; ~राज-कुमार m. Prince of Braj, Kṛṣṇa; [S *vraja*-]

ब्रह्म m. Brahma, the universal spirit, God [S *brahman*-]

ब्रह्मचारी m. celibate student [S *°cārin*-]

ब्रह्मपुर m. name of a city in RN [S]

ब्रह्मसंबंध m. 'connexion with God', initiation (in Vallabha sect) [S]

ब्राह्मन m. brahmin [S *°ṇa*-]

भंडार m. storehouse [9442 *bhāṇḍāgāra*-]

भँव- vi. to roam, wander [9648 *bhramati*]

भक्त, भक्ता, भगत m. devotee, worshipper [S]

भक्ति, भगति f. devotion [S]

भगत see भक्त

भगति see भक्ति

भगवत m. name of poet [S *°t*-]

भगवद् adj. divine [S]

भगवदीय m. devotee, votary [S]

भगवद्धर्म adj. of divine nature [S]

भगवान m. God, the Lord [S *bhagavān*-]

भज-1 vt. to adore, worship [S *bhajati*]

भज-2 vi. to flee, run away [9361 *bhajyate*]

भजन m. adoration, worship [S]

भजा- vt. to make flee, put to flight [9361 *bhajyate*]

भटू f. sister, woman (vocative: cf. बीर in similar usage) [9402 *bhartṛ*- ?]

भट्टी f. kiln, furnace [9656 *bhraṣṭra*-]

भभूक m. blaze, flame [9388 **bhabh*-]

भय m. fear, dread [S]

भर m. burden, load, weight [S]

भर- vt. & vi. to fill, enwrap; to be filled, covered [9397 *bharati*]

भरन adj. & m. bearing, supporting; supporter [S *°ṇa*-]

भरम see भ्रम

भरमा- vt. & vi. to lead astray, allure; to roam [S *bhramati*]

भर्त्तार m. husband [S *bhartṛ*-]

भल—(भली) adj. good; भले adv. well [9408 *bhalla*-]

भव m. existence, worldly existence, the world; ~सागर m. ocean of existence [S]

भवन m. house, dwelling [S]

भवानी f. Bhavānī, Durgā [S]

भस- vi. to drown, float [9654 *bhraśyati*]

भस्म f. ashes [S *bhasman*-]

भाँड़ m. jester, buffoon [9371 *bhaṇḍa*-]

भाँड़ा m. pot, vessel [9440 *bhāṇḍa*-]

भांति f. type, kind, manner [9338 *bhakti*-]

भा- vi. to be pleasing [9445 *bhāti*]

भाइ, भाय m. intention, affection, manner, feeling [9475 *bhāva-*]

भाई m. brother [9661 *bhrātṛ-*]

भाग m. fortune, lot [9434 *bhāgya-*]

भागवत m. *Bhāgavata Purāṇa*, Vaiṣṇava text of c. 9th/10th century [S]

भाज- vi. to flee [9361 *bhajyate*]

भाजन m. pot, plate [S]

भान- vt. to break [9361 *bhagna-*]

भानु m. sun; king, lord [S]

भानुजा f. the river Yamuna [S]

भामिनि f. lady, passionate woman [S °*ī*-]

भाय see भाइ

भार m. burden, load, weight [S]

भारी adj. great, heavy, burdensome [9465 *bhārika-*]

भारो m. burden [9459 *bhāra-*]

भाल[1] (m.) forehead [S]

भाल[2] f. arrowhead; spear [9409 *bhallī-*]

भाव m. sentiment, feeling [S]

भावतो m. beloved [9445 *bhāti*]

भावन— (°नैं) adj. appealing, pleasing [9445 *bhāpayate*]

भावना f. feeling of devotion, contemplation [S]

भावरो (rh.) for भावन—

भाषा f. language, vernacular [S]

भिजा- vt. to soak, drench [9502 **bhiyajyate*]

भिन्न adj. different, various [S]

भीज- vi. to be soaked [9502 **bhiyajyate*]

भीड़, भीर f. crowd [9490 **bhīṭ-*]

भीतर ppn. & adv. in, inside [9504 **bhiyantara-*]

भीन— (°नी) adj. wet, soaked [9500 **bhiyagna-*]

भीर see भीड़

भुज m., भुजा f. arm [S]

भुजंगम m. snake [S]

भुव (f.) ground, earth [9557 *bhūmi-*]

भुवन m. world [S]

भूख f. hunger [9286 *bubhukṣā-*]

भूख्यौ adj. hungry [9284 **bubhukṣaka-*]

भूप m. king [S]

भूमि f. earth, ground, place [S]

भूर— (भूरी) adj. brown [9690 **bhrūra-*]

भूल f. mistake, fault [9538 **bhull-*]

भूल- vi. to forget, err, be mistaken, be forgotten [9538 **bhull-*]

भूषण, °न m. ornament [S]

भृंग m. shrike [S]

भृकुटि, °टी f. eyebrow [S]

भृत्त m. servant [S *bhṛtya-*]

भेंट-, भेट- vt. to embrace [9490 **bheṭṭ-*]

भेख m. frog [9600 *bheka-*]

भेज- vt. to send [9603 **bhejj-*]

भेद m. secret, mystery; category [S]

भेदक m. 'distinguishing', a trope which describes attributes as being in a distinct class of their own [S]

भेष m. appearance, dress, guise; ~ बना- vt. to disguise [S]

भैगाऊं m. Bhaigā̃v, Bhogā̃v, a village in Braj [S *bhaya-/bhava-grāma* ??; see A.W. Entwistle 1987:397]

भो- vi. to whirl, revolve [9648 *bhramati*]

भोग[1] m. food-offering for a deity; offering ritual in the temple [9627 *bhogya-*]

भोग[2] enjoyment; union, (sexual) enjoyment; name of poet appearing in line of verse; ~ कर- vt. to enjoy [S]

भोजन m. food; ~ कर- vt. to eat [S]

भोर f. dawn [9634 *bhorā-]

भोर— (भोरी) adj. innocent, naïve, simple [9539 *bhola-]

भौंन, भौन m. house [S bhavana-]

भौंह f. eyebrow [9688 *bhrumu-]

भ्रकुटि f. eyebrow [S]

भ्रम, भरम m. delusion, error; a trope in which a thing is mistaken for another [S]

भ्रम- vi. to wander, stray [S]

भ्रमर m. bumble bee [S]

भ्रष्ट adj. depraved, corrupt [S]

भ्रांत f. confusion, error, false impression; ~ अपन्हुति f. a trope of 'denial' in which the mistaken attribution of affections is corrected by a second person [S *bhrānti-*]

भ्रुव f. eyebrow [S]

मंग (rh.) f. woman's hair-parting [10071 *mārga-*]

मंगा-, मगा- vt. to procure, send for, buy [10074 *mārgati*]

मंजन m. cleaning, wiping with perfume [10081 *mārjana-*]

मंजवा- vt. to clean, have cleaned [10080 *mārjati*]

मंजुघोषा f. Manjughoṣā, a nymph [S]

मंझारन (rh.) ppn. among [9817 **madhyāra-*]

मंडल m. circle, disk, region [S]

मंडली f. circle, group [S]

मंडित adj. decorated, adorned, jewelled [S]

मंत्र m. prayer, sacred formula [S]

मंत्री m. minister, counsellor [S *matrin-*]

मंद adj. & adv. soft, gentle, mellow, low, dull, blunt; softly etc. [S]

मंदबुद्धि m. 'dimwit', name of a carpenter in RN [S]

मंदर m. a sacred mountain, with which the ocean was churned by the gods and demons to recover treasures lost in the deluge [S]

मंदिर m. house; temple [S]

मंह see मौंह

मकर m. crocodile, sea-monster; मकराकृत adj. shaped like a *makara* [S]

मग m. road, pathway; ~ जोव- vt. to look out for, await [10071 *mārga-*]

मगध m. Magadh (South Bihar) [S]

मगन adj. drowned, immersed, absorbed [S *magna-*]

मगा- see मंगा-

मचा- vt. to stir up, excite [9710 **macyate*]

मछरी f. fish [9758 *matsya-*]

मणि, मनि f. gem, jewel [S]

मटक- vi. to twinkle, move rapidly up and down [9722 **maṭṭ-*]

मत m. idea, tenet, doctrine [S]

मतंग m. elephant [S]

मति[1] f. intelligence, understanding; ~ हीन adj. devoid of understanding [S]

मति[2], मत adv. not (in prohibitions); lest [9981 *mā*]

मतौ m. idea; agreement, concord; ~ कर- vt. to debate, plot, concur [S *mata-*]

मत्त adj. intoxicated, ruttish [S]

मथ- vt. to churn [9839 *manthati*]

मथुरा f. Mathura, Kṛṣṇa's birthplace [S]

मद m. intoxication, passion, frenzy, elephant's rut [S]

मदन m. passion, intoxication; Kāmdev [S]

मधि ppn. in, amidst [S *madhya-*]

मधु m. honey, nectar; ~ रितु f. spring [S]

मधुकर m. bee [S]

मधुप m. bee [S]

मधुमच्छिका m. bee [S °*makṣikā-*]

मधुर adj. sweet, melodious [S]

मधुरता f. sweetness, melodiousness [S]

मध्य ppn. in, amidst [S]

मध्यान्ह m. midday [S *madhyāhna-*]

मन, मनु, मनुआँ m. mind, heart; मन आ- vi. to occur to the mind, to have a whim or idea; मन लाना vi. to apply the mind to, set the heart on; मनमान— (°नी), मनभाइ adj. pleasing to the heart, agreeable; मनमोहन m. 'heart's charmer', Kṛṣṇa; मनरंजन adj. & m. mind's delight; [9822 *manas-*]

मनहुँ see मनु

मनि see मणि

मनु, मनौ, मानो, मनहुँ, मानहु cj. & adv. as if, seemingly [Add[2] 9857 *manyate*]

मनुष्य m. man, person [S]

मनोरथ m. wish, desire, fancy [S]

मनोहर m. & adj. 'heart-stealing', captivating; name of Kṛṣṇa [S]

मनौ see मनु

मन्मथ m. passionate love; Kāmdev [S]

मम poss.pr. my (see I.4.5a) [S]

ममता f. egotism, pride [S]

-मय, -मई suff. composed of, suffused with [S]

मया see माया

मर- vi. to die [9871 *marate*]

मरकट m. monkey [S *markaṭa-*]

मरकत m. emerald [S]

मरगज— (°जे) adj. crumpled [abs. *mara-* + 3960 **gajj-* ?]

मरदन m. crushing, bruising [S *mardana-*]

मरम see मर्म

मरुत m. wind [S *marut-*]

मर्म, मरम m. vital spot, hidden meaning [9893 *marman-*]

मल- vt. to rub [9870 **malati*]

मलयानिल m. wind from the Malaya mountains (Western Ghats); breeze fragrant with Malaya sandalwood [S]

मवास m. refuge, fortress [Ar. *mavāsh* ?? (see J.T.Molesworth 1857:635)]

मवासी m. chieftain, ruler [see मवास]

मसाल f. torch, flambeau [Ar. *mash'al*]

महताब m. moonlight [Pers. *mah-tāb*]

महबूब m. beloved, sweetheart [Ar. *maḥbūb*]

महरि f. woman, lady [9962 *mahilā-*]

महल m. palace; time, occasion [Ar. *maḥall*]

महा adj.(pref.) & adv. great; very [S]

महाप्रभु m. 'great lord', title for religious teacher (e.g. Vallabha) [S]

महाप्रसाद m. food which has been offered to the deity and thus consecrated [S]

महाबिक्रम m. 'very valiant', name of a lion in RN [S °*v*°]

महाराज m. 'great king', title of respect (esp. for Vallabhite priests) [S]

महावर m. scarlet lac dye (applied to the soles of brides' feet as a decoration) [?]

महि ppn. in [9804 *madhya-*]

महिमा f. greatness, majesty, glory [S]

मही f. earth [S]

महेस m. Śiva [S *maheśa-*]

महोछो m. great festival [9979 *mahotsava-*]

माँग f. hair-parting [10071 *mārga-*]

माँग- vt. to ask for, demand [10074 *mārgati*]

माँह, मंह ppn. in [9804 *madhya-*]

माई f. mother; term of address used between women [10016 *mātṛ-*]

माखन m. butter [10378 *mrakṣaṇa-*]

मागध m. bard, panegyrist [S]

माट m. earthen pot [10085 **mārtta-*]

मात, माता f. mother [S *mātṛ-*]

मात्र adj. & adv. mere; just, nothing but [S]

माथो m. head, forehead; ~ धुना- vt. to beat the head (in perplexity) [9926 *masta-*]

मादिक adj. intoxicating [S °*da*°]

माधव m. name of Kṛṣṇa [S]

माधुरी f. sweetness, loveliness [S]

मान m. pride, conceit; show of haughty aloofness contrived in lover's pique [S]

मान- vt. to accept, consider, approve, be appeased, grant, believe, feel, acknowledge (मानो, मनहु see मनु) [9857 *manyate*]

मानिक m. ruby, jewel [9997 *māṇikya-*]

मानुष m. man, human [S *manuṣya-*]

माया, मया f. illusion [S *māyā-*]

मार f. beating [10063 *māra-*]

मार- vt. to beat, kill; to shoot [10066 *mārayati*]

मारे ppn. because of, through [10063 *māra-*]

मार्ग, मारग m. path, way [S]

माला, माल f. garland; rosary [S *mālā-*]

मास1 m. month [S]

मास2 m. flesh [9982 *māṁsa-*]

माह m. the winter month of Māgh [9993 *māgha-*]

माहीं ppn. in [9804 *madhya-*]

मिंता see मित

मिट- vi. to be removed, obliterated [10299 *mṛṣṭa-*]

मिठाई f. sweetmeat [10299 *mṛṣṭa-*]

मिठास m. sweetness [10299 *mṛṣṭa-* + 1452 *āśa-* ?]

मित, मिंता [rh.] m. friend [10124 *mitra-*]

मित्र m. friend [S]

मिथ्या f. falsehood, lie; ~ भाषी m. lier [S]

मिल- vi. to meet, join [10133 *milati*]

मिलन m. meeting, union [S]

मिला- vt. to mix, unite, bring together [10133 *milati*]

मिलाप m. meeting, encounter [10133 *milati*]

मिश्रित, मिस्रित adj. mixed, blended [S °*ś*°]

मिश्री, मिस्री f. a sweetmeat, sugar-candy [Ar. *miṣrī*]

मिस m. pretext, pretence [10298 *mṛṣā-*]

मिस्रित see मिश्रित

मिस्री see मिश्री

मीठ- (°ठी, °ठे) adj. sweet [10299 *mṛṣṭa-*]

मीति (rh.) adj. & m. dear; friend [10124 *mitra-*]

मीन f. fish [S]

मीराँ f. Mīrā [?? Cf. Pers. *mīrān* m. 'the saint Mīrān' (J.T.Platts 1968:1105)]

मुँह m. mouth, face [10158 *mukha-*]

मुकंद m. a name of Kṛṣṇa [S *mukunda-*]

मुकुट, मुगट m. crown, crest [S]

मुकुत m. pearl [S *muktā-*]

मुक्तमाल f. pearl necklace [S]

मुक्ताहल m. pearl [S *muktāphala-*]

मुक्ति f. salvation, final beatitude [S]

मुख[1] m. mouth; ~ससि m. moon-face; ~सँभाल- vt. to speak moderately, to guard the tongue [S]

मुख्य, मुख[2] adj. principal, chief, first [S]

मुगट see मुकुट

मुद्रा f. coin [S]

मुर- vi. to turn [10186 *muṭati*]

मुरझा- vi. to faint, wither, pine [S *mūrchā*- ?]

मुरली, मुरलि f. flute; ~धर m. 'flute-holder', Kṛṣṇa [S]

मुरारि m. 'Mura's foe', Kṛṣṇa [S]

मुसुका-, मुसका- vi. to smile [10227 **muss*-]

मुसुकानि, मुस°, °नी f. smile [10227 **muss*-]

मुहकम adj. firm, strong [Ar. *muḥkam*]

मुहर m. gold coin, mohur [Pers. *mohr*]

मूंड़ m. head [10247 *mūrdhan*-]

मूँद- vt. to close, cover, seal [10202 *mudrayati*]

मूँदरी f. finger-ring [10203 *mudrā*-]

मूठि f. fist, handful [10221 *muṣṭi*-]

मूरख m. fool [S *mūrkha*-]

मूरति f. image, form [S *mūrti*-]

मूरि m. root, source [10250 *mūla*-]

मूल m. root, source [S]

मूषक m. rat, mouse [S]

मूसरा m. pestle, club; ~धार m. pelting rain [10223 *musala*-]

मूसा m. mouse, rat [10258 *mūṣa*-]

मृग, मृगा m. deer [S]

मृगतृष्णा f. mirage [S]

मृगराज m. king of beasts, lion [S]

मृगांकु m. 'deer-marked', the moon [S °*ka*-]

मृदु adj. sweet, tender, delicate [S]

मेखला f. girdle, belt [S]

मेघ m. cloud [S]

मेट- vt. to abolish, remove, erase [10299 *mṛṣṭa*-]

मेरौ, मेरो pr. my, mine (see I.4.5a) [9691 *ma*-]

मेल m. union, intercourse [S]

मेह m. rain [10302 *megha*-]

मैं[1] ppn. in [9804 *madhya*-]

मैं[2] pr. I (see I.4.5a) [9691 *ma*-]

मैन m. Madan, Kāmdev [9775 *madana*-]

मैना[1] m. mynah, a species of starling which can learn to 'talk' [9776 *madana*-]

मैना[2] m. a Rajput bandit caste [S *mainaka*- ?]

मैया f. mother [10066 *mātṛ*-]

मैल m. dirt, pollution [9904 **malin*-]

मो see मैं[2]

मोट f. bundle [10233 **moṭṭa*-]

मोटा adj. fat, stout [10187 **moṭṭa*-]

मोती m. pearl [10365 *mauktika*-]

मोद m. joy, delight [S]

मोदी m. steward [S *modin*- ?]

मोर m. peacock; ~पखा m. peacock feather; ~मुकुट m. crown of peacock feathers worn by Kṛṣṇa [9865 **mora*]

मोर- vt. to twist [10186 *moṭati*]

मोर- (°रे) poss.pr. my, mine (see I.4.5a) [9691 *ma*-]

मोल m. purchase (in *mola mā̃gā*- vt. to purchase, procure) [10373 *maulya*-]

मोष (for मोख) m. salvation, release from worldly existence [10345 *mokṣa*-]

मोह m. delusion, infatuation [S]

मोह- vt. to allure, charm [10362 *mohayati*]

मोहित adj. enchanted [S]

मोहन adj. & m. enchanting, captivating; name of Kṛṣṇa; ~लाल idem. [S]

मौंड़ा m. boy, lad [10191 *muṇḍa-*]

मौज m. enjoyment, ecstasy [Ar. *mauj*]

मौन adj. silent, dumb; ~गह- vt. to remain silent [S]

मौर m. bud, blossom [10146 *mukura-, °la-*]

म्लेच्छ m. non-Aryan, 'barbarian' [S]

म्हाँ obl.pr. me [see note to MP 12.1]

यज्ञ m. sacrifice [S]

यत्न, जतन m. effort, attempt; ~सों adv. carefully [S]

यमुना f. the river Yamuna, Jumna [S]

यसी m. illustrious person [S *yaśasvin-*]

यह, ए, या, ये, यै, इह pr. this, etc. (see I.4.1) [2530 *eṣa*]

यहाँ, हाँ adv. here [1605 *iha*, which is also model for जहाँ, तहाँ, कहाँ, वहाँ etc.]

या see यह

युक्ति f. trick, contrivance; ~करि adv. artfully, dexterously [S]

युद्ध m. war [S]

-युत adj. pref. endowed with [10479 *yukta-*]

ये, यै see यह

यों, यौं adv. thus [2528 *evam eva*]

योगभ्रष्ट adj. & m. fallen from the practice of yoga, ritually defective [S]

यौवन m. youth, youthfulness [S]

रंक m. pauper [S]

रंग m. colour, joy, amusement, sport, revelry; performance; ~महल m. pleasure palace [S]

रँगीलौ adj. merry, sportive, gay, rakish [10571 **raṅgita-* or 10572 *raṅgin-*]

रंध्र m. hole, opening [S]

रंभा f. Rambhā, a nymph [S]

रक्षा f. protection, preservation [S]

रक्षिक m. protector, guardian [S *rakṣaka-*]

रख-, रखा- vt. to put, place, keep; ~वारौ m. keeper, watchman [10547 *rakṣati*]

रघु m. Raghu, Rāma's forefather;
~कुल m. clan of Raghu;
~बंसी m. member of the clan of Raghu;
~बीर m. hero of the Raghus, Rāma [S]

रच-1 vt. to create [10574 **racyate*]

रच-2 vi. to be dyed; to be enamoured [10583/4 *rajyate*]

रचना f. creation, contrivance [S]

रचा- vt. to start up; to celebrate [10574 **racyate*]

रज f. dust [S]

रजधानी f. capital, palace [S *rā°*]

रतन m. jewel, gem [S *ratna-*]

रति f. passion, love-making; ~राइ m. Kāmdev [S]

रती f. a small seed (used as a weight); a tiny amount, a jot [10544 *raktikā-*]

रथ m. chariot, cart, carriage [S]

रन m. battle [S *raṇa-*]

रबि see रवि

रम- vi. to roam, take one's pleasure, have sexual intercourse [10637 **ramyati*]

रव m. sound [S]

रवि, रबि m. sun [S]

रविनंद m. Yama, god of death [S]

रस m. essence, nectar, flavour, joy, love, delight, pleasure, poetic sentiment; a symbol for the number '6'; ~धाम m.

abode of sentiment; ~पान m. drinking of nectar [S]

रस-, रसा- vt. to taste, relish [10655 *rasayati*]

रसखानि, °न m./f. 'mine of sentiment', name of Kṛṣṇa and of poet [S]

रसना f. tongue [S]

रसा- see रस-

रसानंद m. blissful sentiment [S]

रसाल, °ला (rh.) adj. sweet [S]

रसिक m. adj. & m. amorous, voluptuous, impassioned; lover, one who appreciates *rasa*; devotee [S]

रसीला adj. sweet, luscious [10663 *rasin-*]

रह्- vi. to remain, endure, live [10666 **rahati*]

रह्चट- (रह्चटैं) m. desire, thirst [?]

रहस m. secret; privacy, solitaryness [S *rahas-*, and 10669 *rahasya-*]

रहस- vi. to be delighted [10669 *rahasya-*]

रहित adj. (suffixed to preceding noun) without, devoid of [S]

राइ, राय, राव m. prince, king [10679 *rājan-*]

राक्षस m. demon [S]

राख- vt. to maintain, protect, save, keep, place [10547 *rakṣati*]

राग m. joy, delight, pleasure; raga, musical mode; ~रँग m. merry-making, fun and frolic [S]

रागी adj. impassioned [S *rāgin-*]

राच- vi. to be dyed; to be enamoured [10583/4 *rajyate*, or S *rājate*]

राज (in compounds; cf. राज्य) adj. & m. royal; king; ~भोग m. 'royal feast', the fourth daily *darśan* period, when the deity receives his first food-offering; ~सुख m. royal delight; ~हंस m. 'royal swan', goose [S]

राज- vi. to be adorned, shine [10583 *rajyate*]

राजा m. king [S]

राजिव m. lotus [S *rājīva-*]

राजी adj. pleased, contented [Ar. > Pers. *rāzī*]

राज्य, राज m. kingdom, kingship [S *rājya-*]

राणा m. prince (Rajput title) [10680 *rājana-*]

रात f. night [10702 *rātri-*]

रात— (°ते) adj. red, ruddy [10539 *rakta-*]

रात्रि f. night [S]

राधा f. Rādhā; ~कुंड m. a pond in Braj; ~वल्लभ m. Kṛṣṇa as 'lover of Rādhā' — a deity worshipped in Vrindaban [S]

राधिका f. Rādhā [S]

रानी f. queen [10692 *rājñī-*]

राम m. Rāma; God [S]

राय see राइ

राव see राइ

रावन m. Rāvaṇ, king of Laṅkā, Sītā's abductor, Rāma's adversary [S *rāvaṇa-*]

रावर m. palace [10676 *rājakula-*]

रास m. circular dance performed by Kṛṣṇa and the gopis [S, or 10720 *rāśi-*]

रासि f. mass, heap [10720 *rāśi-*]

राह f. road, path [Pers.]

रिचा f. verse, hymn, praise [S *ṛc-*]

रिझा- vt. to delight, enchant [2457 *ṛdhyati*]

रितु see ऋतु

रिस f. anger, huff [1615 *īrṣyā-* or 10746 *riṣ-*]

रिसा- vi. to be angry [1615 *īrṣyā-* or 10749 *riṣyati*]

री see रे

रीझ- vi. to be enchanted, delighted, excited [2457 *ṛdhyati*]

रीति f. manner, way, situation [S]

रु see अरु

रुकमिनि f. Rukmiṇī, Kṛṣṇa's consort in Dwarka [S *rukmiṇī-*]

रुक्का m. note, chit, invitation [Pers. *ruq'a*]

रुख m. aspect, countenance [Pers. *rukh*]

रुच- vi. to appeal, be pleasant [10765 *rucyate*]

रुचि f. taste, relish, liking [S]

रुपैया m. rupee [S *rūpya-*]

रुँध- (for रुंध-) vi. to be restrained [10782 *rundhati*]

रूख¹, रूख- (रूखी) adj. dry, harsh [10799 *rūkṣa-*]

रूख² m. tree [10757 **rukṣa-*]

रूप m. form, beauty; (at end of compound, 'having the form of') [S]

रूपक m. metaphor [S]

रूपा m. silver [10805 *rūpya-*]

रे, री vocative part. (m. and f. respectively) [10808 *re*]

रेख f. line, inscription [S *rekhā-*]

रेंक- vi. to bray [10734 **reṅk-*]

रैनि f. night [10579 *rajanī-*]

रो- vi. to weep [10840 *rodati*]

रोक- vt. to stop [10827 **rokk-*]

रोग m. illness, disease [S]

रोटी f. bread [10837 **roṭṭa-*]

रोम m. hair (on body) [S]

रोष m. anger [S]

लंक f. waist [10877 **lakka-*]

लंघ- vt. to cross, pass over [10905 *laṅghayati*]

लंब—(लंबी) adj. long [10951 *lamba-*]

लकरी f. wood, stick [10875 **lakkuṭa-*]

लकुट m., °टी f. stick [S *lakuṭa-*]

लक्षन m. feature, characteristic [S °*ṇa*]

लख see लाख

लख- vt. to see, look, perceive [10883 *lakṣati*]

लखा- vt. to be seen, be distinguished [10884 *lakṣayati*]

लग, लगि, लगु ppn. up to, until, MSH तक [10893 *lagna-*]

लग-, लाग- vi. to adhere, apply, seem, appear, embrace, be current; fire to catch; (as aux.) to begin [10895 *lagyati*]

लगनि, °न f. attachment, love [10895 *lagyati*]

लगा- vt. to apply, hold, lay out [10895 *lagyati*]

लगालगी f. love, attachment, entrapment [10895 *lagyati*]

लगि, लगु see लग

लघु adj. small, little, minor [S]

लच- vi. to bend, give way [10907 **lacc-*]

लछिमनु m. Lakṣmaṇ, Rāma's younger brother [*lakṣmaṇa-*]

लज-, लजा- vi. to feel ashamed, abashed [10909 *lajjate*]

लटक- vi. to hang loosely, move languidly, loll, saunter [10918 **laṭṭa-*]

लटका- vt. to hang, dangle [10918 **laṭṭa-*]

लटू m. spinning-top; ~कर- vt. to put into a whirl, affect with love; ~हो- vi. to be in a whirl, in love [Add² 10916 **laṭyate* ?]

लदा- vt. to load [10966 *lardayati*]

लपट- vi. to be embraced, entwined, wrapped, covered [10942 **lappeṭṭ-* or 11061 *lipyate*]

लपटा-, लपिटा- vt. to smear, cover, wrap; to encircle, grasp [as लपट-]

लपेट- vt. to wrap [as लपट-]

लर- vt. to fight [10920 **laḍ-*]

लरिका m. boy [10924 **laḍikka-*]

ललचा- vt. to tantalize, tempt [11029 *lālitya-*]

ललन m. boy, darling [S]

ललित adj. charming, wanton [S]

ललिता f. Lalitā, foremost of Rādhā's companions [S]

लस- vi. to shine, look well [10993 *lasati*]

लह- vt. to take, get [10948 *labhate*]

लहर- vi. to wave, undulate [see next]

लहरि f. wave, ripple; frenzy of emotion [10999 *laharī*]

लहलह— (°ही) adj. blooming, luxuriant [10993 *lasati*]

ला-, ल्या- vt. to apply; to bring forth; to make, render [11004 *lāgayati*]

लाख, लख num. 100,000 [10881 *lakṣa-*]

लाग- see लग-

लाज f. shame; modesty [10910 *lajjā-*]

लाटानुप्रास m. 'Gujarati alliteration', when a word is repeated with the same meaning but different applications (named for its currency in Lāṭa, i.e. Gujarat) [S]

लाद- vt. to load [10966 *lardayati*]

लायक adj. fit for, worthy of [Ar. *lā'iq*]

लाल[1] m. beloved; darling, infant son (often as name of Kṛṣṇa) [11030 *lālya-*]

लाल[2] m. ruby [Ar. *la'l*]

लाल[3] adj. red [Pers. *lāl*]

लालच m. greed, hankering [11029 *lālitya-*]

लाहु m. advantage [11018 *lābha-*]

लिए, लिएँ see ले-

लिवा- vt. to cause to be taken or brought [10948 *labhate*]

लीला f. divine sport, play of the gods [S]

लुक- vi. to hide, be hidden [11083 *lupta-*]

लुका- vt. to hide, conceal [11083 *lupta-*]

लुगाई f. woman, women [S *loka-*]

लुटा-[1] vt. to squander, give lavishly [11078 **luṭṭati*]

लुटा-[2] vt. to make roll on the ground [11156 **lorṭati*]

लुप्तोपमा f. incomplete simile (one which lacks subject or object of comparison, or the quality described, or a word expressing comparison) [S]

लू (p. लुवैं) f. hot summer wind [11099 (& Add[2] 11099) **lūṣā-*]

लूट vt. to loot, plunder [11078 **luṭṭati*]

लूनो adj. cropped, cut, destroyed [11094 *lūna-*]

ले- vt. to take, get; (के) लिए, लिएँ ppn. for [10948 *labhate*]

लेख- vt. to consider, regard [11108 *lekhya-*]

लोइन m. eye [11128 *locana-*]

लोक m. world [S]

लोग m. people [S *loka-* >Prakrit *loga-*]

लोचन m. eye [S]

लोट- vi. to roll, toss about [11156 **lorṭati*]

लोटी f. water-pot [11133 **loṭṭa-*]

लोभ m. greed [S]

लोभा- vi. to be allured, desirous [11152 *lobhyate*]

लोय m. people [11119 *loka-*]

लोयन m. eye [11128 *locana-*]

लोल adj. restless, desirous, wanton [S]

लोहू m. blood [11165 *lohita-*]

लौं ppn. up to, as far as, until, MSH तक; like [Add[2] 10893 *lagna-*]

लौंड़ा m. boy, son [10984 **lavaṇḍa-*]

लौकिक adv. & m. worldly, mundane; worldly usage, mankind [S]

लौठी, लौठिया f. stick, club [10991 **laṣṭi-* × *sōṭā* (< 12622 **śoṭṭha-*) ? (Cf. * सौंटि)]

लौन m. salt [10978 *lavaṇa-*]

ल्या- see ला-

-वंत suff. forming possessive adj. from nouns (e.g. बलवंत 'strong'; गुनवंत 'having good qualities) [S *-vat*]

वचन, ब° m. speech, word, promise [S]

वन, बन m. forest, grove, thicket [S]

वर, बर adj. (often suffixed to noun, e.g. नटवर, गिरिबर) fine, choice [S]

वरंगनि f. beautiful woman [S *varāṅgiṇī-*]

वर्णन, बरनन m. description [S]

वर्ष m. year [S]

वस्त्र m. cloth, clothing [S]

वह pr. he, etc. (see I.4.2) [972 *asau*]

वहाँ adv. there [see यहाँ]

वा[1] see वह

वा[2] see बार[1]

वाक्य m. statement, utterance [S]

वार- vt. to sacrifice, offer up [11554 *vārayate* × S]

वारपार adv. & m. round and about, far and wide; locality, limits [482 *apāra-*]

वार्ता f. account, history [S *vārttā-*]

विकसत adj. bloomed, developed [S *°ita-*]

विकास m. expanding, blossoming [S]

विचार- see बिचार-

विटप m. tree [S]

वित्त m. money, wealth, property [S]

विधि f. way, manner, kind; destiny, the creator, God [S]

विन see वह

विभूति f. magnificence, manifestation of power [S]

वियोग m. separation (of lovers) [S]

विरतांत m. report, tale, account [S *vṛtt°*]

विरोधी adj. & m. opposed, obstructing; opponent [S]

विवस्था f. condition, state of affairs [S *vy°*]

विवेकी m. one having the power of discrimination, discernment [S *°kin-*]

विश्व m. world, universe [S]

विश्वास m. belief, trust, confidence [S]

विष m. poison [S]

विषय m. sense, sensuality [S]

विष्नुपद m. hymn [S *viṣṇu°*]

विस्मै m. wonder, surprise [S *°aya-*]

वृच्छ m. tree [S *vṛkṣa-*]

वृथा, बृथा adv. in vain, purposelessly [S]

वृंदावन see बृंदाबन

वृद्ध adj. old, advanced [S]

वृषभानु, °न m. Vṛṣabhānu, Rādhā's father; ~ किसोरी, ~ कुँवरि f. Rādhā [S]

वे see वह

वेणुनाद m. flute-playing [S]

वेद, बेद m. the Veda [S]

वेष m. dress, guise, appearance [S]

वेस्या f. prostitute [S *veśyā-*]

वै see वह

वैष्णव m. Vaiṣṇava, devotee of Viṣṇu [S]

वैस— (वैसियै) adj. & adv. of that kind; in that same way, as before [5760 *tādṛśa-*]

व्यंजन m. condiment, delicacy [S]

व्याकुल, ब्याकुल adj. distressed, agitated [S]

व्याल m. serpent [S]

व्योपारी m. merchant, trader [12205 *vyāpāra-* × 12178 *vyavahārin-*]

व्रत m. vow, pious observance undertaken in order to secure some aim [S]

शक्ति f. power [S]

शत्रु m. enemy [S]

शब्द m. sound [S]

शरणागत m. refugee, sectarian follower [S]

शरीर, स° m. body [S]

शाप m. curse [S]

शिर see सिर

शुद्ध adj. pure, purified [S]

शूद्र m. Shudra, lowest of the four classes of Hindu society [S]

शोभित adj. resplendent, glorious [S]

श्रद्धा f. faith, reverence [S]

श्रवन m. hearing [S °*ṇa-*]

श्री f. beauty, light; Lakṣmī; m./f. honorific title; ~अंग m. divine body; ~नगर m. Shrinagar; ~नाथ m. 'lord of Śrī', epithet of Viṣṇu/Kṛṣṇa (as Govardhannāth); ~निधि m. treasury of fortune; ~पर्वत m. name of a mountain in RN; ~मुख m. divine mouth; ~हस्त m. divine hand; [S]

षट num. six; ~ऋतु f. the six seasons; ~रस adj. having the six flavours (sweet, sour, salt, bitter, acrid, astringent) [S *ṣaṭ-*]

संका f. fear, doubt, apprehension [S *ś*°]

संकुलित adj. grasped, held [S *saṁkalita-*]

संकेत m. 'tryst', a village in Braj [S]

संखनाद m. playing of conch [S *ś*°]

संग adv. preposition & ppn. with, in company of [S]

संगत adj. joined, associated [S]

संगति f. association, connexion [S]

संग्रह- vt. to collect, accumulate [S *saṁgraha-*]

संजोग m. conjunction, combination [S °*y*°]

संत m. holy person, devotee [S *sat-*]

सँदेस, °स– (°से) m. message [12904 *saṁdeśa-*]

संदेह m. doubt, uncertainty, confusion; a trope representing doubt as to the nature of the thing described [S]

संधि f. joint, cleavage, cleft [S]

संपति f. wealth [S *saṁpatti-*]

संपुट m. casket, jewellery box [S]

संबंध m. connexion, relationship [S]

संबंधातिसयोक्ति f. 'hyperbole of relationship', which alleges a connexion between unconnected subjects [S °*ś*°]

संबंधी adj. connected with [S °*in-*]

सँभार- vt. to support, sustain, restrain, moderate [12961 *saṁbhārayati*]

संभावना f. imagination, reflecting [S]

संवत m. & adv. (in the) year according to the Vikram calendar [S]

संवार- vt. to prepare, arrange, decorate [13021 *saṁvārayati*]

संसकृत f. Sanskrit [S *saṁskṛta-*]

संसार m. the world, the cycle of worldly existence [S]

संहार- vt. to destroy [13064 *saṁhārayati*]

सक- vi. to be able [12252 *śaknoti*]

सकल adj. all, whole [S]

सकुच m. shyness, apprehension, bashfulness [12824 *saṁkucyate*]

सकुच- vi. to shrink, be shy [12824 *saṁkucyate*]

सकुचा- vt. to intimidate, make ill at ease [12824 *saṁkucyate*]

सकुचित adj. faded, withered [S *saṁ*°]

सखा m. friend, companion [S]

सखी, सखि f. woman's friend, confidante [S]

सगनौती f. omen [S *śakuna-yukta-* ??]

सगरौ, सगरो, °रौ adj. all [S *sakala-*]

सचा- vt. to soak, cause to be soaked [13394 *siñcati*]

सचु m. happiness, joy [13112 *satya-* ?]

सज- vi. to be adorned [13093 & Add[2] *sajjyate*]

सजनी f. woman's friend [13090 *sajjana-*]

सजल adj. moist, water-bearing [S]

सजीवन adj. bringing to life, reviving; *~mūri* (m.) restorative herb [S *saṁjīvana-*]

सज्जन m. good man, husband, lover [S]

सटकार- (°रे) m. lock of hair [13100 **saṭṭ-* ??]

सटपट f. uncertainty, dilemma [13099 **saṭṭ-* + rhyme ??]

सठ m. fool [S *śaṭha-*]

सतगुर m. the true guru, inner voice, God [S *sadguru-*]

सतसई f. collection of seven hundred (verses) [S *saptaśatī-*]

सता- vt. to torment, oppress, inflame [12886 *saṁtāpayati*]

सती f. virtuous and faithful wife; suttee, woman who commits suicide when her husband dies [S]

सदगते f. salvation [S *sadgati*, locative -*e*]

सदन m. house, dwelling [S]

सदा adv. always, ever [S]

सन- vi. to be steeped, impregnated [12898 *saṁdadhāti*]

सनमान see सन्मान

सनेह see स्नेह

सन्मान, सन° m. honour, reverence [S *sammāna-*]

सपन—(°ने) m. dream [S *svapna-*]

सब adj. & pr. all, whole; ~ कछु everything [13276 *sarva-*]

सबल adj. strong [S]

सब्द, सबद m. sound [S *śabda-*]

सब्दालंकृत f. ornament of sound, alliteration etc. [S *śabdālaṅkṛti-*]

सभा f. gathering, assembly [S]

सम adj. equal, level [S]

समता f. likeness, similarity, equivalence [S]

समय, समै , समैं, समें m. time, occasion [S]

समरथ adj. capable [S *samartha*]

समा- vi. to go into, be contained in [12975 *saṁmāti*]

समाज m. group, assembly, retinue [S]

समाजी m. member of retinue, accompanist [S]

समाधान m. reconciliation, redressing, settlement [S]

समाधि f. meditation, contemplation [S]

समान adj. & ppn. equal, level; like [S]

समास m. compound (of words) [S]

समीप adj., ppn. & m. close, near; proximity [S]

समीर m. wind, breeze [S]

समुंदर m. sea, ocean [S *samudra-*]

समुझ- vt. to understand [12959 *saṁbudhyate*]

समुझा- vt. to explain [12959 *saṁbudhyate*]

समुद्र m. ocean [S]

समूह m. mass, collection, bunch [S]

समेट- vt. to gather up [13026 *saṁveṣṭayati* (cf. Add) or *saṁvṛtta-*]

समेत ppn. with [S]

समै, समैं see समय

समौ m. opportunity, occasion [13185 *samaya-*]

सम्हार- vt. to maintain, keep in order, restrain [12961 *saṁbhārayati*]

सयानौ /°नी adj. & m./f. wise, sensible; wise person; exorcist [13088 **sajāna-*]

सर m. arrow [12324 *śara-*]

सर- vi. to advance, go smoothly, succeed [13250 *sarati*]

सरक- vi. to slip away, retire [13250 *sarati*]

सरका- vt. to move to one side [13250 *sarati*]

सरद f. autumn [S *śarad-*]

सरन f. refuge, shelter [12326 *śaraṇa-*]

सरबर m. pool, pond [S *sarovara-*]

सरमा- vt. to put to shame [Pers. *sharm*]

सरल adj. straight, straightforward, artless [S]

सरस adj. sweet, beautiful, lovely [S]

सरसा- vt. & vi. to delight [S *sarasa-*]

सरा- vt. to complete, bring to an end [13358 *sārayati*]

सरावगी m. Jain adherent [S *śrāvaka*]

सरि f. likeness, equal [13118 *sadṛk*]

सरीख—(°खे) adj. like [13119 *sadṛkṣa-*]

सरीर see शरीर

सरूप m. form, appearance [S *svarūpa-*]

सरोज m. lotus [S]

सर्वज्ञ adj. omniscient [S]

सर्वसु m. one's all, all one owns [S *sarvasva-*]

सर्वोपरि adj. highest, best [S]

सलिल m. water [S]

सलोन—, सलौन—(°नैं) adj. lovely [13286 *salavaṇa-*]

सवार, सबार—(रे) m. & adv. morning; in good time [13290 **savāra-*]

सवैया m. a verse form [13134 *sapāda-*]

ससहर- vi. to feel afraid, to tremble [12435 *śikhara-* ?]

ससि m. moon; a symbol for the number 'one'; ~सीस m. 'he with a moon on his head', Śiva [12363 *śaśin-*]

ससिबार m. Monday [S *śaśivāra-*]

ससुर m. father-in-law [12753 *śvaśura-*]

सह- vt. to bear, suffer [13304 *sahate*]

सहगामिनी f. suttee, woman who burns herself on her husband's pyre [S]

सहचरी f. sakhi, confidante [S]

सहज adj. & adv. innate, natural; spontaneously, easily [S]

सहर m. city, town [Pers. *shahr*]

सहस num. thousand [13307 *sahasra-*]

सहाय, सहाइ m./f. help, support [S]

सहायक m. helper, supporter [S]

सहित ppn. & preposition with, accompanying [S]

सही[1] adj. & adv. true, right, well and good [Ar. *ṣaḥīḥ*]

सही[2] f. sakhi, woman's companion [13074 *sakhī-*]

साईं m. master, Sir [13930 *svāmin-*]

साँकर f. door-chain [12580 *śṛṅkhala-*]

साँकर—(साँकरी) adj. narrow [12817 *saṁkaṭa-*]

साँच, साँचौ adj. & m. true; truth [13112 *satya-*]

साँच- vt. to mould, cast [13096 *sañcaka*]

सांझ f. evening [12918 *saṁdhyā-*]

साँटि f. stick, cane [12622 *śoṭṭha- × lāṭhī (< 10991 *laṣṭi-) ?]

सांप m. snake [13271 sarpa-]

साँवरो adj. dark, handsome [12665 śyāmala-]

साँस f. breath; sigh [12769 śvāsa-]

सागर m. ocean [S]

साज m. apparatus, instrument [Pers. sāz]

साज- vt. to adorn, put on [13093 sajjyate]

साठ num. sixty [12804 ṣaṣṭi-]

सात num. seven [13139 sapta]

सातैं f. the seventh day of the lunar fortnight [13152 saptamī-]

साथ m. company, association; adv. & ppn. with [13364 sārtha-; sārthena]

साधु, साध adj. & m. good; holy man [S]

सामग्री f. provisions, food, stuff [S]

सामा f. provisions [Pers. sāmān]

सार m. essence, best part [S]

सार— (°रे) m. 'brother-in-law' (term of abuse, implying 'I have carnal knowledge of your sister') [13871 syāla-]

सारी f. sari [12381 śāṭa-]

सारो adj. whole, entire [13355 sāra-]

साव m. young of an animal [12417 śāva-]

सावन m. the monsoon month Sāvan, July-August [12699 śrāvaṇa-]

सास f. mother-in-law [12759 śvaśrū-]

साहु m. merchant [13337 sādhu-]

साहब, साहिब m. master [Ar. ṣaḥib]

साहस m. boldness, daring [S]

साहित्य m. poetry; literary or rhetorical composition [S]

साहुकार m. merchant [S sādhukāra-]

सिंगार m. decoration, finery; the amorous sentiment [12592 śṛṅgāra-]

सिंघपौरि f. doorway [13384 siṁha + 8633 pratolī- or 8666 *pradura]

सिंघासन, °ण see सिंहासन

सिंधु m. ocean [S]

सिंह m. lion [S]

सिंहवाहिनी f. lion-rider, Bhavānī, Durgā [S]

सिंहासन, सिंघासन, °ण m. throne (supported by lions) [S]

सिंहोदरि f. & adj. lion-waisted [S °ī]

सिकहर— (°रैं) m. string net in which pots are hung [12428 *śikyadhara-]

सिखा- vt. to teach, instruct [12430 śikṣate]

सिखिर f. peak, summit [S śikhara-]

सिगरो, °रौ see सगरौ

सिच्छित adj. taught, instructed [S śikṣita-]

सिद्ध adj. prepared; available; accomplished, achieved, attained [S]

सिद्धि, सिधि f. one of the eight supernatural powers acquired through austerities or magic: to make oneself extremely small/large/light/heavy, to acquire anything, to have irresistible will, supremacy, power of subjugation [S]

सिधार- vi. to depart [13407 siddha-]

सिया f. Sītā; ~पति m. Rāma [13428 sītā-]

सिर, सीर (rh.), शिर m. head [12452 śiras-]

सिरताज m. lord, great person [Pers. sartāj]

सिरोमनि m. gem worn on the head as diadem: hence 'best of', 'jewel amongst' [S śiromaṇi-]

सिव m. Śiva [12472 śiva-]

सिवार (m.) a water-weed [12493 śīpāla-]

सिष्य m. disciple [S ś°]

सिसिर m. the cold season [12475 śiśira-]

सिसु m. child [12476 *śiśu-*]

सिसुता f. childhood, infancy [S *śiśutā-*]

सिहा- see सुहा-

सींक– (सींके) m. string net in which pots are hung [12427 *śikya-*]

सींग m. horn; ~समा- vi. to be accommodated, find refuge [12583 *śṛṅga-*]

सींच- vt. to water, irrigate [13394 *siñcati*]

सींव f. boundary, border [13435 *sīman-*]

सीख- vt. to learn [12430 *śikṣate*]

सीत m. cold; ~रितु f. winter [S *śīta-*]

सीतकर m. 'cool-rayed', the moon [S *ś°*]

सीतल adj. cool [S *śītala-*]

सीध– (°धे) adj. straight [13401 *siddha-*]

सीर (rh.) see सिर

सीर– (°रे, °री) adj. cold, cool [12487 *śītala-*]

सील m. modesty, moral conduct [12501 *śīla-*]

सीस m. head; ~पट m. veil [12497 *śīrṣa-*]

सुंदर adj. beautiful; °रि, °री f. beautiful woman [S]

सुंदरता f. beauty [S]

सु[1] see सो[1]

सु[2] pref. good, fine [S]

सुक m. Śukdev, narrator of the *Bhāgavata Purāṇa* [S *śuka-*]

सुकुमार adj. tender, delicate; °री f. delicate woman [S]

सुकेसी f. Sukeśī, a nymph [S *-ś-*]

सुख m. happiness, joy, pleasure; ~दाई, ~दायक adj. & m. joy-giving; ~नींद f. sound sleep [S]

सुखद adj. pleasant, joy-giving [S]

सुगंध adj. & m. fragrant; fragrance [S]

सुगम adj. easy of access [S]

सुघर adj. handsome [13460 *sughaṭa-*]

सुचाल f. propriety [*su-* + 4722 **calyā-*]

सुजाति adj. high-born, beautiful [S]

सुजान adj. wise [S *su-* + *jānat-*]

सुढार adj. lovely [*su-* + *ḍhāra* < 5581 **ḍhālayati*]

सुण- see सुन-

सुत m. son [S]

सुदि f. the 'light half' of the lunar month, the fortnight from new to full moon [S]

सुद्ध adj. pure; ~-अपन्हुति f. 'entire denial', a trope in which an object of comparison displaces its subject [S *ś°*]

सुधा f. nectar; ~निधि, ~निवास m. 'store/abode of nectar', the moon [S]

सुधार- vt. to correct, improve, polish [12521 **śuddhakāra-*]

सुधि, सुध, सूधि f. consciousness, memory; सुध बुध f. sense, awareness [12523 *śuddhi-*]

सुधारस m. nectar, ambrosia [S]

सुन-, सुण- vt. to hear, listen [12598 *śṛṇoti*]

सुना- vt. to say, relate [12598 *śṛṇoti*]

सुबरन m. gold [S *suvarṇa-*]

सुबास adj. fragrant [S *suvāsa-*]

सुभट m. great warrior, champion [S]

सुभदत्त m. name of a kayasth in RN [S *ś°*]

सुभाइ, °य m. nature, character, disposition [S *svabhāva-*]

सुमन m. flower, jasmine [S]

सुमिर- vt. to remember, recall [13863 *smarati*]

सुमिरन f. 'recollection', a trope in which a comparison is induced by a memory [S *smaraṇa-*]

सुर[1] m. tone, vowel, note, tune [13498 *sura-*]

सुर[2] m. god; ~लोक m. heaven; ~सरि f. river of the gods, Ganges [S]

सुर[3] see सूर

सुरंग adj. bright, coloured [S]

सुरगुरु m. Bṛhaspati, eloquent sage of the gods [S]

सुरतरु m. wishing-tree, one of the five trees of Indra's heaven, which grants desires [S]

सुरति[1] f. memory, recollection [S *śruti-*]

सुरति[2], °त f. love-making [S]

सुरभी f. cow, cow of plenty [S]

सुरस adj. sweet, delicious [S]

सुरसरिता f. river of the gods, Ganges [S]

सुरी f. goddess [S]

सुरेस m. 'lord of gods', Indra [S *sureśa-*]

सुवन m. son [13569 *sūnu-* ?]

सुहा-, सिहा- vi. to be charmed, pleased [13452 *sukhāyate*]

सुहाग m. wifehood with living husband [13617 *saubhāgya-*]

सुहाना adj. charming [13452 *sukhāyate*]

सूँ see सौं

सूँघ- vt. to smell, sniff [12579 **śṛṅkhati*]

सूख- vi. to dry up/out [12552 **śuṣkati*]

सूत m. charioteer [S]

सूध—(सूधे) adj. & adv. true, direct, straightforward; straight [12520 *śuddha-*]

सूधि see सुधि

सूनो, सूनौ adj. empty, deserted [12567 *śūnya-*]

सूम m. miser [Ar. *shūm*]

सूर m. sun; hero; see सूरदास [S]

सूरज m. sun; the sun-god, Sūrya [S *sūrya-*]

सूरति f. form, face, appearance [Ar.> Pers. *ṣūrat*]

सूरदास, सूर m. name of poet [S]

सृष्टि f. creation [S]

सेज f. couch, bed [12609 **śeyyā-*]

सेठ m. merchant [12726 *śreṣṭhin-*]

सेत adj. white [S *śveta-*]

सेना f. army [S]

सेव- vt. to serve, wait on [13593 *sevate*]

सेवक m. servant, disciple [S]

सेवन m. the act of serving, following [S]

सेवा, सेव f. service, homage, attendance [S]

सेस m. Śeṣnāg, king of serpents, on whom the sleeping Viṣṇu rests [S *śeṣa-*]

सै num. hundred [12278 *śata-*]

सैन f. sign, signal, wink [12874 *saṁjñā-*]

सैल m. mountain [S *śaila-*]

सों see सौं

सोंधो see सौंध-

सो[1] pr. it, he (etc.) (see I.4.3) [12815 *sa*; 5612 *ta-*]

सो[2] see सौ[1], सौ[2]

सो- vi. to sleep [13902 *svapati*]

सोग m. grief [S *śoka-*]

सोच m. anxiety, worry; ~ *bimocana* m. remover of worry [12621 *śocyate*]

सोच- vt. to think, ponder [12621 *śocyate*]

सोधों see सौंध-

सोनो, °नौ, °ना, सौनौ m. gold [13519 *suvarṇa-*]

सोभा f. splendour, beauty; ~युत adj. endowed with splendour [S *śobhā-*]

सोभित adj. resplendent [S *śobhita-*]

सोर m. noise, tumult, din [Pers. *shor*]

सोरह num. sixteen [12812 *ṣoḍaśa*]

सोह- vi. to shine, look beautiful [12636 *śobhate*]

सोहित adj. resplendent [12636 *śobhate*]

सौं, सों, सूँ ppn. with, from, to [13173 *sama-*]

सौंज f. goods, articles [13095 *sajya-* (Thiel-Horstmann 1983:203)]

सौंध—, सोंध— (°धे) m. & adj. fragrance; fragrant; सोंधो, सोधों m. pomade, shampoo [13454 *sugandha-*]

सौंप- vt. to entrust, hand over [13192 *samarpayati*]

सौंह f. oath, vow [12290 *śapatha-*]

सौ[1] adj. & adj.suff. like; -like, MSH -सा [13173 *sama-*]

सौ[2] num. hundred; ~गुनी adj. hundredfold [12278 *śata-*]

सौत— (°तिनु) f. co-wife [13130 *sapatnī-*]

सौनौ see सोनो

स्तन m. female breast, bosom [S]

स्तुति f. praise, adulation [S]

स्त्री f. woman, wife [S]

स्नान m. bath, ritual bathing [S]

स्नेह, सनेह m. love, affection, oiliness, unctuousness [S]

स्पर्स m. touch [S *sparśa-*]

स्याम adj. & m. dark; Kṛṣṇa; ~घन m. 'dark cloud', Kṛṣṇa [S *śyāma-*]

स्यामा f. '[consort of] dark one', name of Rādhā; (but also 'dark one', i.e. Durgā or Yamunā) [S *śyāmā-*]

स्रम m. labour, toil [S *śrama-*]

स्रवन m. ear [S *śravaṇa-*]

स्वच्छ adj. pure [S]

स्वदृष्टि f. one's own sight [S]

स्वप्न, स्वपन m. dream, sleep [S]

स्वरूप m. own form, image [S]

स्वाँग m. mimicry [13203 **samāṅga-*]

स्वान m. dog [S *śvāna-*]

स्वामी m. lord, master, husband [S]

सवारथ m. self-interest [S *svārtha-*]

स्वेद m. perspiration [S]

हँस-, हस- vi. to laugh [14021 *hasati*]

हँसाय f. laughter, ridicule [14021 *hasati*]

हँसी f. laughter [14023 *hasita-*]

हजार num. thousand [Pers. *hazār*]

हट- vi. to recoil, draw back [13943 **haṭṭ-*]

हठ m. obstinacy, pertinacity [S]

हठ- vi. to be insistent [S *haṭha-*]

हथ्यार m. weapon [14027 **hastakāra-*]

हनू, हनूमान m. Hanumān [S *hanuman-*]

हम pr. we, I; us, me (see I.4.5a) [986 *asmad-*]

हमाम m. Turkish bath [Ar. *ḥammām*]

हमारौ, हमरौ pr. our (see I.4.5a) [988 *asmāka-*]

हमेस adv. always [Pers. *hamesha*]

हर- vt. to remove; to steal [13980 *harati*]

हर— (हरी) adj. green [13985 *harita-*]

हरख- see हरष-

हरन m. removal, abduction [13979 *haraṇa-*]

हरष-, हरख- vi. to be delighted, overjoyed; [S *harṣa-*]

हरषित adj. delighted [S *harṣita-*]

हरि m. a name of Kṛṣṇa/Viṣṇu; ~जन m. devotee of Hari, pious person [S]

हरिवंश m. name of a poet [S]

हरुऐं adv. gently [10896 *laghu*]

हर्ष m. joy, delight, pleasure [S]

हल- see हिल-

हलकारा m. courier, factotum [Pers. *har-kāra*]

हलधर m. Balrām, Kṛṣṇa's brother [S]

हवाल m. condition, state, situation [Ar. pl. *aḥwāl* (sg. *ḥāl*)]

हवेली f. mansion, house; Vallabhite temple [Pers. *ḥawelī*]

हस- see हँस-

हस्तिनापुर m. Hastinapur, ancient capital city (near Delhi) [S]

हाँ see यहाँ

हाँस- vi. to laugh [14048 **hasyate*]

हाँसी f. laugh, smile [14048 **hasyate*]

हाड़ m. bone, skeleton [13952 *haḍḍa-*]

हाथ m. hand; के हाथ तें ppn. through, because of [14024 *hasta-*]

हाथी m. elephant [14039 *hastin-*]

हानि f. loss [S]

हाय interj. alas! [14058 *hāyi*]

हार[1] m. garland [S]

हार[2] f. defeat [14062 *hāri-*]

हार[3] m. carrying away, ravishing [S]

-हार[4], -हारो suff. to obl. inf. forming verbal agent (cf. MSH -वाला) [6787 *dhāra-*]

हार- vi. to be defeated [14061 *hārayati*]

हाव-भाव m. blandishments, actions and postures expressive of sentiment [S]

हास, हासु m. laugh [S]

हाहा interj. alas!, ah! [S]

हिंदु m. Hindu [Pers. *hindū*]

-हिं see ही

हित m. & ppn. wellbeing; love; name of the poet Harivaṁś; for the sake of [S]

हिय, हियो, हियौ m. heart [14152 *hṛdaya-*]

हिरणाकुश m. Hiraṇyakaśipu, a demonic adversary of Viṣṇu [S *hiraṇyakaśipu-*]

हिरदै see हृदय

हिल-; हल- (rh.) vi. to shake, tremble [14120 **hillati*]

ही, हिं, हीं emph. enc. only, very, own [S *hi* ?]

हीन adj. low, mean, base; (as suff.) without, lacking in [S]

हीर m. diamond [14130 *hīra-*]

हुँकारी f. grunt of assent, the sound '*hũ*' [14133 *huṁkāra-*]

हुक्का m. pipe, hookah [Pers. *ḥuqqa*]

हुलस- vi. to be delighted [2375 *ullasati*]

हुलसा- vt. to delight [see preceding]

हुलास m. gladness, delight [2375 *ullāsa-*]

हूँ, हू enc.part. even, too, also [3846 *khalu*]

हूँक- vi. to call out, to low [14134 *hūṅku-*]

हृदय, हिरदै m. heart [S]

हेतु, हेत m. cause, motive, purpose; ~ -अपन्हुति f. a trope of 'denial' (see अपन्हुति) showing an implicit cause [S]

हेम m. cold, frost; winter [S *heman-*]

हेमंत m. winter [S]

हेर- vt. to look for, look at, see [14165 **herati*]

हो- vi. to be, become [9416 *bhavati*]

होरी f. Holi, the springtime festival of colours [14182 *holā-*]

हौं pr. I (see I.4.5a) [992 *aham*]

हौस f. lust, strong appetite [Ar. *hawas*]

ह्यां see यहाँ

ह्वां see वहाँ